PONTIFICAL INSTITUTE OF MEDIAEVAL STUDIES

STUDIES AND TEXTS

8

PRINTED BY UNIVERSA, WETTEREN (BELGIUM)

TENURE AND MOBILITY

Studies in the Social History
of the Mediaeval English Village

J. AMBROSE RAFTIS

Professor of Mediaeval History, Pontifical Institute of Mediaeval Studies

TORONTO

PONTIFICAL INSTITUTE OF MEDIAEVAL STUDIES

1964

PREFACE

SOME half-dozen years ago I began an intensive demographic survey of some English villages, but the work had not progressed far before I became aware of patterns underlying the lives of villagers the study of which was a necessary pre-requisite to the *minutiae* of individual lives. Indeed the very detail of the village court rolls, our main source for the behavioural patterns of these villagers, now demands attention by the social anthropologist, sociologist, and perhaps even the social psychologist, as much as by the economic, political, and legal historian. The following volume marks out some lines of study that appear fruitful for the drawing of a sociological map of the village, with the hope of encouraging further investigation into these important communities of our western history. Titles of Chapters and Appendices give a quick reference to the types of village activity to be found treated in the volume. For the reader preferring a rapid assessment one might suggest that the final chapter be read first. Village activities indicated by Chapter and Appendix title are no wise exhaustive. The word 'studies' in the title is intended to designate the lack of unity and the varying degrees of penetration of the different chapters in this introductory study.

It is a curious irony of history that the intricate community life of the village can be fully probed only by a co-operative venture among many historical disciplines. And certainly the following study owes much to assistance from many quarters. First of all one must pay tribute to the generations of scholars who have done pioneer work in the sources employed for this volume. Marjorie Chibnall of Cambridge University, George C. Homans of Harvard University, and Sylvia L. Thrupp of the University of Michigan kindly read parts of the manuscript at various stages of completion. Among my colleagues and confreres particular thanks are owed to M. M. Sheehan for assisting in the laborious task of proof reading, and to A. F. Waligore for assistance with the text of the Appendices. Too much cannot be said for the gracious cooperation of the Department of Manuscripts of the British Museum and of the Public Record Office, London, for making so many manuscripts available. Unpublished Crown-copyright material in the Public Record Office, London, has been reproduced by the permission of the Controller of H. M. Stationery Office. And I am grateful to the Norfolk and Norwich Joint Records Committee for permission to print excerpts from the Ramsey Register as the Norwich City Library. Finally I wish to thank the Nuffield Foundation for a Travel Grant that made possible the initial organization of this project.

J. A. RAFTIS.

Toronto, 1964.

TABLE OF CONTENTS

PART I - THE VILLEIN AND PROPERTY

I - Introduction. II - The Customary Tenant in the Manorial Economy.

I - Succession by the Wife. II - Maintenance Rights in Customary Tenure. III - The Descent of Property Within the Family.

I- Conveyance of the Customary Tenement. II - Subletting on
the Customary Tenement. III - The Tenure of Freehold by a
Villein.

PART II - VILLAGE GOVERNMENT AS GROUP ACTIVITY

I - Government by Officials. II - The Frankpledge System.
III - *Villata* and Group Fines.

LIST OF TABLES

LIST OF APPENDICES

LIST OF ABBREVIATIONS

Add. Ch.   *Additional Charters*, British Museum.

Ault, *Court Rolls*   *Court Rolls of the Abbey of Ramsey and of the Honor of Clare*, editor W. O. Ault, Yale University Press, 1928.

B M   British Museum.

Carte Nativorum   *Carte Nativorum*, a Peterborough Abbey Cartulary of the Fourteenth Century, editors C. N. L. Brooke and M. M. Postan, Northamptonshire Record Society, XXVIII, Oxford, 1960.

Carts.   *Cartularium Monasterii de Rameseia*, 3 vols., editors W. H. Hart and P. A. Lyons, Rolls Series, 79, 1884-1893.

Duby, *Économie Rurale*   *L'économie rurale et la vie des campagnes dans l'occident médiéval* (France, Angleterre, Empire, IXe-XVe siècles), Georges Duby, Paris, 1962.

Elton Manorial Records   *Elton Manorial Records*, 1279-1351, editor S. C. Radcliff, Roxburghe Club, Cambridge, 1946.

Estates   *The Estates of Ramsey Abbey*, J. A. Raftis, Toronto, 1957.

Homans, *Thirteenth-Century Villagers*   *English Villagers of the Thirteenth Century*, George Homans, Cambridge, Mass., 1942.

Maitland, *Manorial Courts*   *Select Pleas in Manorial and Other Seignorial Courts*, I, editor F. W. Maitland, Selden Society, London, 1889.

P R O   Public Record Office.

Ramsey Register, Norwich   *Ramsey Register*, Norwich Central Library.

CHAPTER I

THE EMERGING VILLAGER

I

Introduction

IN the study of mediaeval people the manorial villager is still largely
an unknown person. The reason for this is not that the villager has failed
to leave the imprint of his personality upon the rise of European civilization,
but that the technical terminology of the common law and the mechanism
of the 'manorial economy' have imposed a surprisingly durable 'paper
curtain' between ourselves and the 'humanity' of the mediaeval peasant.
To the economic and legal historian the unfree villager is the chattel of his
lord, an automaton governed by the demands of the manorial economy,
and hence a subject obviously ill-suited to the more human inquiries of the
social historian. As a consequence, and despite the growing insistence by
social historians over recent decades that custom gave a stature, if not a
legal status, to the villager's way of life, the mediaeval historian still
rapidly dismisses this cog in the mediaeval economy to dwell at length
upon men of 'legal status.'

F. W. Maitland was unhappy about the historian's knowledge of the
villein, but tended to find a solution to his queries in the formulations of
common law:

"If now we return to the *villanus* and deny that he is *liber homo* and deny also
that he is holding freely, we shall be saying little and using the laxest of terms.
There are half-a-dozen questions that we would fain ask about him..."[1]

"...Now as regards both the land and the oxen we seem put to the dilemma that
either they belong to the lord or else they belong to the villeins. We cannot avoid
this dilemma, as we can in later days, by saying that according to the common
law the ownership of these things is with the lord, while according to the custom of
the manor it is with the villeins, for we believe that a hall-moot, a manorial court,
is still a somewhat exceptional institution."[2]

---

[1] *Domesday Book and Beyond* (Cambridge, 1897), p. 50.
[2] *Ibid.*, p. 54. Marc Bloch was one of the few writers of the generation after Maitland
to question this absorption of the problem of villein freedom in 'legal history'. For some
references to Bloch's statements on this point, see *Mediaeval Studies*, XXIV (1962), pp. 355,
357.

Non-legal studies have, however, continued to keep Maitland's first queries open. We may cite some examples:

"The sociological interest of these cases lies in the evidence they afford that in the life of a village where intermarriage went on so freely between freemen and villeins there can have been no class barriers along the line of legal freedom and legal serfdom."[3]

"After I had read a hundred deeds or so from the time of Edward I, I became familiar with the names of the free tenants of Wotton. I saw that Wotton was not a manor in which a single lord ruled over a number of villeins, but that it was a community, very like an English village even to-day, but a community united by common practices, within a feudal framework, and directed by a manorial court."[4]

"There are, nevertheless, at least two cognate heresies to which mediaevalists have been prone. One is the traditional conception of a free peasant society gradually reduced to servitude by feudal pressure which has recently been under attack from more than one quarter."[5]

Rarely studied for his own sake, the villager has been given a status from outside rather than inside the village. He has become a man of the king or not, a man of the lord or not, a freeman of the town or not. It is perhaps not surprising that in searching for antecedents of modern civilization historians should have first appreciated the growth of commercial and town life, and the extension of civic liberties through the nation state, rather than the place of the peasant village. Like the family, the village has pervaded human history too widely to attract investigation as the origin of a particular culture. The village is as old as the historical memory of man, and it ranges over the whole known area of human habitation. The village survived in western Europe despite Roman villas, domainal organization, and the rise of the seigneury. Only as social history moves beyond national lines, and the techniques developed by social anthropologists for the study of primitive society begin to be employed, will the place of the village in the history of civilization be adequately studied.[6]

---

[3] H. M. Cam, 'Pedigrees of Villeins and Freemen in the Thirteenth Century', in *Liberties and Communities in Medieval England* (Cambridge, 1944), p. 134.

[4] F. M. Powicke, 'Observations on the English Freeholder in the Thirteenth Century', in *Wirtschaft und Kultur*: Festschrift zum 70. Geburtstag von Alfons Dopsch (Baden bei Wien, 1938), p. 388. F. M. Powicke also noted how Anglo-Norman studies leaped from Carolingian times to Glanvil and Bracton, see *Modern Historians and the Study of History* (Odhams, 1955), p. 145.

[5] H. M. Colvin, in *History*, XLIII (June, 1958), p. 85. One of the most important of these studies challenging traditional concepts to which Colvin here alludes is, no doubt, T. H. Aston, 'The Origins of the Manor in England', *Transactions of the Royal Historical Society*, 5th Series, vol. 8 (1958), pp. 59-83.

[6] A good summary of these new directions in the study of the village may be found in Robert Redfield, *Peasant Society and Culture* (Chicago, Phœnix Books, 1960), p. 14.

So long as the historical method remains based upon written rather than oral sources the study of the village will not be favoured. Even when the village is studied for its own sake, literary remains of a predominantly oral culture are first seized upon.[7] Furthermore, our literary minds seek consistency and uniformity in a society that is very personal and often illogical, more flexible and varied than uniform. Can it even be said that the 'virtues' of the city state or nation, such as individualism, economic enterprise, and indeed civic freedom itself, are suitable criteria for the social history of the village?

Among recent historians, pride of pioneer place must be given Professor C. H. Homans for employing the methods of the social anthropologists to present a 'total picture' of social organization in mediaeval rural England from a wide variety of sources.[8] It will be obvious from the first chapters of the following volume how much is owed to the studies of Professor Homans. But the extremely uneven quality and quantity of sources for different parts of the country would seem to require that henceforth a study in depth must be made for further elaboration of this picture.

The paper curtains of the historians, as with the political curtains of to day, are most readily drawn by personal acquaintance with men of the unfamiliar clime. In the following volume we have not attempted to present the 'total picture' of social organization in mediaeval rural England, nor have we attempted to pull together from a wide variety of sources enough evidence to give, if such were possible, a 'representative' notion of the social life of the times. Rather, from unusually detailed and numerous records we have attempted to approach more nearly the persons and human lives of many villagers in a fixed region over a certain time. Except for the second section of this first chapter that sketches briefly ways by which the individual appears in even the demesne economy, the following study is largely derived from manorial court rolls. Through the court rolls of a score of Ramsey villages from which the following studies have been collected, we meet thousands of mediaeval people. If a traveller had strolled into the court of, say Abbots Ripton, on December 4th, 1299, he would have heard mentioned the names of some ninety villagers, some in one-half dozen contexts, and of whom perhaps eighty were physically present. In such a court matters civil and criminal, public and private

---

[7] The great variety of assumptions implicit to the study of history through the written word are reviewed in Marshall McLuhan, *The Gutenberg Galaxy* (Toronto, 1962). With respect to written records, Lynn White, jr. states the situation succinctly: "The peasant was the last to find his voice." (*Medieval Technology and Social Change,* Oxford, 1962, p. vii). And the same point is stressed in Duby, *Économie Rurale,* pp. 7, 600.

[8] *Thirteenth-Century Villagers.*

that are handled to-day by a dozen or more permanent institutions and officials, all came under the one purview. Since we cannot cross the thresh-hold of a mediaeval court hall we can be grateful at least that the scribe entered the names of the many persons involved, and even more, that he sometimes took pains to report in almost literal fashion the evidence for presentations of a more than routine interest. When the scribe tells us 'the jurors say,' he often follows with a consecutive, ungrammatical, factual resumé, that must be very near to the verbal report of the jurors themselves. Unfortunately, it is impossible to make available these court rolls *in extenso*. Simply the printing of the court rolls used in the following study without notes and commentary would require a dozen volumes. Selection has been necessary, therefore, but in the process an effort has been made to preserve as much as possible of the personal acquaintance with the men of the time by the use of numerous texts from the court rolls.

The limited range of enquiry possible to one volume has also required selection. The following study represents an effort to see the villager only in the two traditional rôles, of tenant and 'native' (*nativus*), in the more complex and varied patterns that these rôles assumed in village life. In the first rôle we sought the ways in which the unfree tenant villager could hold land in relation to the lord and to other men of the village. In short, how did possession add scope to the life of the villager ? In the second rôle, we inquired to what extent the 'native' villager moved abroad, and why. In short, to what extent was the unfree actually a personal possession of his lord ?

In the broadest terms, Chapters One to Five may be said to deal with questions of structure and organization in village life, while the remaining chapters trace out some problems of change and adjustment. But it would be misleading to interpret such division too strictly as the history of 'stability' and 'change' in the village. There was much of change in the traditional structure; there was much that did not change over the four-teenth and fifteenth centuries. Indeed court rolls and maps of open fields indicate that the way of life in many of these villages was as late as 1800 nearer to conditions in 1400 than to 1900. On the whole, however, in our efforts to approach more closely the person of the individual villager our method tends to become an exposition of the elements of variety and change in village social life.

Finally, the following study is not intended to give a legal statement or interpretation of the life of the villein. The structure and activities of village social life traced in this volume move along legal lines in some instances, but in so many instances they do not. Or, to put the point in another way, while the people with whom this volume is concerned are unfree villagers, we cannot always be certain how, if at all, the lack of freedom made any difference. In consequence, we employ interchangeably the terms villein, villager, and customary tenant, as do the court rolls themselves.

II

The Customary Tenant in the Manorial Economy

It is as a tenant in the manorial economy that the villager first makes his personal appearance upon the pages of history. Twelfth and thir-teenth-century extents or manorial surveys give the names of customary tenants, that is, the villagers holding properties that varied in size with the services owed to the lord's cultivable lands or demesne in the village. In these extents the people vaguely enumerated in the eleventh-century Domesday Book as villagers (*villani*), cottars, and bordars, have become persons, like Antony, William the son of Ingeram, or Elena the widow, each of whom held a virgate of land for services at Warboys in the late twelfth century. This contractual relationship in land between lord and tenant marks no doubt a sharp line of contrast between the economic status of slave and that of the manorial villager. In classical terms the slave was one to whom nothing was owed. But the manorial villager, or serf, gave services in return for land. And the measurement of personal obligations according to the tenure of land has properly lead historians to classify serfdom as an institution distinct from that of slavery.

Far from making the villager a mere automaton, a digit in the equation of tenements and services, and as it were a function of the manorial economy, customary land was a villager's means to a fuller social and economic life. The fact that responsibilities attendant upon the tenure of land did not permit the villager to be impersonal, interchangeable and, most important of all for the historian, a nameless unit in the manorial structure, is in part explained in that the tenant was not simply identified with the work required of his tenement. The impersonal nature of servile obligations became concentrated in the servile work to be performed, rather than in the enforced tenure of a servile tenement as such. Services owed to the demesne were measured in work-units, and the performance of the requisite work-unit, not the person so working, was the concern of the manorial reeve and his assistants in the management of the demesne. Just as the lord might commute certain work-units to a money payment[9]

---

[9] This arrangement obtained from at least the time of the twelfth-century extents on Ramsey manors, see *Carts.*, III, pp. 243 ff. The importance of the *opus* (unum opus = i. op. = jobbe = job) in the development of the modern work structure in relation

and hire wage labour in its stead, so the villager might hire others to perform his servile obligations. It is not surprising, therefore, that the names of villagers are not necessary for the calculation on account rolls of works and services performed in the village that year. Except for those instances where the courts indict specific labourers for careless work, it is never possible to be certain who actually performed a certain work owed for a certain tenement. Consequently, the calculus of works and services obtainable from extents and account rolls are invaluable for a technical description of the demesne economy, but such sources do not take us far as an introduction to the personal history of the villagers.

It will not be the purpose of this study, therefore, to add again to the many studies of the manorial economy,[10] that description of the 'exploitation' of demesne and villein. But there is one aspect of the manorial economy with a direct bearing on our area of study that has as yet not received adequate investigation. Extents and account rolls show us that village tenure fostered the recognition of individual villagers from an early date. Furthermore, even these more formal sources indicate something of the variety of the ways by which the opportunities of the individual villager in the manorial economy could change over time.[11] Broadly speaking, until the thirteenth century there was still an uncultivated frontier to challenge the villager; and from the thirteenth century the commutation of works and services transformed the nature of customary tenure.[12] No longer can it simply be assumed that the manorial economy was 'static', and the economic lives of the villagers uniform.[13] Unfortunately there is as yet no adequate formulation of this 'rise of a peasant economy' in mediaeval England, and it is not within the purposes of this volume to provide such a formulation. But the historical image of the villager remains such a passive picture that it may be well to indicate here some of the possible lines of investigation into the emergence of the villager in economic life. It seems logical, therefore, to employ the extents and

---

to 'free time' is now beginning to be investigated. Cf. Sebastian de Grazia, *Of Time, Work and Leisure* (New York, The Twentieth Century Fund, 1962), p. 56. But thus far no concerted study seems to have been made of the place of *opus* in the development of 'freedom' itself in European society.

10 A simple introduction to the mediaeval village agrarian structure may be found in *Thirteenth-Century Villagers*, chapters II, V-VII; or see C. S. and C. S. Orwin, *The Open Fields* (Oxford, 1938).

11 Descriptions of the manorial economy usually move in the opposite direction by employing a dialectic of uniform tenure — servile obligations — increasing serfdom. A simple description of the main arguments in this dialectic may be found in E. Lipson, *The Economic History of England*, I, chapter I.

12 Duby, *Économie Rurale*, provides a good general introduction to this question. See especially Book I, chapter I, Book II, chapter I.

13 See Professor Postan's remarks upon the various natural factors of inequality at work in the village (size of family, age, sex, health, etc.), *Carte Nativorum*, pp. XXXIV-V.

accounts if only for this introduction that they provide to the economic scope of the lives of many villagers, and to move on from there to the court rolls. In the remainder of this chapter we shall look in a general fashion at a number of ways by which the manorial economy fostered a distinction among customary tenants. A beginning can be made with the variety in tenure itself.

The influence of land upon the individuality of the villager may be most clearly seen in the tenurial structure itself. Land not only permitted the serf to escape anonymity with regard to his lord, but land also lead the villager to develop more distinguishing features among his fellows.[14] Indeed, perhaps as noteworthy for the future of the village as the fact of the villein tenement itself, was the variety offered by the early subdivisions permitted to the service-bearing holdings, the so-called virgates. From the time of the twelfth-century extents virgates may be found divided into semi-virgates, and in turn into cotlands that might be one-eighth or one-sixteenth of the virgate. In so far as Domesday Book and twelfth-century extents or surveys[15] may be compared with the detailed extents for the thirteenth century, the common virgate tenement of the late eleventh and early twelfth centuries had in most cases been halved by the mid-thirteenth century; and by that time also some ten to twenty percent of these semi-virgates were usually further subdivided. It is only possible to speculate about the reasons for these subdivisions. Probably the reasons were multiple. Given the fact that the full virgate must supply several men for work upon the lord's demesne at some seasons, it was logical for the lord to guarantee this service by allowing a more immediate responsibility in land. That is to say, in periods of labour shortage a heavy concentration of tenants upon land would provide a greater assurance of labour supply. The competition for men as well as lands seen in Domesday Book is a clear indication of the direction of labour demand at the time. In this respect the disposition of villein tenements paralleled the general pattern of feudal settlement upon land over the late eleventh and into the twelfth centuries.[16] While other factors must have been important, it is not possible

14 A useful study of the variety in size and capitalization of village tenements found in Domesday Book may be seen in Reginald Lennard, 'The Economic Position of the Domesday *Villani*', *Economic Journal*, 1946, pp. 244-64; 'The Economic Position of the Domesday Sokemen', *ibid.*, 1947, pp. 179-95; 'The Bordars and Cottars of Domesday Book', *ibid.*, 1951, pp. 342-71. For the area of the Ramsey villages to be studied in the following volume, H. C. Darby, *The Domesday Geography of Eastern England* (Cambridge, 1952), now provides invaluable maps and tables for the spread of resources in 1086.

15 For a comparative table of the number of tenants at these different periods, see *Estates*, Table X (Property Holders on Ramsey Manors), p. 67.

16 For a study of the movement of the Anglo-Saxon slaves and house-servants on to small parcels of land in a manner parallel to the creation of knight's fees, see M. M. Postan, 'The Famulus' *Economic History Review Supplement, no. 2* (Cambridge, 1954).

to estimate the influence of many of these, such as the increased efficiency in agrarian exploitation and the increased capitalization (especially by livestock) of villeinage and demesne, upon the size of the 'adequate' village tenement.

Broadly speaking, the various forces at work in thirteenth-century England, that brought about on one hand the effort to control subinfeudation, and on the other hand the decline in dependence upon the feudal host with the increased employment of a mercenary soldiery, appear also to have found their parallel in the manorial economy. That is to say, from at least the mid-thirteenth century, there is no further noticeable structural change in the subdivision of village holdings; and from at least the third quarter of the thirteenth century flexibility in demand for work on the demesne was adjusted through the commutation of services owed by the tenant and the employment of wage labour. Indeed the abundant supply of labour in the thirteenth century placed a premium upon the returns from the larger tenement. The availability of cheap labour for obligations upon the demesne as well as the cultivation of his own lands, together with good prices for agrarian produce, combined to favour the larger tenant. The scarcity value of land thus tended to intensify the variations in village wealth first initiated by the division of the virgate. Only over the seventies and eighties of the fourteenth century did easy tenurial terms and the promise of more favourable agrarian profits tempt to a significant increase of the smallholder upon Ramsey manors, although these smallholds were usually let at the expense of the demesne.[17] Over the late thirteenth century, the greater part of the fourteenth century and all of the fifteenth century, economic conditions favoured a greater concentration rather than a subdivision of village tenements.[18]

In some of the manorial rent rolls for the late fourteenth and early fifteenth centuries, the names of village tenants are entered, so that it is possible to tabulate the tenurial structure for such years in the following table. Where possible, available data from extents for an earlier period are entered for comparison. There are usually about one-third more tenants noted in the mid-thirteenth-century extents than in the rolls of the late fourteenth century, a fact largely to be attributed to the mention of very few small holders in the latter documents. At Wistow, Holywell, and Upwood the numbers of those tenants holding more than a cotland had not changed greatly from the mid-thirteenth century to the late fourteenth century. For Abbots Ripton, Houghton and Wyton, the

---

[17] See *Estates,* pp. 275, 281.
[18] It should be noted here again that this chapter is concerned only with one 'level' of tenure, the structure of holdings revealed in account rolls and extents. Two additional levels of tenure will be seen in Chapters Two and Three, below.

tenants holding more than a cotland seem greatly reduced by the fourteenth century, although for the last two manors at least the number of tenants *ca.* 1250 is not certain. Upon all manors in the following table, however, there was by the late fourteenth century a drastic breakdown of the heavy grouping about the one or one-half virgate holdings typical of the previous century. By the fourteenth century too, there were many villagers holding more than one virgate. At Upwood, Abbots Ripton, Houghton and Wyton, the great increase in the number of such tenants would seem to account for the correspondingly greater decline in the total number of tenants with more than one cotland on these manors.[19]

TABLE I

THE DISTRIBUTION OF VILLAGE TENEMENTS[20]

WISTOW

Year (From Court Rolls)	The Number of Tenants According to Size of Holdings					
	Over 1 v.	1 v.	$\frac{1}{2}$ v. to 1 v.	$\frac{1}{2}$ v.	1 cot. to $\frac{1}{2}$ v.	1 cot.
1368	3	11	12	14	10	5
1381	6 (or 7?)	8	9	16	9	4
1388	7	8	11	13	6	$5\frac{1}{2}$
1389	8	9	10	9	10	$4\frac{1}{2}$
1393	5	10	15	6	6	$4\frac{1}{2}$
1394	7	10	12	5	7	6
1413	9	6	7	6	14	$2\frac{1}{2}$
1414	8	8	12	3	10	2

1252 (Extent): 11 at 1 v.; 36 at $\frac{1}{2}$ v.; 12 at $\frac{1}{3}$ v.; 23 smallholders

ABBOTS RIPTON

(From Court Rolls)	Over 1 v.	1 v.	$\frac{1}{2}$ v. to 1 v.	$\frac{1}{2}$ v.	1 cot. to $\frac{1}{2}$ v.	1 cot.
1385	11	20	0	4	5	3
1388	13	15	1	4	3	3
1390	13	16	2	4	3	3
1395	14	10	1	9	4	5

1252 (Extent): 2 at $1\frac{1}{4}$ v.; 8 at 1 v.; 60 at $\frac{1}{2}$ v.; 1 at $\frac{3}{4}$ v.; 1 at $\frac{1}{4}$ v.; 8 at 1 cot.; 4 at 1 manse

HOLYWELL

(From Court Rolls)	Over 1 v.	1 v.	$\frac{1}{2}$ v. to 1 v.	$\frac{1}{2}$ v.	1 cot. to $\frac{1}{2}$ v.	1 cot.	1 cr.
1371	1	12	2	5	4	8	9
1392	2	12	2	4	5	6	$3\frac{1}{2}$
1396	2	11	4	3	3	5	9
						2 of $\frac{1}{2}$	

1252 (Extent): 16 at 1 v.; 6 at $\frac{1}{2}$ v.; 18 at 1 cot.; 14 at 1 cr.; 6 smallholders

[19] The following table may be usefully complemented by a comparison of the actual list of names of tenants from the thirteenth and fifteenth centuries, e.g. for Upwood, *Carts.,* I, 344-51, and *Estates,* pp. 286-7.

[20] The symbols employed below are, v. — virgate, cot. — cotland, cr. — croft.

HOUGHTON

(From Court Rolls)	Over 1 v.	1 v.	½ v. to 1 v.	½ v.	1 cot. to ½ v.	1 cot.	crofts
1372	26	8	4	11	2	4	5 at 2 cr. 4 at 1 cr.
1379	21	12	5	13	5	3	3 at 1 cr.
1383	24	10	4	9	3	6	3 at 1 cr.
1387	29	6	3	7	1	2	3 at 1 cr. 1 at 2 cr.
1394	24	9	4	8	2	4	5 at 1 cr. 1 at 2 cr.
1396	23	11	6	10	1	4	6 at 1 cr.
1399	23	7	3	7	1	5	3 at 1 cr. 1 at 3 cr. 2 at 2 cr. 1 at 5½ cr.
1403	28	4	3	7	1	4	3 at 1 cr. 1 at 3 cr. 1 at 4 cr. 1 at 2 cr. 1 at 5½ cr.

ca. 1250 (Extent, but no names given): 33 v.; 13 cot. at ½ v.; 18 cr. at 1 a.
and Wyton: 30 v.; 10 cot. at ½ v.; 5 cr. at 1 a.

UPWOOD

(From Court Rolls)	Over 1 v.	1 v.	½ v. to 1 v.	½ v.	1 cot. to ½ v.	1 cot.	crofts
1401	11	5	4	5	5		8 at 2 a. 2 at 1 a. 3 at ½ a.
1406	10	6	7	5	5	5	4
1411	10	3	6	5	4	7	5
1412	10	1	8	5	8	5	5

1252 (Extent): 20 at 1 v.; 18 at ½ v.; 23 smallholders (mostly cotlands of 2 a.)

At least as important as the size of the village tenement was the capacity for the villager to render his holding productive by capitalization. Upon this point the size of the holding and the obligation for work upon the demesne combined to 'guarantee' a considerable capitalization of the larger tenements. The expression 'manorial economy' aptly emphasizes the peculiar forces at work in the production and distribution of wealth in such villages. For the village tenement was not an isolated unit of 'private property' but part of a system of co-operative production that must be viewed in the more complex structure of social wealth. This would seem to be particularly important with respect to the plough teams. Since the villagers owed work upon the demesne in addition to the ploughing upon their own tenements, they would seem to have had many more plough animals than the lord upon Ramsey estates. From thirteenth-century extents the estimate of villagers' ploughs necessary for work upon the desmesne alone sometimes equals the ploughs available from the demesne stock proper.

In addition to his work upon the demesne the villager had his own land to plough. Whereas there were few fines for neglect of villeinage, from the thirteenth through to the fifteenth centuries appears consistent evidence in the court rolls that the villager was willing to face a fine rather than forego the needs of his own land for the tsake of the demesne. It cannot be too readily assumed, therefore, that the villeinage was less productive than the demesne.[21] At the same time the interdependence of the demesne villein economy was such that the villager was under obligation to maintain his plough capital and productive resources for the advantage of the lord and other villagers as well as to his own profit. The manor could not prosper with an impoverished or even weakened villeinage.

Since Ramsey manors were divided with four or five virgates to the hide, the virgater would be expected to have two or three plough animals, and the semi-virgater proportionately less. Indeed it is not surprising that the regulations of the extents allow that some of the tenants of smaller holdings have no plough animals. There are many references in extents and court rolls to substantiate the fact that the virgater might have his own plough, but this would not be the large eight-animal plough. An agreement between two tenants of Wistow in 1429 associates the virgater's plough with three horses. In this document John Walgate transferred one virgate to John Onty together with grain for seed, and three horses, and 'aratrum cum apparatu ad tres equos.'[22] As we have seen above, this might be expected from the cultivation requirements of the average virgater.

An attempt to assess the number of animals other than the plough beasts held by the villagers is difficult since such animals only concerned demesne management where the customary rules of common pasture were involved, and the extents refer in the most general terms to such customs. It is even impossible to trace the exact nature of the tax or tallage on village stock as this form of revenue to the lord emerged over the thirteenth and fourteenth-century accounts. Probably, as with the pannage for pigs[23] tax on other stock never lost something of the nature of a payment for use of demesne pasture, or as a sort of commutation for an earlier *quid pro quo*. At Wistow, for example, from 1419 at least the tallage is no longer

---

21 The corn from slightly over six virgates of villagers' land at Warboys that came into the lord's hands because of the Black Death was worth £7.20 d. (ob?). Since the villagers of Warboys held some forty virgates of land, from the above ratios their corn may have been worth at least fifty pounds in 1349. Unfortunately this document (the account roll Add. Ch. 39804) is charred away at many places, but it can be seen that at least nine acres were in corn on one virgate (30 acres), twelve acres on another virgate, nine acres on a one-half virgate (15 acres), and three other one-half virgates each had five acres of corn, four cotlands (of unknown assessment) each had one acre of corn.

22 See text below, Appendix XI, no. 4.

23 See *Estates*, p. 157.

paid for sheep 'because they were kept upon the fold of the lord's demesne.' And at Abbots Ripton the villeins' horses and cattle paid tallage
according as they were not kept upon the lord's marsh.[24] At Holywell,
and probably at Slepe also, the villagers rented pasture in groups or
severally from the late fourteenth century so that there was no tallage
upon their animals as such. Presumably this 'pasture tax' was included
under some other form in earlier account rolls for all Ramsey manors since
no trace can be found of such payments for thirteenth and early fourteenth-
century accounts. Indeed the tallage upon animals is still very difficult
to distinguish from land taxes in late fourteenth-century accounts for
manors like Abbots Ripton, Warboys and Houghton, while at Broughton
it never becomes distinguishable. From early in the fifteenth century, as
the lord's demesne began to be farmed *in toto*, these tallages upon livestock
again disappear from the manorial accounts.

   While the nature of these sources makes it abundantly clear that it is
impossible to obtain a long run comparative picture of village livestock, or
even a satisfactory total of village livestock at any time, there is still enough
evidence to present some notion of the magnitude of the capital stock of
the villagers. For a number of manors there are a few entries 'for agistment
of stock' with rates according to horses, 'beasts,' sheep, and pigs. At
Wistow these rates remained: horses at 1/2d. each, beasts at 1/2d., sheep at
8 for 1d., pigs at 8 for 1d. At Upwood beasts were charged at 1/2d., and
8 sheep at 1d. For Warboys the horses and beasts pay 1d. each, and there
is a 1d. charge for every 10 sheep. At Houghton there was a charge of 1d.
for beasts and 20 sheep were allowed to pasture for 1d. in some years,
8 sheep for 1d. in other years. Since we have the total amounts paid to
the lord for such pasturing it is possible to make some calculations of the
total village stock pastured for these charges during certain years. For
convenience it is assumed in the following calculations that one half of
the total charge was paid by beasts (and horses where such are separately
mentioned) and one half by sheep (and pigs where such are listed separately). For example, at Wistow in 1388 eighteen shillings were paid by
the villagers for pasturing their stock, at the rates given above for this
manor; in the following calculations it is assumed that nine shillings were
paid for horses and beasts and nine shillings for sheep and pigs, and in
turn, four and one half shillings were paid for each of the four categories
of animals. On such a basis the following figures have been derived.

24 P R O, S C 2, Port. 882, no's 6, 8, 9.

TABLE II

VILLAGERS' LIVESTOCK TAXED FOR PASTURE

WISTOW

Year	Horses	Beasts	Sheep	Pigs
1388	108	108	432	432
1389	109	109	440	440
1393	123	123	492	492
1394	97	97	388	388

UPWOOD

Year	Beasts	Sheep
1385	250	960
1386	240	960
1392	240	960

WARBOYS

Year	Beasts	Sheep
1379	336	1680
1404	192	768

HOUGHTON

Year	Beasts	Sheep
1383	91	1820
1387	91	1820
1394	54	432
1396	54	432

Again it might be emphasized that the above data ought not to be taken as any precise indication of the total number of animals owned by the villagers. This point may be underlined by noting that the considerable change in numbers of animals for some manors over several years is quite obviously due to other arrangements having been made for pasture, just as the stable nature of the flocks and herds for some manors reflects the pasture contract rather than the over all pasture needs of the village. At the same time the larger figures do provide useful indications of the magnitudes involved.

Since other livestock, in particular the sheep, represented a 'cash profit' it could be expected that the lord held a much higher proportion of such animals. In some years the lord may have held more than all the villagers together. None the less, the villagers' capacity to pasture sheep was considerable. In Shillington (Beds.) the villagers were warned in 1473 not to exceed the quota of thirty sheep per virgate allowed by custom upon common pasture.[25] Since Huntingdonshire manors had right to common in the extensive fen marshes pasture quotas were probably more liberal for villagers of the fen region. There is a corroboration for this in the fine of twenty shillings imposed upon William Pyherd of Wistow in 1473 for having exceeded the pasture quota of forty sheep to the virgate.[26] As to the disposition of cattle and pigs among the villagers, there appears to be little surviving indication as to quotas or even general patterns.[27] But there is a wide variety of reference to stock in the court rolls. In a Chatteris roll of 1452 it is charged that 400 animals of John Rousson, John Sempool, and others of Chatteris were unjustly seized by officials of the marsh. In the Broughton court of 1437 it was charged that John Judd of Ripton (Abbots) tied and pastured 7 horses unlawfully, and the same John, very likely as a shepherd, lead 320 sheep on to the lord's demesne. In the same court John Berong of Ramsey was fined for leading 40 animals on to the demesne since he was not one who could common there. Seventeen sheep were seized as distress at Houghton in 1309 to bring to court a certain William who had departed with his goods to live in London.[28] At Therfield in 1347 a customary tenant received along with his holding[29] the right to common with 120 sheep. Here are some other typical texts from the court rolls.

WARBOYS,[30] 1424: The animal keeper in the marsh presents that John Baker of Huntingdon had six oxen pasturing in the above marsh, and that three oxen from

---

[25] B M, Add. Ch. 39656.

[26] B M, Add. Ch. 39656. In the Wistow roll of 1451 this quota is mentioned by ordinance, and in the same roll the quota for a virgater of Little Raveley is set at 60 sheep (Et quod nullus inducat plures bidentes quam sexaginta ad 1 virgatam terre cum suis propriis bidentibus quilibet sub pena vis. viiid.) (B M, Add. Ch. 39868). The quota for other manors may have been heavier. The ordinance for Broughton in 1504 was the following: Item ordinatus est quod quilibet habens unam virgatam terre et dimidiam custodiat vi xx oves et non plures sub pena vis. viiid. (B M, Add. Ch. 39487).

[27] In the court roll of 37 H. VIII the following ordinances are found for Wistow and Little Raveley: Et ordinatus est quod nullus custodiat pro uno arabilio supra numerum septem bestiarum sub pena vis. viiid.

Et ordinatus est quod alii qui occupant cotagia non custodiant super communia ultra duas vaccas sub pena vis. viiid.

Et preceptum est quod nullus custodiat in campo de Wistene supra numerum duorum boviculum sub pena ut supra.

(Little Raveley) Et preceptum est quod nullus custodiat pro arabilio suo supra sive ultra numerum septem bestiarum super communia huius ville sub pena vis, viiid. (B M, Add. Ch. 39876).

The Wistow entry for 5 Edw. VI has the following: Et ordinatus est quod nullus fugitat (vel) custodiat pro uno arabilio ultra numerum septem bestiarum sub pena vis. viiid. Et quod nullus cotagiorum custodiat super communia vel infra campos ultra unum equum sub pena iiis. iiiid. (B M, Add. Ch. 39879).

[28] Ault, Court Rolls, p. 250.

[29] P R O, SC 2, Port. 179, no. 33.

[30] B M, Add. Ch. 39865.

Great Raveley were pasturing there. And that John Maddyngle of Hertford had four oxen pasturing there, and that William Purday of Saint Ives had a cow pasturing there. And that John Andrew junior of King's Ripton had one hundred sheep pasturing there. And that Thomas Almer of Hemmingford had eighty sheep there. And that all these have not the right to common there, therefore they are to be distrained to pay the pasture dues, etc.

WISTOW,[31] 1299: Eight sheep, three lambs, eight fleeces, one ring of wheat, hay and straw of John Gernun a naif of the lord are seized, and more is to be taken away until he comes to fine for that virgate of land that Hugh Baron held in the vill of Upwood.

UPWOOD,[32] 1299: The reeve is ordered to reply in his next account roll for the two cows with calf, the ox, the young ox and the two bushels of corn from the chattels of Thomas Godesone, since the latter has not bothered to fine for that half virgate of land that Philip Messor once held.

ABBOTS RIPTON,[33] 1299 : And they say that Andrew at the church had twenty-five sheep abroad, outside the lord's fold, therefore that Andrew is in mercy to sixpence with pledge William the son of John the reeve. And Olyver atte Dam sixpence for the same, with pledge William the son of John the reeve. And Agnes Andreas for the same for thirty-nine sheep, sixpence, with pledge William the woodward.

ABBOTS RIPTON,[34] 1301: And Andrew the son of Allote for having had fifteen sheep beyond the lord's fold in the fold of Robert Gothyrde, sixpence, with pledge Richard Gerold.

BURWELL,[35] 1312: And they say that Alan Idayne overstocked the pasture by fifty sheep. Therefore he is (in mercy) to sixpence, with pledge John Idayne.

GRAVELEY,[36] 1350: John Franceys who held a virgate of land from the lord withdrew from the lord's fee without licence, and he sold a cow worth four shillings, and ten sheep at fourpence each, (these) are accounted through the bailiff to be in the custody of John Ibot, Henry Fern, and John Bugger reeves at Hemmingford Abbots, and other things shall remain on the land.

ELLSWORTH,[37] 1350: And that William le Gray a naif of the lord who died since the last court had on the day that he died two horses worth six shillings, one dene worth four shillings, two cows worth six shillings, three calves worth twelve pence, together with crops and hay and one cover for fen worth twenty-five shillings (escheat to the value of forty-three shillings).

UPWOOD,[38] 1365: The bailiff of Gidding presents that William Hering junior with four horses, John Hackyn with sheep, Richard Warboys with cows, William Alcok with two horses, John Bonde with two horses, and John Hikkesson with three horses, trampled the lord's peas at Bigging.

31 P R O, SC 2, Port. 179, no. 10.
32 P R O, SC 2, Port. 179, no. 10.
33 P R O, SC 2, Port. 179, no. 10.
34 P R O, SC 2, Port. 179, no. 11.
35 P R O, SC 2, Port. 179, no. 16.
36 P R O, SC 2, Port. 179, no. 34.
37 P R O, SC 2, Port. 179, no. 34.
38 P R O, SC 2, Port. 179, no. 37.

Even this very general notion of the magnitude of the capital of the villagers provides a useful key to the flexibility of the villagers' economic resources. Owing to dependence upon manorial extents as sources, it has become so traditional to analyze the economic life of the villager in terms of services that quite often the impression has been conveyed that the wealthiest villagers were the most oppressed ! Not only did the size of the tenement introduce elements of variety, but capital wealth too guaranteed a wide variety in individual condition. From available sources perhaps this variety is best depicted through an economic action that must often have depended directly upon the resources of the tenant: this is the renting of parcels of the lord's demesne. Usually a number of leading tenants got together themselves and rented a substantial field from the lord which they then proceeded to divide according to their private agreement. In such cases the account roll merely states that the land has been rented 'to customaries'.[39] Most of the thirteenth-century rentals and those of the early fourteenth century are of this nature. But for a time in the fourteenth century easy rent terms opened up the demesne as a new frontier for the landless peasant. Occasionally from the late fourteenth century the rolls list the names of all the tenants of demesne parcels so that it is possible to discover the individual nature of the holding.[40] An example is taken below from Upwood in 1406 to illustrate the many ways in which such demesne parcels were held by villagers. Since only five tenants held parcels in more than one field, and none apparently in more than two fields, it has not been thought necessary to enter the tenants' names in the following list.

TABLE III

DEMESNE PARCELS RENTED AT UPWOOD IN 1406[41]

Fenhill (field)	Casle	Castledele	Uphallecroft	Reddele
2 a. 1 r.	3 a. 33 p.	4 a.	4 a.	1½ a.
(3 a.)	3 a. 33 p.	2 a.	2½ a.	1 a. 3 r.
1 a.	6 a. 1½ r.		2 a.	4 a.
2 a.	4 a.		2 a.	2 a.
3 a. 3½ r.	(2 s. 6 d.)	Aspelondele	1 a.	1 a.
1 a.	(2 s. 6 d.)	½ a.		3 a.
2 a. 3 r.	½ r.	1 a.		
1 a.	½ r.	½ a.		
	3 r.	1 r.		
	3 a. 3 r.			
	parcel			

[39] See *Estates*, pp. 273-4 for amounts farmed to such groups of customaries.
[40] See *Estates*, pp. 281-3, where it is shown that 'men of the village', that is, non-customary tenants as well as customary tenants, were renting bits and pieces of land.
[41] B M, Add. Ch. 34857 (account roll).

Tonnestede	Wodedele	Schepecotedele	Hullokdele	
1 a.	2½ a.	2 a. ½ r.	1 a.	1½ a.
4 a.	3½ a.	2 a.	2 a.	1¼ a.
2 a.		1 a.	3 a.	5 butts
1 a.		5 a.	2 a.	1 a.
3 a.	? field	4 a. 3 r.	2 a.	1 a.
3 a.		1 a.	1 a.	1 r.
1 a. 1½ r. 10 p.	4 a.	forland	3 a.	4½ a.
1 a. 1½ r. 10 p.	2 r.		3 a.	2 a.
			8 a.	1 a.

The size of the parcels rented from the demesne varied too with different manors. At Holywell over the late fourteenth century, for example, sizes of individual tenants' parcels ranged from 9 acres 1 rod to 3 rods. Perhaps the broadest picture of this parcelling is obtainable from Holywell pasture to which several manors had access. A rental from one year in the late fourteenth century is given below to illustrate the divisions made in the marsh.

TABLE IV

DEMESNE AND MARSH PARCELS RENTED AT HOLYWELL IN 1371[42]

DEMESNE

Le Smetheys (field)	Schpeynfurlong	Oxhome
John Raven and asociates (socii)—11 a.	Customaries—10 a. 3 r.	Customaries—9 a. 1 r.
John Frere—2 a.		
John Scharp—1½ a.	Elene	Le Brache
Robert Houghton—7 a.		
Sarra Barker—3 a.	Schepherd—3 a.	Nicholas Godfrey—12 a. 1 r.
John Essex—9 a. 1 r.		William and Nicholas Sharp—2 a.
	Middlefurlong	
	Robert Houghton—1 a.	
	John Hammond—1 a.	
	William Rene—1 a.	
	? Hunne—1 a.	
	Nicholas in the lane—1 a.	
	John Hemyngton—1 a.	
	Nicholas Shepherd—3 r.	
	John Shepherd—1 a.	

MARSH

Nicholas in the lane, John Nicholas, and associates—parcel (75 s.)
John Essex—3 a.
John Tretford—6 a.
William Barnwell—2 a.

John Bokenham—2 a.
Thomas Barnwell—1 a.
Henry Parquent' and associates—6 a.
William Botiller and associates—2a.
John at Walde and associates—2a.

42 P R O, SC 6, Port. 877, no. 21.

William Mathlung—2 a.
Simon Fisher—1 a.
John Niel—1 a.
William Ravele—1 a.
Thomas Hogge—1 a.
Nicholas Shepherd and associates—1 a.
William Bigge—1 a.
John Wrgth—2 a.
William (lington?) and associates—2 a.
John Catum—2 a.
Simon Hart—1 a.
John Fynn'—1 a.
Simon Attecrouch—1 a.
Richard Balde—1 a.
John Tretford—4 a.
John Clerk—1 a.
John Reynold—1 a.
John Hemyngton—1 a.
Simon Hauch—3 a.
Robert Cok—1 pec. (18 d.)
John Wrght—1 a.
John Caton—1 a.
William Leighton and associates—2 a.
Hugh Cabe—1 a.

Simon Attecrouch—1 a.
Andrew Pye—1 a.
William Person—1 pec. (44 d.)
Thomas Sewyn—3 a.
Robert Cok—2 a.
William Webester—1½ a.
Thomas Asplon and associates—1¼ a.
John Tolier and John Bronnyng—3 a.
Thomas Caldecote and John Fyn' senior—1½ a.
Edward Hogge de Hyrst—½ a.
Roger Cole—1 a.
Adam Heroff—1 a.
Richard Gernon—½ a.
John Lenchert and associates—2 a.
Robert Sommoner and associates—2 a.
John Herow de Hyrst—1½ a.
John at Wold de Broughton—1 a.
Thomas Couper and associates—1 a.
William Brian—½ a.
John Pope—1 a.
Simon Brunnen—72 a. 1½ r.
John Tretford—1 pec. (2 s.)
Simon Brunne—1 pec. (2 s.)
Hugh (Briae?)—1 pec. (12 d.)

From about 1373 the fen pastures of Holywell began to be rented in larger amounts for a twenty year period so that few individual names appear thereafter in the rentals.

The main entries for the next generation[43] were:

Thomas Huntingdon, William Brunyng, and John Tolier—11 a.
Customaries of Broughton—38 a. 1 r.
Customaries of Holywell—27 a. 1 r.
Thomas Wynegood—gores (5 s.)
Customaries of Woodhurst—23 a. ½ r.
Customaries of Slepe—29½ a. ½ r.

The customary tenant obtained land as ability and opportunity provided. There were many opportunities upon the fenland frontier in the twelfth and thirteenth centuries, and perhaps sometimes all the resources a prospective tenant required were strong arms to dig and to drain.[44] One thirteenth-century source[45] tells of four leagues of marsh grass burnt, one thousand acres of reeds and marsh grass cleared at one time, one hundred acres at another place. Opportunities also existed upon Huntingdonshire uplands at this time for the same sources mentioned newly assarted acreage amounting to six hundred and ninety-two acres, forty one and two-thirds rods, and four perches all held in fifty-seven units. In addition there were eight assarted 'purprestures' of unknown area. Since little is known about the accumulation of capital by villagers at this time it is impossible to

---

[43] P R O, SC 6, Port. 877, no. 22 ff.
[44] For a sketch of some twelfth-century activities, see *Estates*, pp. 71-6.
[45] B M, *Egerton* 3663. The following summaries have been gathered from folios 57-63.

discuss their relative ability to exploit new lands. As lands became scarce new enclosures would be sought by existing tenants as pasture outlets. For example, a waste of more than eighty acres was enclosed at Upwood and Raveley over 1448-9, and the land was strictly apportioned according to the size of the tenements held in the village. Virgaters received two perches, cottagers one, and so on according to the size of the customary holding. Customary tenure had provided the villager with certain rights to village wasteland:

UPWOOD[46] — a certain waste in the marsh next to Snapmede was enclosed for meadow in the twenty-seventh year of King Henry VI with the assent of the lord abbot of Ramsey who is lord of the fee of Nicholas Stukeley, knight, and of John Hore, esquire, tenants of the said abbot. This parcel was measured by perches of sixteen feet and contains in the top lying towards Raveley fifty-two perches, in the other end next Botnale fifty-two perches, along the side towards Walton two hundred and thirty-eight perches, along the other side towards Upvale two hundred and twenty-two perches, which makes in all eighty-one acres, three and one-half rods, and ten perches. This meadow was divided into parcels by metes and bounds in the following manner.

First, the above John Hore will have for himself and his tenants the crops from a parcel in the said waste lying on the edge next Raveley and measuring thirty perches on both ends in the above perch measurements.

And next the above John Hore the almoner of Ramsey will have for tithe three perches in width at both ends.

And next the above almoner the above Nicholas Stukeley, knight, will have for himself and his tenants the crops of another parcel thirty-three perches in width at both ends, both for (his) manor and for the tenement formerly held by John of Raveley.

And next the above Nicholas Stukeley the above almoner for tithe will have widths of three and one-quarter perches at both ends.

And next to the above almoner the lord abbot, who is sole lord of the fee and of the vill of Upwood and Raveley and appurtenants, will have a width of thirteen perches at both ends and not more for in his bounty he remits and assigns all the rest of the said meadow to be divided among his tenants at will at Upwood and Raveley and their heirs as follows: Thomas Newman holds one virgate, John Freeston one virgate, Richard Genge one virgate, Robert Newman one virgate and one-quarter, Richard Aleyn one virgate and one-quarter, John Hendesson one virgate and one-quarter, Henry Skynner one-half virgate, John Aleyn one virgate, John Bukeworth one virgate and one-half, John Edward one virgate, John Leche three-quarters, John Hurre one virgate, Thomas Peny one virgate and one-quarter, Thomas Goular one virgate, William Edward three-quarters, Richard Wrghte one-quarter, and Richard Sewar three-quarters. Each of these will have in order one after the other for each virgate a width of two perches at each end and so according to whether one holds more or less. (Sixteen and one-half virgates).

And the above almoner will have no fen in tithe from these tenants, but as fan' from each virgater he will receive twopence and from each cottager below one penny.

[46] See Appendix I.

RAVELEY — and the tenants at will of the lord in Raveley at this time, namely, William Cusse one virgate and one-half, Walter Baldok two virgates and one-quarter, John Bretham two virgates, John Wrghte one virgate, Thomas Penyman one virgate and one-half, Richard Baron one virgate and one-half, William Colleson one-half virgate, William Skynner one-half virgate, one-quarter formerly held by Richard Skynner now in the hands of the lord, and one virgate formerly held by William Alcok now in the hands of the lord. Each of these will have in order one after the other two perches for one virgate as above ...

And thence each of the above tenants of the lord both of Upwood and Raveley will have in turn for every cottage a width of one perch at each end and according to this ratio according as he holds more or less, namely, for Roger Bryne three cottages, John Ray two cottages, John Broronote one, Henry Baker one, John Jerken one, William Love two, Thomas Newman one, John Hendesson one-half, Henry Skynner one-half, Richard Erle one, Thomas Peny one-half, John Leche one, John Bukworth one, William Skynner one, John Bretham one. And those in the lord's hands, one-half formerly of Christine Wilde, one of William Baylyesman, one of Richard Fraunceys, one of William Dycon, one of Richard Attewelle, one-half of Richard Skynner. And four from Raveley holding pasture are not assigned any fen for cottages.

And there still remains a certain parcel in the north end of the said waste next the ditch that has eighteen perches in the end towards the woods and in the other end facing Walton sixteen perches.

The brief survey of the above section has shown some of the ways by which a variety developed among the customary tenants in the manorial economy. Bound closely as they were to the manorial structure, the villagers developed these differences from that very structure itself. Diversity appeared in both the size and capitalization of holdings. Greater obligations towards the demesne became the basis for larger tenements and heavier stock quotas. Periods of acute labour shortage in the twelfth century, or in the late fourteenth century, brought an opportunity for the appearance of many small tenants. On the other hand an easy labour market facilitated the maintenance of larger holdings by the wealthier villagers. With larger tenements also came greater opportunities for rights in the dwindling frontier of fen, waste, and wood.[47] Distinctions arose among villagers from their opportunity and ability to make many economic decisions.[48]

[47] Long before late mediaeval and early modern enclosures it was clearly arranged that rights in the village common were based upon tenure. Such rights included resources for fencing, roofing, building, heating, etc., as well as the right to common pasture. The tenement in a mediaeval village, as well as the manor, knight's fee, liberty, etc., was a 'bundle of rights'. See below, Chapter V, for examples of these common rights.

[48] It should be clearly understood that the above chapter is merely intended to indicate the nature of possibilities for variety and change *within* the manorial economy. How the 'average' villager fared at a particular time is another matter, involving the investigation of such questions as the following (largely unanswerable from Ramsey sources): How much of his land did the villein sow every year? How thoroughly was he able to manure and to cultivate such land? Was the villein able to purchase better seed varieties for planting? Was the villein better off to have a smallhold, like a cotland, and to hire himself out for wages to other villeins or to the lord, rather than possessing a virgate with

A simple study of the payment of customary services tells us nothing of the personal economic decisions that have promoted the wealth and influence of one villager over his neighbour, or the spread of customary tenements at one time and their concentration at another. For this reason manorial account rolls and extents leave serious gaps as sources for village history.[49] Although invaluable as descriptive sources, account rolls and extents by themselves tend in the final analysis to circular arguments. For from the most complete of these documents the student has ultimately only an equation, the list of obligations for tenancy and the payment of these obligations. Historians have avoided this circular impasse simply by transferring the legal authority of the lord to matters of economic discretion. In this way changes in the structure of the manorial economy can always be said to be directed by the lord and his officials since public actions by members of the manor were only legalized through the lord's manorial court. On this basis the main question has been: was not the manorial economy a collective farm, measured by a strict cost accounting procedure, directed and disciplined by a dictatorial jurisdiction of the lord that could shunt men and lands about at will?

This explanation by authority cannot be accepted, however, without further investigation into the active range of this authority. That is to say, how much independence and initiative may be found in the economic life of the villagers? How and why was it possible that such a variety obtained among tenants that was found in the tables above with presumably a proportionate variety in livestock? To what extent could an ambitious man displace the economic control of the lord by subletting parts or the whole of his tenement? To what degree was hereditary tenure the incentive for the village economy? Upon this basis the main question becomes: was not the manorial economy essentially a peasant economy, geared to the peasant's love for the soil, and ultimately dependent upon the peasant's desire to retain his traditional holding? Fortunately through the generous manorial court rolls for Ramsey manors an investigation can be made into many of these questions. In the following chapter the personal nature of villein or village tenure is investigated through the evidence for succession to land.

---

its heavy servile obligations? Was the larger villein tenant, like the virgater or semi-virgater, better off with a larger or smaller family? That is, would 'many mouths' become the many hands that would allow a villein to control extra labour for use on his own lands and for sale to others, or did many mouths deplete villein capital and induce penury? The extreme difficulty in measuring 'standard of living' in a largely self-sufficient economy makes it next to imposible to get a workable gauge of the 'average' villein condition. But perhaps of greatest difficulty in attempting to gauge villein revenues is our lack of precise data upon the total villein population.

[49] For further strictures upon account rolls and customaries, see the remarks of Professor Postan, *Carte Nativorum*, pp. LIX-LX.

CHAPTER II

THE TENEMENT AND THE FAMILY

Alice Kabe came into full court and gave up into the lord's hands a one-half cotland that she held of him in villeinage. An inquiry was issued by proclamation whether anyone ought to hold that cotland by blood, and no one appeared. Therefore it was judged by the full court that all of the blood of this same Alice were henceforth excluded. And after this Robert the Miller came and paid an entry fine that he might hold the same half cotland according to the custom of the manor. (Wistow, 1339)[1]

THE first feature to be noted of the customary tenant upon the estates of Ramsey Abbey was the fact that he was rooted in the land of his native village. In this respect the villager was one with the traditional peasant type of Western Europe.[2] Upon Ramsey manors the customary tenant retained a close tie to the land because he had a hereditary title, or a right by blood, as documents such as the above example from Wistow say, to the tenure of his holding.[3] The blood-right to land was broken if the property was not taken up after a legally proclaimed vacancy. Over the thirteenth and fourteenth centuries it is rare to find the manorial court roll concerned with the proclamation of a vacancy in customary tenements. Most of the few proclamations obtainable are given below. Appa-

[1] See Appendix II, no. 1. It is of course impossible to include all the available texts in this and following series. The accompanying remarks attempt to indicate the incidence of the texts. Because of the haphazard survival of courts rolls, it is also felt that a subdivision of texts according to periods, or even a listing according to strict chronology, would be misleading. Finally, the significance of a text is far from exhausted by its position here (or under a certain Appendix title). Something is done to indicate this by cross references in the Index. But many texts are as relevant to another place in the study as to their present position; and the titles of Appendices could be easily doubled if an attempt were to be made to cover all the questions raised by these texts.

In these translations simple brackets are used to indicate interpolated words — usually some expression not repeated at every entry in the court roll, or fines from the margin — as well as missing words.

[2] "He (Oscar Handlin, *The Uprooted*, Boston, 1951) then describes that sameness: everywhere a personal bond with the land; attachment to an integrated village or local community; central importance of the family; marriage a provision of economic welfare; patrilocal residence and descent in the male line; a strain between the attachment to the land and the local world and the necessity to raise money crops; and so on." Quoted in Robert Redfield, *Peasant Society and Culture*, p. 60.

[3] Maitland seemed to consider 'right by blood' as rather exclusively pertaining to the villagers of King's Ripton (cf. *Manorial Courts*, p. 105). But the custom appears to have been common to all Ramsey manors. And to recognize this, is to recognize that such villagers' rights did not derive from the peculiar privileges of men on ancient demesne.

3

rently customary succession and demand for land governed the allocation of tenements over this period without the necessity for interference by the manorial court.

From the beginning of the fifteenth century manorial courts had to become very concerned about the shortage and neglect of tenants, although legal pressures to enforce tenure were of little avail. Texts given below from the courts of Barton, Burwell and Lawshall illustrate the early fifteenth-century conditions. At the time of the Black Death the courts were also unusually active in obtaining tenants to replace victims of the plague, as we see by the entries for Cranfield and Burwell below. Texts for Weston, Houghton, and Abbots Ripton, illustrate those rare occasions at other periods when court entries were concerned with obtaining tenants. Responsibility for crops, completion of the legal entry, or reluctance to enter a decayed tenement might be behind such entries, but the entries are too clipped to supply any explanation.

ELLSWORTH,[4] 1306: The jurors say that Adam of Graveley is the nearest heir to Juliana Segrave, and that therefore he has first right to that croft formerly held by Juliana according to the custom of the manor. This same Adam was called (   ) in full court to take the said croft, but did not come. Therefore the croft is delivered to Muriel Cane who gives the lord four shillings as entry fine, as may be seen in the rolls of *gersumae* at Ramsey, and Robert Russel and (   ) Porter are pledges.

WARBOYS,[5] 1347: The jurors announce the death of Robert Berenger who held a messuage and one-quarter land together with a bit of meadow next Boylescroft for the services and customs as listed in the roll of customs. And the court further announces that John his son is nearest heir by blood to that property according to the custom of the manor. This John then came and paid the entry fine and took the oath.

WESTON,[6] 1294: Adam Buncy and Thomas Newman are pledges of Henry de Goseholm that he is to take land from the lord before Easter or else make satisfaction to the lord for not taking that land.

HOUGHTON,[7] 1301: Andrew the son of Emma is chosen to receive and to defend that croft belonging to Margaret le Hyrde now dead, but Andrew is not here. Therefore it is ordered that he be distrained (to take that land) when he comes.

ABBOTS RIPTON,[8] 1299: Andrew West is chosen by the jurors to pay entry to that half virgate once held by Robert Sabyn.

CRANFIELD,[9] 1347: (An inquisition was taken about lands that had fallen into the

---

4 See Appendix II, no. 2.
5 See Appendix II, no. 3.
6 B M, Add. Ch. 39597; a similar entry from this court roll is printed in Ault, *Court Rolls*, p. 230.
7 See Appendix II, no. 4.
8 See Appendix II, no. 5.
9 See Appendix II, no. 6. Several similar entries follow in this roll. The bracketed portions of this text are marginal notes. The xid. is stroked out; perhaps the fine is concelled to encourage the tenancy (cf. *Estates*, Ch. X).

lord's hands). Walter Rideler, Robert Wodehall, Simon Coleman, Ralph Catelin, John Basel, and William Aleyn say on oath that Walter le Erb is able and sufficient to take that messuage and virgate of land formerly belonging to Alice Katelon. And that Walter will maintain this property etc. according to the custom of the manor etc. and he pays as entry fine (xid.) and takes the oath.

BURWELL,[10] 1347: The jurors say that Robert Rolf is able and sufficient to take one half-virgate.

SHILLINGTON,[11] 1290: And they say that the land of Robert West is in the hands of the lord. Therefore the reeve is directed to present the successor to fine for that land before the next court.

HOLYWELL,[12] 1299: The jurors report that a croft formerly held by William Haconn is in the lord's hands. And Robert Mariot is chosen to pay entry for that croft with pledges William Haconn and Absalon Gunne.

BARTON,[13] 1372: The daughter and heir of Nicholas Adam comes to this court and seeks entrance to her inheritance, namely the messuage and virgate that John Richard holds, on grounds that by right of inheritance she should 'defend' that messuage and land after the death of her father Nicholas Adam. And at this the above John Richard comes and says that the above daughter has no right to those tenements and he asks for an inquiry by the court, as does the daughter also. An inquisition was taken on this in the same court. The inquisitors declared on oath that the above-mentioned Nicholas had been seised of the above lands and services a long time ago, and he left the said tenements so that they were taken into the lord's hands because of the customs and services thereby withdrawn by the said Nicholas. Then a proclamation was issued by the same court etc., and afterwards the above-mentioned tenements were handed over to the above John Richard to be held at the will of the lord, etc. And it is therefore decided that the said John may have and hold the above tenements according to the custom of the manor, etc.

BURWELL,[14] 1411: Twelve acres of land that John Paule formerly held for life are ordered to be taken into the lord's hands, for after his death no one came to claim them, etc. And profits are to be accounted to the lord, etc. And a tenant should be provided before the next court, etc.

LAWSHALL,[15] ca. 1400: Robert Jotee came himself to this court and delivered over into the lord's hands one quarter of villeinage land with (messuage), formerly belonging to John Godyng, to be held for service by William Godyng. This land will be held by him and his heirs in bondage at the will of the lord, rendering to the lord every year all the works and services due and accustomed according to the customs of the manor. And he will preserve and maintain that same tenement without neglect. And he takes the oath to the lord accordingly, and he gives the lord five shillings as entry fine. And let it be recalled that at the court held at Lawshall (   ) the feast of Saint Matthew the Apostle in the fifth year of the

[10] See Appendix II, no. 7. Three entries in identical form follow on this roll.
[11] See Appendix II, no. 8.
[12] See Appendix II, no. 9. A similar type of election may be found in this appendix, no. 14.
[13] See Appendix II, no. 10.
[14] See Appendix II, no. 11. Another effort to acquire a tenant at this time may be seen in this appendix, no. 13.
[15] See Appendix II, no. 12.

above king, after a proclamation had been issued at the three preceding court sessions, John the son and heir of the above John Godyng having been summoned and not having come to take his inheritance, he lost this right by the above judgment and thence the above Robert Jotee received that tenement from the lord in the same court, to be held of himself and his heirs according to the custom of the manor as the court roll fully presents.

The right by blood made the tenure at once more than an individual contract, for the family was involved. Who should succeed to the tenement and other effects? How was the division to be made? What relative claims did wives and children and others have in the village tenement? In short, customary tenure was the fundamental act for social involvement in the village economy, and we must properly begin with an exposition of the hereditary nature of customary tenure.

I

Succession by the Wife

The most frequent entry in the court rolls concerned with the tenure of villein properties deals with the succession by the wife upon the demise of her husband. Rights of the wife were such, however, that these entries may be more accurately described as recognitions of co-tenancy, rather than succession. That is to say, the wife is not said to enter the land but to hold the land after the death of her husband. Further proof that the wife does not make a legal entry to the holding may be seen in the fact that she does not pay an entry fine. The following examples illustrate the tenure of the wife in property as it was expressed consistently from the thirteenth to the sixteenth centuries. At Barton, on the other hand, the widow received a specific portion of the lands of her deceased husband as dower, and could only enter the remaining lands by entry fine if there were no heir.

SHILLINGTON,[16] 1347: (The jurors say) that Adam Attewell died, and he held one messuage and two virgates of land from which comes as heriot one cow worth three shillings. And they say that Alice his wife will hold that property first without fine according to the custom of the manor.

GRAVELEY,[17] 1339: The court of jurors presents that John Underbur' who held in bondage from the lord one-half virgate of land, died. And that Katherine his widow will hold that land for the remainder of her life according to the custom of the manor. Afterwards Richard Lake came and paid a fine to the lord in order to take the above Katherine to wife.

16 See Appendix III, no. 1. For a general introduction to partible and impartible systems of land inheritance, see Homans, *Thirteenth-Century Villagers*, Chapters VIII and IX. For the right of widows to land, *ibid.*, pp. 180-4.
17 See Appendix III, no. 2.

ELTON,[18] 1342: The jurors present that Thomas Saleyn who held from the lord in bondage one cottage and one croft died, and that Alice his widow will hold etc. without heriot according to the custom of the manor and she takes the oath.

SLEPE,[19] 1354: The jurors present that John Asplon who held one virgate of land in villeinage from the lord died since the last court. And Margaret his widow will hold that virgate of land according to the customs of the manor, and gives as the heriot (five shillings).

HOUGHTON,[20] 1354: And (the jurors say) that John Wald naif of the lord, who held one virgate of land in villeinage, died since the last court. And Margaret his widow who holds that land while she is alive gives to the lord as the heriot (seven shillings, sixpence).

BROUGHTON,[21] 1369: The jurors present that William Abbot who held a messuage and half-virgate of native land from the lord died since the last court, and Matilda his widow will hold that land according to the custom of the manor. And she gives the heriot as above (two shillings, sixpence).

OVER,[22] 1328: And they say that John atte Grene, who held from the lord in bondage a messuage and a virgate, has ended his days and from him comes as heriot five shillings, according to the custom of the manor. And then Agnes his widow comes and she will hold that tenement for life and takes the oath. And she has as pledge the whole homage that she will repair and maintain the buildings and tenement and perform the services and customs pertaining to that holding.

WYTON,[23] 1428: The jurors present that a certain John Plombe who held from the lord a messuage and two and one-half virgates of land together with meadow according to the custom of the manor, died since the last court, and he gives the lord as heriot five shillings, and his widow will hold that land while she remains single.

BARTON,[24] 1428: And that John Grene who held from the lord a messuage together with one virgate of land and foreland died since the last court, and he gives the lord in heriot an ox that can be driven to Ramsey. And that Etheldreda his widow will have her dower in the above tenement.

BARTON,[25] 1428: And that John Hexton who held from the lord a well-built messuage along with a virgate and one-half of land died since the last court, and he gives the lord in heriot a horse that can be driven to Ramsey. And that Matilda the widow of the above John will have her dower in the above land according to the custom of the manor. And that Joan Forster is the nearest heir of this John Hexton for the above tenement. Therefore she may have entry.

BARTON,[26] 1369: And that Emma the widow of William Roger, who held from the lord a croftland containing one acre and died since the last court, fined for that land and one acre of meadow, eight shillings to come from the heriot sold for cash.

[18] See *Elton Manorial Records,* p. 313.
[19] See Appendix III, no. 3.
[20] See Appendix III, no. 4.
[21] See Appendix III, no. 5.
[22] See Appendix III, no. 6.
[23] See Appendix III, no. 7; and see the same appendix no. 18.
[24] See Appendix III, no. 8.
[25] See Appendix III, no. 9.
[26] See Appendix III, no. 10.

BARTON,[27] 1428: The jurors say that Matilda, the widow of John Roger, will have as dower three rods of land in one messuage and one-half virgate, but she has nothing in (   ). Likewise the same Matilda will have in dower one cottage with a croft called Lynewyk. This Matilda let to John Forster from the stock one brass pot (   ), one (   ) one winnowing-fan, one bushel measure, one cart with wheels, one plough with its own irons as is the custom of the vill. And so also Thomas Wylmote, Simon Fraunces, William Prour, Edward Childe, Richard Childe, John Prour, Thomas Stoucle, John Prour junior, Hugh Hale, and many others will also have (rights to these). And since the land was not fallowed she will have the beans growing on the fallow.

UPWOOD,[28] 1339-40: And the jurors say that Robert del Hill, who held from the lord in villeinage one croftland of two acres, has died, etc. And they further say that his widow Elena will hold that land for life according to the custom of the manor, etc., and with heriot. And she will perform services, etc.

UPWOOD,[29] 1333: The jurors give notice that Stephen le Wrce, a naif of the lord who held from the lord a messuage and two lands in bondage, has died. And at this Agnes widow of the same Stephen came and claimed life tenure of that property according to custom of the manor. And so the land was granted to her and she takes the oath, etc.

GRAVELEY,[30] 1301: William Barun and Walter ad Portam are pledges of Alice wife of Walter Barun who pays ten shillings to the lord, one-half at next Christmas and the remainder at the following Easter, in order to hold her property until Michaelmas next. This property had been taken into the lord's hands because Walter her husband set out for Jerusalem without permission of the lord. And in the meantime (this Alice will pay) all the usual customary services.

WARBOYS,[31] 1309: And the jurors say that the widow Agnes Faber who holds one-half virgate of the lord was convicted in ecclesiastical court of fornication with Richard Ingram. Therefore that land is taken into the lord's hands and the profits are to be accounted to the lord until, etc. And afterwards she fines for twenty shillings (to recover the land) with William the reeve as pledge.

GIRTON,[32] 1291: And the jurors say that Matilda widow of Robert Warewyk was convicted in chapter of fornication with Robert Corebes, and lost some of the lord's chattels thereby. Therefore the land is taken into the lord's hands and the profits are to be accounted to him. The reeve reports that she has fined for three shillings with the chamberlain.

ABBOTS RIPTON,[33] 1299: The fine of Margaret Balle for having withdrawn the lord's ploughing services from six sellions is condoned since her land has been taken into the lord's hands.

[27] See Appendix III, no. 11.
[28] See Appendix III, no. 12.
[29] See Appendix III, no. 13.
[30] See Appendix III, no. 14.
[31] See Appendix III, no. 15.
[32] See Appendix III, no. 16.
[33] See Appendix III, no. 17. An interesting claim by Alice wife of Richard le Bonde to a croft held by Richard Faber was defeated in Wistow court in 1305 and again in 1309 by Agnes the widow of that Richard Faber. But this text has badly deteriorated at several points.

And the jurors say that Alice atte Dam who holds one-half virgate of land is not performing services required from that property, nor is she maintaining the buildings. And afterwards pledges were found, namely John le Bonde and William son of John the reeve, that she will perform these obligations.

Andrew Bonde and John of Hyrst were pledges for Alice atte Dam to enter and hold a lot in Wennington for which she had fined with Brother Reginald of Peterborough. For this she was to pay two shillings a year, and yet nothing has been paid nor is she living there. Therefore it is ordered that this payment be levied from the above pledges. And so it is to be done every year until, etc.

Since the widow held such a well established right to her husband's land it may be asked why the court rolls bothered to enter this fact with such regularity. The explanation for this entry seems to be that this tenure for life by the widow was not recorded in the usual record, the *gersuma* rent roll at the abbey, probably simply because no *gersuma* (that is, entry fine) was required of the widow. At the same time recognition of tenure by the widow also provided an opportunity to record the payment of the heriot. Heriots were substantial amounts and bore the relation to the villein's capital goods that the entry fine bore to the customary tenement. That is to say, payment of a heriot was the recognition by the villager that the lord was ultimate owner of his chattels even though the heriot had become a tax set according to the size of the tenement.[34] A heriot may be looked upon, therefore, as the commutation of the lord's right to inherit the chattels of his tenant. The customary tax upon goods represented by the heriot was always paid upon the death of the tenant, however, not upon entry by his successor. As a consequence the heriot was paid even when there was not the widow, not anyone else, to take over the holding. Frequent examples of holdings left vacant after the death of the tenant, but from which nevertheless the heriot was collected, occur from the late fourteenth century. But over most of our period the recognition of a widow's tenure provided the only occasion when a heriot was noted in an account or court roll. When the heir succeeded at once after the demise of his father, presumably the heriot was recorded with the *gersuma* at the abbey.[35]

In view of the fact that labour upon the lord's demesne was one of the

34 From over 150 available entries it would appear that the heriot fine had been fixed on Huntingdonshire manors from an early date at five shillings for one virgate and over, and two shillings, sixpence, for one-half virgate and over, and so proportionately. These are actually twelfth-century values for major animals! For non-Huntingdonshire manors better beasts were usually taken as heriot — a horse or cow for the virgate, a sheep for the one-half virgate — and sold from the manor.

35 But see Broughton, 1409 (P R O, SC 2, Port. 179, no. 52) where the heriot was cancelled 'since the wife died before the husband.' Cancellation of the heriot as in this instance as well as the entry fine was likely one of the many forms of discount in the early fifteenth century, in order to encourage the heirs to take up land.

conditions for customary tenure, and that such labour by family (husband, wife and perhaps children) rather than employed 'hands' may have been essential to a profitable management of the customary tenement over most of the mediaeval period, it would be virtually impossible for a widow to maintain the larger tenements by herself. This has been the explanation adduced for the fact that some women were ordered by the court to find husbands.[36] But such court orders disappear from the records after the early fourteenth century despite the large number of widows left with estates. And on the whole such orders are very rare for the earlier period. No doubt younger widows with property had little difficulty in finding husbands, and older women would in any case be anxious to hand on such responsibility for property so long as their maintenance was secured. Other possible arrangements open to the female tenant will be discussed in chapter three. In any case, there does not seem to have been any question of the widow's right to property over all others so long as she could maintain the tenement.[37] At Warboys in 1313, for example, William Fyne gave the court twelve pence in order to have his rights ascertained in Sixpennyworthland held by his mother. The court determined that William's mother had a proper title to the land, and that as long as she was alive it was the custom of the vill that her son could make no claims upon the property.[38]

The man marrying a widow holding customary land always seems to have paid an entry fine. He received a title to the property as her husband, rather than simply by payment of the entry fine. Often, as with the example from Chatteris and Wistow below, or Graveley above, the one marrying a widow is only said in some general terms to pay a fine. But it seems clear from all references to such fines that the *gersumae*, the legal entry fines, are indicated. There is no evidence that the widow paid a merchet for this second marriage. Indeed the two acts of marrying a widow and entering her property had become so telescoped in legal formulation that the husband was merely said to 'enter so and so' and we only know from the conjunction of the reference to a widow with a fine for property and the promise to fulfill tenurial obligations, that the dual acts are involved. Where the marriage and entry agreement is illicit owing

36 See Ault, *Court Rolls,* p. 277.
37 This right of the woman to property is also well illustrated in twelfth and thirteenth-century extents where it is normal for several women to be listed as tenants. At the same time it should be noted that among scores of entries where the word *gersuma* is used for fines for widows re-marrying, there is no reference to land.
38 See B M. Add. Ch. 34324. Further texts illustrating the ready acceptance of heiresses' right to land will be found in the next section of this chapter.

to the lack of permission from the lord, as with the examples from Girton and Abbots Ripton given below, the court roll entry tends to be more explicit. But since succession to the land was the widow's right, there is no reason why she should not marry an outsider — a freeman — with permission, and still hold her land.[39]

CHATTERIS,[40] 1273: Richard Turpyn paid the fine for eight acres in the fields of Chatteris which Baldwin the carpenter had held. And the above Richard gave twenty shillings to the lord to take as his wife Agnes the widow of the above Baldwin and (to take) the above land, and he will do the services and customs owing from that land, and he finds as pledges Andrew Alberd and Stephen Tydd.

WISTOW,[41] 1347: The jurors present that William Sabyn entered to Matilda widow of Andrew Sabyn, virgater, and he fined and took the oath.

GIRTON,[42] 1312: Evidence was given in the last view that a certain foreigner, William of Ten'esham entered one messuage and ten acres of customary land by *gersuma* to Juliana who had been the wife of Robert of Warwick, villein. And since the said William is free and a foreigner it was ordered that the messuage and land were to be taken into the lord's hands and the profits to be accounted for. Therefore the reeve Galfridus is directed to account to the lord for one and one-half quarters of wheat, one and one-half quarters of barley, and two quarters of beans and peas, from the returns of that land. And again the said land is to be held as above until, etc.

KING'S RIPTON,[43] 1292: It was established that Katherine widow of John of Ramsey and tenant of a three-quarter land and one messuage in King's Ripton married Roger of Kenlaw a foreigner without permission of the lord. Therefore it is ordered that all the above land be taken into the lord's hands unless the said Roger is able to be licenced by the lord abbot before the feast of St. Martin.

ELLINGTON,[44] 1311: After the death of Bartholomew in Inlond who had held from the lord one-half virgate of land the reeve together with all the customary tenants of the vill allowed a certain John Brymbel, foreigner, to enter the above property to the widow of the said Bartholomew by a *gersuma* agreed upon among themselves without the permission of the lord and against the customs of the vill. Therefore they are all in mercy at forty shillings. And the above property was taken into the lord's hands and there still remains. Therefore it is ordered that the profits be accounted for. And afterwards it was testified through G. Duboys that satisfaction had been made.

GIDDING,[45] 1290: And the jurors say that Sarra le Monek held a cottage from the lord abbot into which she took (by marriage) a man of the homage of Lord Reginald

---

39 See Cranfield, Appendix VII, no. 14, below, for an example of this.
40 For text, see Ault, *Court Rolls*, p. 268. For the right of the widower in a wife's land, see Homans, *Thirteenth-Century Villagers*, pp. 184-7.
41 See Appendix IV, no. 1.
42 See Appendix IV, no. 2.
43 See Appendix IV, no. 3. This injunction was repeated in 1294, see Ault, *Court Rolls*, p. 218.
44 For latin text, see Homans, *Thirteenth-Century Villagers*, p. 454.
45 See Appendix IV, no. 4.

le Grey. Therefore that cottage was taken into the lord's hands by the reeve of Gydding who hung a lock on the doorpost of the house of the same Sarra. And the said Sarra came and broke that lock with a stone and committed hamsok. Therefore she is in mercy to threepence, with John Monek as pledge. And since she was married without licence of the lord she is to be distrained to pay for this licence. And still that messuage is taken into the lord's hands and (his officials) will reply for the profits thereof. And the above Sarra is in mercy to sixpence.

BURWELL,[46] 1312: William Swyn and Hugh Edward act as pledges of Elena daughter of William Prime who holds a messuage with croft and three acres of the lord that she will only marry someone of the lord's fee.

CRANFIELD,[47] 1347: Richard Taylor and Richard Milneward recognize by oath that they hold from the lord for the lifetime of their wives two messuages and one-half acre belonging to their wives. And they give the lord as fine for entry ninepence.

Lawrence of Barton pays the lord two shillings entry fine for entry to a messuage and one-half virgate by Isabella Aleyn.

William Attehurst pays the lord forty pence fine for ingress to one messuage and one acre of Pennyland by Margaret widow of Simon Attecros.

William Aleyn receives a messuage and one-quarter land formerly belonging to Robert Godhale. And he pays forty pence as entry fine.

Roger Longe fines to enter a messuage and three-quarter land, formerly of William Wykyng, by Cecilia Attefield. And he pays in fine (fifty shillings is cancelled with note 'no fine'). He is to hold by custom of the manor etc. and takes the oath, with William Heryng as pledge.

HEMMINGFORD ABBOTS,[48] 1347: The jurors present that William Warde entered to Christina Carter, virgater, and paid the fine.

And they present that Alan Syer entered to Matilda White, virgater, and paid the fine. And they order that he be distrained to take the oath.

HOUGHTON,[49] 1347: And John Whryghte is granted permission for entry to Emma Bedill in one messuage and one virgate of land, and he pays threepence as fine.

II

Maintenance Rights in Customary Tenure

Of the same species as the widow's rights in land were the claims to maintenance from a tenement that could be established by several members of a family. The customary tenant who was too old or decrepit to work his tenement might hand the land over to some more able member of his

---

[46] See Appendix IV, no. 5.
[47] See Appendix IV, no. 6.
[48] See Appendix IV, no. 7.
[49] See Appendix IV, no. 8. In a parallel entry for Upwood in 1344 (B M, Add. Ch. 39854) Margaret the widow of Robert Crane had paid the heriot in the entry before she was married by William del Wold who took the oath for the land.

family, or to a fellow villager, in return for an agreement whereby he should be maintained for the remainder of his days. This was no doubt a common recourse for elderly parents. Such maintenance agreements were strictly enforced by the manorial courts. In the case given below from Warboys in 1334 Stephen the Smith lost possession of his tenement for failing to keep his mother as well as he had promised. However, it is interesting to note that Stephen did not lose his right of succession to this land. The redress given to Elena Martyn at Wistow in 1318 is another valuable example of this legal protection.

Despite enforcement by court there does not seem to have been a special legal form for maintenance arrangements. The parent would often likely remain in the old home with right to a 'reasonable maintenance,' as we see below for the case of Nicholas the son of Adam at Upwood in 1311. At the court of Cranfield in 1294 Elyas de Bretendon' took the unusual step of specifying the amount of maintenance to be paid if he and his wife were unable to live peacefully with their son John. In the case cited below from Warboys in 1343 Bochardus waives all inheritance claims in certain lands in return for maintenance rights.[50] However, it is clear from many texts such as those for Graveley and Over below, that children had claims in the property of their parents. Probably Bochardus expected to make provision for heirs from other lands if he should marry.

WISTOW,[51] 1318: The jurors convicted John Catelyne with having evicted Elena Martyn from a certain house that she held for life according to the custom of the manor, and of afterwards pulling down that house. Therefore he is in mercy to twelve pence, with Henry Thedwar and John Whyte as pledges. And by the same pledges he is to rebuild that house well before next Easter. And in the meantime he must find a suitable residence in which she can stay until Easter.

UPWOOD,[52] 1311: Godfrey Hales surrendered, etc., one messuage and two acres of land to be held for services by his son Thomas as shown in the *gersuma* roll of last year. He (Thomas) is to have and hold this tenement after the death of the above Godfrey. However, the same Thomas may have freely one room on the above land during the lifetime of the above-mentioned Godfrey.

UPWOOD,[53] 1311: Nicholas the son of Adam likewise surrendered, etc., one virgate of land to be held for services by his son John as is shown in the *gersuma* roll, etc. Nicholas is to have a reasonable maintenance in that land until the end of his life.

---

[50] For further agreements, see below, Chapter III, especially section I.
[51] See Appendix V, no. 1.
[52] See Appendix V, no. 2.
[53] See Appendix V, no. 3. An agreement in this same form was made at Therfield in 1306 (P R O, SC 2, Port. 179, no. 12) where John de Paynes was to give Alice de Paynes certain produce for the remainder of her life in return for the tenure of one-half virgate. However, the amounts to be rendered to Alice are partly rubbed out in the manuscript. Another agreement in this form may be seen in Appendix V, no. 20.

And the above John agreed to grant the same Nicholas every year for the rest of his life one ring of wheat, one ring of barley at Christmas, one ring of wheat and one ring of oats, etc.

WARBOYS,[54] 1334: And since Stephen the Smith did not keep his mother according to their agreement he is (in mercy) etc. to sixpence. And afterwards the above jurors ordered that the said land be given back to his mother and that she should hold it for the rest of her life. And the above Stephen may not have anything of that land while his mother is alive.

WARBOYS,[55] 1343: An agreement was reached between Bochardus Rolf appellant and William le Loonge, tenant of a virgate in villeinage of Caldecote at one time belonging to William Rolf father of the above Bochardus. It was drawn up in this form, that is, that the above Bochardus should receive annually for life from the above William le Loonge one ring of wheat, two bushels of dredge, and two bushels of peas. And the same Bochardus will have for life one acre of land from that virgate of which one-half acre lies in Harewell and is now sown with wheat. The same Bochardus will have the harvest from that acre for this year while giving to William le Loonge the amount of seed sown on that acre as estimated by the neighbours. Moreover, the above Bochardus will have for life after the death of his mother, that messuage with the house on it where his mother now lives. While it is permitted to Bochardus to marry nevertheless, the quarter of corn, the acre of land, and the messuage shall accrue to him for life. And upon the death of the same Bochardus all the above quarter of corn, acre of land, and messuage shall entirely devolve to the above William and his heirs so that neither the widow nor children of the same Bochardus should receive anything. And for the above quarter of corn, acre of land, and messuage as agreed and specified the same Bochardus surrendered and quit-claimed to the same William le Loonge and his heirs all rights and titles that in any way should ever be sought in that virgate of land by Bochardus.

CRANFIELD,[56] 1294: Elyas de Bretendon' surrendered in open court a messuage and half-virgate of land in Cranfield at money rent together with the accompanying woods, appurtenants, and three acres of foreland, to be held by his son John for services. This same John, through his attorney William le Moyne of Barnwell, fined for three marks with the lord abbot to hold this land. And he is to pay this amount, one mark at the feast of the Translation of St. Benedict in the eighth year of Abbot John, another mark at the feast of St. Michael in the ninth year of this abbot, and the third mark at Christmas of the following year, with pledges Thomas atte Hache, Simon of the Meadow junior, William Smith, John the Hawker and Thomas Godwyne. And the above Elyas will cultivate that land and sow it well at his own expense until the next feast of St. Michael, and he and his wife shall receive one-half of the whole harvest in the autumn. And in addition the above John will provide suitable food and drink for Elyas and his wife Christine while they are alive and they will have the residence with John on the capital messuage. And if it should happen, though may it not, that trouble and discord should in the future arise between the parties so that they are unable to live together, the above John will provide for Elyas and Christine, or whichever of them should outlive the other,

---

[54] See Appendix V, no. 4.
[55] See Appendix V, no. 5.
[56] See text in Ault, *Court Rolls,* p. 236. The same type of entry is found in Houghton for the year 1274, but the text is destroyed at several points.

a house and curtilage where they can decently reside. And he will give each year to the same Elyas and Christine or whichever of them is alive, six quarters of hard corn at Michaelmas, namely three quarters of wheat, one and one-half quarters of barley, one and one-half quarters of peas and beans, and one quarter of oats. And in addition, the said Elyas and Christine by this agreement will have all the mobile and immobile chattels of their house as these were on the day the land was surrendered into the lord's hands.

GRAVELEY,[57] 1312: John Hughloc together with Thomas and Robert brothers of this same John, and their sister Alice, give twelve pence to the lord to have the vill investigate their rights in that land formerly belonging to their mother that come to them according to the customs of the manor on the death of their mother. And therefore the above jurors together with the whole vill are ordered to see that they have the portion which according to the above custom they ought to have from their mother's land. And afterwards it was determined that they should have lodgings and six bushels of corn of all types.

OVER,[58] 1301: Roger Ive gives the lord sixpence in order to determine whether or not he has a dwelling in the messuage of Robert Ive his brother according to the custom of the vill. Therefore the jurors are ordered to go there to see what ought to be done and to act accordingly.

ELLINGTON,[59] 1278: William Koc acknowledges that he is in arrears for the grain owed his father for the year, (   ) of wheat, one bushel of barley, and one bushel of beans and peas. And for the present year he is in arrears for the payment of Michaelmas last, (   ) of wheat, three bushels of barley, and three bushels of beans and peas. Therefore John Smith and Richard the reeve, his pledges for such payments, are amerced, sixpence on John and sixpence on Richard, with each other as pledge. And the said William comes and makes an agreement with his father Walter whereby the latter concedes the arrears of this and the previous year on condition that for Michaelmas last William pays now to his father Walter six bushels of wheat, two bushels of barley, and two bushels of beans and peas. And the same amounts are to be paid at the feast of the Purification of Blessed Mary, and so on accordingly every year while Walter remains alive, with Richard le Hunter and Richard in Hale as pledges. And the fine for the above William unjustly withholding payment is condoned, with the above as pledges. And the above Walter under this contract grants to the same William all his land in Ellington. And the same Walter, to assure the above agreement, and for licence to withdraw from the village with his chattels, pays the lord abbot annually two shillings from the above grain with Richard the reeve as pledge.

OVER,[60] 1300: Roger Syward and Adam Syward are pledges of Margaret Syward for two shillings paid the lord's cellarer that she might have the court consider what portion pertains to her from the virgate of villeinage formerly belonging to her late father so long as she remains unmarried. The villagers come and say that according to custom of the manor the said Margaret and her sister Amicia will have lodging and a ring of corn, that is one-half ring of wheat and the other half of

---

57 See text in Homans, *Thirteenth-Century Villagers*, p. 432, no. 14.
58 See text in Homans, *ibid.*, p. 433, no. 14.
59 See Appendix V, no. 6.
60 See Appendix V, no. 7.

peas. Roger Syward their brother pays one-half of this and Alan the other brother the remaining half since they now hold that land between them.

WISTOW,[61] 1297: Thomas Palmer was convicted by the jurors in this court of having broken the contract made with Joan and Sarra, daughters of Mariota Martin, whom he was to have taken in marriage according to the court roll of the last view. And since it is ascertained that Joan has married, the obligations of this contract to that Joan may be considered quitted. But the said Thomas owes Joan's sister Sarra according to that contract one ring of wheat, one ring of barley, and a ring of beans and peas for her maintenance from the last court of view right to the present. And hereafter the said Sarra is to be supplied adequately in food and clothing and other needs. Since the contract was broken Alexander Frere and Michael Palmer, pledges of the above Thomas, are amerced twelve pence. And by these same pledges that Sarra is to have her due as prescribed above.

ABBOTS RIPTON,[62] 1294: Agnes Hubert acknowledges that she owes Alice Martin as marriage portion for the daughter of the said Agnes one horse worth six shillings, one pig worth twelve pence, four bushels of wheat, and three goats to be delivered to Alice before Easter. And for failure to deliver (Agnes) is amerced sixpence. Pledges for both parties are William Howlond and William Olyver.

UPWOOD,[63] 1295: Juliana the widow of Adam the son of John gives the lord sixpence in order to have the court investigate her portion in that virgate of land formerly belonging to her husband, and her son Nicholas is the pledge. And the twelve jurors say that according to the custom of the vill she ought to have a house with the small lot of the messuage, and every year for life one ring of wheat, one ring of beans and peas, and one ring of oats.

Chattels

There are negligible references in the court rolls or extents to the laws governing the descent of chattels upon the customary tenements of the manors of Ramsey Abbey. It only remains to suggest that the disposition of chattels was a matter for the last will and testament, and hence within the jurisdiction of ecclesiastical courts.[64] Villagers were permitted, sometimes without the supervision of manorial officials, to make wills upon at least several Ramsey manors.[65] The texts below from Weston and Wistow probably indicate a usual disposition of chattels for support of children who were not to succeed to land, or whose lands were in wardship. Of course rights to chattels were also established by marriage agreements,

---

[61] See Appendix V, no. 8.

[62] See Appendix V, no. 9.

[63] See Appendix V, no. 10. See also no. 11 of this appendix for a good reservation text.

[64] See M. M. Sheehan, *The Will in Medieval England* (Toronto, 1963), Index *s. v.* Bequest: *chattels*, and villein.

[65] *Carts.*, III, p. 384 (Hemmingford Abbots): "Faciet testamentum suum libere, etiam in absentia servientis et prepositi"; *ibid.*, p. 477 (Barton): "Faciet testamentum per visum ballivi"; *ibid.*, p. 411 (Ringstead): "Faciet testamentum sine visu ballivi abbatis."

as was illustrated by texts for Wistow (1297) and Abbots Ripton (1294) in the previous section of this chapter. Since it was the practice for the lord to seize the chattels of the tenant who died intestate tenants were no doubt very careful to draw up their last will, and this may explain the paucity of references to chattels. In the text below for Upwood in 1435 the lord is seen seizing chattels of an intestate. It would destroy the very 'laws' of his manorial economy were the lord to strip the villager's tenements, so very probably there were arrangements, as at Warboys below, where a compromise had been worked out whereby the lord received one-third of the chattels of the intestate, or at least of the intestate without heirs of his body. There are numerous entries in court rolls, like the example given below for Wistow in 1306, of executors raising debts for the heirs.

WESTON,[66] 1294: Alice Robat enters a plea against her mother Isabella and Robert de Salene for two rings of wheat, two rings of barley, one ring of peas, the third part of the harvest of one-half acre of wheat, the third part of the utensils, and five sheep, as her portion by the bequest of her father. And the above Robert and Isabella have come to put themselves at the disposal of the village jury for this plea of the said Alice. And the same jurors come and say that the plea of that Alice is just and right, and it is determined by those same jurors that Isabella mother of this Alice in whose hands remained the third part in question should pay Alice four shillings sevenpence, farthing, for the same. For her illegal tenure (Isabella) is amerced sixpence. And the jurors determine that Robert, in whose hands remained the other two parts of the plea of the above Alice should pay her for these nine shillings, fourpence, halfpenny, farthing before Michaelmas, and for illegal retention he is amerced threepence. Pledges are Adam Bunty, William Neweman, Stephan Porter, and Roger Man.

UPWOOD,[67] 1435: And that John Gouler a native who held one messuage and three quarters of land died intestate since the last court. Therefore it is ordered that his goods and chattels be seized into the hands of the lord.

WISTOW,[68] 1294: Before Michaelmas next Ralph Keyse must pay two rings and two bushels of wheat, two rings and two bushels of barley, to Andrew Gylemle and Thomas Keyse executors of Sarra Keyse for the use of the sons of this same Sarra, and for the unjust withholding of this payment he is amerced sixpence. The pledges for both parties are Robert Bronnenote and Simon le Bonere.

WISTOW,[69] 1306: Robert Bronnote and Simon Le Bonere were pledges of Ralph Keyse at the last view that the said Ralph would pay before the feast of St. Michael next to Andrew Gilenyle and Thomas Keyse executors of Sarra Keyse, two rings and two bushels of wheat and two rings, two bushels of barley for the use of the

[66] Ault, *Court Rolls*, p. 231.
[67] See Appendix VI, no. 1. For the will of a smallish villager in 1293 see *The Archaeological Journal*, III, pp. 65-6.
[68] See Appendix VI, no. 2.
[69] See Appendix VI, no. 3.

children of the same Sarra, and that the corn has not yet been paid. Therefore the above Robert and Simon are in mercy to sixpence with pledges Nicholas Palmer and John Andrew. And it is directed that the said corn be raised from Ralph Keyse as the principal debtor if he has it, and if he does not, it is to be raised from his pledges.

WARBOYS,[70] t. Eliz. I: At this court the homage were ordered to inquire about a certain custom in the above manor. These having been charged and sworn say on oath that the matter is in the vill of Warboys as follows — it is the custom that if any customary tenant holding land of the lord should die without an heir of himself and his wife, that then the lord of the above manor should receive all the mobile and immobile goods both of the deceased and of his widow such as these are found to be on the day he died, and according to the above custom the third part of the said goods shall remain exactly and entirely in the hands of the lord. And such is the custom both after the death of the wife and of the husband if it should happen that they should die without a legitimate heir as is stated above. And therefore it is determined and agreed by the above homage that the above custom entirely in all things as above reiterated is to be observed in the above vill of Warboys. And the above jurors present that Robert Pankerell alias Benson and Robert West alias Borowe, one of whom held a virgate of customary land and the other six quarters of customary land, died since the last court without heirs of themselves and of their wives. And that John Pankerell alias Benson brother and executor of the said Robert Pankerell, and James West alias Borowe nephew and administrator of the goods of the above Robert West alias Borowe paid fines to the lord for the third part of the above goods of the above Robert Pankerell and James West in accordance with the above custom.

WARBOYS,[71] ca. 1300: ...And accordingly, upon the death of Richard Plumbe who held a virgate of land, without heirs of himself and his wife, Matilda the widow of the same Richard came and paid a fine of five marks to the lord following this custom, as is established in the *gersuma* roll for the twenty-fifth year of Abbot J.

III

The Descent of Property Within the Family

Customary law gave to the son the first title in properties after the decease of his parents. As already noted at the beginning of this chapter in explanation of the rare necessity for proclamation, the son usually entered his property so automatically that no record of this was made on the court

---

[70] See Appendix VI, no. 4.

[71] For text see *Carts.*, I, p. 307, note. The first part of this text is the statement of the custom as given in the above text from the time of Elizabeth. It should be noted that this fine, that may be compared to the payment of a feudal 'relief' for the transfer of seisin from the hands of the lord, is distinct from the heriot. On the other hand, the heriot lost its meaning when all the goods of the deceased came into the hands of the lord, so that very possibly the heriot was then absorbed in the fine for one-third of the chattels.

rolls, and the account rolls note only the receipt of the entry fine. A permanent record of these tenures was kept in a court book at the abbey, but this court book has only survived from the fifteenth century.[72] Occasionally, as with the texts below from Wistow in 1339, and Weston in 1358, some circumstance has brought a note concerning the entry of sons on the court rolls. The entries from Shillington in 1339, and Hemmingford Abbots in 1291, illustrate the entry of sons to property before or after the death of their mothers. At Shillington in 1358 it was enough for John the son of Walter to establish that his father had held and died in seisin of a one-third virgate tenement for John to recover this holding from Henry Lewyne. That strong title of the widow noted earlier in this chapter did not allow a son to lose his inheritance by the marriage of his mother, as we see illustrated from Hemmingford Abbots (1301) below. Even the absence of Sampson the son of Adam from Holywell, when his sister received their father's land, did not disallow Sampson's claims in that property in 1294. At Warboys in 1313 the son was able to recover his property inheritance that had been leased by his aunt with the consent of the lord. It would be expected of course, that the hereditary right to succession would take precedence over time leases, and the following text from Knapwell shows customary law being invoked to this purpose. One of the best illustrations of the strength of this customary title may be found in an entry for Hemmingford Abbots in 1312[73] whereby William, son of Peter the Miller, was given seisin of a family croft even during his father's lifetime owing to the fact that the latter had received another holding through his wife. The son could lose his right to inheritance by various means, and from the roll of Chatteris in 1273 Richard is seen to have lost his land to his brother Robert since the land was escheated to the lord. When Robert son of Mabel of Warboys vacated his land for a trip to the continent, some of his neighbours were given temporary responsibility, but Robert was not disseised at once.

WISTOW,[74] 1339: The jurors present that Robert Haukyn, who held a one-half virgate from the lord, died. And Thomas his son does not come to-day to fine for that land and take the oath for he is ill. (A note is added in another hand, 'afterwards he takes the oath).'

WESTON,[75] 1358: And that John Baroun who held from the lord in villeinage one-half virgate died since the last court. And Roger his son is a native of the lord and

[72] See *Estates*, Appendix I, p. 321 ff.
[73] For latin text, see Homans, *Thirteenth-Century Villagers*, p. 443, and translation, *ibid.*, p. 199.
[74] See Appendix VII, no. 1.
[75] See Appendix VII, no. 2.

nearest heir, and they say that the lord will have nothing from the death of this John save what the heir will give in entry fine at the will of the lord. Therefore he is to be distrained to take the oath, etc.

SHILLINGTON,[76] 1339: The jurors present that Agnes in the slade who held in bondage from the lord one virgate of land at Stondon has ended her days, and from her is sent one cow worth five shillings as heriot. And Walter her son fined for that land and took the oath.

And that Matilda atte Grene who held a virgate of the lord in bondage at Shillington ended her days, and from her comes as heriot one cow worth five shillings ...

Godfrey the son and heir of Isabella Okolt came to this court and having proved that he was of age asked to be admitted to an acre of land formerly of the heritage of the said Isabella that was in the lord's hands after the death of the same Isabella owing to the minority of this same Godfrey. And he is thereby granted seisin. And he takes the oath.

HEMMINGFORD ABBOTS,[77] 1291: And they say that the messuage and adjacent croft once held by Thomas Thykene is in the lord's hands. And the seneschal by the exercise of his own office granted that messuage and croft to Emma Ange. And the same Emma (in person) in full court with the assent of her husband Ange transferred all her rights (in that land) to the service of her son John but only that first he should fine for that messuage and croft with the lord abbot by sixteen shillings.

SHILLINGTON,[78] 1358: It was established by the jurors that Henry Lewyne unjustly deforced John son of Walter (Pechat) of the third part of a virgate of land that Walter father of this John had formerly held and in which he died in seisin. Therefore it is ordered that it be recovered, etc.

HOLYWELL,[79] 1294: Sampson the son of Adam Gilbert of Niddingworth pays twelve pence to the lord with John the physician of St. Ives as pledge in order to have an inquiry by the court as to whether he has the greater right in that messuage and virgate of land formerly belonging to his father than his sister Maycusa the tenant. This same Maycusa fined for the said messuage and virgate of land with lord Abbot John to be held for services by her son Robert owing to the absence of the said Sampson. And the inquisitors come and say that the said Sampson had the greater right in the said land after the death of his mother than the said Maycusa his sister according to the custom of the vill. And afterwards an agreement was reached whereby Robert and Maycusa his wife ? will acquit Sampson of the promised twelve pence to the lord and will give the same Sampson twenty shillings. And (they will give) the lord abbot one-half mark, with pledge Walter Grey.

WARBOYS,[80] 1313: Nicholas Oseburne gave the lord two shillings... to have an inquiry concerning a land that is called Sixpennyworthland that Richard Godwyne now holds. And the same Nicholas says that he has right, etc. And the jurors say that a certain Richard Oseburne father of the above Nicholas held the said land

---

[76] See Appendix VII, no. 3. And see Broughton, 1339, in no. 11 of this appendix for a parallel entry. A good example of wardship arrangements for a villein's son may be found in no. 32 of this appendix.
[77] See Appendix VII, no. 4.
[78] See Appendix VII, no. 5.
[79] For latin text, see Ault, *Court Rolls*, p. 225.
[80] See Appendix VII, no. 6.

as of his right and he handed over that land to his sister Cristina to hold by service, and the said Cristina paid the fine for it to the lord. And she handed this land over to be held by the above Richard Godwyne who fined for it with the lord and now holds it. And the case is reserved to be put to the lord. And the above lord abbot by a special grace conceded and delivered the said land to the above Nicholas Oseburne who renders to the lord twelve pence in fine for which the reeve is held to account in his roll, and he is to pay yearly eightpence at the usual times. And he is to find one man for the lord's boon in the autumn and another at lovebones and to remove fen grass, and he pays fowl and eggs and all other services and customs to be done according as they were accustomed to be done for that land.

KNAPWELL,[81] 1316: Nicholas Isabell gives the lord twelve pence in order to have an inquiry of the court concerning a one-half virgate of land against Anna widow of William Alred who holds that land through the death of her husband. The above Nicholas seeks and claims this one-half virgate as of his right and heredity in so far as a certain Robert Isabel his father held this land during his life when he handed it over to the above William Alred to be held for service for life. Consequently the above Nicholas says that according to the custom of the manor the above land should resort to him after the death of William Alred. And that this is so he puts himself on the *gersuma* roll of Ramsey. And he is told to inquire in the said rolls before the next court.

CHATTERIS,[82] 1273: Richard Charite comes and gives the lord two shillings to have an inquiry as to whether his brother Robert Sichrich has a better right to the land that this Robert holds... and he find pledges, namely Ivo the reeve and Stephen Sichrich. The inquest was held and says that the above land... (was held) by the ancestors of the above Richard and Robert but it was escheated to the lord abbot and the above Robert made satisfaction to the lord abbot for the above land, and therefore it is judged that it remain with the said Robert.

HEMMINGFORD ABBOTS,[83] 1301: The jurors established that Henry Trappe had purchased one and one-half rods of land from Alice Hering by charter, and one-half acre from Matilda Hering by charter. And then Thomas son of Simon of Stukeley who had married the widow of the above Henry showed these charters in court and took the oath to hold these lands. The court orders that the rod and one-half bought by Henry Trappe from Alice Hering by charter, as well as that one-half acre that the same Henry bought of Matilda Hering, should be seized into the lord's hands until John the son and heir of Henry should come to claim that land. And eighteen pence are to be levied from Emma Ingel, widow of the above Henry, for the crop of dredge from that land gathered by the same Emma. And note that the charters of the above-mentioned lands are delivered to the custody of Thomas Marshall, the reeve, until etc. Then afterwards the said John came and paid the lord as entry fine to hold these lands at the will of the lord (two shillings, in margin). He shall perform the usual required services. And in addition he will pay the lord at Easter every year one capon as increment. Let it be noted that Adam Hog and Thomas the Marshall are pledges of John son of Henry Trappe that the latter will be obedient to the lord and pay the services commonly owed for that land for which he has fined as noted

---

81 See Appendix VII, no. 7.
82 For latin text, see Ault, *Court Rolls,* p. 267.
83 See Appendix VII, no. 8.

more fully above. And John will be responsible for the two charters for that land delivered to him in full court when these are required of him.

HEMMINGFORD ABBOTS,[84] 1313: (   ) Richard the Fyssher held that land from the lord and after his death the title to the land fell according to custom to Christina daughter and heir of the same Richard. This Christina married a certain John Trappe (who entered) that land without fine and generated by that Christina William the Fyssher father of the above (John) now entering the plea. And the above-mentioned William held and had a virgate of land. When the said John Trappe had died, the above Christina who outlived him gave that land through the farmer of the vill to be held by services by John the Fyssher son of the above William the Fyssher. Therefore it is determined that the above Thomas may receive nothing from the above land and that the above John may recover that land. And he gives the lord two marks as entry fine.

WARBOYS,[85] 1301: The virgate of land belonging to Robert son of Mabel of Caldecote who has gone overseas without permission from the lord has been seized into the lord's hands together with the chattels thereon. And now this property is handed over to four men, namely, John Segely, Robert Harsyne, Simon son of Robert, and Richard son of Robert, who are accountable to the lord for all the dues and customs pertaining to that land, until, etc.

The daughter's rights to land were also clearly affirmed in customary law. At Lawshall in 1394 we see a woman establishing the right to inherit a property. Alice Planterose recovered an inheritance at Chatteris in 1289, even when she had been forced by poverty to release the holding for some time. Alice the wife of Hugh Waryn presents her hereditary right against a life lease in the court of Shillington in 1306. At Cranfield the 'foreign' husband of Alice, Godfrey of Crawley, obtains the right to hold Alice's inherited land through a special agreement with the lord. Incidentally, it is interesting to note that this agreement practically repeats the customary laws of the manor as found in the extents, even to the point of requiring residence on the manor, since an outsider like Godfrey, unlike a native of Cranfield, was not ordinarily bound by customary laws. On the other hand, an unfree woman who had married a freeman before receiving her customary inheritance would appear, following the text from Hemmingford Abbots below, to have lost her right to customary inheritance by that act. From the court roll of King's Ripton in 1297 we have an example of how the father had purchased property for the support of his daughter. Since this property was purchased and bequeathed by will it was likely freehold, however, rather than customary land.

LAWSHALL,[86] 1394-5: John Bedford of London, carpenter, and Sabina his wife and daughter of Alice Couper, come and claim the right and inheritance after the death

[84] See Appendix VII, no. 9.
[85] See Appendix VII, no. 10.
[86] See Appendix VII, no. 12.

of the above Alice mother of the same Sabina, to a ten acre tenement that Godfrey Walter now holds as let to him by William Togood, and (she) seeks to be admitted to the above tenement. And an inquest was made about this by twelve jurors of this court who say on oath that the above Sabina is the nearest heir to the aforesaid Alice, and that the above Alice mother of the same Sabina died in seisin of the said tenement according to the customs of the manor, and that the above Sabina has right to the said tenement. Therefore it is agreed that the above Sabina should recover the said tenement, to be held from the lord for the services and customs therefrom due and customary according to the customs of the manor. The whole court determines that she is to pay to the above William Togood for expenses and repairs he has done one hundred shillings, which are to be paid through the hands of the lord's bailiff Simon, who also is to be her pledge for this. And she gives the lord as a fine for having the entry, three shillings fourpence, with the same pledge.

CHATTERIS,[87] 1289: Alice Planterose gives the lord twelve pence with Nicholas Sarle as pledge in order to have the court consider whether she has the greater right in that messuage and yard than the tenant Margaret le Blodlade. And Godfrey the Red and his companions the jurors coming say that that Alice fined for the said tenement after the death of her father and mother, and after nine years left the said tenement for which she was not able to provide the due and accustomed services. Thence Lord Berengarius delivered that tenement to the above Margaret, but afterwards the said Alice has now come again and is prompt to pay the lord all the arrears, saying that she has the better right to hold that tenement than the above Margaret... (the court determines that this land) will be defended by Alice as hers by right of heir, on the condition that this Alice pay twentypence to the above Margaret for the costs borne in correcting the due and accustomed services for the period of ten years as assessed by the court.

SHILLINGTON,[88] 1306: Hugh Waryn and his wife Alice come and give the lord twelve pence, with Walter Lamb as pledge, to have the court inquire about three acres of land now held by Roger Carter. These three acres the above Hugh and Alice seek as of right belonging to the said Alice, because the above land belonged to a certain Richard le Bole father of Alice who now seeks the land as heir. This land was let during his lifetime by the above Richard to the said Roger for a term of years. And they ask that an investigation be made. And the above Roger comes and says that he fined for the above land with Abbot William of Ramsey. And he puts himself on the *gersuma* roll at Ramsey as proof of this. Therefore he is told to search those rolls before the next court.

CRANFIELD,[89] *ca.* 1300: To all the faithful in Christ who shall see or hear read this document John by the grace of God abbot of Ramsey sends greetings in the lord. We inform you that for a fine of twenty marks which our beloved Godfrey of Crawley paid to us, we grant that he may have entry on our customary land at money rent at Cranfield by our special permission to Alice the daughter of Cristina de la Burne and may take her in marriage with that whole messuage in Cranfield, with its lands, meadows, and adjacent woods, which messuage with lands and woods the same Alice daughter of Cristina de la Burne fined for after the death of the above Cristina

---

[87] For latin text see Ault, *Court Rolls*, p. 280. Lord Berengarius was a Le Moigne from whom Abbot William of Godmanchester bought this property in the thirteenth century.
[88] See Appendix VII, no. 13.
[89] See Appendix VII, no. 14.

her mother. Accordingly the above Godfrey must hold as a unit for his whole life that tenement together with its appurtenants, and he must continually reside in the same place with his chattels. He must perform for us and our church every year the ploughings, harrowings, boon works, carrying services, tallages, and all other services customarily owed except the office of reeve from which service we exempt the same Godfrey perpetually by this document. Moreover, the said Godfrey will maintain and preserve the buildings on that tenement, as well as the walls, and hedges, in the same state or better than when he received them, and he will return from what is grown on that land to that same property. Nor shall it be permitted to the same Godfrey to sell or give away or take beyond the fee anything from the woods of that tenement or from the vines and hedges, nor shall he destroy any of these things nor cut them for his own use, except only for the reasonable repair of the buildings and hedges and for fire, and to repair and rebuild ruinous buildings, except with a special licence from us. In witness of which etc.

KING'S RIPTON,[90] 1297: John Pege gave the lord sixpence in order to have the court consider (his rights in) a grange and land formerly in the hands of Cristina Umfrey his sister who has died. John le Malker and his companions the twelve jurors say that William Umfrey once bought the said grange and land, and he bequeathed it upon his dying to Cristina for life that after her death it should go to his son John. Therefore it is decided that he may have seisin etc.

HEMMINGFORD ABBOTS,[91] 1313: Agnes daughter of Nicholas le Hunne comes and requests entry by fine after her father's death to a croft formerly her father's. And it is established that this Agnes is married to a certain freeman. Therefore that croft is to be taken into the lord's hands and the profits accounted for. And the said Agnes retains no claim in that land. It is shown that afterwards someone else fined for that property.

WESTON,[92] 1300: Adam of Goseholm holds from the lord that half virgate of land once belonging to Henry Randolf. From this land a certain Mariota daughter of that Henry had by right of custom of the manor two rods after the decease of her parent Henry. That Mariota let that land at farm for several years to a certain Adam Buncy. And since the said Mariota was living at a distance from Weston and did not want to come to Weston, the above Adam Buncy was instructed to have the said Mariota come in person by a certain day under penalty of losing that land. On the day appointed the said Adam Buncy did not have her so that those two rods of land were taken into the lord's hands so that the lord received the revenues and esplees from them for two years. Now the above Adam of Goseholm comes and gives the lord two shillings with William of Bythorn, Adam son of Roger, Godfrey Carter, and Simon Buncy as pledges, to have a proper inquiry as to whether those two rods are appurtenant to his half virgate or not. And the inquisitors come and say that those two rods are appurtenant to the half virgate of the above Adam de Goseholm, and through ignorance as to whether the said Mariota was still living or married, they deliver those two rods of land to the above Adam de Goseholm to cultivate and hold so long as he shall be responsible to the above Mariota should she come. And the pledges are as above.

[90] See Appendix VII, no. 15.
[91] See Appendix VII, no. 25.
[92] See Appendix VII, no. 26. See also no. 27 of this appendix for an interesting inquiry concerning a woman's title.

ELTON,[93] 1306: Of Emma Gocelyn for having the judgement of the court for appointing and delivering to her the portion which belongs to her of that messuage and place formerly her father's, sixpence, pledge Robert Gocelyne. Therefore it is commanded to the jurors that they go there in order to do and appoint according to what is fitting for the above Emma in the foregoing.

An order for the direct descent of property seems to be clearly taken for granted in customary law. But when it comes to defining precisely what principles directed the establishment of a certain order of precedence in family claims to property our evidence is most vague. For example, the following account from the court of Ellington gives us an interesting survey of the evidence presented in court in response to the inquiry by Richard in Estate. But this evidence fails to tell us upon what principle the issue was decided among the family beyond indication of apparently important facts such as, the claimant had not made his plea at the proper time, and was not propertyless in any case. It was the establishment of a new blood-right to property by marriage that occasioned a lawsuit at Shillington in 1356.

The brisk control of the allocation of dwellings as well as lands, indicated in the following example from Hemmingford Abbots, leaves one with the impression that customary law was far too vital a part of the daily life and circumstance of the villagers to require exposition in the court rolls. Whether it was a simple matter of alienating customary land as in this example from Hemmingford Abbots, or an involved succession such as that found in the example below for Shillington in 1306, where the villagers went back three generations to establish a direct line that would take precedence over the heir of the last tenant, or over the collateral heir of the last one in this family to hold the tenement, the villagers seemed equally competent to establish the proper blood title to property. If the order of precedence in the direct line of descent cannot be clearly seen from the records, it is not surprising that the rights to property in collateral descent are even less discernible. The lawsuit over the property of the late William Huck of King's Ripton who died intestate in 1483 cannot be taken to suggest that the will of the deceased would have had any authority in determining the bequest of the customary property, beyond perhaps certain chattels.

The intriguing tenure by Borough English also appears among village customs. But the importance of Borough English on Ramsey properties is difficult to determine. This system of succession through the youngest son in the family seems to have been introduced to Graveley in the third

[93] See text in *Elton Manorial Records,* p. 118.

quarter of the thirteenth century[94]; a younger brother had also inherited family lands in the text from Woodhurst (Slepe) below. The right of children of the second marriage over those of the first, as seen in an example from Ellington, may indicate the same emphasis. But the reasoning behind succession by younger members is not easy to assess. Lawyers have argued at least from the time of Littleton that Borough English ensures support for the most dependent members of the family. That is to say, by Borough English the needs of the family as a community take precedence over the narrower concern with the guarantee of direct succession. However, such explanations are inadequate as they stand. Indeed there is an equally strong argument for Borough English at a time of land plenty in that this type of inheritance ensures that a mobile group — the older members of the family — are made available to take up vacant or newly-cleared holdings. In addition, in a mobile society the youngest child would be most clearly discernible as of the blood because of his being the last of the children associated with their parents, and at least in tribal days this would be an important consideration. Since Borough English dates from before the Norman Conquest this argument cannot be lightly dismissed. But finally, Borough English is not easily explicable in terms only of labour demand. The peasant virgate, or even the half virgate, needed more than one labourer at many seasons of the year. It was logical to encourage this assistance from the older members of the family. But primogeniture, rather than Borough English, encourages the interest of the older sons. In fact the common opinion among students of the matter is that primogeniture ensures better control of the property by the immediate family. And, by the same token, Borough English increases the likelihood that land will be inherited by a minor, a very undesirable situation for the demesne economy.

ELLINGTON,[95] t. Ed. III: (Richard in Estate) gives the lord one-half mark, with pledges Walter Smith and Henry Attebrok, to have the court inquire about one virgate against Nicholas Burgeys who holds that land, on the basis that he has a better right (   ) according to the custom of the manor. Accordingly he claims this land against Nicholas in that Hugh, whose nearest heir is Richard, held the said virgate as his of proper right according to custom, and in this died in seisin, and so after his death (Richard) as nearest son and heir of the said Hugh ought to defend the land according to custom, etc. And to establish that such is his right he asks that

---

94 See Homans, *Thirteenth-Century Villagers*, for latin text, p. 430, and translation, p. 126. The same type of emphasis may be seen at King's Ripton in 1307 where a sister's son is said to have prior right by custom to a certain land over the brother of the former tenant, Thomas Arnold who died childless. For this text, see *Homans, ibid.*, pp. 122 and 429, and Maitland, *Manorial Courts*, p. 106.

95 See Appendix VII, no. 16.

an inquiry be made. An inquisition was therefore taken for a decision on the above through Richard of Hayward, Bartholomew in Lynland, Simon son of John son of Walter, William Aldych, Thomas Godman, William Burneys, Roger Aldych, Godfrey Buk, John son of Sarra, William son of Walter, William Lennard, and Adam the reeve. These say on oath that a certain Hugh in Estate held the said virgate as his of right and died in seisin of this tenure. And they say that the above Hugh had three sons, namely Thomas, Adam, and Richard the present claimant. The above Adam married a certain Juliana who held a virgate of land, and the above Thomas son of that Hugh married Agnes daughter of the above Juliana (with an agreement) made among themselves that the above Thomas and Agnes would have the forementioned virgate after the death of the said Hugh. But indeed the above Hugh (   ) lived for a long time in possession of that land so that Thomas died before him (   ) finally at the death of Hugh the above Agnes (received) the said land (   ) and for eight years and more held it in that vill. The jurors being asked whether the said Hugh (   ) Thomas or Agnes had received this land through the lord or not, they say no. And so it is judged (that the vill?) let the land to Agnes contrary to custom (   ) it was submitted that the above Thomas her husband never was in seisin during his life, but that she was still given seisin, (the vill) in mercy to twenty shillings. The jurors being asked whether the above Richard claimed that land after the death of his father as son and heir, they say no. But they find clearly that with his own goods and chattels of his father an entry fine was made by the said Richard to a three-quarter land of the abbot in the same vill, (and so) no further claim ought to be made for the above virgate, nor any right expected. Therefore it was determined that the above Richard should receive nothing of the above land, which afterwards by grant and licence of the lord was committed to Nicholas Burgeys who first held it, and he pays forty shillings to the lord in *gersuma*.

SHILLINGTON,[96] 1356: It is recalled that Walter Pechat fined at the last court for a virgate of land that Adam Lewyne first held, to be held for services by John son of the above (Walter) and Margaret daughter and heir of the forementioned Adam according to the custom of the manor. Concerning this Walter atte Wode came to this court and claims the above land as heir and relative of a certain Alice atte Wode mother of Walter atte Wode father of the above Walter in so far as that Alice held according to the custom of the manor as he maintains. And now come both John son of Walter Pechat and Margaret daughter of the above mentioned Adam (and they defend themselves against the claims of this Walter   ) and they say that the above mentioned Alice atte Wode through whom he makes the claim was incapable of maintaining the above tenement (so that   ) with the assent of the same Alice herself the lord's steward at that time directed a naif Silvester Lewyne to (enter so) that through marriage (to Alice) and the payment of entry fine that land should be held by him and his heirs according to the custom of the manor. And Silvester and Alice defended (   ) Henry as their son and heir defended the (right to this tenement), to the same Adam son and heir of Henry (from whom) came the fee and right to the above Margaret as daughter and heir of the said Adam, and she is the present tenant (   ) through the twelve jurors it is submitted that a certain Alice atte Wode etc., etc. Judgement is given in favour of the above John and Margaret his wife and not to

96 See Appendix VII, no. 17.

Walter; Walter is considered to have nothing in this and to be in mercy for a false claim, and the above John and Margaret will hold in peace.

HEMMINGFORD ABBOTS,[97] 1293-4: On Simon Koc naif of the lord since to the prejudice of the lord he conceded to John le Sachere a house along with his sister whom the latter took in marriage, twelve shillings...

On all the vill and the jurors... since to the prejudice of the lord and against the custom of the vill they permitted Simon Koc to grant a house along with his sister in free marriage gift.

SHILLINGTON,[98] 1306: From Walter Cobbe that the court might consider an inquiry into the right he claims to have in a messuage and virgate formerly of Hugh the Carter, twelve pence, with William Le Hauscomp pledge. From Robert Gill' for the same, twelve pence, Adam Richard the pledge. From Hugh the Carter for the same, twelve pence, William Le Faycour pledge.

There died Hugh the Carter who held from the lord a messuage and virgate. And a certain Walter Cobbe comes and seeks to hold that land with permission of the lord as of his right. And he says a certain Juliana died without heirs of her body. And as her nearest heir he asks for the tenement. And at this a certain Hugh, son of the above Hugh (Carter) comes and claims the tenement as his by reason of the fact that Hugh his father outlived the said Juliana. And the above Hugh married Joan the mother of this Hugh, and in this very tenement was born this Hugh who now asks for his right. Both the above Walter and Hugh ask for an inquiry to establish which has the greater right. And (an inquisition) was made by twenty-four true and lawful men of the above vill who say on oath that according to the custom of the manor the right is found in the above tenement in that a certain Robert Cobbe (father?) of the above Juliana through whose death the said Juliana entered the said tenement and died without heirs of her body, had three sisters, namely Agnes, Matilda, and Joan. And by custom of the manor such succession falls to the eldest son of Agnes as heir. And from the above Agnes this right descends to a certain Richard as her son and heir. And from the above Richard to a certain Nicholas as son and nearest heir who is eligible and present. And he is told that he may proceed to fine for that land.

KING'S RIPTON,[99] 1483: They (i.e. the jurors) say that William Hrech died intestate since the time of the last court and without issue. And they also say that he has two sisters, one named Juliana married to Richard Baker of Holme, and the other Agnes married to Robert Fabyon of this vill. That same Juliana has a son John Baker who claims as nearest heir the right to half of that land and tenement formerly of the above William Hrech his uncle in that vill. And he asks to be admitted to these in full court according to the common law of England and according to the custom of this court. And the other sister, the above Agnes wife of Robert Fabyon, claims sole possession of all lands and tenements formerly of William Hrech her brother as nearest heir, (seeking entry?) to the above lands and appurtenants. And the said Robert Fabyon her husband came into court and seeks to be admitted as sole possessor of the above lands and tenements as belonging to his wife of right according (he is fully admitted   ).

[97] For latin text see Homans, *Thirteenth-Century Villagers*, p. 433, no. 18, and for discussion of the free marriage gift, *ibid.*, Ch. XIII.
[98] See Appendix VII, no. 18.
[99] See Appendix VII, no. 19.

WOODHIRST,[100] 1395: In the nineteenth year of the reign of King Richard II and the seventeenth year of Lord Abbot Edward, on the twenty-fourth day of July, John in le Wroo received from Brother Richard of Schenyngdon, the custodian, a messuage and virgate of land, an empty plot, and one-half virgate of land, that his father had first held and that his younger brother Thomas entirely refused to have and to hold according to the customs of the manor. These lands are to be held by the same John in bondage at the will of the lord for life. And he is to pay the lord every year thirty-nine shillings at the usual times, equal parts at Saint Andrew's, the Annunciation, Saint Benedict's, and the Nativity of Blessed Mary. And he is to perform annually the boon works, ploughings, and autumn works, and other services and customs owed and determined as done by others of like circumstance according to the customs of the manor. And the above John will well and suitably preserve, repair, and maintain all the houses and enclosures of the said tenement at his own expense during all that time. And it is not allowed to the said John within that time to transfer or lease that tenement in part or in whole without the licence of the custodian of the moment. And he gives the lord as entry fine, six shillings, eightpence.

ELLINGTON,[101] t. Ed. III: And William of Cotenham gave the lord (four) shillings with Richard son of Alice and Simon Pen'el as pledges, to have the court investigate a messuage and a virgate in Ellington and a messuage (   ) the above virgate against Walter of Cotenham who holds the said messuages and virgates (   ) claiming to have the better right in the above messuages and land over the above Walter according to the custom of the vill (   ) in that William Smith, the father of this William who is his nearest heir, held the above two messuages and land as of his right and in this died in seisin, after whose death the above messuages and land ought to come to William as nearest heir and son of his father's first wife according to the custom of the manor to be defended and held by him. And that such is his right he asks for inquiry. And the above Walter who holds all the above messuages and lands says that he has the better right in these messuages and lands than William according to the custom of the manor in that he married Isabella daughter of William Smith by his second wife... and he likewise asks for an inquiry to be made. An inquisition was then composed by Richard Hayward, (   ), Simon son of John son of Walter, William Aldych, Thomas Godman, William Burneys, (   ) Buk, John son of Sarra, Walter son of Wate, William Lennard and Adam the reeve (who say) that a certain William Smith from a time before they remembered held the said two messuages and virgate in entirety as of right and never was known to have separated them, and that (this William) married a certain Cristina from whom was born the above William the claimant. Then Cristina having died, the same William Smith took to wife a certain Emma from whom was born Isabella wife of the above Walter who now holds the two messuages and virgate. And they (i.e. the jurors) say that the sons and daughters of the second wife, as in the above case, have a greater right according to custom to the land of their fathers than the sons and daughters born of the first marriage. Therefore it is judged that the above William son of William Smith may have nothing of the two messuages and the virgate, and

[100] See Appendix VII, no. 20.
[101] See Appendix VII, no. 21. A woman's right to inherit a cottage, according to the custom of the manor, for which a fine had been paid that it might be defended by her and her heirs, is established at Cranfield in 1306 (P R O, SC 2, Port. 179, no. 12) against a male claimant. But the text is too defective to merit transcription.

60   THE TENEMENT AND THE FAMILY

that the above Walter may retain peaceful possession of these. And Walter gives two shillings to the lord that this be well enrolled.

HEMMINGFORD ABBOTS,[102] 1278: Henry son of Godfrey gives sixpence, with Simon son of Godfrey as pledge, in order to have the court give him custody of two rods of land that Henry son of Roger and Agatha the widow hold. And the jurors come and say that never during the previous fifty years has any ancestor of this Henry been seen holding those two rods of land. Therefore the said Henry will receive nothing for his claim, and the above Roger and Agatha may continue to hold, etc.

HEMMINGFORD ABBOTS,[103] 1296: Simon of Benelond gives the lord sixpence in order to have the court determine rights to a half-rod of land between himself and Thomas son of Henry. And a day was fixed before Easter for Ranulph at the top of the vill, William the Warde, Adam Hog, Thomas Marsh, Simon of Stukeley, Nicholas the Farmer, Reginald son of the Smith, Adam Almar, William son of Peter, Nicholas of Ellsworth, William Selede, Jordan Tuppe, Reginald son of Peter, William ate Style, and Simon son of Godfrey to inquire which of the above Simon and Henry has the greater right to the above half-rod of land. These inquisitors say that the said Thomas has complete title to that property. And therefore it is ordered that he be put in seisin.

ELLINGTON,[104] 1329: Agnes (Alet) gives the lord threepence, with the reeve as pledge, in order to have the court establish her rights in a certain plot in the garden formerly belonging to her father.

ELLINGTON,[105] 1306: William Brun comes and gives the lord twelve pence, with Richard West as pledge, in order to have the court determine by inquiry (his rights in) one rod of land that Roger Aldych for a long time has kept from him and still keeps. An inquisition having been taken with the above jurors, these say on oath that according to the custom of the vill the above William Brun has the greater right to that rod of land than the above Roger. Therefore it is determined that this William should recover that rod of land, and that the said Roger be amerced sixpence for illegal tenure. The pledge is Richard West, reeve.

SHILLINGTON,[106] 1290: Adam Richard gives the lord twelve pence, with Reginald de Hamscomb as pledge, to have an inquiry whether he has the greater right to a rod of meadow than Matilda his aunt now holding that property.

As well as being an obligation contracted with his lord, customary tenure was an intimate personal and social act in the life of the villager. Rights to land through blood remained even in periods of intense competition for land, remained even when a woman succeeded, or when she married an outsider; such rights remained even when the legitimate heir had been illegally outside the manor and for long periods, or when the land had been illegally sublet.[107]

[102] See Appendix VII, no. 22.
[103] See Appendix VII, no. 23.
[104] See Appendix VII, no. 28.
[105] See Appendix VII, no. 24.
[106] See Appendix VII, no. 29.
[107] It is clear from many sources that common law was not the 'law' for the villager: e.g. *Casus Placitorum and Reports of Cases in the King's Courts*, 1272-8 (Selden Society, vol. 69,

Perhaps the most striking feature of customary tenure was the adequacy of this system of succession until the late fourteenth century. By the time of our extant court rolls in the late thirteenth century a system of inheritance was running so smoothly that questions of disputed right to customary lands rarely reached the manorial court to require attention by the lord and his officials. Among a peasantry who were not particularly law-abiding, and who were often greedy for land, this uninterrupted history of inheritance can only be explained by very well-known and very wide laws of succession. Rights to customary land were so clearly seen that succession was usually automatic; and rights to succession were so well worked out among various degrees of blood relationship that the failure of certain family lines to provide heirs posed no legal difficulties.[108]

For the purpose of this study, an immediately practical consequence of the vitality of customary family laws is the fact that court records are inadequate sources for an analysis of succession in village family tenements. Court records tell us that there were family laws; but the local court did not pass judgement upon the rationale of these laws. On the one hand the principle of premier individual right by blood emerges strongly as the kingpin of the local legal structure. But over against this is another principle of 'group rights' — wife, daughter, son, brother can present a variety of claims to maintenance. What were the limits set for application of the latter principle? Inexplicable applications, for example in the custom of

---

ed. W. H. Dunham, 1952), p. 13, no. 61—"A woman claimed dower; it was answered that she was a villein, therefore she could not have dower..." *ibid.*, p. 17, no. 78: "Two sisters divide a heritage, one marries a villein, the other a free man; the one who has the free man may hold all the land by reason of the (other's having married a) villein..." But historians of common law continue to pass judgement upon the nature of freedom and law in the village upon the bases of these common law negations: e.g. G. J. Turner, *Brevia Placitata* (Selden Society, vol. 66, 1951), p. cxli, "He was not eligible to serve on a jury, nor on an assize; nor could he take orders in the church unless first emancipated. He could make no will. His chattels were his lord's. His children, like himself, were adscriptitii glebae; no one of them was properly described as his heir. They were mere sequelae, suit or issue. Such a man was not free if the word has any meaning." In view of the villager's extensive service on local juries, of the evidence for his making a will, of the right of the widow to dower, the rights of villagers to hereditary tenements, to maintenance from land and chattels, etc. seen in the above chapter, such statements by historians are irrelevant to local life; and even more, the dominance of the common law historian in the writing of social history has caused historians to neglect the meaning of the existence of another law for the villager. Indeed, it is interesting to note that the terms 'bondage' and 'villeinage' have a less repulsive overtone in the context of customary law where the naif becomes a sort of vassal of the lord with his own 'rights' and 'law'.

108 It may be expected, of course, that wide family rights to land by blood have an ancient tradition reaching back to the tribal culture of early mediaeval England. Lack of evidence for definite lines of cleavage between lineal and collateral rights to property is evidence for the very vital persistence of the wide kin relation. Social anthropologists have found a wider kinship relation in all areas of life in more primitive societies, see A. R. Radcliffe-Brown, *Structure and Function in Primitive Society* (The Free Press, Glencoe, Illinois, 1952), p. 52.

Borough English, only serve to underline the gaps in our knowledge. Beneath the administrative structure of the local court lay kinship connections to which the court deferred in dealing with the tenure of customary land. Where administration of customary land was temporary, as with tenure by the widow or maintenance arrangements, the court roll frequently served as a record and we can see how some decisions were made. But the permanent pattern of rights in land was a matter of blood relationships which were recognized but not established by court records. For the disposition of chattels too, the last will and testament of the villager often took the administration of mobile goods out of the local court.

The tension between the varied and multiple claims of the 'community family' upon a tenement and the claims of the lord must have been very great in times of economic distress. What would happen to the rights of parents, brothers, and sisters in a villager's tenement, when the latter's crop was inadequate to pay the rents and services owed to the lord? The material of the above chapter indicates at least that the 'manorial nexus' between lord and villein had not supplanted a vital community right in land.

Does the regular flow of proprietary rights in customary land through blood mean that the commercial market for land failed to attract the manorial properties? From the thirteenth century there was an active market in freeholds on Ramsey villages. In the following chapter we shall see some of the ways by which customary land too could enter this market.

CHAPTER III

CONVEYANCE AMONG CUSTOMARY TENANTS

I

Conveyance of the Customary Tenement

CUSTOMARY tenure and hereditary rights to properties tell us little about the actual variety in land transactions on the manor. It is true that tenure by service remained the only proper title to a customary holding. Adopting a terminology from feudal legal formula, the villeinage tenement was said to defend (*defendere*)[1] itself for work (*ad opus*) on the demesne. It was only under this title that such property could be transferred through the courts (*reddidit in manu domini ad opus*). However, since servile obligations had become impersonal and fixed as conditions of tenure (that is, *secundum consuetudinem manerii*),[2] rather than burdens inherited by villein status as such, servile obligations might be divided and transferred. In this way the villein had wide possibilities for conveyance of land within the legal framework of customary tenure. Family rights by blood still left discretion to the tenant in the disposition of customary lands. Brother might convey land to brother, as we see in the example from Hemmingford Abbots below. The failure of brothers to complete terms of a land transfer at Abbots Ripton has left an interesting account in the court of that village. More frequently, of course, the father or mother transfers property to a son during the former's lifetime. As far as the lord was concerned, the latter type of conveyance was the same as inheritance, for it may be noted in the examples given here from Shillington that the property was consequently taxed for the heriot as well as the entry fine. The case of John Edrich in Burwell suggests that the son could receive land through the father, but whether in this the son was a minor or the father was merely representing him at court, is not clear.

---

[1] The term 'defend' has already occurred in several texts in Chapter Two, above; see Appendices.

[2] The fixed conditions of tenure indicated by this formula in the conveyance entries are most readily observed first, in the static structure of services detailed by the extents, and secondly, in the history of the stable commutation rates for these services. Extents available for Ramsey Abbey manors are listed in *Estates*, Appendix A, and work obligations are discussed particularly in Chapter VIII, Section I; for commutation in the same study see the Index under that title.

HEMMINGFORD,[3] 1316: William the son of Simon Koc came and delivered through the lord's hands the virgate of land formerly held by his father to his brother Lawrence to be held for services. And the latter gives the vill a ploughshare for entry fine as is required in the *gersuma* roll of Ramsey. And he must perform the services and customs.

SHILLINGTON,[4] 1347: Robert Sammer gives the lord one mark for permission to stay abroad for life, finding as pledges Robert West, Nicholas Attemade, Henry del Abbey, Walter Attewode. And the same Robert Sammer delivers through the lord's hands to William his son one messuage and two virgates to be held for services. And the latter gives the lord in *gersuma* etc., and there also comes one mare for heriot according to the custom of the manor. And William presents the same men as pledges, and he will repair the buildings, perform the customs, services, etc.

Robert Attegrene junior delivered through the lord's hands to his son John one messuage and one virgate of land. And he gives a mare as heriot, and the said John pays the fine and swears the oath. The lord then gives him entry so that he and his heirs will hold according to the custom of the manor. And he must perform all services and customs.

Lucy Wayn delivers to her son Henry through the lord's hands one messuage and a virgate to be held for services. And Henry gives the lord the fine etc. And there comes in heriot according to the custom of the manor one sheep.

BURWELL,[5] 1347: John Edrich receives from the lord a messuage and fifteen acres of land formerly belonging to his father, and he gives in fine two shillings. The same John receives from the lord a built up place to be held for services by his son John by paying eighteen pence yearly. Thomas Rolf once held this property, and for it threepence are given as fine.

CRANFIELD,[6] 1312: Roger son of William Smith pays four shillings in fine for a cottage and croft formerly belonging to Emma Muriel to be held for services by his son William.

HOUGHTON,[7] 1347: And the jurors say that William Froyl handed over a half-virgate of villeinage to be held for services by his son Roger who fines and takes the oath.

ABBOTS RIPTON,[8] 1274: Ralph Attehyl caused waste in a messuage that Hugh Attehyl now holds (   ). The above Hugh fined for that messuage and land from which trees were cut down and removed (   ). Therefore he is amerced for two shillings, with the beadle as pledge.

Simon the son of Thomas, Richard Gerold, and John the Vernoun are pledges of Ralph Attehyl (   ) to the lord for having withdrawn with his chattels from the lord's fee in order to live married on the land of Philip of the Hall. There he has built and established a house with wood from trees cut down and removed from the lord's fee. These trees had been growing in the above half-virgate that Hugh Attehyl

---

3 See Appendix VIII, no. 1.
4 See Appendix VIII, no. 2.
5 See Appendix VIII, no. 3.
6 See Appendix VIII, no. 4.
7 See Appendix VIII, no. 5.
8 See Appendix VIII, no. 6; and see numbers 7-9 of this Appendix for further examples, also the Index, *s. v.* Tenure.

now holds, as mentioned above. And afterwards he fines for two capons to be delivered at Easter every year, with Thomas Onty as pledge, and for forty pence that he paid personally, that he may have licence to remain on the land of the above Philip. And he is to come to the view of frankpledge once every year, with the above as pledge.

The jurors convict Ralph Attehyl of having removed a 'langsetel' from the home of Hugh Attehyl. Therefore they order that this be returned and that satisfaction be made to him for the said 'langsetel.' And for this transgression he is amerced threepence, with Nicholas the beadle as pledge.

The jurors convict Hugh Attehyl of failing to pay the elevenpence farthing to Ralph Attehyl that this Ralph had paid to the lord for him as rent from his land. Therefore he is to make satisfaction to him. And for this illegal debt he is amerced sixpence, with the beadle as pledge.

The jurors convict Hugh Attehyl of owing his brother Ralph Attehyl twenty shillings which (   ) that the same Hugh should hand over for services to the said Ralph all his rights in a one-half virgate (formerly ?) his father's when these should accrue to him. And in addition he is charged with owing him four shillings (   ) that he received for the same agreement, which agreement indeed the same (Hugh) afterwards broke on Ralph. Therefore it is ordered that the said Ralph should recover from Hugh that twenty four shillings, and for the unjust debt the above Hugh is amerced two shillings, with John of Hurst, William Haulond, Nicholas Hubert, and Nicholas the beadle as pledges.

When a customary tenement was conveyed beyond the family the court was usually concerned only that the conveyance be through the manorial court and that the entry fine be paid. Some typical entries are given below. The two entries for Wistow in 1349 allow comparison of conveyances within and beyond the immediate family. Such texts tell us nothing about the terms of arrangement among villagers themselves.[9] Heriots were no doubt paid, since there are no references to the waiving of heriots. But, as it was the custom to enter the heriot in the account roll or the *gersuma* roll at the abbey, it is rare to find a heriot noted in a court roll before the late fourteenth century.

So long as proper legal procedure was followed, the lord was apparently indifferent to the conveyance of customary land out of the hands of the family of the current tenant. The courts seemed indifferent also to conveyance for life as against hereditary tenure. Since life tenure required conveyance through the manorial court, customary services and the entry fine[10] were guaranteed by movements of land in this manner as surely as

---

[9] Such as the maintenance arrangements discussed in Chapter Two, above.

[10] Much more detailed information about entry fines is available for the Ramsey town of St. Ives in the fourteenth century. From St. Ives it can be seen that the lord varied the entry fine with the prospective period of tenancy, the state of repair of the property, etc. (see 'Rent and Capital at St. Ives', *Mediaeval Studies*, XX, 1958, pp. 85-6). Beyond these *ad hoc* variations, the maximum entry fine for properties according to different sizes was apparently established upon fairly common bases throughout Ramsey properties (*Estates*, pp. 248-9), although the entry fine rapidly became insignificant during depressions (*Estates*, Chapter IX, and below, Chapter IX).

by the descent of property through a family. Before the court book, which provides great detail on tenure from the late fourteenth century, evidence for life tenure was noted in court rolls often only when an heir was attempting to recover his family tenement. Examples of this from Knapwell[11] in 1316, Warboys[12] in 1313, and King's Ripton[13] in 1297 were given above in Chapter Two. The two texts from the court roll of Graveley given below show some ways in which the villager was employing the time lease. The entries below for Weston in 1370 and 1375 indicate that life tenure was given until hereditary tenure could be established through one person, that is, until tenure by blood was established. Where there were no heirs, life tenure could be extended to other members of the tenant's family, as to the widow in the example from Therfield below. But this was only confirmation of the usual life tenure by widows on Ramsey manors. To judge from the large number of conveyances of customary land entered in account rolls where the new entrant was not said to be a relative of the former tenant, life tenancies may have been very numerous in the late thirteenth and early fourteenth centuries. At the same time the villager may not have been allowed to concentrate too much land in his family by this process. Peter the Miller at Hemmingford Abbots[14] (1312) and Richard at Ellington[15] found that possession of acquired lands weakened their claims to traditional family holdings.

GRAVELEY,[16] 1307: William Shepherd, who twelve years ago surrendered a messuage and ?acres of land into the lord's hands to be held for services by William the son of Dyke, comes with his wife and they ask permission of the lord for re-entry to that messuage and land. And the said abbot ordered inquiry to be made as to how much cost and (expenditure) the above William Dyke had invested and spent in the above messuage and lands since the time he fined for them, both in buildings and lands. Upon the evidence of the appointed clerks they say that from all costs and expenses made by the above William to the said messuage and lands it is now truly worth sixty shillings more than its value at the time he fined for it, in addition to his fine of one-half mark paid to the lord for entry to the above messuage and land, etc.

GRAVELEY,[17] 1321: And they say that Walter at the gate, a native of the lord, let his messuage and half virgate of villeinage to a certain John Onty, native, for a term of years without permission of the lord. And that Walter withdrew from the domain and lives without permission in foreign parts. Therefore it is ordered that all that

---

11 See above, Chapter Two, p. 51. Evidence from other parts of England that ownership might only be alienated for a lifetime may be found in Homans, *Thirteenth-Century Villagers*, p. 197.
12 See above, Chapter Two, p. 50.
13 See above, Chapter Two, p. 54.
14 See above, Chapter Two, p. 49.
15 See above, Chapter Two, p. 57.
16 See Appendix IX, no. 1.
17 See Appendix IX, no. 2.

property be taken into the lord's hands and that the profits be accounted to the lord until, etc. Afterwards he came and fined with the lord.

WISTOW,[18] 1349: Andrew Maunger surrendered to the lord one hideland formerly belonging to John Maunger to be held for services by Robert Barker. He will hold according to the custom of the manor, etc., and gives the lord for having entry, etc. (*gersuma* — two shillings is stroked out and an entry added to indicate the fine is already in the *gersuma* book). The pledge is William Warin.

WESTON,[19] 1370: Richard Moltisson came to this court and surrendered into the lord's hands a messuage and one-half virgate to be held for services by John Moltisson his son, saving the rights of Richard brother of John. (And John) will hold for life at the will of the lord doing the service and customs pertaining to that tenement, and he gives six shillings eightpence as *gersuma*.

Godfrey Godeford comes to this court and gives five shillings fine as licence to hold a messuage and one-half virgate in common with Walter Penyell at the will of the lord for the lifetime of that Walter. And after the death of Walter the above Godfrey will have and hold the above tenement for himself and his heirs at the will of the lord according to the custom there established.

WESTON ?,[20] 1375: Robert Smyht of Bythorn and his wife Margaret come to this court and surrender to the lord a one-half messuage and one-half virgate to be held of services by Richard the son of Richard Makynesson. Richard is to hold from this time for life on condition that he serve the above Robert and Margaret till the end of their lives. After their death Richard will have the other half of that messuage and virgate to hold to himself and his heirs at the will of the lord performing all the yearly services to the lord as the above Robert had done and paying through the farmer the *gersuma* as required of that vill for he is a *nativus* of the above vill and not an outsider.

WARBOYS,[21] 1322: Nicholas Palmer surrendered into the lord's hands an acre of land to be held for services by John Wariner, one rod of this lying at Hotel,' another rod at Waterlond, one rod at Longelond, and one rod at the three oaks. And the said John gives the lord threepence as entry fine, and takes the oath.

ELLSWORTH,[22] 1316: And Joan the daughter of John Broun gives every year at Easter one chicken in order to have for life a certain part of the place of Henry Notte. And in addition she will give every year as long as she lives twelve pence to the above Henry or to his successors for that lot, with her father John Broun as pledge.

THERFIELD,[23] 1321: Ralph of Crishale comes into the full court and gives the lord ten shillings in order that his wife may be able to hold for life all that land that he holds from the lord should she outlive the said Ralph, and she would pay yearly for the same tenement sixteen shillings at the regular times.

ABBOTS RIPTON,[24] 1343: The order is given to take into the lord's hands the half

18 See Appendix IX, no. 3.
19 See Appendix IX, no. 4.
20 See Appendix IX, no. 5.
21 See Appendix IX, no. 6.
22 See Appendix IX, no. 7.
23 See Appendix IX, no. 8. This form of arrangement became very common from the late fourteenth century.
24 P R O, SC 2, Port. 179, no. 31. This manuscript is too decayed for transcription.

virgate let to Thomas Hilmar for life (   ) the half virgate let to John Hawelond in similar fashion, as well as the one quarter land let to Andrew Bouk, the (one-half virgate?) to John atte Lane, the (one-half virgate?) to Martin Onty, and the one-quarter land let to (   ) Colle, all in similar fashion.

THERFIELD,[25] 1306: Thomas of Brancaster comes and takes the oath to hold for life all the property formerly belonging to John of Harpefield.

THERFIELD,[26] 1321: John of Brancaster comes into full court and gives the lord thirteen shillings fourpence for entry to twelve acres to be held for life. His rent shall be ten shillings annually to be paid at the regular intervals.

CRANFIELD,[27] 1300: Joan daughter of Richard de Campo came and paid the lord an entry fine of twenty shillings for eleven acres of land formerly held by Elias Hog and for the three acres that the above Richard held of the lord. Payment is to be made at the feast of the Nativity of Blessed Mary. And she must render to the lord every year all the services and accustomed dues. The pledge is Richard de Campo.

SHILLINGTON,[28] 1332: Richard Crouche fines thirteen shillings fourpence to enter the virgate that Mariota Crouche held for life.

ST IVES,[29] 1305?: And they say that Robert the tailor rented for life from Robert Parys a rod of land lying at the lane facing Ocle. While ploughing this rod of land the same Robert the tailor appropriated from the common land of a perch in length and breadth. Therefore he is to be distrained to answer for this.

Since the manor court protected the lord's rights in customary land these local courts were very jealous of their jurisdiction over such lands. A lawsuit to enforce conveyance through the manor court at Slepe after 1311 is given below. However, the court roll entries tell us little about the status of the tenant William of Gilling. In the text from Burwell in 1312 we are given the exact status of lands and persons involved. It may be assumed that the land was taken into the lord's hands at Burwell for not being conveyed through the manorial court. Properties not required to be conveyed through the manorial court were conveyed by charter, so that villeinage conveyed by charter was in danger of being lost to the lord. Two examples of this are given below for Hemmingford Abbots and Ellsworth. If land might lose its customary status by sale to a serf outside the manorial court, the land was doubly in danger of losing its status by sale to a freeman. The courts came down hard, therefore, on the sale of villeinage to freemen. An illustration of this is given below, where John West of Slepe sold his villein tenement to a freeman and the property was seized by the lord and returned to its original condition. But there is no doubt but that through marriage a freeman might become associated with

---

[25] See Appendix IX, no. 9.
[26] See Appendix IX, no. 10.
[27] See Appendix IX, no. 11.
[28] P R O, SC 2, Port. 179, no. 26.
[29] See Appendix IX, no. 12. See also numbers 13 and 14 of this Appendix.

villein property. Examples of this will be found in another part of this study.[30] There is also an indication in the entry from Weston[31] in 1375 that 'outsiders' could be admitted to village lands under certain conditions. The text from Elton court for 1300 provides us with remarkable evidence of an outsider and his family becoming to all intents and purposes naifs of the lord for a tenement. When a proper licence was obtained there seems to have been no limit to types and varieties of persons who could hold customary land; but customary land could not be enfeoffed, even when held by the relative of an abbot, as we see in the example from Hemmingford Abbots below.

SLEPE,[32] 1313: The reeve and beadle are ordered to account to the lord for fifty-eight shillings and twopence from the sixteen rings of wheat, sixteen rings of dredge and twelve rings of peas from the crop of all the lands of John West that had been taken into the hands of the lord because the said John, a naif, had independently allowed Adam the son of William the son of Hugh a freeman to add to his freehold from the land that John had held in villeinage so as to disinherit the lord, etc. And it is ordered to keep that land in the lord's hands until, etc. And afterwards it was shown that the above land had been returned to its previous condition. And the above John paid a twelve penny fine to the lord that he might have and hold the above land.

SLEPE,[33] 1311: It is ordered that the one-half messuage and perch that William of Gilling first held as a gift of Alice the daughter of John Pak' by charter be kept in the lord's hands since the above half messuage was not surrendered through the lord's hands in court as directed in the last view.

SLEPE, 1313 ?: It is also ordered that the one-half messuage and perch that William of Gilling first held as a gift and enfeoffment of Alice the daughter of John Pak' by charter be kept in the lord's hands since the above half messuage was not surrendered through the lord's hands in court as directed in the last view. And evidence is given that the above William occupies the said half (messuage) against the will of the lord's bailiff and the above William in full court says that the above half belongs to the lord abbot alone, and yet he has held the seneschal in great contempt. Therefore for contempt one-half mark.

---

[30] See above, Chapter Two, and Index, s. v. Marriage.
The legal machinery that had developed under common law to protect the freedom of freemen who had performed villein services can be taken as evidence that freemen would often hold villein tenements. See for example, *Brevia Placitata*, pp. CXLIII-V; or *Casus Placitorum*, p. LXXVII, no. 20; or *Abbreviatio Placitorum*, p. 90.

[31] This permission is tacit in the entry of a naif to this manor in the same year, see above, p. 67 (Appendix IX, no. 5). An ordinance of 1396 indicates how a licence might be obtained for anyone to hold villeinage at Houghton: "Ordinatum est per dominum quod nullus de cetero dimittat terram nativam domini liberis hominibus nec nativis sine licentia speciali domini, sub pena xxs." (P R O, SC 2, Port. 179, no. 44)

[32] See Appendix X, no. 1. Most frequently, however, the court seized land because a female tenant had married a freeman. E.g. Weston, 1307-8: "Preceptum est capere in manu domini messuagium et terram Roysie uxoris Ricardi Molendarii eo quod dictus Ricardus liber est et non nativus. Et de exitibus inde provenientibus domino respondere donec, etc."

[33] See Appendix X, no. 2, for these two Slepe entries.

BURWELL,[34] 1312: And they say that Goderob' a native of the lord sold to Ralph le Ber a native a messuage at money rent. Therefore it is to be taken into the lord's hands and a faithful account made of the profits accruing from it.

ELLSWORTH,[35] ?: And they say that Henry Fynche, one of the lord's men, sold by charter to Thomas Leg' and his son William a messuage with an attached croft. And afterwards it was established that the father of the above Henry, who together with his ancestors was a man of the lord, purchased the above land from the fee of Bokesworth. And the lord abbot of that period rented that messuage and croft as villeinage at five shillings a year. Those properties he (the abbot) handed over in the beginning to the said Henry to be held in villeinage for the above rent and other services owed as well as for an entry fine, etc. And now that land has been sold by charter to the above Thomas Leg' and son William who showed that charter and by the above evidence the charter is nullified in full court. And therefore it is ordered that the above land be taken into the lord's hands and the profits accounted to him until, etc.

HEMMINGFORD ABBOTS,[36] 1307: And they say through the jurors that a certain William Gapup in the time of King Henry (III) held of the lord a messuage and two virgates in the above vill without a charter, and for entry fine at the will of the lord abbot that time, and for the above land he was at law with all of the above vill just like any others who hold servile land in that vill. And they say that the said William begot of his wife Lyn a certain daughter Agnes who is still living, (and) who married a certain Thomas of Acolt brother of the lord William of Acolt, abbot. From her Thomas begot Thomas Onpron and his sister Agnes who are still living, while the said Thomas of Acolt died. William Gapup died, and after his death his daughter Agnes fined to hold that land at the will of lord William of Godmanchester, abbot. Afterwards a certain Simon Byle Whyt, naif of the lord, came and fined for two marks of silver to enter that land by marriage to the above Agnes, so that he should hold that land by such services as others who hold by service in that vill. And they say that the said Simon and Agnes then enfeoffed by a charter to one-half of that messuage and land Thomas Onpron, which charter the same Thomas shows and it is identified. And they say that afterwards the said Thomas enfeoffed to a certain part of the above messuage the said Agnes his sister, by a charter that the said Agnes shows. And they are told that it was at the grace of the lord that the above lands were held at the will of the lord, and they hand over their charters (   ) in open court (   ). And therefore it is directed that all the above land be taken into the lord's hands both that land as well as the part held by Simon and Agnes because they enfeoffed by charter so as to disinherit the lord to (the advantage of) Thomas with servile land to which the same Thomas was by them enfeoffed, etc.

WESTON ?,[37] 1375: And from James Piteman an outsider as a fine for a messuage and quarter land formerly of Thomas Bacheler, who will perform all yearly services as the above Thomas did (five shillings).

ELTON,[38] 1300: Because it is testified in full court as well by the free tenants as by

---

[34] See Appendix X, no. 3.
[35] See Appendix X, no. 4.
[36] See Appendix X, no. 5.
[37] See Appendix X, no. 6.
[38] See *Elton Manorial Records*, p. 96. Compare the Cranfield entry, above p. 53 (Appendix VII, no. 10).

others, that Richard Turne who held of the lord one cottage with a curtilage in the vill of Elton is a native of the vill of Fodringeye from the land of the abbess of Northampton, and that upon the death of the said Richard a certain Gilbert his son entered the said cottage to hold it of the lord by the services therefrom due and accustomed for an entry fine which he made with the lord, and because it was found and proved by all present in the same court that the said Gilbert is not a naif of the lord but rather the son of a newcomer from the homage of another, the said Gilbert was told by the steward that he should surrender the said cottage and seek an abode for himself where he should see more fit, or that he should find four safe and substantial pledges that he the said Gilbert and all those issuing of his blood will do in all things to the lord abbot and his successors all manner of unfree customs as any cottar or naif does more fully in the same vill. Wherefore the said steward at the request of the above Gilbert received the underwritten pledges that he will fully perform all the aforesaid things, to wit John Trune, Richard Gosselyn, Andrew Gamel and Reynald de Brynton, each of whom is a pledge and surety in all the aforesaid things.

It has been seen that manorial courts were largely concerned with the record of conveyance in so far as it involved failure in obligations between lord and villein or among villagers. At the same time there is evidence that the transfer of land among villeins involved an actual sale or life rental by private agreement. The articles for conveyance within a family, and especially from parent to child, would usually contain a maintenance clause, as has been illustrated in the previous chapter.[39] But maintenance agreements could just as readily be made with in-laws or strangers, as the examples below for Graveley, Girton, Abbots Ripton and Warboys (1347) illustrate. Information about other conditions of sale can only be gleaned from lawsuits among villeins in the manorial court. The examples given below suggest that the capital investment on the tenement may have provided the main terms of the sale. At Ellsworth, Alan the son of Philip possibly left adequate corn with Henry of Warboys for the sowing of his crops, but the latter failed to repay this amount. At Elton, the amount in dispute would appear to represent a capital investment by the former tenant through the lord. The exchange of land between two men at Wistow indicates a combination of maintenance arrangements and capital costs. Over and Ellington provide further examples for the allocation of capital costs.

ELLSWORTH,[40] 1299: Henry of Warboys was convicted by the jurors for being in arrears by five rings of wheat, two rings of barley, two rings of dredge, and one ring of peas to Alan son of Philip from whom Henry had received his land to be held for services. And Alan remits one ring of wheat and one ring of barley, and so there remain eight rings to be paid at the times indicated below, namely one ring of wheat

---

[39] Chapter Two, Section II.
[40] See Appendix XI, no. 1.

and one ring of barley at the feast of the Purification of Blessed Mary, and the remainder at the feast of St. Michael, with pledges William Simond, William Baldwin, Henry son of Eustach, and Simon Brun. And for the unjust detention of goods he is in mercy to sixpence, with pledges as above.

ELTON,[41] 1308: John the son of John Abovebrok was convicted by the jurors for owing Robert of Teyngton two shillings eightpence and thirty shillings, the amounts that the same Robert had paid the lord for the decay of a certain property afterwards transferred to the said John upon the agreement that the same John should recompense him to this amount. Therefore he makes satisfaction to Robert for the said money. And for unjust retention is in mercy — with pledges — (cancelled).

GRAVELEY,[42] 1290: Robert Beneyt complains that John Herneys senior has unjustly deprived him of one-half mark of silver in one way, twelve pence in another and three rings of wheat, three rings of barley, two rings three bushels of dredge from the agreement made to marry his daughter. And he petitions for an inquiry, and the said John does the same. And the jurors of the neighbourhood come and say that this was the agreement made between them, that the said John should give the above Robert one-half mark on the same day that he should fine to enter his land, and he did not pay the half-mark on that day. And the twelve pence he was to give on the day when he purchased a brazen pot, which day has not yet arrived. As to the above corn, they say that a day for its payment was not determined, unless it be at will and as John should be able to pay it. Therefore it was decided that the same John should pay the above Robert the half mark, fifteen pence at the feast of the Purification of the Blessed Virgin and forty pence at Easter. And the above twelve pence (will be paid) at the buying of the pot, and the corn as the above agreement indicates. And the above John is in mercy to sixpence for the unjust deprivation, with no pledges as he is poor. And the above Robert is likewise in mercy for his false charge to sixpence, with William Koc and Robert at the bridge as pledges.

GIRTON,[43] 1291: Margaret at the green paid the lord twelve pence to have enrolled the agreement she had made with Thomas Rodbaund to which Thomas recognized in open court that he had agreed and was bound. And this is the agreement, namely, that the said Thomas for a certain half virgate let to him by the same Margaret will pay the same Margaret every year two quarters of wheat, two quarters of barley, and two shillings of silver in equal amounts at the four times in the year. And he will provide a residence for that Margaret in a certain solar in his hall. And in the same home where Thomas and his family live he will allow Margaret to eat at her own expense separate from the vessels and food belonging to Thomas, providing for Margaret the same provisions as his own. And he will bake bread for Margaret whenever he bakes his own bread. And Margaret will also have a cow in the courtyard of Thomas (   ) at the expense of Margaret in the summer and of Thomas in the winter. And the same Margaret may keep a pig, a hen and five chickens all year in the courtyard of Thomas at her own expense. And since this Thomas admits to be in arrears to fourpence and one ring of barley for the last payment owed by the agreement, and also later was proved by jurors of the vill to owe threepence in

---

[41] See *Elton Manorial Records*, p. 153.
[42] See Appendix XI, no. 2.
[43] See Appendix XI, no. 3.

addition to that threepence and one ring of barley, the same Thomas is in mercy to sixpence, with Peter the son of Roger and William Sbyrrene as pledges. And the costs to Margaret were established at sixpence, which are given to the clerks.

WISTOW,[44] 1429: John Walgate surrendered into the lord's hands a messuage and virgate to be held for services by John Onty the son of John Onty junior... John Walgate also granted to the same John Onty his meals this next year, wheat to sow three and one-half acres of land, three quarters and six bushels of barley for seed, and three horses, that is a bay, crossed, and dun, and after this year will give him a plough with equipment for three horses. He grants to the same John Onty the maintenance of three horses for this next year. And in return the above John Onty grants to the same John Walgate a room with entrance, one carthouse, rights in the garden and the foreyard, and one virgate of land.

WARBOYS,[45] 1347: It was established through evidence from the examination of neighbours that William Cowherd surrendered a messuage and nine acres to be held by Thomas Gerold at services, under these conditions, that the same William and his wife will have for life a part of the messuage bounded by pine trees and two acres of arable from the above land, and will pay two shillings to the same Thomas every year at Michaelmas. And the above Thomas will plough and cultivate those two acres very year at the proper time as often and in the same way as other like land is ploughed. And if the same Thomas should be unwilling to plough the two acres at the proper time William and his wife may keep the annual two shillings payment and provide for the ploughing of the two acres by someone else. It was also agreed by the same villagers that the above part of the messuage was not designated in length and breadth by feet but as bounded by the pine trees. And they would find in the *gersuma* roll the length and breadth were not by common measure but by estimation.

LAWSHALL,[46] 1395-6: William Togood came to the same court and surrendered into the lord's hands a ten-acre tenement with appurtenance called Auncelles, that John King formerly held, to be held for services by John Underwood and his wife Joan after the term of Robert Peek who now holds that tenement for a certain number of years by the grant of the said William. This land is to be held by the same John and his wife Joan and their offspring in bondage at the will of the lord once the above tenure has been completed. And they will pay and render to the lord annually all services and customs thereby due and accustomed according to the customs of the manor. And they will keep and maintain that tenement without damage. And if any heir should wish to claim that tenement, he will have to pay back all the costs and expenses incurred by John, Joan and their offspring, as determined by the sworn inquiry of the court and tenants of the lord. And the above John takes the servile oath to the lord. And they give the lord as entry fine ten shillings to be paid before the next court following.

OVER,[47] 1308: William the son of William Ive and his wife Margaret were

[44] See Appendix XI, no. 4.
[45] See Appendix XI, no. 5.
[46] See Appendix XI, no. 6.
As heirs were less and less available from the late fourteenth century, this provision for expenses should heirs resume the tenure seems to have become common form, e.g. *ibid.*, p. 22 (twice).
[47] See Appendix XI, no. 7.

convicted of a debt of eighteen pence owed to Robert Ive for expenditures on the land once belonging to John Lawe while Robert held that land at farm, and the above William Ive now has that land. Therefore this sum is to be paid that Robert, one-half at Easter and the other half at the feast of St. Lawrence, with the reeve William Ive as pledge.

ELLINGTON,[48] 1299: Richard le Beaumeys pledges that Emma daughter of Henry le Bok will build a house on that lot formerly belonging to her father before the next court. For (construction of) this house she has received one-half mark from William son of Bate.

ABBOTS RIPTON,[49] 1296: Robert Sabyn comes to demand from Agnes Sabyn six rings of wheat, six rings of barley, and six rings of beans and peas which she owes him from the arrears of the past six years as well as two and one-half ells of red or russet cloth a year and three ells of linen the alternate year for the six years, and along with this lodging on the property. And he asks that this be certified by inquiry of the vill. And all of the vill come and say that it is not required that Agnes be responsible for the above payments of corn to Robert since at the last view of frank-pledge a settlement was agreed upon, all to the contrary notwithstanding, in the following terms: that the above Agnes should in the future pay Robert one ring of wheat at the Purification of Blessed Mary, one ring of beans at Easter, and a ring of barley at the Gules of August, and every (   ) ell and one half of linen cloth and three shillings tenpence for three ells of linen cloth, these to be rendered at Michaelmas. Twentypence (are paid the lord?) that the said Agnes should have peaceful tenure of the property for the above annual payments to the said Robert. Richard the hayward and Andrew Onty are pledges.

II

Subletting on the Customary Tenement

The customary tenement, like the military fee, was subject to heavy pressure to extend the tenurial ladder. Despite the obvious danger that the very services by which the villein tenement was 'defended' should be prejudiced, a further step was allowed in the manorial ladder of tenure. Upon Ramsey manors it was a common custom to permit subletting of the villein tenement, or parts of the tenement, for one, two, or three years. Examples are given here for a variety of manors.

WARBOYS,[50] 1306: Godfrey Scut came and admitted that he had broken the agreement made with Amicia Bugge about one sellion of land let to the same Amicia for four years in part payment for the debt of one cow. Therefore he is in mercy to sixpence. And since it was established that no customary tenant is permitted to lease or to let any portion of his villein holdings to anyone for a term other

48 See Appendix XI, no. 8.
49 See Appendix XI, no. 9.
50 See Appendix XII, no. 1.

than two years according to the custom of the manor, it is directed that the said sellion of land be taken into the lord's hands until, etc.

SHILLINGTON,[51] 1455: The bailiff is ordered to take into the lord's hands one messuage with sixteen acres of land formerly belonging to John Waryn since the whole homage gave evidence that the said John leased this land messuage and sixteen acres during his life beyond the one-year term against the custom of the manor, etc. And profits are to be accounted to the lord, etc.

ABBOTS RIPTON,[52] 1306: John the Carpenter was convicted by the jurors for breaking an agreement with Martin Onty whereby he had let one rod of land to him for two crops, but Martin had received but one crop so that he suffered the loss of eighteen pence to be paid to him. And for this default he is in mercy to threepence, with pledges both William Elynn and Oliver atte Dam. And the said amount must be paid to him by the Nativity of Blessed Mary.

HEMMINGFORD ABBOTS,[53] 1311: Agnes the (Geminn) was convicted by the jurors of having broken an agreement with Ralph Bischop concerning the three crops of the land let to her so that he suffered the loss of three shillings and threepence. Therefore she does satisfaction. And for the unjust detention is in mercy to threepence with pledge Ralph Vernoun.

BROUGHTON,[54] 1288: The reeve and beadle are to be asked about the crop of one and one-half acres that John Rob' let to John Stake and which they ought to take for service to the lord. But since the said John Stake took that crop away against the prohibition of the said reeve and beadle with the warranty of John Rog' who was not able to warranty, he is in mercy for sixpence, pledges Richard Parson and William the son of Ralph. And through the same pledges he must make satisfaction to the said reeve and beadle for the crop accounted to them. The amount of the crop (is) three rings, three bushels and one-half of barley, and of peas two rings, three bushels.

John Rog' admitted that he gave warranty to John Stake for the crop of one and one-half acres held for service to the lord when he was not able to warranty. Therefore in mercy (   ) with pledge John of Wistow.

Andrew Onty was attached to reply to the charge that though forbidden he removed the crop of one-half acre of land that John Gere had let to the same Andrew, but because it was testified by William Nuncius that he had a licence to do this, he was therefore acquitted.

HOLYWELL,[55] 1288: And they (the jurors) say that Roys' the Frankeleyn let an acre of arable and one-half acre of meadow for two crops to Walter the Shepherd. Therefore they are to be seized, etc.

SHILLINGTON,[56] 1313: John Hamond who holds a one-half virgate of land let that land by parcells to several people so that the lord lost ploughing and other services which neither John nor the others who held his land were able to supply.

---

[51] See Appendix XII, no. 2.
[52] See Appendix XII, no. 3.
[53] See Appendix XII, no. 4.
[54] See Ault, *Court Rolls*, pp. 198-9.
[55] See Ault, *Court Rolls*, p. 189. Two similar entries occur in this same roll.
[56] See Appendix XII, no. 5. Five other semivirgaters were indicted for this same offence at Shillington this year.

Therefore it is directed that the land be taken into the lord's hands and its profits be accounted for. They did the ploughing.

SHILLINGTON,[57] 1288: And they say that Amicia Atewode is the tenant of a one-half virgate that John Hamond sowed for one-half the crop for one year and more, from the feast of Saint Michael until now, and that the same Amicia ought to plough four acres a year, for which she will give sixteen pence and for the withdrawal of this ploughing is in mercy to sixpence, with John Ategrene as pledge. (It is reported) to the lord that the reeve was ignorant of this since the man is an outsider. But the beadle is guilty of this concealment. Therefore he is in mercy to sixpence with Robert de Uppenande as pledge.

HOUGHTON,[58] 1311: They say that Ralph the son of Thomas let to Ralph Perot three rods of land for a term of seven years. Therefore it is ordered that this land be taken into the lord's hands and that the profits be accounted for, etc.
And they say that Ralph the reeve let to the said Ralph one rod of land in a croft for a term of five years. Therefore it is to be taken into the lord's hands as above. And he must account for the returns until, etc.

WESTON,[59] 1312: And they say that a naif of the lord named William Prat rented a quarter of land to Roger Attehill for a period longer than that allowed by custom of the vill. Therefore it is taken into the lord's hands, and the profits are to be accounted until, etc.

ELLSWORTH,[60] 1278: Robert son of John (is presented in court) with having rented to William Elene beyond the limits of two sellions for one crop. The fine is condoned for poverty.

ELLSWORTH,[61] 1294: The reeve is to account for revenues from a croft and house taken into the lord's hands because Robert le Gage rented this to Alan Dylle junior for four crops.

GRAVELEY,[62] 1290: Walter Barun, William Barun, and Robert Algar, executors of Robert Berkar, come to demand four shillings from Simon Halyday senior. The latter comes and says he owes nothing since that Robert had one-half acre from him for four crops by which he had over that time two bushels of wheat and four rings and two bushels of dredge for that payment. And to support this statement he is prepared to swear three handed, his pledges are William Hulot and Richard Danyel.

WARBOYS,[63] 1290: And the jurors say that William Lucas let a certain part of his messuage along with one-half rod in his croft to Ralph Wrench for the life of that William. For this transgression he is amerced sixpence and that land is taken into the lord's hands.
And they say that the same William let a certain part of his messuage to John the tollman, and it is ordered as above.

WARBOYS,[64] 1294: And the same John the tollman gives a capon in order to hold

[57] See Ault, *Court Rolls,* p. 194.
[58] See Ault, *Court Rolls,* p. 259.
[59] See Appendix XII, no. 6.
[60] See Appendix XII, no. 7.
[61] See Appendix XII, no. 8.
[62] See Appendix XII, no. 9.
[63] See Appendix XII, no. 10.
[64] See Appendix XII, no. 11.

for two years that messuage let from William Lucas. He is to pay to the same William sixpence a year after first paying this sum to the lord abbot.

WARBOYS,[65] 1294: Threepence a year are to be paid for that part of a messuage that Margaret de Hawegate rented to Richard Derward upon which a shop is to be built.

John the tollman will send a capon every year to be able to hold one half messuage for three years. This property was let from William Lucas who is to be paid eightpence a year after this amount has first been paid to the lord abbot.

HOUGHTON,[66] 1316: From Robert Trappe for subletting his vacant house without apprising the bailiffs, sixpence fine, with Richard Plumbe as pledge.

From Richard son of Agnes for letting his house to Robert Trappe, twelve pence, with Alexander son of Agnes as pledge.

WISTOW,[67] 1297: Ranulph son of Andrew was convicted by the jurors of having broken his contract with John Gernun concerning the crop from one acre. He must pay twelve pence to him in satisfaction for this, and is amerced sixpence for the transgression with Richard Long as pledge.

ABBOTS RIPTON,[68] 1294: And the jurors say that John the son of John sublet a certain part of his yard to Stephen the shepherd for ten years. Therefore that same John is amerced sixpence, and it is directed that the said part of the yard be taken into the lord's hands until, etc.

ABBOTS RIPTON,[69] 1299: And William Huwelot is amerced sixpence for removing the harvest from one-half acre of wheat sown by Nicholas le Tyneker. For this land had been sown by Nicholas while William Palmer held it and before the above William Palmer fined for that land. The pledge is John of Hyrst, and it is ordered, etc.

Payment of services would provide a seasonal check upon subletting, and no doubt complications following upon the failure to pay services, as with the examples for Shillington in 1313 and 1288 and Broughton in 1288 given above, supplied the main reason for the short term regulation. The regularity with which abuses of subletting had to be checked in the late thirteenth and early fourteenth centuries suggests that subletting was widely employed on the villeinage. Villagers often sublet to men of a neighbouring homage from isolated Ramsey manors like Chatteris, or to freemen who were present on all Ramsey manors. The manorial courts were sensitive to the loss of villeinage to outsiders or freemen, and as the following examples illustrate, such violations were strictly corrected by taking the land into the lord's hands. On the other hand, the entries from Shillington (1339, 1409), Barton (1420), suggest that licence could be obtained for a freeman to hold land. Licences for short tenancies at

[65] See Appendix XII, no. 12.
[66] See Appendix XII, no. 13.
[67] See Appendix XII, no. 14.
[68] See Appendix XII, no. 15.
[69] See Appendix XII, no. 16.

Hemmingford Abbots in 1316, and Burwell in 1321, were likely to out-siders. It would appear certain that only 'foreigners' and freemen were excluded from the manorial custom permitting land to be sublet for short terms without licence from the lord.

WESTON,[70] 1318: And they (the jurors) say that Thomas Randolf leased (   ) of land to a certain Richard the Carter, a freeman. Therefore it is ordered to be taken into the lord's hands, and that the profits be accounted for.

SHILLINGTON,[71] 1333: (The reeve) therefore is to account for the crop of one-half acre of wheat that Edith Hammond a naif of the lord leased to Simon Shepherd, a freeman, without licence.

SLEPE,[72] 1301: And (it is charged) to the reeve and beadle that they did not take into the lord's hands as they had been ordered to do the crop of one acre sown with dredge which Robert Baldwin had let to John Moring', a freeman, this was valued at four shillings which he pays (   ) they are pledge for one another.

CHATTERIS,[73] 1289: And they (the jurors) say that Maurice of Somersham let to Gilbert the Clerk, a man of the abbey (of Ely), one-half acre of land sown at lent, for the period of three crops, and to John Andrew, a man of the abbey (of Ely), one-half acre sown at lent. Therefore he is in mercy to sixpence, pledge Richard Clement. (It is ordered to be seized, etc.).
And they say that Roger Sarle let to Alice Blysse of the homage of the bishop (of Ely) one-half acre sown in lent, against the statute. Therefore he is in mercy to sixpence, pledge Stephen Gilbert. And it is ordered that the said land and crop be taken into the lord's hands.
And they say that William of Hunneye let one-half acre sown at lent to Thomas the son of Ralph of Kareseye of the homage of the abbey (of Ely). Therefore he is in mercy to sixpence, pledge Richard Clement. And it is ordered that the land and crop be seized, etc.

HOUGHTON,[74] 1306: The order is given to take into the lord's hands the half-acre sown with dredge that Thomas the Bouyer let to Andrew le Mayngne, a freeman. And also that rod sown with wheat that John atte Pole let to John Smith... And also that acre of land sown with wheat that Richard of Walsingham permitted Robert of Segrave to sow in exchange for park.

HOLYWELL,[75] 1318: And they say that John of Upwood, a naif, holds of the lord one-half virgate of customary land, and from the cellarer one virgate of customary land

[70] See Appendix XIII, no. 1.
From evidence for subletting found in several regions in England, R. H. Tawney suggested that a fully developed machinery for land marketing existed among customary tenants from the thirteenth century; see *The Agrarian Problem in the Sixteenth Century* (London, 1912), pp. 80-1. Where information is available in the following texts, it appears that sharecropping was the usual arrangement for subletting among villagers. For a reference to subletting at King's Ripton, see Maitland, *Manorial Courts*, p. 114, under the son of Thomas the Reeve.
[71] See Appendix XIII, no. 2.
[72] See Appendix XIII, no. 3.
[73] See Ault, *Court Rolls*, pp. 278-9.
[74] See Ault, *Court Rolls*, pp. 240-1.
[75] See Appendix XIII, no. 4.

together with a croft. He let from these to John de Hermingo, a freeman, two acres and one-half for three years, and to John the Clerk two acres for the same term. And all the rest of the above land, beyond the three acres that he kept (   ) he let to the same John and John for this year for one-half of the crops on these lands. Therefore it is directed that all the above lands be taken into the lord's hands. And the profits from these are to be accounted to the lord.

SHILLINGTON,[76] 1409: And Peter Cook gives fourpence fine as a licence to let his villeinage at farm to a certain man from outside the village.

BARTON,[77] 1420: And Agnes Sare fines at fourpence a year to let her land to farm while she is outside the manor. And in addition she finds pledges, namely Richard Wodward and Walter Wodward that a heriot worth six shillings eightpence will be returned if she should die outside the domain.

HEMMINGFORD ABBOTS,[78] 1316: And (a fine) of two shillings on Nicholas Denmeys to hold a virgate of land of Nicholas Pate for three years by the grant of this said Nicholas. The reeve is the pledge.

BURWELL,[79] 1321: John Jukyn came into this view and gives the lord two shillings to hold twenty three acres of servile land from the feast of Saint Michael in the sixth year of Abbot Simon for the next five years. And he will perform for the lord all the services and customs pertaining to that land.

WESTON,[80] 1300: William le Newebonde was convicted for attempting to deceive the lord by renting to Walter son of John (   ) a rod of land to be held for services by John the son of Lawrence, a freeman, and this same John paid Walter to do this. Both are ordered to be amerced, William for twelve pence with Simon Bacheler as pledge, Walter for twelve pence with Bartholomew (Curteys?) as pledge.

HEMMINGFORD ABBOTS,[81] 1299: (They come) and present that Nicholas Lawrence sublet to William son of Martin le Longe of the homage of lord Reginald de Grey two acres of rye (   ). And that the same burned a certain grange and sold timbers from this. He also sold trees growing in his yard. Therefore he is to be amerced twelve pence. And since the customary tenants all allowed this, they are amerced one-half mark.

ELLINGTON,[82] 1306: And they say that William Aldych, a naif of the lord, let two rods of customary land to a certain freeman, Thomas the skinner. Therefore that land is to be taken into the lord's hands, and the reeve will account for any profits accruing therefrom.
And they say that Juliana Le Neweman, a naif of the lord, let to Matilda Kannt one-half acre of customary land to be held at farm beyond the lord's fee. Therefore that land is taken into the lord's hands, and the profits are to be accounted for.

[76] See Appendix XIII, no. 5. Since this entry was repeated in following years, Peter Cook, and Agnes Sare in the next entry, apparently paid this licence fee every year.
[77] See Appendix XIII, no. 6.
[78] See Appendix XIII, no. 7.
[79] See Appendix XIII, no. 8. Two similar entries follow in this court roll, although there is no certain evidence that any of these lands are being sublet through the lord by another villager. As the text in this Appendix, no. 14 indicates for Lawshall, longer periods of subletting were probably permitted from the end of the fourteenth century.
[80] See Appendix XIII, no. 9.
[81] See Appendix XIII, no. 10.
[82] See Appendix XIII, no. 11.

ELLSWORTH,[83] 1312: And the jurors say that Christina widow of Thomas Smith, who is from the parson's homage, let to two chaplains a messuage that the above Thomas her husband had held from the lord. Therefore this property is to be taken into the lord's hands, and the revenues accounted for until, etc.

WARBOYS,[84] 1333: The reeve is to account for the crop of that one rod sown with peas that William Semar sublet to a certain freeman without licence.

Another source for information about subletting is the contract (*conventio*) reference in the court roll. There were a very great number of lawsuits over broken agreements among villagers in Ramsey manorial courts. Usually the court roll entry specifies a debt owing from the agreement, without indicating what the agreement had been about. Some agreements obviously dealt with the ordinary sale of farm produce among villagers. But the *conventio* might also be concerned with the lease of land, as the following examples show.

HEMMINGFORD,[85] 1316: The bailiff and reeve are ordered to look at a certain piece of meadow about which an agreement has been made between Adam Cademan, naif of the lord, and John Porthos. And (also an agreement) between Thomas Oremund, naif of the lord and the above John.

OVER,[86] 1316: Roger Molle was convicted by the jurors of having unjustly broken an agreement with Muriell Linene about one rod of land to the extent of sixteen pence damages that he pays to her. And for this transgression, etc., (he pays) threepence with pledges Eudo Kylle, Robert the reeve, John Ine. And by the same pledges the above Muriell will have that rod of land for one autumn crop.

HOUGHTON,[87] 1321: John the son of Brayerson was convicted by the jurors of having broken the agreement that he made with John Child about one and one half acres of land that he received from the same John for a five year term (the term was to end in lent the next following). And since he unjustly withheld from the same John one-half bushel of corn valued at sevenpence, this he pays. And for this transgression, etc. he pays sixpence, with Reginald Gomesson' as pledge.

OVER,[88] 1328 ?: The six jurors convict Agnes Garyn of having broken her contract with William Garyn about the letting of a grange so that the latter suffered a loss estimated at two shillings. For this transgression she is amerced sixpence, and the beadle is the pledge for both.

---

[83] See Appendix XIII, no. 12.
[84] See Appendix XIII, no. 13. See further examples in numbers 15 and 16 of this Appendix. Further useful texts, especially on the subletting of land to freemen, may be seen in the 1300 roll for Over (Add. Ch. 39600), the 1300 roll for Cranfield (Port. 179, no. 10), 1311 for Ellington (Port. 179, no. 16), 1292 and 1294 for Warboys (Add. Ch. 34335 and 39597), 1297 for Broughton (Port. 179, no. 9), 1299 for Wistow (Port. 179, no. 10). An interesting suit was arrayed against Alice widow of Robert Smith at Wistow in 1309 (Add. Ch. 34342), charging that the property had only been sublet to Robert. But the text is too decayed for transcription.
[85] See Appendix XIV, no. 1.
[86] See Appendix XIV, no. 2.
[87] See Appendix XIV, no. 3.
[88] See Appendix XIV, no. 4.

CRANFIELD,[89] 1312: Hugh the son of Cecilia acknowledges that he broke an agreement with William the cooper concerning the land sold to the latter. William suffered a loss estimated at eighteen pence which is paid to him. And for this transgression Hugh is fined twelve pence, with John of Bretenden and Roger of Pyre as his pledges.

GIDDING,[90] 1312: The jurors find John Bynethetown guilty of owing John le Monek fourteen pence from a loan, eighteen pence from a croft, a bushel of beans, and in addition with having broken a contract about a bit of meadow at a loss of sixpence, all of which is paid him. For this illegal debt he is amerced sixpence, with William Graunt as pledge, and the sixpence goes to the clerk.

WARBOYS,[91] 1294: The villagers, free as well as others, say on oath that John of Higney broke an agreement with Reginald of Sutton concerning a house thereby causing him twelve pence loss. Therefore he is amerced twelve pence with Alexander the chamberlain as pledge.

WARBOYS,[92] 1320: The jurors find Thomas Puttok guilty of wrongly withholding from Richard Puttok part of a certain messuage, six rings of wheat, two rings of barley, one ring of beans and twelve pence from a certain contract formerly drawn up between them as is established from the manorial court. This debt, together with damages assessed at tenpence, are now paid, with Hugh Beneyt and Ralph Semar as pledges. And for this illegal debt, etc., sixpence, with the same pledges as above.

ABBOTS RIPTON,[93] 1318: The jurors find Alice the daughter of Stephen of Burcester guilty of breaking a contract drawn up with John the son of Robert by which a house was rented from the latter. He suffered a loss of threepence which is now paid. Therefore she is amerced threepence, and Roger son of Bartholomew is to be pledge of both.

III

The Tenure of Freehold by a Villein

Tenurial possibilities for serfs were not limited to the unfree tenements on Ramsey lands. In the case below from Ellington in 1311 it is clearly accepted that a villein, Alice daughter of Bartholomew in Inlond, inherited freehold from her father. The principle is enunciated in this same entry that Alice should not alienate such land without permission of the lord, nor marry any but a villein. The latter part of the principle was waived very soon, however, when for an entry fine Alice was allowed to marry a freeman. And the freeman thereby apparently assumed full seisin of this

[89] See Appendix XIV, no. 5.
[90] See Appendix XIV, no. 6.
[91] See Appendix XIV, no. 7.
[92] See Appendix XIV, no. 8.
[93] See Appendix XIV, no. 9. And see again Appendix XI, above, for further uses of the *conventio*.

land, although he is not shown to have performed any obligations peculiar to a freeman such as homage.[94]

ELLINGTON,[95] 1311: Robert the son of Richard the reeve, Roger in the Hale, John the Woodward, Richard of Cotenham, and Simon son of John are pledges of Alice daughter of Bartholomew in Inlond who holds of the lord one messuage, ten acres, one rod and more of land freely that she will not sell that land in part or in whole, nor will she marry anyone, without permission of the lord, and then not to anyone but a villein. Some time after the lord abbot, during easterweek, and at the request of lord Robert of Hereford, granted to the same Alice permission to marry a certain Godfrey Unterhyl a freeman for forty shillings as in the *gersuma* rolls of the twenty sixth year of the same abbot. And so he may have the said land in peace, void of any claim, etc.

It is interesting that the villager does not seem to have had to receive his freehold from the lord's hands. Manorial jurisdiction was maintained over freehold held by villagers by two steps. First, the charters by which the villager received such lands had to be shown in court, and secondly, the villein had to pledge himself not to sell such lands without permission of the lord. Fines were imposed for having failed to obtain from the lord licence to purchase freehold, as we see below in examples from Hemmingford Abbots and Girton in 1321. But the court entries record granting of licences without fines at Little Stukeley (1318) and Cranfield (1321). And no evidence has been found that the lord always exacted a licence fee with this permission. These acts guaranteed the jurisdiction of the lord over his villein, but the charter and right of alienation preserved the proper nature of the freehold. Villein tenure of freehold was a regular feature of the manors of Ramsey Abbey from the earliest available court rolls in the thirteenth century. A few of the many entries have been translated below. From the sources it would appear that villeins were gaining control of considerable local freeholds. The entries for Hemmingford in 1316 (William atte Grundehous) and 1321, or for Abbots Ripton in 1318, show a villager inheriting freehold for the payment of a fine. From these texts, and other documents such as that concerning Alice at Ellington above, it would appear that in some instances at least the villein had free disposition of his freehold by will, as well as by sale (see below, Cranfield, *ca.* 1318).

The court rolls do not always identify the purchaser of freehold as villein

---

[94] Since manorial officials assisted the lord's steward by taking cognisance of the conveyance of freehold within the abbot's liberty, the manorial courts regularly report improper conveyance among freemen themselves. From such reports it would appear that homage and the oath, rather than conveyance through the lord's manorial court and the oath, are the significant notes of the freehold transfer. But see further below, note 96.

[95] See Appendix XV, no. 1.

or free. The reason for this is that *everyone* purchasing property must show his charter to the lord of the fee. The manorial court was first interested in seeing all new charters, and most of the court rolls record the charge that some new charter be shown. Sometimes, as in the case of Richard the son of Serbinus probably of Over in 1291, the fact had to be established that the purchaser was a villein. But in most instances this fact seems to have been taken for granted, and we may only tentatively recognize villeins as those who pledge not to alienate without permission, and freemen as those who pay homage for their purchases. But for many freehold purchases by villeins the manorial court entry hardly differs from the record of purchase by a freeman (e.g. Upwood, Appendix XV, no. 27), and indeed after the mid-fourteenth century there appear to be no more references to the obligation of the villein to pledge himself not to sell freehold without the permission of the lord.[96] Apparently the villager, like the freeman, had henceforth only to show his charter. As a consequence, from this period it becomes impossible to distinguish freehold purchases by villagers from those of freemen. The court rolls do not bother to indicate whether the purchaser of a freehold is a freeman or a villager. Occasional inquiries do confirm, however, that villagers continued to purchase freehold into the fifteenth century.[97]

---

[96] At this point in the present study we leave consideration of the tenure of freehold by villeins through charters, not for lack of evidence, but to the contrary, for the very reason that such villein tenure enters the whole structure of freehold. There are scores of detailed references to land charters in Ramsey Abbey manorial court rolls that evoke the statement of the editors of the *Carte Nativorum* (p. XVII): "Some of the *Carte Nativorum* deal with free land, some with bond; some of the parties were free men, some villeins. But the striking thing about them is that the status of the land and the parties very rarely affects the form of the documents; ..." In addition to the above reasons of space, but also because it is felt that a more useful study of such charters can be made *after* a complete demographic study of the region, no attempt is made here to present a representative selection of these texts.

The student anxious to review current evidence for villein tenure by lease from the twelfth century will find Professor Postan's remarks invaluable (*Carte Nativorum*, pp. XLIX-LVIII). To this should be added the comments on the manors of the Bishops of Winchester (*ibid.*, p. LXIII) and the estates of the abbey of St. Albans (*ibid.*, p. LXIV).

As already noted, the purpose of this study is to bring out the scope of customary law, that is the accepted local practice. To what extent local law deviated from a wider system of law is another matter and not of concern here. In the above mentioned study (Section III, p. XLI ff.) Professor Postan surveys the evidence for this deviation or negative approach to villein tenure by charter. I cannot yet agree with Professor Postan's suggestion of a new legal attitude or 'reform' on Ramsey manors (XLVII-XLVIII). Large groups of land transfers occur over a long period in Ramsey court rolls (cf. below, p. 90). The changing economic conditions (cf. *Estates*, Chapter Eight) could have been adequate for varying attitudes on the part of the lord without reference to legal ideas.

[97] E.g. at Ellington in 1405 (Port. 179, no. 50) the jurors report that the naif Thomas Botman has three acres by inheritance from his father, the naif John Burgeys one and one-half acres by purchase, the naif William Burgeys one acre by purchase, the naif Thomas Burgeys three rods by purchase, the naif Walter Burgeys two acres of pasture by purchase, the naif John Hikkesson two acres by purchase.

LITTLE STUKELEY,[98] 1318: And they say that Henry Houlot bought two acres of land from William Brekespere. And that (Henry bought) from John Wale three and one-half rods of lands; which Henry comes and finds a pledge, namely Robert Ben'eth, that he will not sell that land.

And they say that William le Daye naif of the lord bought from the same William an acre and one-half. And John the son of Robert Clerk is his pledge that he will not alienate this land.

William Rolf is pledge of Robert Ben'eth that he will not alienate a rod of land that he bought from William Brekespere.

And they say that Rycherus Ben'eth bought an acre of land from the above William Brekespere, and two ? acres of land from John Wale, and one-half acre and one-half rod of land from Matilda Sutor. This Rycherus finds pledges, namely Hugh, Thomas and Robert Ben'eth, that he will not alienate those lands.

CRANFIELD,[99] 1321: A naif of the lord, John Catelyne, comes and shows his charter for the one-half acre of land that he bought from Nicholas Clerk, and he finds pledges, namely Simon Catelyne and Robert Catelyne, that he will not alienate the said land.

Lawrence Hayn comes in full court and shows the charter by which John the Chaplain enfeoffed him with one acre of land. And he finds a pledge that he will not alienate (that land), namely Simon de Barton. The charter (is seen ?).

And they say that Lawrence Hayn bought one-half acre of land from Sir John the Chaplain, and he finds pledges, namely Robert Gardiner and Peter Aleyn, that he will not alienate that land and will show his charter at the next court.

HEMMINGFORD ABBOTS,[100] 1321: And they say that William Plumbe a naif of the lord bought two acres, one and one-half rods of land from Ralph Bischop a freeman without licence from the lord, therefore he (is fined) forty pence with Simon at the style as pledge. And he pledges through the same that he will not alienate that land.

And they say that Peter Sley a naif of the lord bought an acre of land from a freeman Ralph Bischop, therefore (he fines) for two shillings, with John Roger as pledge. And he pledges through the same that he will not alienate that land.

GIRTON,[101] 1321: And they say that a naif Ralph Faber bought two acres of freehold and therefore (is fined) sixpence, with pledge John in the willows. And by the same pledge he will not alienate that land without permission from the lord; he comes and shows his charter.

LITTLE STUKELEY,[102] 1294: And they say that Godfrey Wisdom bought a house and one-half acre of arable on Langelong from Ralph of Stowe. Therefore he is to be distrained to show his charter.

And they say that John le Warde bought an acre of land from Alice le Warde. Therefore he is distrained to show his charter.

And they say that John le Man bought from Simon Chacede four sellions of land in Madfurlong, two sellions of land on le Lowe, one-half acre of land on Wydenhale

98 See Appendix XV, no. 2.
99 See Appendix XV, no. 3.
100 See Appendix XV, no. 4.
101 See Appendix XV, no. 5.
102 See Ault, Court Rolls, p. 214.

and one-half acre of meadow in Michaelmede. Therefore he is to be distrained to show his charter.

WESTON,[103] 1294: It is ordered that Henry the son of Hugh of Molesworth correct his charter on the three acres of land that he bought from John Ellington and which must be held *in capite* of the lord.

CRANFIELD,[104] 1294: William Robert was pledge of Nicholas of Crawley who was to come and show his charter for the tenement he bought from the same William, but nothing has been done. Therefore the same William is in mercy to threepence with the beadle as pledge. And it is again ordered that he show his charter.

Walter le Daye finds pledges, namely Ralph Marshall and William Robert, to correct his charter on the tenement bought from the same William before the next court.

OVER,[105] 1316: Robert le Baxster and Henry Walt are pledges of William of Temesford that he will show his charter on the messuage, three and one-half acres one rod of arable, and three rods of meadow, that he bought from Thomas Aylward as was presented. And (he is to do this) before the feast of St. John.

John bought one acre of land from Thomas Gilbous. Therefore he is to be distrained to show his charter at the next court.

ABBOTS RIPTON,[106] 1318: Philip of the hall is pledge of William le Bateman that he will show his charter on the one messuage bought from Stephen of Norfolk.

LITTLE STUKELEY,[107] 1318: And they say that someone from Brampton whose name is not known bought from the above William Brekespere an acre and a rod of meadow. Therefore he is to be distrained to show his charter at the next court.

WESTON,[108] 1318: And they say that Roger the son of Michael bought one-half acre of land from Hugh the son of Walter Gautron who will show his charter at the next court, with William Faber as pledge. Afterwards he does homage (for that land).

And they say that William the Hayward bought a cottage from Richard the Chamberlain, and he comes and shows his charter. And that charter was found to be defective, and he finds a pledge, namely John Baronn to correct that charter at once.

OVER,[109] 1332: And they say that John the son of Giles of Holywell bought an acre of land from Thomas Gon in the lord's fee. Therefore he is to be distrained to show his charter.

OVER, ?[110] 1291: Richard the son of Serbinus claimed that he was not one of the lord's men (*nativus*). But it was established by twelve men that he is of servile status. Therefore he finds a pledge, namely William Bonde, that he will henceforth be obedient to the lord and his officers. And since the same Richard is going to purchase two acres on the lord's fee of which one sown with wheat and valued at two

103 See Ault, *Court Rolls,* p. 230.
104 See Ault, *Court Rolls,* p. 234.
105 See Appendix XV, no. 6.
106 See Appendix XV, no. 7.
107 See Appendix XV, no. 8.
108 See Appendix XV, no. 9.
109 See Appendix XV, no. 10.
110 See Appendix XV, no. 11.

shillings is accounted for by the reeve, he finds a pledge, namely Alan Maynor, that he will fine to hold that land (twelve pence).

ELLINGTON,[111] 1311: Simon Pen'el and William the hunter are pledges of Walter Burgeys that he will not alienate a freehold, of three acres more or less, that he has purchased without licence of the lord.

HEMMINFORD ABBOTS,[112] 1316: And the whole village, for having permitted William atte Grundehous to enter an acre of free meadow after the death of his father without paying an entry fine, pay forty pence to the lord. Afterwards he fines for that acre of meadow as is recorded in the *gersuma* roll at Ramsey.

LITTLE STUKELEY,[113] 1321: Also it was ordered to distrain William the son of Robert the farmer by pledges to do homage and fealty for the acre and rod of meadow that he bought of William Brekespere.

KNAPWELL,[114] 1316: On the reeve of Knapwell for not having distrained Ralph the son of William and his wife Eleanor to do homage, relief, and fealty for the land they hold of the lord in Knapwell, threepence (fine). And it is ordered also that they be distrained to do this.

OVER,[115] 1316: And (fines) to John of Over and William Smith pledges of John Bycardun of Stanton for not having him do homage and fealty to the lord for the one acre of land bought from Thomas of Ellsworth. The fines are condoned. And it is also presented that they be distrained as before. And it was established that they hold nothing from the lord save through (   ) Hence nothing is due from them.

   John of Over is also pledge of John Freysel to do homage for six cottages and six acres bought from Mariota Fynor before the feast of the nativity of John the Baptist.

BURWELL,[116] 1321: And on the reeve and beadle for not having distrained Thomas the son of Paukn of Halt' to do homage, relief, and fealty for the tenement formerly belonging to Thomas de Beyville in Burwell, twelve pence (fine). And it is ordered that they distrain.

WESTON,[117] 1318: The jurors say that William son of John Adekoc purchased a cottage from John son of Roger the Shepherd. And he finds a pledge, namely Roger the reeve, that he will not sell that cottage.

WESTON,[118] 1300: And the jurors say that John son of Wylke, who is a naif of the lord, bought one-half acre from John of Ellington. And it is established that he hold this from the lord as tenant-in-chief. And he performs the enfeoffment to the lord.

   And they say that Walter son of Juliana purchased a rod and one-half of land from the same John. And it is established that he holds from the lord as tenant-in-chief. And he performs the enfeoffment to the lord.

---

[111] See Appendix XV, no. 12.
[112] See Appendix XV, no. 13.
[113] See Appendix XV, no. 14.
[114] See Appendix XV, no. 15.
[115] See Appendix XV, no. 16.
[116] See Appendix XV, no. 17.
[117] See Appendix XV, no. 18.
[118] See Appendix XV, no. 19.

OVER,[119] *ca.* 1310: And the jurors say that William Howe junior, a freeman, bought three acres from John Payn. Therefore he is to be distrained (to show his charter).

And they say that William Lord, a naif, bought as freehold a messuage from Walter Fynor. And this William gives the lord ( ) in order to have peaceful tenure of that messuage.

And they say that Robert Syleby bought as freehold an acre of land from Walter Fynor. And he gives the lord twelve pence to have peaceful tenure of that land with the beadle as pledge.

And they say that Richard Wylle, a man of the bishop (of Ely), bought two acres from John Payn. Therefore he is to be distrained to show how he obtained entry to the lord's fee.

And they say that Roger Crane a naif of the lord bought freely one messuage from Robert Fynor and he pays the lord twelve pence to have peaceful tenure of that holding.

And they say that William the son of Howe junior, a freeman, bought an acre of land from Richard Baudre. Therefore he is to be distrained for entry to the fee.

And they say that William Taby junior a naif of the lord bought a built up rod from Richard the ( ), and some land from Richard Baudre, as well as an acre from John son of Letitia. And this William gives the lord twelve pence for peaceful tenure of these lands.

CRANFIELD,[120] *ca.* 1318: (The jurors say) that lord John Morite bought from Thomas Fychyer, a naif of the lord, a plot with five acres, an acre of meadow, and an acre of woods from the lord's fee. Therefore he is to be distrained to perform all those obligations to the lord that are required.

CRANFIELD,[121] 1321: Walter the woodward, naif of the lord, is fined sixpence for puchasing one rod of freehold from Richard the marshall without licence. Henry at Wood is pledge.

And they say that Thomas Terry, a naif of the lord, bought two acres from Ralph Dumbely without licence. Therefore he is amerced two shillings with Hugh ( ) pledge. And it is ordered that this Thomas be distrained to show his charter before the next court.

HEMMINGFORD ABBOTS,[122] 1321: And they say that Thomas son of Thomas Marshall, a naif of the lord, bought one-half rod of freehold from Thomas Jordon and he comes and shows his charter. Therefore, etc., twenty shillings, with the reeve as pledge. And he pledges by the same that he will not alienate this land.

John son of Thomas of Stukeley gives the lord forty pence for entry to three rods of freehold that his father had bought, and the reeve is pledge.

ELLINGTON,[123] 1292: The reeve and Richard West are pledges of William Brun that the latter will do what is necessary for the lord in order that his daughter Chris-

---

119 See Appendix XV, no. 20.
120 See Appendix XV, no. 21.
121 See Appendix XV, no. 22. There are two other entries in this roll of villeins showing charters and swearing not to alienate lands without the lord's permission. A roll for this manor likely for the following year (Port. 179, no. 26) notes freehold purchases by three villeins without licence from the lord.
122 See Appendix XV, no. 23. Similar entries for this manor may be found in rolls for 1299 (Port. 179, no. 10), 1320 (Port. 179, no. 19), 1325 (Port. 179, no. 22).
123 See Appendix XV, no. 24. Further detailed examples for this manor are to be found for 1311 (Port. 179, no. 16) and 1318 (Port. 179, no. 18).

tina may freely hold that one-half virgate of freehold that William bought from the abbot of (   ) the above Christina (   ) at Ramsey before the lord abbot.

SHILLINGTON,[124] 1290: Robert Smith, naif, who bought freely one acre of land from Godfrey of Aldebyry gives the lord a rent of a penny per year as increment.

ABBOTS RIPTON,[125] 1318: Joan, a naif of the lord and widow of Clement of Eltyslo, came and showed her charter for a certain part of a garden that she and her husband Clement had bought from Thomas le Ladde and his wife Mariota. And she finds pledges, namely William le Hawelound and John le Vernoun, not to alienate that bit of land.

It is difficult to obtain a total picture of the market for small free-holdings at any time. There are some entries, like the sale of various properties by William Brekespere at Little Stukeley in 1318 above, or at Over *ca.* 1300, that suggest freeholdings were commonly fragmented among villagers. Further examples of multiple divisions in village tene-ments that might be freehold or customary are illustrated below for King's Ripton (1306), Shillington (1306), and Weston (Bythorn in 1308). At the same time there is a steady stream of evidence that villagers were consoli-dating their holdings by exchange of scattered units.

SHILLINGTON,[126] 1306: The jurors established that Robert of Ocolt held a virgate from the lord in Shillington for the service of five shillings, eightpence. And he sold that land to various tenants. And then Ralph of (   ), one of the tenants, came and asked for his section worth eighteen pence. And Matilda of Stondon (seeks) her part of elevenpence, Alice of Stondon of (eightpence), John the Baker of twopence, Robert the Chaplain of one penny, John of Barton of a halfpenny, Ralph the Chapman of a halfpenny, Ralph the Smith of a halfpenny, William of Hames-compe of twopence, Master John of Shillington of threepence a halfpenny farthing, Williams the widow's son of fourpence, Alice (   ) of thirteen pence halfpenny farthing.

KING'S RIPTON,[127] 1306: It was established by the whole court that Stephen Rabat during his life purchased in the vill of King's Ripton three acres and one rod of land, ... of which one-half acre lies at Mortelande, one-half acre at Langelond next to John the Stalker, one-half acre at Watlondum next to John Wyllyam, one rod at Lang(bred) next to John the son of Simon and one rod towards the meadow next to Henry Hanetok, one-half rod at Hyhyl, one rod next to Hugh in Angulo, one rod at Lytlemere next Nicholas the Newman, one rod towards the meadow next to Nicholas Carpenter. These same lands the above Stephen bequeathed to John the son of John the Palmer as is found in the will of the said Stephen. Therefore it is determined that he may obtain the said land in peace.

WESTON,[128] 1308: It was determined by the jurors that Reginald the son of

---

[124] See Appendix XV, no. 25.
[125] See Appendix XV, no. 26.
[126] See Appendix XVI, no. 1.
[127] See Appendix XVI, no. 2.
[128] See Appendix XVI, no. 3. Another example of this problem may be seen in Maitland, *Manorial Courts*, p. 78 (Pleas in the Court of the Abbot of Ramsey's Honour of

Andrew the Freeman had held from the lord William of Godmanchester, abbot of Ramsey, one messuage and thirty acres of land and meadow. Of these lands Reginald died in seisin under age and they were in the custody of the said lord abbot. After his death Petronilla, Letitia, and Alice, sisters of the said Reginald succeeded to that land as co-parceners, and so they held until Petronilla gave her part to Simon the son of William of Ellington who in that portion enfeoffed John his brother and the above Petronilla on the day that she married him, to be held of him and his heirs. And afterwards the above Alice gave her part to the said John and Petronilla to hold of them and their heirs. And the same John and Petronilla sold all the above land to diverse tenants, except for the messuage and an acre three rods of land of which the said Petronilla died in seisin after the death of her husband John. After her death Thomas her son came and asked for that land in which his mother the said Petronilla had died seised according to the donation of the above, and it was given to him. And since the whole of the above land in which the said Reginald died seised is held of the abbot by military service, by homage and fealty, and by the service of two suits yearly to the court of Broughton and one suit to the court of Weston, and whosoever was the tenant of that land by the above service was to come himself to the autumn boon works with one labourer. And it is ordered that the said Thomas be distrained as tenant of one messuage containing one acre of arable and one acre, three rods of land in the meadows of Bythorn; and Philip the son of Lawrence of Bythorn holding one-quarter of a messuage and two acres of land; and John the son of Lawrence holding two acres and one-half and one rod of land; and Michael of Bythorn holding one acre, and Henry of Millesworth holding five and one-half acres, John son of Emma holding one acre; Matilda the Ploughwryte holding one and one-half acres and one and one-half rods, Walter Shepherd holding one and one-half rods, William Faukes one acre one rod, Simon Secour one acre one rod, Richard Smith one and one-half acres, Reginald Delbyrg one and one-half rods, William Smith one-half acre, William Smith and Letitia his wife and co-heir of the said Reginald tenants of the third part of the one messuage, and of ten acres of the above land. (All are distrained) to do all the above service.

HEMMINGFORD ABBOTS,[129] 1301: Peter Miller gives two shillings to the lord for an inquiry about the three rods of land that Thomas the son of Henry holds unjustly as he (Peter) claims since this land belongs to that virgate for which Peter has fined with the lord abbot. And the jurors, examined on this point, say under oath that the above land was exchanged by a certain tenant of that land with a predecessor of the above Thomas at a time long since forgotten, so that no inquiry can be made even of the names of those who exchanged because of the lapse of time. Therefore the above Peter is told to make a request of the lord abbot whether anything can be done, or to come to some agreement with the other party.

WARBOYS,[130] 1325: And for twelve pence Robert Bronnote, Stephen Aubyn and Robert Atebrok are licenced to exchange land as is found in the rolls of the manor, and they will be pledges for one another.

Broughton) where it is complained that the fee of Silvester L'Enveyse had all been sold in parcels over the previous generation so that tenants had to be distrained for services due to the king and for suit to the lord's court.

The embarrassing complications that could arise when villeins had to be distrained according to common law are well illustrated in Casus Placitorum, pp. 80-1.

[129] See Appendix XVI, no. 4.
[130] See Appendix XVI, no. 5.

WISTOW,[131] 1347: And the jurors present that Thomas del Halle who held a part of the messuage of John Bonde, cotman in Little Raveley, in exchange for an acre of demesne at farm on the Osshes of the manor of Upwood has died. And Sarra the widow of this John will hold this for life, etc. and takes the oath.

WISTOW,[132] *ca.* 1300: Thomas Onty pays a twelve pence fine to the lord for permission to hold a rod of land below his yard that he had received in exchange with Mariota Gernon for a rod of land on Lytlehyl in the time of William the abbot without licence. And Nicholas Gernon gives the lord twelve pence for the exchange in order to lawfully hold that land of the said Mariota, and they are to be pledges of one another.

In the above chapter evidence from manorial court rolls has made it possible to catch a glimpse of the various ways by which the villager was trafficking in land. How heavy was the traffic? The court rolls give no exact answer to this question since it was not regularly necessary to enroll any of the various types of conveyance in the court rolls. The customary conveyance proper was enrolled in the *gersuma* book which has not survived for the thirteenth and fourteenth centuries; subletting within the permitted limits required no licence; those who had purchased freehold had to present their charters for examination in court, or perhaps only to the lord's officials when the court was not in session. Only at King's Ripton was the court roll employed as regular record of smallhold conveyance. At the other manors a large number of conveyances will inexplicably appear on the court roll now and then, suggesting that the court session just happened to coincide with a heavy conveyance period. Some examples from these years of more numerous entries are given below in Appendix XVII.[133] But for the most part the tempo of the traffic in conveyances escapes the calculus of the investigator since the lord himself did not control this traffic by a rigid record.

It is difficult to find what would in reality be described as an absolute prohibition to the traffic in customary or freehold by villagers, or to the conveyance of customary land by freemen. Freemen only obtained customary land through village laws, that is through a villager (by marriage) or at other times by special licence of the lord. Once willing thus to submit to village laws, the freeman's possibilities for customary tenure were considerable. In order to maintain personal responsibility for services

---

131 See Appendix XVI, no. 6.

132 See Appendix XVI, no. 7. Some other examples of these exchanges may be seen: e.g. for Therfield in 1296 (P R O, SC 2, Port. 179, no. 9), for Weston in 1290 (B M, Add. Ch. 34908) and 1321 (Port. 179, no. 21), for Hemmingford Abbots in 1320 (Port. 179, no. 19), for Cranfield in 1312 (2) (Port. 179, no. 16) and 1321 (Port. 179, no. 21), for Warboys in 1333 (Add. Ch. 39470), for Gidding in 1342 (Port. 179, no. 30), for Houghton in 1308 (2) (Port. 179, no. 15). Except for Hemmingford, where virgates were exchanged, these exchanges were all for small units of land.

133 See Appendix XVII (King's Ripton, 1321, 16 entries; Therfield, 1347, 15 entries).

any customary tenant might either let his land only for very short periods of a year or two, or allow his property to be conveyed through the courts for a life tenure to a lessee who assumed all responsibilities vis-à-vis the lord. Both the short term and the life tenure offered many opportunities for a brisk traffic in land. And finally, nothing stood in the way of the unfree villager's tenure of freehold, so long as the charter was recognized by the lord or his official.

The great numbers and variety in village land tenure illustrated by the general survey of this chapter indicate a 'village economy' underlying that manorial economy better-known to the historian. Whereas the hidage assessment, with the virgate and other subdivisions, was the basis for the manorial economy of the villager, the key to the village economy proper seems to lie in very small, variable, and perhaps often irregular and enclosed units. How little we know about the existence of these small units from ordinary sources is most easily seen by an effort to reconstruct the village, buildings, lots, and gardens, from a manorial survey or extent. Extents tell us practically nothing about the existence of these things, and yet we know that there were buildings, lots, and gardens! And furthermore, the small unit was the focus for the most active land market among villagers! While the small unit of land was vital to the subsistence economy of the villager, the small unit was fostered also by wider economic uses. Over the twelfth and thirteenth centuries scores of servants from Ramsey Abbey were partly paid in kind with small holdings, or the crops from these. Servants on the manor continued to be paid in part by special small units of land until the fifteenth century. In addition, the initial unit of production in the clearing of arable seems to have been the small enclosure. While these enclosures were incorporated in the manorial assessment of hides and virgates in many parts of England, and probably in Ramsey villages also, perhaps students have assumed too readily that the smallhold then ceased to remain a common unit of tenure and a practical unit of production for the villager! Whether scores of arable smallholdings were assessed separately, as in twelfth and some thirteenth century extents like that of Warboys, or whether these small units were assessed within virgates and then sublet in the manner seen in the above chapter, might not make a great deal of practical difference. In any case, as the above chapter has indicated, there was a machinery for the maintenance of smallholds, and there appeared to be an active market in smallholds, until the close of the fourteenth century.[134] With the concentration of

---

[134] At the same time it should not be too readily accepted that the wide existence of smallholds merely involved a fragmentation of larger holdings. The wide variety of claims in land seen in Chapter Two above, and the variety of term tenures noted in

lands from the end of the fourteenth century the smallholding tends to disappear as a separate unit in the economy of the village.

Chapter Three, reduce the practical significance of partible and impartible inheritance systems to something nearer a family management. In some ways the systems may have merged: partible inheritance may be held jointly (cf. Homans, *Thirteenth-Century Villagers*, p. 116), but joint tenure of virgates was not infrequent in twelfth and thirteenth-century extents of Ramsey manors where a custom of impartible inheritance prevailed.

No doubt our knowledge of the smallholding must be seen in the widest context of European history as well as from the detail of the above chapter. See D. Herlihy, 'The Carolingian Mansus', *Economic History Review* (1960), pp. 79-89, for the features of the smallholding at an earlier period. Some useful suggestions for the economics of the small family unit, plot or garden, may be found in Duby, *Économie rurale*, pp. 59-60, 61-2, 166 ff., 191-2, 377-9, 473.

CHAPTER IV

VILLAGE ADMINISTRATION

IN the thirteenth century the villagers under the jurisdiction of
Ramsey Abbey exercised a range of responsible action remarkable in
view of their servile status. The lord's demesne might be farmed to the
villeins of the village as well as to any other farmer.[1] As we have seen in
Chapters Two and Three above, the succession to and subletting of lands
were, within certain limits, varied, flexible, and autonomous. In order
to exert such responsibility over the demesne or customary tenement, it
must be assumed that the villager also had a relatively free access to
markets[2] and a relatively free control of his revenues.

In addition, however, much of this economic organization was only
possible owing to the governmental structure of the vill. Self government
has always been an outstanding feature of the village community.[3] It is
difficult to envisage villagers farming a desmene if some of the villagers,
especially the reeve, had not exerted already a genuine responsible authority over demesne-villeinage obligations, whether the demesne was farmed
or not. It is difficult to envisage a spontaneous movement of lands among
villagers if the mutual responsibility of these men was a matter for the
personal discretion of the lord rather than dependent upon 'one of their
own' — the villager's neighbour, his pledge. And behind reeve and
individual pledge there also stood clearly a corporate responsibility in the
late thirteenth century. There was, first, the corporate responsibility of
the *villata* to be fined as a body, and secondly the frankpledge system,
whereby the individual pledge was tied into a complicated system of
mutual responsibility.

The village was such a closely woven social and legal unit that many
elements basic to the tenurial structure can only be seen by going beneath

---

[1] See *Estates,* p. 124.
[2] The scanty amount of research as yet devoted to study of local exchange markets, as
against the fair and 'international' market, poses a serious problem for the student of
village life in mediaeval England. The schedule of villagers' transactions, payments,
rents, debts, fines, wages, etc., in account and court rolls leaves no doubt as to the market
'involvement' of the villagers. Restrictions were placed on village marketing where stock
essential to the function of the manorial economy were concerned, see *Estates,* p. 192,
note 7.
[3] See the fourth quality of the little community in Robert Redfield, *The Little
Community* (Phoenix edition, Chicago, 1960), p. 4.

manorial extents and land contracts to probe deeper folds in these levels
of local administration. Court records for reeve and beadle, group fines,
frankpledge organization, and indictments of the *villata* will be studied in
this chapter in order to be able to understand more clearly the place of
village government in the questions under consideration in this volume.
Needless to say, this chapter does not pretend to give a complete picture
of village government. Village administration may be looked upon as an
extension of those social relations already seen in the manorial structure,
the family community, and the village economy. This chapter indicates
some basic lines along which this extension developed.

I

Government by Officials

Court rolls are largely the record of convictions and fines, and are not
therefore concerned to summarize the ordinary government of the village
or even the range of activity of the village officials. Quite frequently,
however, village officials were concerned so closely in the responsibility
or irresponsibility of the carrying out of these convictions that their duties
were spelled out clearly in the records. Since such detailed entries abound
in the court rolls, and every series of texts in this volume supplies further
examples, illustrations are given below from only two rolls. Furthermore,
as we have dealt in another place with the obligations of these officials,
and in particular the reeve[4] with respect to the administration of the
lord's demesne, the following examples will be restricted to relations
between officials and their fellow villagers. It must be kept in mind that
demesne administration was the first reason for the important position
of reeve and beadle in village government. But, while the reeve and
beadle were responsible for their lord's economic interests, at the same
time such responsibility was guaranteed to bring them into contact with
every facet of village life. Even more, in the exercise of their duties these
officials reveal the social structure of the village upon which demesne
administration depended.

Because the reeve and beadle were responsible for distresses, these officials, although themselves unfree men, might be charged with distraining
freemen to do homage for their lands in the Ramsey liberty. Two examples
of this may be seen in the Burwell entries of 1321, below. In order to

---

4 See *Estates*, index *s. v.* reeve, and especially pp. 125-7.

ensure that the lord's interest had not been violated, the reeve might be delegated to look at the charters of land transactions among villeins and others, as in the case given below for Hemmingford Abbots in 1316. Offences against the common and demesne rights, such as Matilda Edward wrongly gleaning at Hemmingford Abbots in 1316, or Goderobbe cutting and carrying off fen grass at Burwell in 1321, left an obligation upon the reeve to bring the culprit to court.

By dint of many of these functions the reeve was also, of course, a servant of his fellow villagers. At Hemmingford Abbots in 1316, for instance, we see below that the reeve must collect a claim for Thomas son of Adam, and he must force John of Hagenham to reply to a charge of transgression by William Plumbe. A good example of reeve and beadle collecting debts among villagers may also be seen for Upwood, under 1297. The court would seem to have left to the reeve the solution of the complicated problem that arose at Broughton in 1294 when William Catelyn sold an ox that the reeve had taken from Thomas Cobbe as a distress and left with William. The duty of the reeve to collect piecemeal the debt owed by Robert Godrich to Hugh Albyn in Warboys, in 1326,[5] suggests that villagers' affairs may have taken up a good part of his time. The great effort involved in collecting debts is also seen in the case of John Beneyt at Broughton in 1291.[6]

From the nature of his obligations the reeve was bound to become involved in the more personal affairs of his neighbours. When Matilda Warewyk of Girton was sentenced to lose her property for immorality in 1291, it was the reeve who reported that she had compounded for the delict by a fine. The most frequent involvement on the personal level was, however, with fleeing serfs. Manorial officials would seem to have jurisdiction over such men and women in the first instance because they carried their chattels with them from the manor. But the line between movable goods and villagers themselves as chattels of the lord was not very clearly drawn in customary law, so it is not surprising to find the reeve being held responsible for the person of these fleeing serfs. The reeve, or the reeve and beadle, usually had the duty of arresting the runaway and keeping him in custody.[7]

BURWELL,[8] 1321: And (it is presented to the) reeve and beadle that they did not

[5] See the text below in this chapter, p. 103.
[6] B M, Add. Ch. 39849.
[7] See further below on runaway serfs, Chapters Six and following. The reeve's position with respect to recovery of properties, management of escheated properties, purview of charters and land entry, etc. may be seen in the texts of the previous two chapters.
[8] See Appendix XVIII, no. 1. Several excerpts are taken from the same court roll in these examples in order to underline the multitude of duties of the reeve and beadle in *every* village.

distrain Thomas the son of Panham of Halt' to pay homage, relief, and fidelity to the lord for the tenement formerly held by Thomas de Beyville in Burwell, twelve pence (fine). And they are ordered to distrain him.

John Ideyne and Henry the Drynere are pledges of William the Oryner for the recovery of the goods and chattels that he took away from the lord's fee. This same William was delivered to the custody of the reeve and beadle, but since they do not have him, they (are in mercy to) sixpence. And it is ordered that the said William be distrained to reply at the next (court).

And to the reeve and beadle for not having distrained Nicholas Arfick to do homage to the lord for one acre of land that he had bought from Bartholomew son of Bartholomew as had been directed in the last view, threepence. And they are ordered to distrain him to do this before the next view.

And to the reeve for not having arrested Nicholas the Clerk, as he had been ordered to do in the autumn court, for having gone abroad from the lord's fee with his chattels without permission from the lord, threepence. And he is ordered to be distrained to make good for those things he removed before the next court.

And to the reeve and beadle for not arresting Goderobbe for having cut and taken away some of the lord's marsh grass, threepence. And it is directed that he be arrested to account to the lord for this before the next court, etc.

HEMMINGFORD,[9] 1316: And to the reeves for they did not arrest Thomas Neel to give an account for what he took away, etc., sixpence. And it is directed that he be arrested, etc.

And to the reeves for not having recovered from Thomas the Marshall twenty-two pence owed to Thomas son of Adam. And it is ordered that it be collected.

And to the reeves for they did not bring Matilda Eduard to account for having wrongly gleaned in the autumn.

And the bailiff and reeve are ordered to look at a certain piece of meadow about which an agreement was drawn up between Adam Cademan and John Porthos, and between Thomas Oremund, a naif of the lord and the said John. So that etc.

And to the reeves for not having distrained John of Hagenham to reply to a charge of transgression by William Plumbe, threepence. And it is directed that he be distrained to reply as before.

Despite these many disagreeable tasks there is little evidence that the reeve and beadle were detested officials in the village.[10] The reeve's

---

9 See Appendix XVIII, no. 2.
10 In any case the villagers seemed to be quite able to keep officials in line. Here are a few examples of this control. First, a failure to pay threshers: *Wistow*, 1299 (P R O, SC 2, Port. 179, no. 10): De Thoma Onty quondam preposito pro iniusta detentione xxx denarios versus Ricardum le Clerk, Thomam Herny, Ranulphum Fabrum, et Simonem Tannatorem pro trituratione bladi in curia abbatis inter festum Sancti Michaelis et festum Omnium Sanctorum anno preterito, condonatur, plegius utriusque Thomas Clericus de Wystowe.
A beadle is fined for harming villagers: *Wistow*, 1316 (B M, Add. Ch. 34896): Et dicunt quod Johannes Waryn bedellus non est idoneus commorandus in officio bedelli pro eo quod parcet quibusdam de homagio pro donis ab eisdem receptis, vexatque et onerat quosdam alios de homagio ultra modum ad dampnum et gravamen maioris partis totius villate. Ideo ipse Johannes etc. vid., plegius Galfridus le Rede.
A miller is fined for poor service to villagers: *Wistow*, 1313 (B M, Add. Ch. 34917): De Smale Ade Molendario quia male custodit blada et saccos vicinorum in molendinum sicut

obligation to take runaway serfs was not a very practical one, as we shall see in a further chapter,[11] so he may in fact have gained in popularity by opportunities of non-enforcement in restraint of the movements of villagers. At other times, we have clear evidence of the reeve or beadle favouring his fellow villager against the rights of the lord. Cases of this are illustrated below for Ripton,[12] Holywell,[13] and Ellsworth.[14] But the in final analysis the villagers must have co-operated with these men because they were servants of the whole village as well as the lord's officials. A good example of this may be seen below from Hemmingford Abbots in 1332. Here we see a villager treated as a veritable traitor, ostensibly because he had betrayed the village to royal tax officials. Every kind of charge is made against this man who had taken his civil service obligations too literally. In the enforcement of penalties the reeve is the main agent of the village.

HEMMINGFORD ABBOTS,[15] 1332: And they say that Thomas Jordan by ploughing appropriated to himself a furlong called Watelond, forty perches in length and a foot wide, to the damage, etc. Therefore he is in mercy to sixpence, with the reeve as pledge. And it is ordered that this be repaired.

And they say that the same Thomas took from the common at Langemerch a section four feet in length and three perches wide to the loss, etc. Therefore he is in mercy to sixpence, with the reeve as pledge. And it is ordered that this be repaired.

And they say that the same Thomas in digging caused damage to the lord's meadow at the head of the croft of this same Thomas. Therefore he is in mercy to forty pence, with the reeve as pledge. And it is ordered (that this be repaired).

And they say that the same Thomas and his servants unceasingly mow on their neighbours' lands to the damage of the whole homage. Therefore (he is in mercy) to twelve pence.

And they say that the same Thomas arranged to represent his fellow villagers with the collectors of the fifteenth, and then revealed to the said tax collectors hidden things of his fellow villagers so that the whole vill was taxed for a greater amount through the efforts of this said Thomas to the sum of forty shillings. Therefore, for this transgression he is in mercy to twenty shillings.

And they say that the same Thomas gave the bailiffs of the lord king and the other magnates warranty in order to procure the office of tax assessor over his fellow

presentatum fuit in ultimo visu, vid., plegius Willelmus Rolf. Bailiffs are forced to return land appropriated from the villagers: *Houghton*, 1295 (P R O, SC 2, Port. 179, no. 9): Juratores dicunt per sacramentum suum quod ballivi abbatis appropriant culture domini de terra custumariorum apud Estcroft. Ideo preceptum est quod emendetur, etc.

11 See below, especially Chapter Six.
12 See below, p. 274 (no. 12).
13 See below, p. 274 (no. 13).
14 See below, p. 140. Some villagers were found bribing the beadle to avoid work at Warboys in 1325 (B M, Add. Ch. 34898): Et dicunt quod Galfridus bedellus est inoportunus serviens domino et comitati nativorum pro eo quod accepit munera diversis custumariis percendis eis de operibus debitis domino ad grave dampnum domino. Ideo ipse etc. xld., plegius prepositus.
15 See Appendix XVIII, no. 3.

villagers and so spent the lord's chattels to the amount, etc. And since he is a common flatterer against the good of the whole homage to their harm, etc., forty pence, with William Trappe as pledge.

And they say that the same Thomas keeps four shillings belonging to the whole vill. Therefore the reeve is ordered to get those four shillings for the profit of the whole vill, with a sixpence fine.

II

The Frankpledge and the Personal Pledge

Despite the fact reeve and beadle were paid officials of the lord, with specified duties on the manor, it will have been noticed in the previous section that certain obligations were often placed upon these officials by appointing them pledges to various persons. In this way the lord was tying in seigneurial jurisdiction with the traditional method of village governance whereby the villager must carry a certain responsibility for his neighbour.[16] The best known use of the pledge, and an institution basic to local law and order throughout most of mediaeval England,[17] was the frankpledge system. By the frankpledge system every male in the village over twelve years of age must be in a tithing, a group of varying sizes, organized under a headman, or under a capital pledge as he was called in Ramsey villages.

In the earliest extant court rolls the capital pledges seem to occupy a position of prominence comparable to the jurors. For example, in 1288 there were listed for Shillington eight jurors and eight capital pledges, for Holywell, eight and eight, for Houghton, twelve and twelve, for

---

[16] The pledge may be looked upon as a means of identification or 'mergence' with the group, and is therefore very likely a much more intimate relationship than the formal text of the court rolls reveals. In the study of primitive peoples in modern society, where the student has the advantage of personal observation, this identification is often traceable through kinship relations. For example, A. R. Radcliffe-Brown, *Structure and Function in Primitive Society, op. cit.*, p. 25: "In primitive society there is a strongly marked tendency to merge the individual in the group to which he or she belongs. The result of this in relation to kinship is a tendency to extend to all members of a group a certain type of behaviour which has its origin in a relationship to one particular member of the group." But whether or not the personal pledge tended to be chosen along blood lines, the function of the personal pledge was central to the stable social behaviour of the village. The capacity of the villager to always find a personal pledge only underlines the uniformity of behaviour: "The first condition of fitting human beings together into a social system depends on obtaining a certain uniformity of behaviour. Society is fiduciary. You cannot live in a society unless you can on reasonable grounds expect that people will behave in a certain way." (A. R. Radcliffe-Brown, *A Natural Science of Society*, The Free Press, Glencoe, Illinois, 1957, p. 99).

[17] W. A. Morris, *The Frankpledge System* (Harvard Historical Studies, no. 14, 1910), see pp. 90-5 for duties of the pledge, pp. 96-7 for duties of the tithing proper, pp. 98 ff. for relations to other legal institutions, pp. 103-110 for duties of capital pledge.

Broughton, twelve and thirteen. The main obligation of the capital pledge was to have all his men in tithing that should be there. The court rolls noted failures by capital pledges to have all their men in tithing. For example, in 1297 at Upwood one capital pledge 'had not thirteen men,' another six, another three, and another three. At Warboys in 1301 one capital pledge was short eleven men; at Upwood in 1307 one capital pledge had not one man, another had not four, another had not two. Such entries indicate a more or less wholesale neglect of his duties on the part of the capital pledge. Throughout all the court rolls references to the failure of capital pledges to have 'their men' are on the whole, however, very scattered. Usually the court indicts a villager or two for not being in any tithing without attaching blame to any capital pledge. In order to carry out his obligation the capital pledge would seem to have had some coercive powers, at least to the extent of being able to present delinquents in court. For example, at Wistow in 1297 the court ordered that John Carter be distrained for disobedience to his capital pledge, Richard at the spring. In this way, from the evidence of the early court rolls that are available, the capital pledge would seem to be the official liaison between the manorial court and the frankpledge.[18]

From the beginning of the fourteenth century the capital pledges would seem to have ceased to take an active part in the manorial court. Their names no longer receive prominence along with the jurors, and in fact the capital pledges gradually cease to be fined in manorial court for not having men in tithing. This withdrawal of frankpledge personnel from the manorial courts may be but one area of the general decline in private courts at this time.[19] The immediate explanation for the disappearance of the

---

[18] The chief pledge does not appear to be obliged to do the distraining himself, however, for his name is not mentioned in this context. E.g. *Over, ca.* 1300: Item preceptum est quod braciatrices et homines manentes super feodum domini abbatis in tenementum Roberti de Fueges in Overe distringantur de die in diem donec satisfecerint super hoc quod non venerunt ad visum franciplegii. Postea venit Hugo serviens Person de Overe, et dat domini iiiid. quod habeat pacem de omnibus contencionibus usque festum Sancti Michaelis proxime sequens. (Norwich, *Ramsey Register,* fol. 45d.)

For further on the chief pledge with respect to jurisdiction of those beyond their tithing, see below, Chapter VI, beginning of Section I.

[19] See Ault, *Court Rolls,* pp. xxiii-iv, for a discussion of the decline in private courts from the late thirteenth century. At the same time there was a vital relation between the villagers and the king's courts in the thirteenth century. Fines upon villagers in the late thirteenth century show that these were kept strictly to their task of enforcing law and order for the king. E.g.: Item vicecomes reddidit compotum de villata de Terfeld xxs. quia non fecit sectam sicut continetur ... Et de decenna Radulphi Wynegor in Therfeld xld. pro fuga Johannis Wynegor fugantis sicut continetur ibidem (Egerton 3663, fol. 34). It must have been difficult to distinguish the obligations of free and unfree villagers with respect to these 'external' legal obligations. Another lord, as well as the king, could claim certain rights over Ramsey freemen and villagers, e.g.: Et salva integra sunt eidem Abbati de Burg' amerciamenta fines et proficua provenientia de liberis hominibus ipsius

capital pledge from the manorial records appears to lie in the commutation of his obligations. From sometime around the beginning of the fourteenth century it became no longer necessary for every person in frankpledge to be present in person at the annual view of frankpledge. Henceforth an annual fine was paid, the *capitagium*, in commutation of this personal appearance. In the spring of the year 1306 at Over the lord withdrew this right to commutation (for that year), and in so doing describes for us the meaning of this payment: "Since the lord abbot does not intend any more to receive the half mark that he had been accustomed to receive from Over in *capitagium*, it is directed that the bailiff and reeve instruct the capital pledges to have at the next view of Over all men of their tithings."[20] Once this obligation of attendance had been waived, however, the capital pledge would apparently have little more to do than collect the annual penny and hand in the full amount.

From the fourteenth century the manorial court itself rather than the

---

Abbatis de Ramesiae ad visus predictos. Et similiter integre de villanis ipsius Abbatis de Rameseae de forinsecis terris que ad visum franciplegii pertinent. Amerciabuntur et villani ipsius Abbatis de Rameseye per pares suos proximores predictorum et vicinarum villarum . . . (*ibid.*, fol. 127).

See also an entry from the honour court of Broughton, likely for the year 1285, copied into the Norwich *Register* (fol. 24), and following upon a usual list of essoins: "... Preceptum est villate de Gyddynge quod assideant v marcas reddentes pro transgressione sua infra diem dominicum proximum.

Villate de Elyngton in defalt' quia non veniunt set memorandum quod inquisitio commissa fuit facienda. Willelmus le Noreys, villate de Caldecote in misericordia de dimidia marca quia non secuti fuerunt uthesium levatum per bercarios de eadem super bercarios de Woldehirste. Woldehirste in defalt' quia non venit ad presentandum uthesium super ipsam levatam per bercarios de Caldecote amerciantur ad dimidiam marcam et preceptum est quod tenentes Prioris auxilientur ad predictam marcam. Broughton in defalt' quia non venit ad inquirendum veritatem de uthesio noctanter levato secundum quod irrotulantur ad curiam predictam." For some general remarks on the problems of interdependence of free and villagers in the administration of frankpledge, see Morris, *The Frankpledge System*, especially p. 125 and p. 146.

20 See P R O, SC 2, Port. 179, no. 12. Only five other entries of this nature have been noted:

Ellington, 1290 (P R O, SC 2, Port. 179, no. 7): Preceptum est Galfrido Gerold capitali plegio de homagio persone quod habeat ad proximum visum omnia capita in decenna sua contenta eo quod nichil dant ad dimidiam marcam cum villate.

Hemmingford Abbots, 1291 (Port. 179, no. 7): Et dicunt quod Willeldus le Eyr, Henricus filius Simonis tannator, et Hugo Haryng sunt liberi et extra decennam. Ideo preceptum est distringere ipsos. Et dicunt quod liberi decennarii nichil dant ad capitagium. Ideo vocentur omnes per capita.

Upwood, 1448 (B M, Add. Ch. 34826): Et preceptum est omnibus capitalibus plegiis quod faciant parare capitagium annuatim solvendi coram seneschallo qui pro tempore fuerit (annuale) veredictum suum dicendum sub pena xxs. Et si aliquis decenare non vult distringatur per eius capitagium.

? , 1470 (Port. 179, no. 90): Et Symon Bocher, Ricardus Wilkinson et Roulandus Holde electi sunt capitales plegii, ad colligendum et levandum communem finem totius ville et pro solvendo veracitim senescallo, in visu precedenti curie.

Houghton, 1290 (Port. 179, no. 7): Capitales plegii et eorum decene nichil dant ad capitagium. Ideo vocandi sunt omnes per capita.

chief pledges dealt directly with those not in tithing, that is, the court imposed a fine upon those who received men not in tithing, and from the late fourteenth century fined directly the men not in tithing.[21] The obligations of the capital pledge to those of his tithing beyond the manor without permission seems to have disappeared also from the early fourteenth century.[22]

While the frankpledge system was the framework for peace and good order in the village, the personal pledge had wider and more varied applications. It is well known that the structure of feudal relations became shot through and through with manifold uses of the personal surety.[23] But the personal dependence or responsibility in the feudal relation was but one species of the use of a personal surety, guarranty, or warranty, in the widest compass of mediaeval society. In its own way, too, the mutual responsibility that made possible a frankpledge system merely sponsored a wide use of the personal pledge. This does not mean that the tithing gradually encroached as a system of control over all aspects of the villager's life. On the contrary, beyond the very narrow range of obligations to keep peace and to take offenders that has been described above, the chief pledge, or the tithing, are not held finally responsible for other sureties. The pledge in other matters was a specific, personal, commitment. Whether the villager was restricted to his tithing in choosing a pledge cannot be ascertained, but in any case there is no evidence that the tithing bore ultimate responsibility for failures of individual pledges. No doubt, however, failure to pledge successfully, or to honour his pledges, redounded ultimately upon the lawworthiness of the villager himself so that he could in fact be evicted from the tithing.

How then was the pledge chosen ? Apparently the one who required the pledge had to present (to find — *invenire* — is the technical form employed in the rolls) a suitable person as surety. The husband was the obvious pledge for his wife, as the husbands of ale-wives often experienced.[24] Fathers were usually expected to be responsible for their children.[25] But for no type of responsibility is there described a necessary relation between the kinship connection and the pledge. Where an element of charity was perhaps predominant, as in the sponsoring of a transient,[26] we are told

---

[21] See below, p. 130 ff.
[22] See below p. 141 ff.
[23] See for example Marc Bloch, *Feudal Society* (Chicago, 1961), Chapter X 'Character and Vicissitudes of the Tie of Kinship'. On the other hand the personal pledge was a very ancient institution. See for example, T. G. E. Powell, *The Celts* (London, 1959), p. 77.
[24] Of the dozen or so ale-wives fined for breach of the assize in nearly every roll, very often the husband was the pledge for more than one half.
[25] See below for some examples, pp. 168-9.
[26] See below, Chapter Six, Section I.

that pledges stepped forward to offer their surety. Very likely the transient would be engaged as a servant to his pledge in this circumstance as part of the private agreement. In most cases, however, the procedure is less easily ascertained. But there is at least no evidence that obligations of surety were imposed either for faults of omission or commission, by selection or imposition of the court, unless there is clearly common involvement. Thus when customary villeins were fined severally for group violations of some manorial law or other, they were often placed as pledges of each other (*alter alterius*) against future violations. But where the charge was upon an individual only, the choice of a personal guarantor would seem to be a matter for personal agreement, no doubt at a price determined by the degree of risk involved.[27]

The function of the pledge was much more limited than the area of responsibility of manorial officials like the reeve. That is to say, there is no suggestion from the evidence that the personal pledge could distrain his man, present him in court for delicts, and so forth. The personal pledge merely stood to pay a fine for non-performance by his principal. The obligation here was reasonable. If the pledge had failed to prevent something because it has been done under cover of night, he was usually excused. For repeated faults on the part of the principal, it would appear that the pledge had limited responsibility. That is to say, he was only fined once or twice, and then the pledge was changed or some other action taken by the court. Illustrations of this personal pledge activity are found in texts throughout this volume, so that a special list of examples does not seem necessary at this point.

In contrast to these many uses for the pledge, the pledge seems to have been called upon rather infrequently to answer for his charge. When so called upon, the pledge was usually fined threepence for failure to produce his man and cautioned to have him next time, or the manorial officials had to distrain the principal.

UPWOOD,[28] 1318: And to Stephen Albyn for not having Richard Baroun for whom he was pledged to account for his sow having harmed the lord's demesne, threepence. And it is ordered that this said Richard be distrained to reply to this charge at the next court.

---

[27] At Graveley in 1290 a villager was unable to find a pledge because he was poor, see above, p. 72.

[28] *Upwood,* (B M, Add. Ch. 34803): Et Stephano Albyn quia non habuit Ricardum Baroun quem replegiavit ad respondendum de hoc quod sus eius dampnum fecit in marisco domini, iiid. Et preceptum adhuc distringere dictum Ricardum ad respondendum ad proximam curiam.

Et Roberto Newman plegio Willelmi filii Laurentii le Bone quia non habuit ipsum ad respondendum de hoc quod apportavit virgas extra Rokesgrove, iiid. Et preceptum distringere dictum Willelmum ad respondendum ad proximam curiam.

And to Robert Newman pledge of William the son of Lawrence le Bone for not having him to account for having removed sticks from Rokesgrove, threepence. And it is ordered that this said William be distrained to reply to this charge at the next court.

Although it would appear to be almost a general rule that the pledge was fined threepence for not having his man appear personally in court to answer a charge, responsibilities of the pledge could be more onerous. This seems to have been the case particularly when contracts and land were involved, as in the following examples.

BROUGHTON,[29] 1314: Godfrey de Bir gave the lord sixpence, with the beadle as pledge, that a plea of his be heard about customary lands let and leased, so that from this plea he may take steps to recover this land, etc.

WARBOYS,[30] 1326: The jurors convicted Robert Godrich of unjustly retaining two rings of wheat and one ring of beans from Hugh Albyn. Therefore for this unjust retention he is in mercy to threepence, with pledges the beadle Godfrey son of Cecily, and Robert Mercar. And it is directed that the said grain be raised from the same Robert and his pledges day by day until, etc.

ST. IVES,[31] 1307: And (the fine) to Nicholas the reeve, pledge of Robert Abbot for not having the same Robert give his warranty that he is in a tithing at Stanton as pledged in the last view, sixpence. And it is ordered that the same Robert be distrained to put himself in tithing. And it is ordered that Robert Gernoun be distrained to account for the fact that he received the above Robert while he was not in tithing.

In the second quarter of the fourteenth century a rapid decline in the use of the personal pledge becomes noticeable. But it is always difficult to trace historically a 'negative development' such as this gradual abandonment of an institution. Court rolls became shorter from this time as entries became more clipped and some items were probably omitted altogether. Where comparisons can be made the village does not seem to be any more or less law abiding from this time. Rather violations of village law were penalized directly by a reasonable fixed fine that was apparently always paid without the use of a pledge, unless of course the

29 *Broughton*, (B M, Add. Ch. 39463): Galfridus le Bir dat domino vid., plegius bedellus, ut querela sua audiatur que ad terras custumarias locandas et conducendas, et audita querela sua ut potest inde recuperare, etc.

30 *Warboys*, (B M, Add. Ch. 39760): Convictum est per iuratores quod Robertus Godrich iniuste detinet Hugoni Albyn duas ringas frumenti et unam ringam fabarum. Ideo pro iniusta detentione in misericordia iiid., plegii utriusque bedellus, Galfridus filius Cecilie et Robertus Mercar. Et preceptum quod dictum bladum levetur de eodum Roberto et plegiis suis de die in diem quousque etc.

31 *St. Ives*, (P R O, SC 2, Port. 179, no. 15): De Nicholao preposito plegio Roberti Abbot quia idem Robertus non habuit warrantum suum quod est in decennam apud Stanton sicut manucepit in ultimo visu, vid. Et preceptum quod idem Robertus distringatur ad ponendum se in decennam. Et preceptum est distringere Robertum Gernon ad respondendum de hoc quod recepit dictum Robertum extra decennam.

fine was waived because of poverty. In short, the personal pledge seems to have lost its practical use. After the Black Death pledges are no longer entered for the main categories of the court rolls, that is, fines for bad brewing, for avoidance of work on the demesne, and for transgressions upon common wood and pasture by livestock. In addition, fines become smaller and more routine from this time.

But it was the period after the Black Death that best demonstrates how the pledge had lost its vitality as an instrument for manorial administration. When, after the mid-fourteenth century, there was an attempt to strengthen the traditional organization of the manor, the pledge was invoked at the most crucial point of control, the movement of the villeins from the village[32] and the maintenance of villein tenements.[33] But in neither case is there evidence for successful penalties upon pledges for failure to control their man, and when suitable opportunities arose villeins moved at their will and deserted properties with apparent disregard for pledges.

III

Villata *and Group Fines*

Frequently in the late thirteenth century the whole village (*villata*) was held responsible for certain areas of government.

SHILLINGTON,[34] 1288: And upon the whole village for not having observed the watch, and upon the capital pledges for several concealments and false proclamations, and upon the jurors for false presentations and concealments, six shillings, eight pence.

ELLINGTON,[35] 1290: And upon the whole village for not having pursued the hue and cry justly raised against William of Stow, nor having arrested him, and for not keeping the watch, eight shillings.

In these police duties the *villata* was not required to go beyond the usual regulations required by king's courts of the villages of England.[36]

---

[32] See Chapter VI below, especially Section II.
[33] See Chapter IX below.
[34] *Shillington*, (P R O, SC 2, Port. 179, no. 5): Et tota villata pro vigilia non observata, et de capitalibus plegiis pro pluribus conceleamentis et falsis proclamatibus, et de juratis pro falsis presentatibus et conceleamentis vis. viiid.
[35] *Ellington*, (P R O, SC 2, Port. 179, no. 7): De tota villata quia non prosecuti sunt hutesium iuste levatum super Willelmum de Stowe nec eum arrestaverunt, et quia non vigilaverunt, viiis.
[36] See Morris, *The Frankpledge System*, p. 90 ff.
Such police duties of the villager are now generally recognized as congenial to village psychology. E.g. George H. Mead, "The Psychology of Punitive Justice", *American*

There is nothing in the court rolls to suggest that the whole village was an organ of government separate from the reeve, capital pledges, or jurors. That is to say, the village does not seem to have appeared before the lord's steward as a body, nor was there any particular agent representing the *villata* beyond the above-mentioned officers. Fines imposed upon the whole village underline the fact that there was a universal responsibility for village law and order. But it would be more than evidence supports to suggest that the *villata* was the body of *final* responsibility, after the exoneration of officials, capital pledges, and jurors. Rather it must be said that fines upon the *villata* represent that very small area where village government is not entirely the responsibility of these various officials. In similar fashion to such enforcement of the king's law, the lord abbot seems to bind the whole village to some particular obligation in the texts below. Whether this was simply to further guarantee that the village court and officials should do their job is impossible to determine. For in reality there is no evidence that the whole village ever was fined under this title by the abbot. Rather, the village court would take steps to distrain or indict the particular offender.

The *villata* in a more limited sense of the word did however often speak and acts as a corporate person. It is in this sense that the *villata* of Ellington was said to have overstepped its powers by conveying villein tenements against the customs of the manor.[37] The *villata* here refers to the customary land tenants only. These 'customaries' (*customarii*), as they are usually called, had common rights upon fen, pasture and wood, and they had common obligations upon the lord's demesne. Furthermore, lands of customaries were so intermingled that it was to their common utility to co-operate in the carrying out of laws of drainage, trespass, seasonal enclosure, and so forth. It is not surprising to find such customary tenants

---

Journal of Sociology, 23, 1918, p. 591: "...that attitude of hostility towards the lawbreaker has the unique advantage of uniting all members of the community in the emotional solidarity of aggression. While the most admirable of humanitarian efforts are sure to run counter to the individual interests of very many in the community, or fail to touch the interest and imagination of the multitude and to leave the community divided or indifferent, the cry of thief or murderer is attuned to profound complexes, lying below the surface of competing individual efforts, and citizens who have been separated by divergent interests stand together against the common enemy." Quoted in Robert K. Merton, *Social Theory and Social Structure* (The Free Press, Glencoe, 1957), p. 61. And see further references for the study of this question on the same page.

37 *Estates*, p. 124. Some useful remarks on this organized village activity may be found in Duby, *Économie rurale*, section 'De village et les entrepreneurs,' especially pp. 263-4, 266-71. Duby's concluding remarks are particulary worthy of our attention (p. 271): "On peut considerer l'assolement réglé, avec l'ultime aménagement des rotations de cultures, comme l'un des remèdes que chercha, pour s'évader de la pénurie alimentaire, une population dont le progrès agricole et l'essor des échanges avaient permis la libre expansion pendant trois long siècles, mais qui, à l'approche de 1300, se trouvait de nouveau trop nombreuse dans presque tout l'Occident."

coming together as a body to rent a fifty acre field from the lord's demesne at Upwood in the mid-thirteenth century, or in other instances to lease the whole of the demesne. Unfortunately there are no extant copies of the agreements that these villeins drew up among themselves. On the other hand it is easy to reconstruct the main elements of such agreements. The rights of customary tenants in common lands were strictly ordered according to the size of the tenement, so it is reasonably certain that the portion of each villein in the cost and profits of the farmed demesne would be directly proportioned to his villein tenement. The actual management would still rest, of course, in the hands of the reeve and beadle.

It has been necessary to stress the positive nature of group action among customaries as a regular feature of manorial life, since thirteenth and fourteenth-century court rolls usually report this group action only when it has involved opposition to the interests of the lord. But, contrary to the parallel sometimes drawn between such opposition and the rise of revolutionary groups in modern industrial societies, the rebellious customaries did not represent a new, and incipient from, of group activity. Even with the most sensational case on Ramsey estates, where the *villata* of King's Ripton carried their case to the king's court, the joint activity as such was never challenged.[38] Upon nearly every other manor of Ramsey the customaries challenged the lord from time to time in terms of the customary law itself. Such joint action was an accepted expression of village life.

WISTOW AND LITTLE RAVELEY,[39] 1297: All the customary tenants of Wistow and Little Raveley sought a respite until Christmas at the last view in order to search the register with leave of the lord about the custom of taking and carrying beyond the lord's meadow on mowing day, against the penalty of twenty shillings to be paid to the lord. And from that time till now they have done nothing, nor have they found anything in the register to support their claim. Therefore the above fine is to be levied on them.

All the customary tenants of Wistow and Little Raveley are held for contempt of the lord and for having denied that they are to mow the meadow at Thurnbrugg for a day in return for their work obligations of the next day as had been requested of them on behalf of the lord by William of Beaumeys, then serjeant. Therefore they are in mercy to two shillings.

WISTOW AND LITTLE RAVELEY,[40] 1299: Since all the customary tenants of Little Raveley have not yet (arranged) with the lord abbot to (burden) the separate pasture of the said lord at Assedyche, still these customaries pastured the same pasture with their animals for the past two years so that they owe satisfaction to the lord to the sum of twenty shillings for these beasts and have not done it. Therefore

---

[38] *Estates*, p. 227.
[39] See Appendix XIX, no. 1.
[40] See Appendix XIX, no. 2.

it is ordered that the said money be raised from them, or that they seek recourse from the lord.

WISTOW AND LITTLE RAVELEY,[41] 1301: And the whole vill of Little Raveley, except William Marger and Thomas Beneyt, is fined four shillings for not coming to carry the lord's fen to Ramsey when summoned. And the above William and Thomas (are fined) twelve pence. They are all pledges for each other.

And the whole vill of Wistow and Little Raveley for refusing to collect nuts in the woods, whereas of right they ought, to an amount estimated at six bushels worth thirty pence. And for transgression they are in mercy to six shillings.

And the reeve is ordered to collect twenty shillings from all the customary tenants of Little Raveley for the lord since they pastured on the separate pasture of the lord at Assedyche for three years, as was established in the last court.

WISTOW AND LITTLE RAVELEY,[42] 1306: It is charged to the customary tenants of Wistow and Raveley that they withheld ploughing for the lord in the week immediately after the Nativity of Blessed Mary, in the 21st year of King Edward. And they put themselves on the register that this ploughing was not owed, as is found in the last court, in which court they were directed to search the register and have not done so. Therefore they are in mercy to two shillings, pledges one of the other.

ABBOTS RIPTON,[43] 1306: All the customary tenants of the vill of Ripton who ought to perform carrying services are in mercy, for as they were often summoned to go beyond the manor to carry to Ramsey the next day sacks were filled for them. And yet the filled sacks are left in the following day until the first or third hour before these customaries come to perform this carrying service to Ramsey to the great harm of the lord and convent. (They are fined) one-half mark, and are to pledge one another.

BURY,[44] 1297: It is noted that the customaries of Bury withdraw and do not plough, and have not when they ought, the accustomed ploughing services owed to the lord, namely one ploughing service on a Friday or Wednesday of every week. At the same time these same customaries plough their own land or even land of others, and for this ploughing of outsiders they are paid in cash. However, these customaries expressly state that they are not obliged to perform any ploughing services for this same lord once their own land has been completely ploughed. A day is arranged for them to discuss this matter with the lord and his officials, namely the next Sunday after the feast of Saint Lucy the virgin at Ramsey, at which time all are obliged to appear there under penalty of one-half mark.

HOUGHTON,[45] 1274: All the customary tenants of Houghton and Wytton, namely sixty-nine virgaters and semi-virgaters, are accused in this court by the steward of having gone to Huntingdon and St. Ives for penny ale at other times than during a fair. And this is done against the licence and ordinance established by Abbot William of Godmanchester as may be found in the rolls for the autumn court of the fifth year of that abbot, and has now been renewed by Abbot John, as may be found in the autumn court held on Saturday the morrow of the feast of Saint

---

[41] See Appendix XIX, no. 3.
[42] See Appendix XIX, no. 4.
[43] See Appendix XIX, no. 5.
[44] See Appendix XIX, no. 6.
[45] See Appendix XIX, no. 7.

Margaret in the tenth year of this lord abbot, that if any of the above customaries should be convicted of the above offence he should pay a twelve penny fine to the lord. These customaries come and admit that truly none of them is able to acquit or absolve himself of other than guilt against the above licence and ordinance (   ) that the above fine, namely sixty-nine shillings, be levied on these customary tenants, namely twelve pence from each of them.

BROUGHTON,[46] 1291: It is noted that all the customary tenants of the vill of Broughton in contempt of the lord, and especially as in his presence, withdrew from the great autumn boon works leaving their work from the ninth hour until evening (   ). These maliciously and wrongly say in explanation that they had not received bread in the amount that by custom they had the right to receive. But it is found in the register of services and customs that unless the lord wishes such customaries do not have the right to more bread than may be purchased so that two men together have bread worth three farthings. And since the said customary tenants in contempt of the lord were not willing to take such bread, but withdrew from the lord's autumn works to his serious loss, they are amerced to forty shillings.

GRAVELEY,[47] 1290: The whole vill was ordered to go and get a millstone at St. Ives since it was believed that such was the custom. But they denied they were to do this, admitting only that they were bound to assist in transporting the stone while not being obliged to do so entirely at their own expense. Therefore, an order is issued to search the register of their customs and services.

After the early fourteenth century there is no more evidence for concerted action against the lord on Ramsey estates. How is this to be interpreted? As the victory of seigneurial power over common action? In so far as we can investigate the problem from extant documents, this question of seigneurial victory is not significant. A glance at some of the elements in the context of these common actions is of primary importance here. First, there does not seem to have been a vigorous and prolonged effort by the lord to revive centralized demesne farming after the second decade of the fourteenth century. In other words, the fulfillment of many common obligations by the villeins must have been of less importance to the lord from this time; not only would there be less reason for opposition by villeins, therefore, but not surprisingly fixed fines and commutations replaced heavier penalties. Secondly, despite the group action taken by villagers, fines were imposed upon tenants only. The villeins took united action because common interests were at stake, but these interests followed

46 See Ault, *Court Rolls,* p. 201, note 35.
47 See Appendix XIX, no. 8. Smaller groups of customaries of course can be found acting in the same manner. For example, at Houghton in 1313 (Add. Ch. 34324) all the cotmen refused to work at Easter. Or at Broughton in 1290 (Add. Ch. 39754) ten villagers 'sowed in the fallow where they ought not to the harm of free and customaries who have common pasture there.' A good indication of how the customaries tended to assume the domainal jurisdiction of the lord after farming the village of Ellington is given below, Appendix XXXII, no. 9.

from the fact that each was a tenant. Fines were ultimately imposed upon individuals as tenants. In short, the tenant ultimately acted as an individual for his own economic interests. It is no surprise that fines were more and more placed upon the individual from the early fourteenth century.

In addition, despite the occasional group avoidance, penalties were obviously set by the decision of the villagers themselves as well as by the lord in cases like the above example regarding the cutting of reeds at Wistow in 1306. The common laws of the village were set by those implicated.[48] The establishment of these ordinances, as they were called, seems to have been an old tradition by the time of the first extant court rolls. And these laws would appear to be a necessary complement to the demesne-villeinage complex, for extents give only the static list of obligations. The ordinance would continue so long as village life centred about communal economic activity. In this wider context opposition to the lord was only one phase in the history of communal organization. Ordinances would continue with or without the lord. In fact when, after the early fourteenth century, the violation of an ordinance no longer came to be treated as opposition to the lord, ordinances began to be invoked with more frequency. The ordinance gradually becomes from this time a valuable evidence for agrarian administration, and an important indication of various crises in village economic life. In the following chapter we shall see something of the breadth and variety of questions settled among the villagers by means of the ordinance.

---

[48] The function of the villagers in expressing the laws of maintenance and tenure is seen in the work of the jurors in the texts of Chapters Two and Three, above.

CHAPTER V

THE VILLAGE ORDINANCE[1]

THE village ordinance or byelaw was not a product of the fourteenth or fifteenth century. Those most commonly proclaimed byelaws of the late mediaeval period, laws governing the regulation of open fields, must have been as ancient as the open field system itself. These regulations stand out in the court records from the fourteenth century because in a changing legal and economic environment, the open field system retained its traditional form. As the lord withdrew from exploitation of the demesne, and as village tenements fell out of hereditary hands, the open field system lost much of the traditional support of the 'custom' of the village. The increased promulgation of byelaws from the fourteenth century underlines a new administrative urgency especially with respect to the open field system. But these byelaws still describe for us the age-old dynamics of customary law: the necessity for collective action in the village economy.[2]

For Ramsey villages the local statute, byelaw, or ordinance is a source as fundamental as account rolls and extents for our knowledge of the organization of the village. These regulations have properly been called 'village byelaws' since they come from all the village, and the implementation of these laws was of a material concern to the whole village. In the late

---

[1] This chapter is merely intended to suggest some of the scope of the material available on this question from manorial courts. I have not attempted to indicate fully the value of the byelaw as a source for the study of the social history of the village in late mediaeval and early modern periods since I understand that Professor Ault has a definitive volume ready for publication.

[2] Students of primitive tribes to-day have drawn attention to this dynamics. E.g. A. R. Radcliffe-Brown, *Method in Social Anthropology* (Chicago, 1958), p. 54: "But my own view is that it (the desire to understand) is of comparatively minor importance amongst primitive peoples, and that amongst them the basis of the development of custom is the need of action, and of collective action, in certain definite circumstances affecting the society or group, and that the custom and its associated beliefs are developed to fill this need."

The concentration of evidence in the late mediaeval period should not lead to the notion that the group activity of the villagers, their 'socialization' or 'togetherness', became any greater in the late mediaeval period. Besides all the evidence that may be found in court rolls for that very urgent implementation of the ordinance discussed in this chapter, some villagers altogether refused to take common responsibility with their neighbours. Entries such as the following are not uncommon. *St. Ives*, 1305 (B M, Add. Ch. 34774): Et dicunt quod Radulphus de Houghton non vult esse ad scot et lot cum vicinis suis. Ideo distringatur. *Weston*, 1360 (Add. Ch. 34812): Et quod Jacobus Martyn est rebellus et non vult justificare per pares suos.

thirteenth century the court rolls frequently referred to village byelaws as
'statutes' (*statuta*). But from the fourteenth century the term 'ordinance'
(*ordinatio*) became universally accepted in Ramsey villages. The byelaw
or ordinance was made, although issued in various forms, 'by the common
consent of the whole vill.' For example, from Hemmingford Abbots[3] in
1299 there is the entry:

(Since) with the assent of all the customaries it was ordained in court four years
ago that if any of the above customaries were convicted of buying ale for other than a
halfpenny they should be liable to a twelve penny fine to the lord. And it is presented
upon inquiry that all bought ale at a penny except William Dargon, that is sixty-
four shillings fine on the customaries. And they fine for twenty shillings for now.

In a text from the village of Warboys[4] in 1326 we find free and customary
tenants for the protection of their own interests introducing a byelaw
for which they obtain the consent of the lord (that is, through his officer
in court):

The whole homage of Warboys, freemen as well as the rest, request in full court
that henceforth it be forbidden to anyone of the township to sell or give away any
reeds (trimmed and bundled) in the marsh of Warboys until the reeds (   )
have been collected and bound on his own lands, under penalty of one-half mark
to be paid to the lord for each offence against that ordinance in any way by any of
them. And this was granted in full court etc. in the above form.

Changes in the economic organization of the demesne and of the village
do not seem to have altered the legal form of the ordinance. A text from
Houghton in 1274, already cited in Chapter Four,[5] referred to violation
of an ordinance as against the 'permission and ordinance made through
Abbot William of Godmanchester'. Fifteenth-century texts were much
the same, as may be illustrated from the Broughton[6] roll for 1405:

It was ordered by the lord together with the whole homage that no one should
enter a field to harvest or to cart corn during the whole autumn either in the evening
or morning while it is still dark, under penalty of forty pence. And that no one
should trample the stubble of another with any animals during the whole autumn
until the feast of Saint Michael unless each on his own lands, under the same penalty. And that no one should pasture with any animals about any corn in the
fields until that corn is entirely removed for the distance of one stadium, under
the same penalty.

3 See Appendix XX, no. 1.
4 See Appendix XX, no. 2. See also numbers 4 and 5 of this Appendix.
Very frequently the reason for the promulgation of a particular ordinance in a court
session can be seen from the indictments of previous months. For example, for the year
prior to the promulgation of this ordinance, there were thirteen convictions for wrongfully
selling reeds from Warboys.
5 See above, p. 107.
6 See Appendix XX, no. 3.
A list of ordinances usually begins with 'Ordinatum est' for the first ordinance only, the
following ordinances simply beginning 'Et quod'. Occasionally, however, a list of ordinances
begins with 'Ponitur in pena.'

Violation of an ordinance was a threat to the common good of the whole village. Obviously such violations tended to occur in those areas of village life where common interests were involved more immediately, that is, common pasture and the open fields. By far the greatest number of infringements of common rights appear in court rolls under fines for livestock breaking into corn fields. Infringements were penalized according to the damage done, and villagers sought to protect their crops by regulations governing the enclosures about sown fields and the movements of pasture animals. Common fields had to be closed off from pasture animals at certain seasons and villagers were responsible for the construction of the 'gappes,' ditches, etc., closing off these fields from their own lands.

ABBOTS RIPTON,[7] 1428: And that Catsherdgap be closed before the feast of Saint Lawrence under penalty of fourpence.

LITTLE RAVELEY (Wistow),[8] 1438: It was established under pain of fine that all gaps from Ontyescroft corel to Rowdich be closed before the feast of the Annunciation of Blessed Mary under penalty to each of sixpence to the lord and sixpence to the church.

UPWOOD,[9] 1534: And under pain of fine all the tenants of both Upwood and Raveley are to make fences and ditches facing newmedow before the feast of Saint Hugh next, under penalty to each of three shillings, fourpence.
And no one is to put any animal in that newmedow from the feast of Saint Lawrence to the feast of Saint Michael under penalty of six shillings, eightpence.

WISTOW,[10] 1430: It was promulgated under pain of fine that each make his enclosure between le Hathe and the (arable) field before the feast of Saint Martin, under penalty of twelve pence to the lord and twelve pence to the church.

WARBOYS,[11] 1483: And under pain of twelve pence fine everyone in the vill is to build his gaps along the edge of the woods of the said Warboys before the feast of Saint Martin, bishop and confessor, in the winter next following, under penalty (of twelve pence).

UPWOOD,[12] 1483: And it was established under pain of fine that all ditches of this vill be cleaned and all openings in the fences be closed before the feast of the Nativity of the Lord next under penalty to each of forty pence.

HEMMINGFORD ABBOTS,[13] 1454: And it was ordered under pain of fine that everyone enclose the end of his garden good and well from hoxtensday to the feast of Saint Peter in Chains next following under penalty of six shillings, eightpence.

ELLINGTON,[14] 1443: And everyone is ordered to make an enclosure around a one-half virgate within the octave of Martin next etc. under penalty of forty pence.

---

[7] See Appendix XXI, no. 1.
[8] See Appendix XXI, no. 2.
[9] See Appendix XXI, no. 3.
[10] See Appendix XXI, no. 4.
[11] See Appendix XXI, no. 5.
[12] See Appendix XXI, no. 6.
[13] See Appendix XXI, no. 7.
[14] See Appendix XXI, no. 8.

UPWOOD,[15] 1452: And that whoever holds land along Nesthaledyche and Boc
nalesyde is to build an enclosure between the field and the marsh before the fea
of Saint Martin next following under penalty of twelve pence each.

CHATTERIS,[16] 1452: And under pain of fine every tenant (is ordered) to repair h
section of the manor enclosure before the feast of Saint Peter in Chains und
penalty of two shillings.

LITTLE RAVELEY (WISTOW),[17] 1457: And under pain of fine everyone is to bui
an enclosure from the croft of William Onty to Huntingdonwey before the fea
of All Saints under penalty of sixpence to (be paid to) the lord.

GREAT RAVELEY (UPWOOD),[18] 1454: And everyone is ordered to build his ow
enclosure between the marsh and highmadefeld within a fortnight under penal
(   ).
And everyone of Raveley is ordered not to allow anyone to go beyond his gard
either on foot or on horse under penalty (   ).

WARBOYS,[19] 1455: And everyone must make his enclosure from goodmanstile
Burywodeend before the said feast and under the above penalty, etc.

The temporary enclosures could be removed for re-entry to pastu
only on specific days. Dates of entry to pasture were determined by th
location and the nature of the pasture. The variety of regulations governin
entry to pasture can be seen from the following selections.

UPWOOD,[20] 1411: And that no one is to drive his animals into the arable fields n
along the edge of the fen before the feast of Saint Martin under penalty of twen
shillings.

WISTOW,[21] 1411: And that no one is to re-enter the meadow before the feast
Saint Benedict under penalty of twelve pence.

UPWOOD,[22] 1428: And that no one is to come into the Frith until the fen grass ha
been removed, under penalty of forty pence.

WARBOYS,[23] 1428: It was decreed under penalty of fine that no hog should l
allowed to come into the pasture between Logehill and Wolfhay before the feast
the Finding of the Holy Cross under penalty of six shillings, eightpence to each offende

SHILLINGTON,[24] 1473: And under penalty of twelve pence no one may keep h
sheep in Stokkynge before the feast of All Saints.

BRINGTON,[25] 1473: And that no one may henceforth put any animals in Marty

---

15 See Appendix XXI, no. 9.
16 See Appendix XXI, no. 10.
17 See Appendix XXI, no. 11.
18 See Appendix XXI, no. 12.
19 See Appendix XXI, no. 13.
20 See Appendix XXII, no. 1.
21 See Appendix XXII, no. 2.
22 See Appendix XXII, no. 3.
23 See Appendix XXII, no. 4.
24 See Appendix XXII, no. 5.
25 See Appendix XXII, no. 6.

Slade unless (as was the custom?) of old, namely, until the feast of the birth of Saint John? under penalty of?

UPWOOD,[26] 1473: And that no one may keep any animals in the meadow of the township after the (feast of) the Purification under penalty also of three shillings, fourpence.

LITTLE STUKELEY,[27] 1536: And it is directed that no one place any lambs or sheep nor any other animal in the three gorse pasture except with the consent of all the tenants, under pain of a twenty shilling fine to each offender.

CHATTERIS,[28] 1473: And that henceforth no one may keep any animals in Elehalf under penalty of an eightpence fine to the lord and eightpence to the church, etc.

ABBOTS RIPTON,[29] 1428: It is decreed that under penalty of fine no one may pasture within the demesne unless he lives within the demesne, under penalty of forty pence to the lord and forty pence to the church.

GREAT RAVELEY (Upwood),[30] 1473: And that henceforth whosoever puts his hogs outside the township pasture (is to be fined) under penalty of three shillings, fourpence.

LITTLE RAVELEY (Wistow),[31] 1534: And it is decreed that no one put any of the animals called bullocks on the demesne from the feast of Saint Elene until the feast of Saint Michael under penalty of three shillings, fourpence.

UPWOOD,[32] 1534: And that no tenant is to place any animal in Higham Feld, unless it be horses and calves called wenelyng calffe, from the end of autumn until a time agreed upon by those tenants, and furthermore, that no one not having at least a cottage put any animals in that field under penalty of three shillings, fourpence to each.

WARBOYS,[33] 1440: And that no one tie or keep his animals in the leyes of Caldecote under penalty of twentypence on every offender.

WARBOYS,[34] 1483: And under penalty of fine no resident of that vill may tie his colts, horses, or mares on the common throughways there until? the feast of the Ascension of the Lord next following, under penalty to each of twelve pence.

WESTON,[35] 1457: And it is prohibited under penalty of fine to all tenants that any one drive horses in the summer time unless these are tied up, under pain of sixpence.

WISTOW,[36] 1453: And it is prohibited under penalty of fine to all tenants that any one allow beasts or sheep to go into the field called Wodefeld from the feast of Saint Peter in Chains to the feast of Saint Michael the Archangel, under penalty to each of twelve pence to be paid to the lord and twelve pence to the church.

26 See Appendix XXII, no. 7.
27 See Appendix XXII, no. 8.
28 See Appendix XXII, no. 9.
29 See Appendix XXII, no. 10.
30 See Appendix XXII, no. 11.
31 See Appendix XXII, no. 12.
32 See Appendix XXII, no. 13.
33 See Appendix XXII, no. 14.
34 See Appendix XXII, no. 15.
35 See Appendix XXII, no. 16.
36 See Appendix XXII, no. 17.

Once a certain pasture was opened to the villagers, the number of animals that each villager could pasture in the common was strictly determined by the size of his tenement. Examples of these common rights have already been given in Chapter One.[37] Villagers were still responsible for the behaviour of their animals after these had been driven to the common, and in some instances at least, the villager had to provide a herdsman for the pasture. Pigs had to be ringed to prevent harm to the turf.

UPWOOD,[38] 1438: It is decreed that under pain of a fine no one may keep foal or beasts around Botnale from the feast of the Purification to the feast of Saint Michael without a custodian, under penalty of forty pence each.

SHILLINGTON,[39] 1473: And under a penalty of three shillings, fourpence every tenant of Stondon is bound to keep custody of pasture ? until autumn ?
And under a penalty of three shillings, fourpence every one of them must carry on and maintain well the duties, namely each his said custody.

BRINGTON,[40] 1473: And that no one may keep any animals or any fowl in ? unless ? with the custodian obliged to have them in his custody, under penalty of three shillings, fourpence.

WARBOYS,[41] 1483: And likewise under pain of a fine of six shillings, eightpence, no one of the said vill may put his hogs (in) the Herth unless they are ringed.

UPWOOD,[42] 1457: And it is ordered for all tenants that henceforth no one may keep hogs unless they have been ringed, under penalty of twentypence to each.

WISTOW,[43] 1398: It is ordered with the assent of the lord that no one may pasture his livestock on the stubble of the township before the feast of the Nativity of Blessed Mary under penalty of twelve pence.
And that no one may pasture sheep or oxen in Chanereth until the same feast, and also that every tenant must tie his own horses on his own meadow and not elsewhere under the same penalty.

WISTOW,[44] 1483: And that John Randolf (   ) promulgated in the last view, that no one may put his cows in the fields there unless with a custodian (which) he did against the same ordinance, and therefore is in mercy.

WARBOYS,[45] 1334: It is ordered that no shepherd or any other custodian of beasts henceforth keep or bring dogs into the marsh, under penalty of twelve pence.

WISTOW,[46] 1347: And that Robert Milner had (twenty) hogs inadequately watched by one boy (so that they went into) the corn of neighbours and damaged it, (fine) threepence.

---

[37] See above, p. 23 ff.
[38] See Appendix XXIII, no. 1.
[39] See Appendix XXIII, no. 2.
[40] See Appendix XXIII, no. 3.
[41] See Appendix XXIII, no. 4.
[42] See Appendix XXIII, no. 5.
[43] See Appendix XXIII, no. 6.
[44] See Appendix XXIII, no. 7.
[45] See Appendix XXIII, no. 8.
[46] See Appendix XXIII, no. 9.

Wistow,[47] 1550: And it is ordered that everyone will drive his foals tied while going through sown fields after (their) fourth week under the same forfeiture for every foal of twentypence.

Broughton,[48] 1496: And that no one may keep a horse in the common fields among horses of his neighbour for any year henceforth, under penalty to each offender of three shillings, fourpence.

Brington,[49] 1454: And it is ordered that no one tie any animal by the head in the common without the consent of the tenants, under penalty to each of three shillings, fourpence to the lord and three shillings, fourpence to the church.

Towards the close of the summer months pasture fields must often dry up and villagers then became anxious to turn their animals into the open fields where grass could be found on the balks between sown strips or in the undergrowth left after the mown corn. At the same time crops were harvested early or late according to the type of growing season, so that it was not possible to establish a date for entry to stubble that would be suitable for every year. Village self-government must have been most active in this area as ordinances were constantly being proclaimed in an attempt to control entry to stubble pasture. Villagers may pasture animals only at an agreed time, the ordinances emphasized. But apparently there were varied viewpoints about the time for entry to stubble: some villagers tried to pasture animals among the shocks of corn, probably by tying the animals to stakes or trees; others herded animals into the fields before all the corn was removed, under the impression perhaps that if the animals were kept from harming the corn no damage would be done by having them nearby.

Wistow,[50] 1483: And under penalty of fine no one resident in that vill may put any hogs in the fields of the township before that day fixed by their common consent, under penalty of six shillings, eightpence, of which forty pence go to the lord and forty pence to the church.

Girton,[51] 1498: It was ordered on this same day that no one of this vill allow hogs, young pigs, horses, cows, bullocks (   ) in the sown fields until the public proclamation of the 'hokey' be proclaimed by the rector of this vill publicly in church under penalty of twopence to every delinquent for every offence, etc.

Upwood,[52] 1453: And that no one may keep any beast in the fallowfield because of the harm to the wheat, under penalty to everyone of twelve pence to the lord and twelve pence to the church.

[47] See Appendix XXIII, no. 10.
[48] See Appendix XXIII, no. 11.
[49] See Appendix XXIII, no. 12.
[50] See Appendix XXIV, no. 1. In these documents the field (campus) is the sown arable field; and the 'autumn' period refers to the harvest season.
[51] See Appendix XXIV, no. 2.
[52] See Appendix XXIV, no. 3.

BROUGHTON,[53] 1496: And under pain of fine no one may tie horses in the wheat stubble from the feast of Saint Peter in Chains until the feast of Saint Michael the Archangel for any year under penalty to anyone for every offence of six shillings, eightpence.

UPWOOD,[54] 1369: It is ordained with the assent of the lord and of the whole township that no man may have his animals running in the stubble from the time (   ) after the mowing of the corn for a period of three weeks following and more if the lord should consent, unless these be carthorses and there tied, under a penalty to everyone of forty pence.

WISTOW,[55] 1363: It is ordained with the consent of the lord and the township that no one may have his foals running in the fields until all corn has been garnered under penalty of forty pence.
And that no one may allow his animals to come among the shocks under penalty of forty pence. And that no one may pasture his horses in the meadow of Chenereth before the feast of Saint Michael under penalty of forty pence.

WISTOW,[56] 1365: It is ordered by the consent of the lord and the township that no one may have foals running in the corn of the lord and the township from the gules of August until that corn will have been garnered, under penalty of two shillings to be paid to the lord.

ELLSWORTH,[57] 1358: It is ordered by the assent of the whole township that no one pasture among the corn of his neighbour nor in the stubble with oxen under penalty of two shillings to be paid to the lord.

BROUGHTON,[58] 1411: And that no one is to drive his animals into the wheat stubble before the feast of Saint Michael, unless these be plough animals, under penalty of twelve pence.

WYTTON,[59] 1473: And that no one may henceforth pasture his horses in the Schirefeld after the corn has been removed without the common consent of the whole vill, under a penalty of twelve pence to every offender.

UPWOOD,[60] 1534: And that no tenant of Upwood or of Ramsey is allowed to put any animals in the wheat field or in the peas field for a period of thirteen weeks after the end of autumn, except for dray-horses and milch animals and newly-freshened cows, under penalty to anyone of six shillings, eightpence.

KING'S RIPTON,[61] 1483: And that under pain of fine no one of this vill may put his sheep, oxen, or horses or mares in the fields of the township within fifteen days after the rector of the church here has completely removed his peas from the fields of this same vill, under penalty to each of twelve pence for each offence.

LITTLE RAVELEY (Wistow),[62] 1536: And that no one may put his hogs in the sown

53 See Appendix XXIV, no. 4.
54 See Appendix XXIV, no. 5.
55 See Appendix XXIV, no. 6.
56 See Appendix XXIV, no. 7.
57 See Appendix XXIV, no. 8.
58 See Appendix XXIV, no. 9.
59 See Appendix XXIV, no. 10.
60 See Appendix XXIV, no. 11.
61 See Appendix XXIV, no. 12.
62 See Appendix XXIV, no. 13.

fields before the end of autumn without the consent of all the tenants, under penalty to anyone of three shillings, fourpence.

Upwood,[63] 1411: And that no one may chase his foal into the stubble before the lord's corn has been removed, under penalty of twelve pence to anyone.

Wistow,[64] 1411: And that no one will fetter his cattle on the land of a neighbour before the corn has been removed from it, under penalty of sixpence.
And it is ordered that no foals be left loose in the corn from the feast of Saint Peter in Chains to Michaelmas, under penalty ( ).

Abbots Ripton,[65] 1411: And that no one may pasture his animals in the stubble before the feast of the Nativity of Blessed Mary, under penalty of twelve pence.

Upwood,[66] 1428: And that no hogs or sheep may be driven into the arable without the permission of the autumn reeves, under penalty of twelve pence.
And that no beast may be driven into the wheat stubble before the feast of the Nativity of Blessed Mary under penalty of twelve pence.
And it is decreed under pain of a fine that no one may tie his horses in the field with foals left loose, under penalty of twelve pence.

Wistow,[67] 1428: And that no one may have pasture in the wheat stubble before the feast of the Nativity of Blessed Mary, under penalty ( ).

Abbots Ripton,[68] 1428: It was decreed under pain of fine that no one have pasture in the wheat stubble before the feast of Saint Michael, under penalty of twelve pence to the lord and twelve pence to the church.

Broughton,[69] 1496: And under pain of a fine no one may keep hogs during the autumn on the wheat stubble until all the grain remaining on a furlong has been removed, (and so) for every year, under penalty of twentypence to each.
And under pain of a fine that no one fold in the pea field until the peas have been removed, and so for every year, under penalty of twelve pence to each.

Warboys,[70] 1369: It is ordered with the assent of the lord and the township that no man pasture his livestock among the shocks until all corn has been fully removed to a distance of a stadium, under penalty of forty pence.

Elton,[71] 1411: And that no one drive his foals among the haycocks in the autumn under penalty of twelve pence.

Upwood,[72] 1459: And under pain of fine no one is to tie his horses in a sown field with foals running loose among the corn (until) the end of autumn, under penalty of twelve pence.

Wistow,[73] 1411: And that no one is to drive his animals loose into the stubble

[63] See Appendix XXIV, no. 14.
[64] See Appendix XXIV, no. 15.
[65] See Appendix XXIV, no. 16.
[66] See Appendix XXIV, no. 17.
[67] See Appendix XXIV, no. 18.
[68] See Appendix XXIV, no. 19.
[69] See Appendix XXIV, no. 20.
[70] See Appendix XXIV, no. 21.
[71] See Appendix XXIV, no. 22.
[72] See Appendix XXIV, no. 23.
[73] See Appendix XXIV, no. 24.

unless the distance of a stadium is kept on the side (of the corn), under penalty
of twelve pence.

BROUGHTON,[74] 1411: It is ordered that no one drive his animals into the arable
field before the corn has been first removed to the distance of one stadium, under
penalty of twentypence to the lord and twentypence to the church.

ABBOTS RIPTON,[75] 1411: And that no one lead or tether his animals in the stubble
until it has been raked, under penalty of sixpence to be paid to the church and
sixpence to the lord.

UPWOOD,[76] 1428: And that no foals are to follow the carts in the fields during
autumn, under penalty of twelve pence.

LITTLE RAVELEY,[77] 1428: And that no one may pasture in the field until it has been
raked, under penalty of twelve pence.

GRAVELEY,[78] 1398: And that no one should have his horses tied during the night
in the fields and among the corn of the township in the autumn, under penalty of
forty pence.

Draining and ditching were important for Ramsey manors, especially
those fronting on the fens. The most detailed thirteenth-century source for
land improvement in Huntingdonshire shows that ditching figured as
prominently as assarting.[79] Drainage was essentially a community project
since a stoppage of water at one poorly kept ditch could flood properties of
all those on the same outlet. As a result the courts were quick to fine
for neglected drains, and ordinances were frequently issued to warn of the
importance of this work.

ABBOTS RIPTON,[80] 1428: And that all ditches within the demesne be cleaned before
the feast of Saint Michael, under penalty of a fourpence fine to each offender.

BRINGTON,[81] 1473: And that the ditches pertaining to the lord next Eston Place
be cleaned, and all other ditches harming elsewhere be cleaned, before the feast of
Saint Andrew, under penalty of twelve pence to each.

UPWOOD,[82] 1473: And that all having ditches towards Nerthalfdich and Neumede
have these improved before the feast of the Purification of Blessed Mary, under
penalty of three shillings, fourpence.

GREAT RAVELEY (Upwood)[83] 1534: It is ordered that every tenant shall clean
out his ditches before the feast of Saint Michael under penalty of three shillings,
fourpence to each.

[74] See Appendix XXIV, no. 25.
[75] See Appendix XXIV, no. 26.
[76] See Appendix XXIV, no. 27.
[77] See Appendix XXIV, no. 28.
[78] See Appendix XXIV, no. 29.
[79] See B M, Egerton, 3663, folios 57-63.
[80] See Appendix XXV, no. 1.
[81] See Appendix XXV, no. 2.
[82] See Appendix XXV, no. 3.
[83] See Appendix XXV, no. 4.

GREAT RAVELEY (Upwood),[84] 1483: And under pain of fine to all residents there, all ditches of this same vill are to be repaired before the feast of the Finding of the Holy Cross next following, under penalty of threepence each.

KING'S RIPTON,[85] 1483: And under pain of fine to all likewise resident here all ditches not cleaned are to be cleaned out before the feast of Saint Thomas the Apostle next following under penalty of two shillings to every one.

WARBOYS,[86] 1350: The whole homage is ordered to make its required ditches at Wodemer and Stokkyng under penalty of forty pence.

The upkeep of roads was organized along the same lines as drainage, that is, the tenant was responsible for roads fronting on his property. However, for special projects like bridges and the main roads, the villagers apparently worked as a gang under a foreman or supervisor. Often, as in the case from Ellington below, the supervisor would be the reeve. With large open fields spread throughout the countryside villagers would be tempted to take short-cuts through fields or along balks, and some of the entries below show efforts made to prevent such trespassing.

WISTOW,[87] 1438: It is decreed under pain of fine that each tenant build the king's road facing his tenement with stones, and that he clean his own ditches before the feast of Saint Michael under penalty of sixpence to each.
And since the farmer (twopence) did not clean the watercourse nor build the bridge called Paddokbrgge so that water is allowed to wander from its right course, therefore he is ordered to repair under penalty of twelve pence.

WISTOW,[88] 1534: And it is ordered that every tenant build (his own section of the road with stones) before the feast of Saint Michael next, and that John Syder and Silvester Campyon' will be supervisors of the said road and that everyone follow their directions for that road, under penalty to each of six shillings, eightpence.

WISTOW,[89] 1406: It is ordered through the whole homage that every man of (Little) Raveley who has lands and tenements is to gather two cartloads of stones and put these in the weir next the gate of John Cleryvaux in the king's road, under penalty to each of twelve pence.

UPWOOD,[90] 1448: And that no one is to make a road on the land of Thomas Newman towards Richewewroke, under penalty of twelve pence.

UPWOOD,[91] 1459: And that no one is to make a road beyond Longewong to (   ) under penalty of sixpence.

WARBOYS,[92] 1536: And that nobody from Wistow may come across the fields of

84 See Appendix XXV, no. 5.
85 See Appendix XXV, no. 6.
86 See Appendix XXV, no. 7.
87 See Appendix XXVI, no. 1.
88 See Appendix XXVI, no. 2.
89 See Appendix XXVI, no. 3.
90 See Appendix XXVI, no. 4.
91 See Appendix XXVI, no. 5.
92 See Appendix XXVI, no. 6.

Warboys with his ploughs unless along the village street, under penalty to each of forty shillings.

And that no one may come along the said balk with his ploughs from any other village, under penalty of twenty shillings.

ELLINGTON,[93] 1375: It is directed with the consent of the lord and of the whole township that every tenant follow the orders of the reeve in the building and repairing of the king's road at Thornhill before the feast of Saint Martin, under penalty of forty pence.

HEMMINGFORD ABBOTS,[94] 1316: It is ordered that all customaries repair the road to the mill before the next view under penalty of twenty shillings to be paid to the lord.

WARBOYS,[95] 1322: The vill is ordered to clear the bank next the bridge which has become so overgrown that the king's road is being flooded. And that they are to do this before the feast of Saint Michael under penalty of one-half mark.

Reeds and willows growing in common pastures, or on balks in the open fields, had many uses for the villagers as thatch, fencing, or firewood. Ordinances had to be invoked to control the use of these resources. The ordinance seems to have been especially necessary to prevent the sale of reeds, perhaps to upland people who had not common rights in the fen marshes.

UPWOOD,[96] 1406: It is ordered throughout the whole homage that no tenant who lives within the lord's domain will cut or mow rushes growing along the shore of the marsh or in the marsh from Easter day until the feast of the Nativity of Blessed Mary under penalty of six shillings, eightpence each.

UPWOOD,[97] 1413: And that Robert Jurdon (threepence), of Wenington, Robert Juell (threepence) from the same place, William Wattes (threepence), John in the Hirne (threepence), William White (threepence), Walter Shepherd (threepence), (cut) rushes in the marsh and overburdened the common pasture, and they have not common there, therefore each of them is in mercy.

WISTOW,[98] 1483: And under pain of fine to any of this same vill, no one is to cut any ashes growing in the common balks there, under penalty of two shillings.

RAMSEY,[99] 1536: And since the said John Aston (fourpence) cut willows on Newlodebanke, he is in mercy. And he is threatened that if he henceforth cuts there the will endure the fine of forty shillings.

WISTOW,[100] 1413: And that John Plombe (sixpence) of Caldecote came into the marsh and cut reeds and carried them to Caldecote. And that Richard the parson of

[93] See Appendix XXVI, no. 7.
[94] See Appendix XXVI, no. 8.
[95] See Appendix XXVI, no. 9.
[96] See Appendix XXVII, no. 1.
[97] See Appendix XXVII, no. 2.
[98] See Appendix XXVII, no. 3.
[99] See Appendix XXVII, no. 4.
[100] See Appendix XXVII, no. 5. In 1297 eight men were fined in this manor for cutting reeds 'against the statute.'

the church of Wistow sold reeds beyond the vill, namely a thousand to Lawrence Merton. And that William Derworth sold eighty reeds outside the village.

It is ordered that no one shall cut reeds in the marsh from the feast of Saint Peter in Chains until Easter under penalty of one-half mark fine.

And that no outsider cut in the marsh under penalty of one-half mark fine to the lord, and one-half mark to the church.

WARBOYS,[101] 1350: The whole township ordered that no one may measure and cut in the marsh from this day until the feast of Easter, and from the feast of Pentecost until the feast of the Assumption of Blessed Mary, under penalty of twenty shillings, and if anyone has more than five hundred reeds non-bound, beyond (the quota ?) (they are to be seized and he will be in mercy).

WISTOW,[102] 1294: It is ordered that henceforth no one shall enter the marsh of Wistow to cut reeds until all together and at one time enter to cut, just as it was formerly decreed with the common consent of the whole vill, under penalty of two shillings. This (ordinance) can be found in the court held at Wistow the Monday after the feast of the translation of Saint Benedict, in the eighteenth year of Abbot William.

WARBOYS,[103] 1334: And they say that the whole township of Broughton, both free and natives, during the night enter with their carts and labourers into the marsh of Warboys, and throughout the night they cut and carry both the reeds cut and bundled by the people of Warboys as well as their own reeds, to the damage of the lord and of the whole township. It is ordered that this is not to be done again under penalty of one-half mark fine.

WARBOYS,[104] 1412: And that no one may cut reeds in the marsh from the feast of Saint Martin until the feast of the Finding of the Holy Cross, under penalty of one-half mark.

WISTOW,[105] 1365: And that no one may cut reeds except with the permission of the fenreeve, under penalty of ten shillings.

WISTOW,[106] 1410: It is directed through the lord and the whole homage that no one will cut young reeds in the marsh until all the old reeds have been cut, under penalty of ten shillings.

And that no one may cut reeds in the marsh from the feast of Saint Peter in Chains until the feast of Easter under penalty of ten shillings to be paid to the lord.

The sternest measures were taken by ordinance against those who abused common regulations governing the cutting of turves. In some

---

[101] See Appendix XXVII, no. 6.
[102] See Appendix XXVII, no. 11.
[103] See Appendix XXVII, no. 7. It must have been almost impossible to control the movement of reeds beyond the village marsh in one way or another. At Warboys in 1372 William Hugeneye was fined (iiid.) for selling 700 reeds beyond the manor, William Atehill, iiid. for selling 160, William Hiriebrok vid. for selling 600, John Attewode iid. for selling 200, John Lenot Fyshere vid. for selling 600, William Bonde and Robert Colle viiid. for selling 800, William Wilkys ivd. for selling 400, and John Herresson ivd. for selling 450.
[104] See Appendix XXVII, no. 8.
[105] See Appendix XXVII, no. 9.
[106] See Appendix XXVII, no. 10.

villages turves could only be cut under supervision, perhaps to avoid waste as well as clandestine sales. It will be noted that the fines are very heavy for these ordinances. At the same time there is evidence that villagers were repeatedly fined for selling turves to outsiders.

GREAT RAVELEY (Upwood),[107] 1473: And that henceforth no one may dig or have dug turves in the marsh, except according to the ancient ordinance, under pain of twenty shillings fine to each.

UPWOOD,[108] 1413: It is ordered that no one may dig turves on lelakelonde on the Fayway under penalty of forty pence.

UPWOOD,[109] 1453: And it is ordered that all dig hassocks of grass throughout the whole marsh and not ( ) unless with the permission of the custodian of the marsh, under penalty of twelve pence each.

WARBOYS,[110] 1372: And that henceforth no one is to dig turf between Newlode and Gateslyrne under penalty of twenty shillings.

WISTOW,[111] 1403: It is ordered by the lord and whole homage that henceforth no one shall cut or dig turves in the marsh between the boundaries of Wistow and Warboys for a distance of forty feet in width along the said boundaries, under penalty of forty pence each.

WISTOW,[112] 1347: It is ordered that no one take or carry turves beyond the manor except in carts, under penalty of forty pence.

UPWOOD,[113] 1411: The jurors also say that various tenants of Ramsey during the past year came into the marsh of Upwood called Upwoodturffen, and dug turves and made diverse cuts called lodes to the great damage of the tenants of Upwood, so that it is not possible to run or drive their animals beyond the above marsh as they have been wont to do.

And that diverse tenants of Bury and Heitmongrove came into the above marsh and dug turves on the west side of the Fenbrg where they ought not to have common rights to dig.

UPWOOD,[114] 1428: It is noted that Abbot John granted that every virgater of Upwood and Raveley could dig ten thousand turves and the semivirgater seven thousand, the cottar holding three acres of land four thousand, the cottar of two acres three thousand, the cottar of one acre two thousand, the cottar with no land in the fields may not dig any turves. This grant was discovered in an old book belonging to the steward.

UPWOOD,[115] 1450-1: And that no one working or his servant may dig turves in any place in the marsh except under the direction of the master by whom the work is approved every day, and it pertains to the overseeing of the custodian of the

107 See Appendix XXVIII, no. 1.
108 See Appendix XXVIII, no. 2.
109 See Appendix XXVIII, no. 3.
110 See Appendix XXVIII, no. 4.
111 See Appendix XXVIII, no. 5.
112 See Appendix XXVIII, no. 6.
113 See Appendix XXVIII, no. 7.
114 See Appendix XXVIII, no. 8.
115 See Appendix XXVIII, no. 9.

marsh that no labourer should sell any turves in (   ). And those who have tenements are not to sell turves until the turves come up to (   ) under penalty of a fine of ten shillings to the lord and ten to the church. And through the view of four men and the marsh reeve whoever etc. (violates this is presented).

And (   ) will not grant licences to men of Ramsey or of any other villages to come within the marsh to dig turves etc.

And (   ) Tollesson was able to bring men into the marsh to dig turves in the marsh for outsiders, therefore, etc.

And that (   ) may dig beyond Upvale, nor is (anyone) able henceforth to 'shoteneldyng' beyond the limits allowed by inquisition, under penalty of three shillings, fourpence fine to the lord, three shillings fourpence fine to the church by each transgressor.

And no one from Ramsey may dig turves beyond Sheggelode under penalty of a twenty shilling fine.

And (it is presented that) John Sewer of Bury dug turves in the marsh and carried these away. Therefore, etc. (twopence).

The recent ordinance. That whoever has a messuage and one virgate of land may dig sixteen thousand turves, one-half off the land and one-half out of water, and not more. And that whoever has one-half virgate may dig eight thousand turves and not more. And whoever is a cottager may dig five thousand turves and not more, under penalty of twenty shillings.

And under penalty of a fine of three shillings, eightpence, no land holder may bring any foreigner into the lord's domain in order to dig turves.

The machinery that we have seen so widely applied to the government of common rights could act equally well in other areas of village life. Some examples are given here of ordinances not dealing with the common agrarian and pastoral structure. The village activity most closely approximating the commercial and industrial activities of mediaeval towns and cities was the brewing and selling of ale. Consequently, it was upon the village brewers that price and trade controls were concentrated. In a great variety of ways the villager's individual rights had to be protected in his daily life in the village as well as his work in the common fields or pasture. The neighbour's cart ought not to be left blocking one's door; ploughing must be closely restricted to one's own land; animals that can be left in the marsh should not overburden the village pasture, etc. Some of these varied ordinances are given below.

ELTON,[116] 1473: And that no one of this vill may keep others at the tavern or at

[116] See Appendix XXIX, no. 1. In the context of these entries it might be further added that only in the wide range of fines and indictments recorded in the court rolls can the full significance of the ordinance be seen. Through such entries may be seen how the ordinary villager was protected against all, the most powerful as well as the most humble, the neighbour as well as the neighbouring village. At Wistow in 1278 (Port. 179, no. 4), for example, the rector is ordered to repair his encroachment on a public way. At Broughton in 1306 (Add. Ch. 39459) the lord abbot himself and a leading freeman John de Broughton are ordered to make amends for the same type of encroachment. Further examples are added to this Appendix XXIX.

any other illicit place after the eighth hour of the evening, under penalty of twenty shillings each.

ELLINGTON,[117] 1322: The prohibition is decreed through the lord's steward and with the consent of all free and customary men lest any of the above customaries be charged henceforth a penny at a tavern, or that he purchase ale for more than a halfpenny a gallon, within the village of Ellington. And if any of the above customaries should be convicted of this, he will give a sixpenny fine to the lord. And with this it is ordered that if the tasters should find any brewer who is selling to a native of the lord for more than a halfpenny a gallon, that ale is to be taken into the hands of the same taster, seized, and sold. And the money thereby acquired is to be faithfully accounted to the lord. It is also prohibited to any brewer who is free to sell within the above vill ale for more than a halfpenny a gallon. And if any should be convicted of this, forty pence fine should come to the lord upon each conviction.

BROUGHTON,[118] 1464: And under pain of fine to each brewer, none of them is to keep his tavern open after the eighth hour of the night, under penalty of twenty shillings each.

And likewise under pain of fine if anyone should be found sitting in a tavern after the eighth hour of the night he must be seized and put in jail there under a good guard, etc., under penalty of six shillings, eightpence.

HEMMINGFORD ABBOTS,[119] 1454: And it is presented that no brewer may henceforth be allowed to brew unless she will brew for the whole year, under penalty of six shillings, eightpence.

ELTON,[120] 1454: And it is presented that no brewer be allowed to brew unless she will brew one-half quarter at a time, under penalty to each of forty pence to the lord and forty pence to the church.

And it is presented that whoever will brew must send for the tasters before any sales shall have been made, under the same penalty as above to each.

UPWOOD,[121] 1453: And it is ordered to every brewer that after she has begun brewing she must continue to brew for that whole year, under penalty to each of three shillings, eightpence for the lord and three shillings, eightpence for the church.

LITTLE RAVELEY (Wistow),[122] 1301: And since all customaries of Little Raveley agreed that none of them would buy ale in that vill for more than a halfpenny a gallon, investigation is made (concerning one penny sales?) etc., (under) penalty of sixpence.

ABBOTS RIPTON,[123] 1492: In addition the provision is promulgated throughout the whole court that henceforth all common brewers, if there should be more than one in any one vill throughout the whole hundred (   ), should not all together brew on the same day unless it is necessary, but should have an agreement governing what is brewed and should be brewed. (This is decreed) so that the villagers should not suffer from a lack of drink as they have suffered in the past, to their harm and

117 See Appendix XXIX, no. 2.
118 See Appendix XXIX, no. 3.
119 See Appendix XXIX, no. 4.
120 See Appendix XXIX, no. 5.
121 See Appendix XXIX, no. 6.
122 See Appendix XXIX, no. 7.
123 See Appendix XXIX, no. 8.

to the damage of the liegemen of the lord king. And so all common brewers within the hundred must henceforth provide in season and out of season an adequate service, especially for those of the neighbourhood and for other liegemen of the lord king, under penalty of six shillings, eightpence to each for every such offence.

And henceforth no brewer, tapster, or seller (   ) may sell to any liege of the lord king whosoever in pots, cups, dishes, or bowls, but only in true measures that have been properly marked as the law requires, and this obliges all under the penalty of twelve pence for each offence.

WISTOW,[124] 1428: And that no one shall labour in the fields on feast days, under penalty of sixpence to the lord and sixpence to the church.

BROUGHTON,[125] 1411: And that no one shall cart his corn by night, under penalty of twentypence to the church and twentypence to the lord.

UPWOOD,[126] 1483: And that John Genge has incurred the penalty decreed by the edict of the last court that no one resident in this vill should (   ) beyond the vill, under penalty of six shillings, eightpence to every tenant for each offence.

BROUGHTON,[127] 1536: And it is ordered that no tenant of this manor shall plough more arable with his ploughs than is strictly his anywhere throughout the homage of the lord, under penalty of ten shillings to each.

BROUGHTON,[128] 1507: And that no one should encroach on common balks and ridges under penalty of three shillings, fourpence each. And whoever has so encroached must repair the loss inflicted before the next court under the same penalty.

HEMMINGFORD ABBOTS,[129] 1462: And under pain of fine all tenants are to present themselves before the ninth hour, under penalty of twelve pence each.

BARTON,[130] 1493: And under pain of a fine no one is henceforth to fish or to cast a net or any other thing to catch fish in the Myllebroke, under penalty of three shillings, fourpence.

WARBOYS,[131] 1412: And that no one may set his carts at his neighbours' gates or move the 'alestakes', under penalty of twenty shillings.

And that no one may hinder any tenant from commoning in the crofts in straytyme, under penalty of one-half mark.

WISTOW,[132] 1451: And that no one tie any animal in the field that is able to be driven or run to the marsh, under penalty of twentypence to the lord and twentypence to the church.

And under pain of fine (as decreed) in the preceding year, no one is to turn his plough in the meadow under penalty of twelve pence to the lord and twelve pence to the church.

---

[124] See Appendix XXIX, no. 9.
[125] See Appendix XXIX, no. 10.
[126] See Appendix XXIX, no. 11.
[127] See Appendix XXIX, no. 12.
[128] See Appendix XXIX, no. 13.
[129] See Appendix XXIX, no. 14.
[130] See Appendix XXIX, no. 15.
[131] See Appendix XXIX, no. 16.
[132] See Appendix XXIX, no. 17. And for further examples, see numbers 18 to 22 of this appendix.

CHAPTER VI

PEASANT MOBILITY IN THE THIRTEENTH
AND FOURTEENTH CENTURIES

AFTER a study of the finely woven web of manorial, kinship, economic, legal, and co-operative relations that bound the villager to his local community, to inquire next whether the village was a closed community may not appear immediately relevant. And yet these relations are far from discouraging the inquiry. A manorial economy did not turn the villein in upon the local village. Rather, through the manorial economy the villein participated in the regional organization of the lord's liberty. For example, the villager on Ramsey manors, or his servant, would be required to go as far as twenty or thirty miles, perhaps a dozen times a year, in order to bring food rents to the abbey and produce to the various markets of the region.[1] Family ties were frequently extended by marriage with outsiders.[2] By freehold tenure villagers broke through limitations of the 'manor.'[3] Procedures for the enforcement of law and order brought villagers into courts of all types. As a consequence of rights to common,

---

[1] See the various thirteenth-century extents in *Carts.*, I.

[2] A gloss on *Britton*, while it may be pseudo-Roman law, could well be taken as descriptive of the confused and changing picture of status in Ramsey villages depicted in tenure in Chapters Two and Three above: "Naif is he that has come of such lineage that they have been in servitude for several generations. Villain is he that has come afresh into servitude, from which he cannot depart though he be of a free stock. Serf is he who is not absolutely a villain, nor absolutely free, but is *de facto* in servitude, as a freeman who marries a nief and enters into the villain tenement, and does for his wife's lord the villain customs which belong to the land held in villeinage. Wherefore this freeman and the issue he has by the nief, are serfs *de facto* and freeman *de jure*, and are called serfs for the servitude in which they are. Wherefore if the issue of this freeman remains in servitude, and his issue the same for all their lives, and so on to the fourth degree, the fourth will be a villain forever, and those who come of him." (*Britton*, notes and tr. by F. M. Nichols, Washington, 1901, p. 160, note 2).

[3] It is worth recalling that in such relations with freemen the villager was on an equal footing. Cf. *Brevia Placitata, op. cit.*, p. cxli: "Now the villain or naif, for there is no distinction between them, was certainly free against all men but his lord. He could sue in debt and trespass, and the law protected him against assault and maltreatment, as if he were a free man." Again let it be stressed that according to this statement there was no distinction in common law, which is of course the only law as such for the author of the above remarks. Contrast the multitude of distinctions given by *Britton*, note 2 above, and the actual life of the village. The fact that historians now seem to be recognizing a decline in importance of the writ of naifty after the Anglo-Saxon period (e.g. Sidney R. Packard, *Speculum*, 36, 1961, p. 358) may open the way to more study of these distinct realities of the village life.

the villager mixed with freemen and men from several neighbouring villages in the exploitation of meadow, marsh, and wood. Perhaps most important of all, the pull of the fen economy forced Ramsey manors to be 'outward-looking'. For example, men from Broughton, Woodhurst, Slepe, and Holywell, were renting in Holywell fens. Our sources are not adequate to a presentation of the relation between the villagers and the outside world as an extension of the basic relations within the village. But there is much in the court rolls about the movement of various individuals in and out of villages, and in the next three chapters we have attempted to reconstruct the overall picture of such movements.

I

Natives, Outlaws, and Foreigners

The legal position of the serf in his home manor may be usefully described as that of a citizen. In the manorial court he was recognized to be a resident by birth (*nativus*), while the visitor from beyond, whether from near or far, was an alien (*extraneus*). Legal status was acquired at the age of twelve on Ramsey manors, from which time all males must be in a tithing (*decenna*) for police and surety. The new citizen was apparently assigned to a certain tithing, no doubt determined by his place of residence, and thereafter it was the duty of the head of the tithing to 'keep his man in tithing'. There is practically nothing in the court rolls to indicate the method of appointment of this headman or chief pledge. Only in the one instance in our records, that of Over in 1301,[4] was a villager found to be distrained by the court to take this office: 'An order is issued to distrain Gilbert Wrek to come to the next view to receive the office of chief pledge in place of Robert son of William Hobbe and thence to take the oath, etc'.

The chief pledge had a definite jurisdiction over the members of his tithing, as can be seen in the terms of the entry from Warboys below. But there is no evidence to suggest that the chief pledge had coercive authority such as that exercised by the reeve, beadle, and bailiff. As the following examples from Ellsworth, Upwood, and Ellington illustrate, the chief pledge must first give an account of his missing member, but unlike the personal pledge, the chief pledge was not as often fined for being unable to present his man. Once the chief pledge had failed to have

---

4 P R O, SC 2, Port. 179, no. 11.

his man, the responsibility for the man was often passed on to the reeve or to some personal pledge to find him, or if he was resident in the vill, to distrain him till he came into a tithing.

WARBOYS,[5] 1299: It was presented in the last view that Nicholas Kannt was useless and disobedient to Nicholas Lone his chief pledge. And Nicholas Kannt (father?) is his pledge to have him at the next court.

SHILLINGTON,[6] 1313: And John of Barton, pledge of Adam of Batlesden for not having him put himself in tithing. And it is ordered that he be distrained to put himself in tithing. And afterwards he came and put himself in a tithing.

UPWOOD,[7] 1295: And they report that Robert of Wenyton lives married at Ramsey. Therefore it is ordered that John of Wenyton, his chief pledge, have him at the next court.

ELLSWORTH,[8] 1294: And then they report that Robert son of Robert at the wood lives at Trumpington, not rendering anything to the lord. Therefore Mathew at the wood, his chief pledge, is in mercy for not having him as he was ordered to at the last court. And his pledge is the reeve. However the former did come afterwards and fined for one chicken, with pledges Thomas at the wood, and William Baldewyne.

WISTOW,[9] 1320: The jurors present that William Coppyng lives within the precincts of the lete and is not in tithing. Therefore it is ordered that he be attached to put himself in tithing at the next view.

UPWOOD,[10] 1294: And (a fine on) John Curteys capital pledge for not having John Eldman, John Wodekoc, John Cook, Henry Coqun and John Coqun senior, sixpence with pledge Robert Alkoc. And the vill is prohibited to Henry Coqun since he is not in a tithing.

HOLYWELL,[11] 1288: And they say that Robert le Ster living on the land of Richard Franceys is not in tithing. Therefore he is in mercy to sixpence. And it is ordered that he be prohibited the vill unless he puts himself in tithing.

HEMMINGFORD ABBOTS,[12] 1296: And on Thomas son of Henry Clerk for not having William his brother who lives at Blackerwyk in tithing, threepence. And it is ordered that he (William) be arrested if he should come on to the fee.

ABBOTS RIPTON,[13] 1301: It is ordered that William the son of John at the Green, Andrew his brother, and Peter the miller be attached if they should come since they have put themselves outside the tithing of Philip of the hall.

Richard the hayward, capital pledge, is ordered to have at the next court William the son of Thomas who now lives married at Heytmongrove.

[5] See Appendix XXX, no. 1.
[6] See Appendix XXX, no. 2.
[7] See Appendix XXX, no. 3.
[8] See Appendix XXX, no. 4.
[9] See Appendix XXX, no. 5.
[10] See Appendix XXX, no. 6.
[11] See Appendix XXX, no. 7.
[12] See Appendix XXX, no. 8.
[13] See Appendix XXX, no. 9.

St. Ives,[14] 1306: The jurors of the Green say that Richard the brother of the vicar is living on the lord's fee but is not in tithing. Therefore it is ordered that he be distrained to put himself in tithing.

St. Ives,[15] 1299: And it is ordered that no one henceforth receive Bartholomew the cooper for he is disobedient to his capital pledge.

William of Gilling is pledge of Emma Wygar and her son John that they will behave while they are living in the vill.

Holywell,[16] 1299: Again it is ordered that William Bogge and John of Graveley be distrained since they were disobedient and unwilling to give to the headtax.

Ellsworth,[17] 1299: The jurors of Ellsworth say that William the son of Simon, Aspelon Gag', and Walter Gag' withdrew before the coming of the justice and before the day of the view. And it is testified that they are outlaws. Therefore they are to be taken, etc.

Perhaps the crux of the difference in status between the serf and the slave of classical times may be seen in the comparative punishments for disobedience. The intransigent slave was incarcerated and punished in various ways; the unamenable serf was banished from his village. The punishment of a slave was that of an animal owned by its master; the punishment of a serf was that exile from family, friends, and security — that status of outlaw — so feared by members of all primitive societies.[18] At Niddingworth in the late thirteenth century, for example, after the capital pledge William son of Adam had been unable to keep two men in tithing even when fined to do so, the onus was then placed upon the two men themselves. They were outlawed; no one could lawfully receive them. Here are other examples of this form of expatriation.

Ellsworth,[19] 1306: And to John Gang' the chief pledge for not having Henry the

---

[14] See Appendix XXX, no. 10.

[15] See Appendix XXX, no. 11.

[16] See Appendix XXX, no. 12.

[17] See Appendix XXX, no. 13. Further examples of the variety in this type of entry are given in numbers 14 and following of this Appendix.

[18] Again, of course, the discipline of village solidarity has multiple expressions. The number of fines condoned for poverty is remarkable, for example, in contrast with the rare seizure of a tenement for incapacity. Or, the petty fines for thievery in the village are in striking contrast with the penalties of the king's law. On the other hand, the village could enforce conformity in many ways, as in the following text likely from the court of Over. "Prohibitum fuit omnibus et singulis custumariis domini sub pena dimidie marce quod nullus eorum emerit cerviciam Johannis Mayner' pro eo quod noluit se iusticiare in curia domini sicut de iure debuit." (1316, P R O, SC 2, Port. 179, no. 18) The villagers would even evict a landholder, as is seen in Appendix XXXI, no. 19. A general description of outlawry in terms of the king's law may be found in Maurice Keen, *The Outlaws of Medieval Legend* (London, 1961), especially pp. 9-10. See also R. F. Hunnisett, *The Medieval Coroner* (Cambridge, 1961), pp. 61-8, for outlawry in the county court.

[19] See Appendix XXXI, no. 1. In the county courts, outlawry was proclaimed after four calls and non-appearance. Cf. Hunnisett, *op. cit.,* p. 61.

son of William Merchant and William the son of Ralph who are off the fee in his tithing (sixpence?). And it is ordered that no one receive them.

OVER,[20] 1301: It is ordered that no one henceforth receive either Alan the son of Robert Galeway or John his brother who are put out of the tithing.

It is ordered that no one receive Henry Fengers who is put out of the tithing of Walter Ode until, etc.

And they report that Donte Goldyene received John Cissor who was not in tithing. Therefore he is in mercy to threepence, with pledge William Sire. And it is ordered that no one receive him (i.e. Cissor) until, etc.

And it is ordered that no one receive Richard of Caxton henceforth who has been forbidden the village.

ELLSWORTH,[21] 1301: It is ordered that no one henceforth receive John Alderman who is put outside the tithing of Robert King for being disobedient to his chief pledge, nor (receive) Ralph Pyk who is put outside the tithing of Ralph at the spring for the same.

It cannot be said for the estates of Ramsey Abbey that the outlawed villein usually, or perhaps even in the majority of instances, was one who had fled his native village. Very often the outlaw attempted to stay on with relatives or friends. Obviously the harbouring of such outlaws could be best curtailed by the co-operation of law-abiding neighbours, and from the late thirteenth century many are fined for 'receiving those beyond tithing' or 'beyond the assize'.

Strangers from neighbouring villages were often associated with outlawed natives in the court rolls, for if the stranger had not taken the trouble to acquire legal residence he would also be treated as an outlaw whom no one might receive. An example from King's Ripton[22] indicates that the stranger was not put in tithing, but was pledged: 'Walter of Den is the pledge of William Russel that henceforth he will behave well and faithfully so long as he is a resident in the vill of Ripton'. Another entry, from St. Ives,[23] suggests that the illegal status of a resident was sometimes discovered only upon the occasion of his prosecution for crime: 'And they report that Agnes wife of William Moryte and Emma of Earith took possession of the stall of William the Spycer and there keep a fire at night. And yet legally the said Emma is not a resident of the vill. Therefore it is directed that they be ejected from their house unless they are able to find

[20] See Appendix XXXI, no. 2.
[21] See Appendix XXXI, no. 3. And see further number 6. Henry Mayhew's remarks appear particularly relevant to the village: "Almost every tribe of people who have submitted themselves to social laws, recognizing the rights of property and reciprocal social duties, and thus acquiring wealth and forming themselves into a respectable caste, are surrounded by hoards of vagabonds and outcasts from their own community..." (*London Labour and the London Poor*, London, 1851, I, p. 1).
[22] See Appendix XXXI, no. 4.
[23] See Appendix XXXI, no. 5.

sufficient security that they will henceforth behave themselves truly and honestly'.

Criminals who were forbidden entry to the village seem to have been quite numerous. We are frequently told why such persons have been proclaimed malefactors, but again the most common reference to this group is found because of fines upon villagers for having received such people.

WARBOYS,[24] 1313: And they say that Agnes Malitras is not worthy to be let stay in the vill because she gleans wrongly taking sheaves and other small things. Therefore the vill is prohibited to her. And Alan Haugate received her, therefore (in mercy to) threepence, pledge Ralph Haugate.

And they report that Elena Baroun is the same type. Therefore she is prohibited the vill as above. And Ivo of Hurst received her. Therefore etc. threepence.

And they say that Matilda the daughter of William Pylche gleaned wrongly in the autumn. Therefore etc. threepence, pledge Reginald Beneyt.

And they say that Nicholas Kannt received the above Matilda. Therefore etc. threepence, pledge Richard Puttok.

WISTOW,[25] 1297: And they report that Walter Pellipar is useless and unfaithful. Therefore it is ordered that no one henceforth receive him.

WISTOW,[26] 1318: And they report that Matilda Crane is in the habit of taking the chickens of her neighbours and other small things[27], and is not suitable to live among her neighbours etc. And therefore it is ordered that no one henceforth receive her under serious penalty to whomsoever it be etc.

---

24 See Appendix XXXI, no. 7. The great importance of gleaning in the welfare organization of the village is seen in the serious concern with violation of gleaning regulations. Those who were able to earn by regular employment were not allowed to glean, as is illustrated in the following texts. *Upwood*, 1294 (B M, Add. Ch. 39769): Custodes autumpni de Upwode dicunt quod Matilda filia Willelmi le Koc potuit conduci et noluit sed glenavit contra statutum et ideo in misericordia iiid. (Three others were fined for the same on this roll).

Wistow, 1318 (Add. Ch. 39757): Et dicunt quod Sarra le Puskere glenavit ubi posset locari pro uno denario et pro mensa sua contra statutum. Ideo ipsa etc. iiid., plegius Johannes le Whyte. (And so with five others on this roll).

Shillington, 1294 (Add. Ch. 39597): Custodes autumpni dicunt quod Elena uxor Willelmi filii prepositi recepit quemdam Umfridum qui noluit conduci in autumpno et glenans dampnum fecit. Ideo in misericordia vid., plegius Samuel Godard.

The amounts that could be gleaned seemed to be considerable, e.g. *Warboys*, 1313 (Add. Ch. 34910): Et dicunt quod Adam garcon Laurentii Wodeward malo modo glenavit L garbas frumenti et illas posuit in bosco domini. Ideo distringatur ad respondendum. Et juratores testificant quod habuit de predictis garbis et aliis simili modo adquisivit V bussellos frumenti, et ordinatum est per senescallum ut distribuantur ad reparandum calceti et alibi ubi necesse fuerit pro viid. emendandis etc.

Wistow, ca. 1320 (Add. Ch. 34915): Quia custodes autumpni presentant quod ceperunt et attachiaverunt male glenantes in autumpno unam ringam pisarum, sex bussellos drageti et dimidium bussellum frumenti, concessum est per senescallum cum assensu et voluntate proborum hominum totius curie quod predictum bladum detinetur et solvatur ad reparandum pontis de Wystowe, etc.

25 See Appendix XXXI, no. 8.

26 See Appendix XXXI, no. 9.

27 Such references to petty thievery are fairly frequent. E.g. around this time, *Warboys* 1313 (Add. Ch. 34324); Wistow, 1316 (Add. Ch. 34896); Upwood, 1318 (Add. Ch. 34803).

WISTOW,[28] 1339: And the order is issued throughout the whole homage of the lord that no one receive Robert Michel an exceptionally contumacious man, and that no residences be let to him under penalty of forty pence.

It is difficult to gain a fairly complete picture of the number of persons illegally resident in a village at any particular time. The court rolls were usually concerned with various stages of the legal process — the identification of those not yet in tithing, the employment of chief pledge, pledge or official to obtain the man, the proscription, the fine for harbouring the proscribed. But at no time before the fifteenth century was there the issue of a general list that might serve as a summary picture of the status of all within the demesne; and since gaps in the rolls prevent an accumulative picture, it is impossible to draw together the consequences of these legal processes. Nevertheless, a long run tabulation of various categories of those illegally resident does give some idea of the movements of these groups. The vast majority of the entries could be gathered under the general heading of those unlawfully received, but for convenience in tabulation each column in the following table also includes those of the various categories who have been proscribed even when it is not mentioned that such have been wrongly received. That is to say, the column 'not in tithing' includes those banished for not being in tithing as well as those wrongly received for not being in tithing; the column 'malefactors prohibited' is derived from those officially exiled for crimes as well as references to the reception of malefactors; the column 'foreigners' includes those outsiders ordered to leave as well as references to foreigners wrongly received.

Since no particular trend is discernible in the data, the following table has not been organized on the basis of manors, nor are the entries exhaustive. Grouping all manors together chronologically indicates a broad parallel with the intensity of movements from the manors of Ramsey to be seen in the next table (VI), but in itself this table showing those unlawfully received hardly indicates cycles. St. Ives and Ramsey naturally attracted more strangers because of their important markets, and many of these apparently stayed on without warrant. But it is impossible to discover how many foreigners actually were received in one year, whether many not in tithing actually were excluded, whether most foreigners were drifting seasonal helpers who left before the court caught up with them, or the reason why the names of exiled natives or outlaws were usually not repeated year after year. In short, it would be hazardous to suggest that the following table is in any way a 'total' picture. And yet these figures indicate a continual movement to Ramsey manors. It is not surprising, of course,

---

[28] See Appendix XXXI, no. 10.

that the economic conditions that brought many Ramsey natives to leave their home manors, as we shall see in the next section, should also have occasioned the trespassing of many foreigners on Ramsey territory.

Despite the large numbers excluded from certain villages on occasion, our information does not indicate that the village was a 'tight little island' likely to exclude all and sundry. Although we do not know how many were legally accepted into the village from year to year, at least there is no evidence that outsiders were formally excluded by general practice at any time in order to reduce a problem of unemployment, crowded housing, and so forth. In fact there is no reason to believe that considerable numbers of outsiders could not be accepted. The lack of record by the courts again prevents further analysis. For a period before 1350 a large percentage of the court rolls make no mention of any outsiders being received. After the Black Death the manorial courts do not even record the illegal reception of malefactors and others who have been prohibited the vill.

In addition it should be noted that reception into the village was as much an individual act — the finding of a personal pledge — as it was the reception in public law into a tithing. Some texts are given here to illustrate this point. It should also be borne in mind that the number of natives who unlawfully received outsiders manifests a lively individual welcome for the foreigner.

WARBOYS,[29] 1316: And they say that Richard Neel and Agnes his wife are useless, evildoers, and not worthy to live in the vill. And at this William the reeve came and pledges for them that they should henceforth behave themselves. And the fine is condoned since they are poor.

And they say that Margaret Fyne received a certain Thomas Gabyon against the assize, nor is he worthy to live in the vill. Therefore (she is in mercy to) threepence, with William Fyne as pledge. And the vill is forbidden to the above Thomas Gabyon.

WARBOYS,[30] 1320: And they say that Beatrice Puttok is a common wrongdoer who stole several little things. Therefore the vill is prohibited to her unless someone now receives her, under penalty of twenty shillings. However, she came and found pledges, namely J. Deward and J. Caton that she would behave, etc.[31]

---

[29] See Appendix XXXI, no. 11.
[30] See Appendix XXXI, no. 12.
[31] Further entries of this type are added to this Appendix. Note especially how villeins are forbidden to visit relatives, numbers 20 and 21.

TABLE V

PERSONS UNLAWFULLY RECEIVED

Manor	Year	Not in Tithing	Foreigners	Malefactors
Upwood	1279	—	9	—
Wistow	1279	—	4	—
Broughton	1288	—	2	—
Houghton	1288	2	1	—
Holywell	1288	2	—	—
Shillington	1290	1	—	—
Slepe	1291	—	4	—
Ellsworth	1290	1	5	—
Ellsworth	1294	2	—	—
Abbots Ripton	1295	—	2	—
Wistow	1294	3	7	—
Ramsey	1294	10	—	—
Broughton	1294	—	2	—
Houghton	1294	2	1	—
Little Stukeley	1294	—	2	—
Hemmingford Abbots	1294	3	1	—
Slepe	1294	4	1	—
Holywell	1294	1	—	—
Cranfield	1294	6	1	—
Walsoken	1295	9	7	—
Therfield	1296	—	4	—
Abbots Ripton	1296	—	3	—
Hemmingford Abbots	1296	—	3	—
Houghton	1297	—	1	—
Burwell	1299	—	2	—
St. Ives	1299	14	—	—
Hemmingford Abbots	1299	1	—	—
Graveley	1299	2	1	—
Broughton	1299	—	1	—
Weston	1300	2	—	—
Shillington	1300	—	2	—
Ellsworth	1301	—	—	3
Graveley	1301	1	—	1
Over	1301	—	—	5
Ellsworth	1306	—	2	—
Over	1306	—	8	—
St. Ives	1306	2	6	—
Elton	1306	1	—	5
Graveley	1306	1	—	4
Cranfield	1306	—	—	7
Over	ca. 1306	—	6	—
Over	ca. 1306	1	3	—
Houghton	1307	1	1	—
Hemmingford Abbots	1307	1	—	1
Graveley	1307	1	—	—
Cranfield	1307	1	—	1
Therfield	1307	1	—	11
St. Ives	1307	20	3	—
Gidding	1307	1	—	—
Hemmingford Abbots	1311	—	3	—
St. Ives	1311	8	12	—
Holywell	1311	2	—	—
Graveley	1312	—	1	—
Ellsworth	1312	1	—	—
Weston	1312	1	—	1
Elton	1312	—	—	8

Manor	Year	Not in Tithing	Foreigners	Malefactors
Hemmingford Abbots	1312	—	3	—
St. Ives	1313?	8	2	—
Shillington	1313	4	—	—
Elton	1313	1	—	—
Ellsworth	1316	1	3	1
Knapwell	1316	3	2	6
Over	1316	7	3	8
Hemmingford Abbots	1316	1	—	—
Elton	1316	—	—	2
Ramsey	1316	—	—	3
Weston	1316	1	4	—
Ellington	1316	1	—	2
Cranfield	1316	—	—	12
Over	1316?	3	2	6
Abbots Ripton	1318	1	—	2
Little Stukeley	1318	1	—	2
Ellington	1318	—	—	1
Hemmingford Abbots	1320	—	—	1
Cranfield	1321	3	—	—
Shillington	1321	2	—	—
Burwell	1321	2	1	2
Girton	1321	2	—	2
Ellsworth	1321	4	—	—
Houghton	1321	2	—	—
Abbots Ripton	1321	3	—	—
Warboys	1322	1	—	—
Houghton	1322	1	—	—
Ellington	1322	8	—	—
Weston	1322	3	3	4
Elton	1322	1	—	—
Cranfield	1322	3	—	—
Ellington	1325	3	—	—
Ramsey	1325	—	—	3
Ramsey	1326	—	—	3
Ellsworth	1326	1	1	—
Over	1328?	1	7	—
Hemmingford Abbots	1328	4	—	—
Slepe	1328	1	—	—
Holywell	1328	—	1	—
Graveley	1332	4	1	—
Houghton	1332	—	3	—
Over	1332	2	2	—
Graveley	1333	—	2	—
Shillington	1339	4	—	—
Over	1339	4	—	—
Ellsworth	1339	1	—	—
Hemmingford Abbots	1339	1	—	—
Slepe	1339	1	—	—
Holywell	1340	1	—	—
Abbots Ripton	1340	1	—	—
Elton	1342	15	—	—
Abbots Ripton	1343	—	1	—
Warboys	1353	2	1	—
Little Stukeley	1356	2	—	—
Ellington	1356	1	—	—
Slepe	1356	6	—	—

II

Movement Beyond the Manor

The emigration of the serfs from their home manor or at least from the domain of the lord, with or without permission of the lord, was a regular feature of manorial life upon Ramsey Abbey estates from the time of the earliest extant court rolls. Permission to remain abroad was granted the villein for a nominal annual fine of a chicken or two, or the corresponding money payment. In addition, this licensed exile had to remain in the tithing, and for this purpose he must appear in person at the yearly view of frankpledge in his home manor. Ordinarily the court rolls merely list the names of the persons licensed to be abroad and the fine paid, but occasionally an exceptional circumstance allows the scribe to give more detail about the granting of such licences. A good instance of this may be taken from Upwood in 1313:[32]

The charge was laid upon Alexander Gallon who lives on the fee of John Clervaux that he is a naif of the lord, and he in full court denied this, saying that he is a naif born of John of Clervaux. But it was established by a true inquiry of the above jurors that the same Alexander was born as a naif of the lord, and both he and his father before him were naifs of the lord. And therefore he is given a day to come before the lord at Ramsey to reply to the above, the reeve being his pledge. And afterwards the above Alexander fined with the lord for twelve pence to be paid now, and for two chickens every year at Easter, with his pledge John Bygge, while he lives on the fee of the above John. And he must come to the view of frankpledge.

There are some entries that suggest the villein paid a lump sum before he would be licensed to go abroad. But whether such lump fines were usual is difficult to determine. Surviving examples of these larger payments are relatively few, and largely included below. On the whole one is inclined to conclude that initial large fines were exceptional. The strongest evidence for this conclusion that there were not regular payments of substantial initial fines comes from entries describing the easy terms for licensing of villeins who had previously been away from the manor without permission. Typical examples of such arrangements are given below.

SHILLINGTON,[33] 1288: Juliana Hakel sixteen years ago married a certain Rythmundus without licence from the lord and withdrew to live on the land of the rector, making herself to be free. (The fine) is pardoned for she is poor. And henceforth she will be obedient, with pledges Reginald of Hauescomb and William of Thywell.

32 See Appendix XXXII, no. 1.
33 See Appendix XXXII, no. 2.

ELLSWORTH,[34] 1312: And on the reeve and beadle for not having arrested Walter the son of John Smith to account for having withdrawn from the lord's fee and to be living at Papworth, sixpence. And on Adam the Typper, brother of the said Walter for having received this Walter often but has not wished to warn the bailiff of his coming. And afterwards the above Walter himself came and is in the custody of the reeve and beadle. And afterwards he arranges to fine for two chickens yearly to be paid at Easter while he is outside the fee, with pledges John Attegrene and Adam the Typper. And he must come to the view of frankpledge by the same pledge.

HEMMINGFORD ABBOTS,[35] 1313: And they report that Thomas Canoun lives at Earith beyond the lord's fee. And afterwards he comes and pays a twelve pence fine now, and two capons at next Easter, and thereafter one capon yearly at Easter with the reeves as pledge..., that he may legally remain there. And he must come to the yearly view of frankpledge.

OVER,[36] 1301: Nicholas Smith, villein, fines with the lord John, abbot of Ramsey for forty shillings of silver to be able to go and to stay on the fee of the bishop of Ely in the vill of Over till the time of the death of the said Abbot John. He is to be attentive and obedient to him (the bishop) and to his cellarers and their bailiffs just as other villeins in the same vill, and to come yearly to the view of frankpledge held by the said lord abbot. And he is to pay yearly at Easter two chickens; pledges William Atefen, William Thurston, John Derman, and William Felipe.

GIDDING,[37] 1307: From John son of Stephen le Graunt two chickens at Easter while he remains outside the lord's fee with his chattels; pledges John le Bonde and John Monek. And it is ordered that the two chickens be raised from the said John for the previous year.

Nicholas the son of John le Lathe of Gidding gives the lord ten shillings by his own hands. And two chickens yearly at Easter while he remains outside the fee with his chattels; pledge John le Lathe.

HOLYWELL,[38] 1311: Nicholas Laweman gives the lord every year two chickens at Easter; pledges Richard the son of Ralph and William Gray. And by the same pledge he must come once a year to the view of frankpledge while he lives at Cotton, and he gave first one mark as is found in the *gersuma* roll.

WESTON,[39] 1312: Reginald the son of William Hakun gives the lord with his own hands one-half mark, and every year (will give) one chicken at Easter, pledges Godfrey Hakun and Hugh Hakun, for licence to stay outside the lord's fee. And by the same pledge he must come every year to the view of frankpledge.

Walter the son of Godfrey Bacheler paid a fine of five shillings to the lord at Ramsey as is found in the *gersuma* roll that he be able to stay beyond the lord's fee.

---

[34] See Appendix XXXII, no. 3.
[35] See Appendix XXXII, no. 4.
[36] See Appendix XXXII, no. 5.
[37] See Appendix XXXII, no. 6.
[38] See Appendix XXXII, no. 7.
[39] See Appendix XXXII, no. 8. And see further number 9 of this Appendix for a general statement of the practice. The following fines for permission to be beyond the domain have also been noted: 2s.—Cranfield, 1307 (Port. 179, no. 15); 40d.—Upwood, 1318 (Add. Ch. 34803); 2s.—Graveley, 1312 (Port. 179, no. 16); 10s.—Graveley, 1313 (Port. 179, no. 17); 2s.—Ellington, 1308 (Port. 179, no. 15); 1s.—Hemmingford Abbots, 1321 (Port. 179, no. 21); 1s. & 2s.—Warboys, 1316 (Add. Ch. 34896).

And every year at Easter he must give two chickens, and come every year to the view of frankpledge; pledges William the son of Walter and Godfrey Bacheler.

The relatively insignificant fine for those who stayed abroad, and the readiness with which licences were granted for this purpose (even to those who had originally moved without permission), all indicate that there was not great pressure to retain villeins on their 'home' manor. This may also be reflected in the lord's reluctance (or perhaps inability) to invoke the assistance of the king's courts to recover his villeins. Only in the case of William Wyldefoul does there appear to be recourse to a royal writ: '...he withdrew and is living at Newnham on the land of the abbot of St. Albans. Therefore a brief.'[40] Of course there was a regular manorial machinery that might be invoked to retain or to recover the villein. As with most regulations concerning serfs, the directives about runaways are awe-inspiring in form: 'let him be taken', 'let his body be taken', 'he is to be arrested', etc. But at a closer glance there is little evidence for physical coercion in retaining the villein on the manor.[41] Indeed manorial regulation seems to have been largely innocuous in this area. In part this must have owed much to the fact that the manorial court was usually only concerned to keep the villein under the lord's jurisdiction, not to have him back on the lord's demesne. To this end the villein might be distrained, after his pledges had been fined, as with the example of Robert of Wenyton of Upwood, John West of Ellington, or John the Chaplain of Warboys.

UPWOOD,[42] 1299: And upon John of Wenyton and Robert Crane (pledges) because Robert of Wenyton who is living at Ramsey has not yet arranged with the lord for permission to stay at Ramsey with his chattels, sixpence, pledge each other, etc.

UPWOOD,[43] 1302: Robert of Wenyton, a naif of the lord who is living married at Ramsey, where he brought his chattels without licence, is ordered to be distrained.

ELLINGTON,[44] 1318: And they say that John the son of Philip West is living at Waltham with his chattels. Therefore it is ordered that two marks worth of goods be raised from his brother William West, from the goods of the above Philip on the property of that William. Afterwards he (Philip) comes and fines, as is recorded in the *gersuma* roll.

WARBOYS,[45] 1318-19: John the Chaplain of Warboys finds pledges, Robert the

40 See Ault, *Court Rolls*, p. 194. For invoking royal writs about land problems with neighbouring lords, see *ibid.*, p. 193 (3).
41 Despite some historical myths about marks and iron collars, there was nothing to identify the villein from other men on the road or in a village. There is also no evidence for any concern in court of one lord about the return of villeins of his neighbour.
42 See Appendix XXXIII, no. 1.
43 See Appendix XXXIII, no. 2.
44 See Appendix XXXIII, no. 3.
45 See Appendix XXXIII, no. 4.

son of Henry the bailiff the son of Seman, and his whole tithing, that he will come (to court) at the feast of Saint Michael, and will drive all his chattels on to the land of the lord abbot.

This taking of distress suggests that the villein may sometimes still have had some property in his native manor. However, the villein seems almost always to have taken his chattels with him when he left his lord's jurisdiction. Before the Black Death, the losses of chattels are as prominently mentioned as persons in court records. Indeed, since in the ordinary course of events many villagers must have left without chattels, one wonders whether the lord was not more interested in the chattels at this time to such an extent that the propertyless who departed is not even mentioned![46] Frequently the villein was given licence to be abroad in the first instance, and then only gradually withdrew, as with the example from Elton below. Failure of distraint upon the property of the runaway, and of fines upon his pledges, left the lord with no practical recourse. The last step was to issue a general warrant for the arrest of the culprit if he should re-appear upon the lord's lands.

ELTON,[47] 1307: Robert Gamel and John Dunnyng pledges of Walter the son of Henry the Marshall (are charged) because the same Walter has not yet paid the lord the one chicken that he is obliged to give every year at Easter while he remains outside the lord's fee with his chattels. And since he is four years in arrears, he is in mercy to sixpence. And it is ordered that the said chickens be raised from the pledges for the arrears. From the same Robert and John pledges of Simon the brother of the said Walter for the same through the same time, sixpence. And it is directed as above that the arrears be raised from the said pledges.

HEMMINGFORD ABBOTS,[48] January 13, 1320: And William of Mollesworth and Richard Boyken, pledges of Thomas Neel, (are charged) for not having the latter to fine with the lord for having withdrawn with his chattels and remaining married at Offord. It (the fine) is pardoned. And it is ordered that the said Thomas be given better pledges for the next court.

HEMMINGFORD ABBOTS,[49] November 23, 1320: Again it is ordered, as several times before, that Thomas Neel naif of the lord be arrested if he should come on the lord's fee, to account for having withdrawn with his chattels to live at Offord.

SHILLINGTON,[50] 1300: William Byrd has married at Osseley where he brought his goods without permission, and moreover it is discovered that he is believed and testified by several in the present court to have deceived the lord in the five shillings fine made. Therefore he is to be arrested if he comes on the fee until etc.

[46] The readiness with which the names of villeins *extra dominium* were dropped from the court rolls is one of the reasons for this suggestion.
[47] See Appendix XXXIII, no. 5.
[48] See Appendix XXXIII, no. 6.
[49] See Appendix XXXIII, no. 7.
[50] See Appendix XXXIII, no. 8.

BYTHORN,[51] 1306: Thomas Randolf (is charged) for not informing the reeve of Bythorn that Walter the son of Reginald the Bacheler secretly stayed in his house at night. And this man ought to be arrested as directed in the last court for he withdrew with his chattels from the lord's fee, sixpence, pledge William the son of Walter. And it is ordered again that he be arrested. And the said Thomas is his pledge to be at the next court.

ELTON,[52] 1306: It is ordered that John the son of John Jolly be arrested if he should come, for having withdrawn with his chattels. And afterwards Michael in Angulo and John of Pappele are pledged to have the said John at the next court to answer for this neglect in obedience.

The reversal of the supply and demand relationship for land and labour after the Black Death is clearly reflected in the court rolls of Ramsey manors. For the first time in our extant records the manorial officials have to seek out tenants. At Houghton in 1356 three pledges were ordered to have Stephen Bidell 'come to the demesne of the lord abbot at Houghton and to take land from the villeinage at the feast of Pentecost next.' At Shillington in the same year the court pronounced that 'John Richard was the nearest heir and able to take the virgate held formerly by his father, and the same John was to be distrained for the services and customs of this virgate.' It is not surprising, therefore, that in place of the casual form 'let them be taken if they return,' a sharper note enters the legal orders with respect to fugitives from the domain. At Weston in 1354 it was noted that Agnes Michel was living at Islope and Hugh Michel, presumably her pledge and father, was ordered to have her person at the next court under penalty of 20 shillings. Or at Barton in 1356 John Child and Robert Taylor, pledges of John son of William Sonter naif of the manor, were fined four shillings 'quia non habent ipsum ad curiam istam sicut ipsi manuceperunt et preceptum est quod habeant eum infra viii dies, sub pena xxs.'

This effort to maintain labour and tenants was also reflected in the heavier fines for licence to leave the lord's manor. Whereas the traditional fine had been one or two capons *per annum*, in 1356 at Cranfield licence was given to the woodward to be abroad for life at 40d. *per annum* (with two pledges), and to John Ter' of the same manor under the same terms (but with one pledge). Two licences were granted at Shillington in 1356 for the same amount, but with two and three pledges respectively. The increase in the number of pledges required for those permitted to leave was often remarkable. One pledge would normally be a requirement before 1349, but two and even three became common requirements thereafter

[51] See Appendix XXXIII, no. 9.
[52] See Appendix XXXIII, no. 10. And further numbers 11, 12 and 13.

and occasionally even more were demanded. At Weston in 1356 Walter the son of Adam was permitted to remain beyond the manor for life upon the annual payment of 6s. 8d. and with the presentation of four pledges. From the same court John Hakon was given the same permission for a fee of two capons and one pledge, while Walter the son of Thomas was allowed to go abroad annually for two capons and two pledges. Another effort to control movements abroad may be seen in the limitation of this licence to a specific number of years. From Weston in 1356 John Wyly was given permission to be away for only one year, for the payment of 17d. At Elton in the same year John son of Andrew was given licence to stay abroad for three years, for the annual fee of 12d. (and two pledges). From Abbots Ripton in 1356 William Bank was allowed licence to be abroad for ten years, at the yearly fee of 2s. All licences were of course only granted under condition that the villein report annually to the view of his home manor.

However, despite the distraining of villeins to secure tenants, the distraining of pledges to recover fugitives, the increase in fines and pledges for movement abroad, and the shorter term for such movement, Table VI below shows no decline in the numbers of those leaving the manors after 1350. Why was this so? First, it is noteworthy that there was no general promulgation against the licensing of villeins to leave the lord's domain. As we have seen in the previous chapter, the general ordinance was a powerful instrument in the establishment of law and order in the local village, and if at all possible it should be expected to be invoked at this time as a local supplement to the Statute of Labourers. But such promulgations, and the group fine of the *villata*, had fallen into disuse. From the immediate significance of evidence in the court rolls it must be said that movement from the demesne had become too traditional, and the conditions for this movement too customary, to be changed by even the dire necessities of the post-Black Death manor.[53]

Unfortunately, with the exception of the occasional apprentice or cleric, the court rolls do not usually enter the title, if any, under which the villein was given licence to be abroad. But the persistance of such licences under customary conditions would seem to be ample proof of the force of custom. At Houghton in 1356, for example, John Redere was permitted to stay at Brington for only one year at eighteen pence, but in the same court Robert

---

[53] No doubt the Black Death only drew attention to traditional movements in other parts of England too. See, for example, *Winchester Cathedral Chartulary*, ed. A. W. Goodman (Winchester, 1927), p. 152, no. 346, *ca.* 1355, where Prior John replies to John, abbot of Beaulieu, that a shortage of servants (*servi*) and ministers forces him to recall scattered servants to their proper condition of service.

son of Aleyn, William Dawes, and John Skinner were given permission to be abroad for an indefinite period at one capon, two capons, and two capons *per annum* respectively. Or at Ellsworth in the same year, while John William and John? Porter had to pay forty pence each to be abroad, licences were given to Richard William, William Ketel, William son of Aleyn, and Robert Robous? at one or two capons each. In the same year at Holywell William Hamond was giving two shillings for licence to be abroad, but four others had this licence at one capon; or at Slepe, William Aleyn was paying three shillings, fourpence, but Robert Cole only two capons. This variety apparently continued. At Ellsworth in 1365, for example, John William had a licence to be *extra dominium* at forty pence *per annum*, Thomas Page at twenty (shillings ?), Alan Dille for ten years at five shillings, John Porter at forty pence, and five others at one or two capons. As one can readily see from the following table, there was apparently no distinct break in the tradition of allowing villeins to live abroad despite the acute labour needs after the Black Death. And it must be kept in mind that it was the nominal customary fee, rather than the higher and more representative demand rate, that regained prominence over the late fourteenth century.

TABLE VI

MOVEMENTS BEYOND THE MANOR

Manor	Year	Licensed	Unlicensed
Therfield	1296	—	1
	1299	—	2
	1307	3	3
	1390	4	—
Hemmingford	1278	4	1
	1291	6	—
	1294	—	5
	1296	5	2
	1297	9	—
	1299	3	4
	1301	2	2
	1306	?	2
	1307	4	3
	1311	1	1
	1312	3	3
	1316	1	1
	1320	( )	3
	1321	—	2
	1322	1	2
	1326	8	—
	1328	7	—
	1332	7	—
	1339	8	—
	1356	1	—
	1359	1	—

Manor	Year	Licensed	Unlicensed
Ellsworth & Knapwell	1278	—	1
	1290	4	2
	1294	17	5
	1296	19	4
	1299	17	6
	1301	17	6
	1306	20	11
	1307	20	5
	1312	17	7
	1316	—	4
	1321	—	1
	1326	—	4
	1333	—	1
	1339	11	—
	1356	6	—
	1365?	13	—
Knapwell	1278	4	—
	1291	—	1
Elton	1278	1	1
	1300	7	1
	1301	4	5
	1306	7	8
	1307	7 (+ ?)	10
	1307?	1	9
	1312	9	5
	1313	—	1
	1322	—	1
	1342	7	1
	1356	1	—
Shillington	1278	1	—
	1288	—	2
	1288	—	8
	1290	2	10
	1300	7	1
	1313	—	2
	1321	—	—
	1339	5	1
	1356	2	1
Slepe	1291	—	2
	1297	4	2
Slepe (St. Ives)	1306	—	3
	1307	—	1
	1311	—	1
	1313?	—	1
Slepe	1328	—	2
	1339	6	—
	1356	2	—
Wistow	1278	—	1
	1279	—	1
	1291	—	1
	1294	1	—
	1294	—	2
	1297	—	1
	1299	1	—
	1301	—	1

Manor	Year	Licensed	Unlicensed
	1307	1	3
	1313	2	1
	1316	—	1
	1318	1	1
	1326	3	—
	1333	3	—
	1333	2	—
	1339	4	1
Broughton	1288	—	1
	1294	1	2
	1294	—	4
	1297	—	3
	1299	—	—
	1306	2	—
	1316	—	2
	1318	—	2
	1329	2	—
	1331	1	—
	1333	2	—
	1337	3	1
	1339	3	—
	1340	7	—
	1390	1	—
Burwell	1299	—	—
	1307	1	2
	1312	1	1
	1321	—	5
Graveley	1299	4	4
	1301	5	3
	1306	(6)	1
	1306	1	—
	1307	9	1
	1312	8	—
	1313	9	—
	1321	—	3
	1321	—	1
	1332	—	—
	1333	8	1
	1339	9	—
	1358	—	1
	1363	—	1
Warboys	1294	9	7
	1294	3	14
	1299	7	12
	1301	—	7
	1301	7	—
	1306	1	—
	1306	10	7
	1306	4	1
	1313	22	3
	1316	2	2
	1320	1	1
	1322	2	2
	1325	1	1
	1326	8	1
	1331	9	2
	1333	—	1
	1333	8	—

Manor	Year	Licensed	Unlicensed
	1334	11	—
	1339	7	1
	1353	1	1
	1371	2	—
	1372	1	—
	1390	1	—
King's Ripton	1292	—	1
	1294	—	1
	1299	—	2
Houghton	1274	6	—
	1288	—	3
	1288	5	—
	1294	1	1
	1296	2	3
	1297	2	2
	1299	4	0?
	1300	4	—
	1306	—	2
	1306	7	—
	1306	—	1
	1307	?	8
	1307	—	1
	1308	—	1
	1311	—	1
	1312	—	1
	1316	—	3
	1321	—	1
	1322	—	1
	1325	—	1
	1328	6	—
	1332	—	—
	1340	5	—
	1356	4	—
	1371	4	—
Upwood	1279	—	2
	1295	—	4
	1297	2	4
	1299	1	3
	1302	1	1
	1307	3	1
	1308	4	—
	1311	—	2
	1313	4	—
	1318	1	1
	1320	—	1
	1328	—	2
	1332	3	—
	1333	3	—
	1334	4	—
	1339	5	—
	1340	7	—
	1353	2	3
	1390	1	—
	1391	1	—
Abbots Ripton	1274	1	—
	1295	—	2
	1296	—	4
	1299	—	3

Manor	Year	Licensed	Unlicensed
	1301	—	2
	1318	—	—
	1321	—	—
	1332	3	—
	1340	8	—
	1343	9	—
	1356	5	—
Ellington	1292	—	1
	1299	5	—
	1306	6	2
	1311	9	4
	1316	1	—
	1318	—	2
	1322	7	—
	1325	—	—
	1332	—	2
	1356	—	1
Weston	1294	—	—
	1300	2	1
	1307	—	—
	1308	3	2
	1312	12	1
	1316	—	—
	1318	—	1
	1322	—	—
	1354	—	5
	1356	4	—
	1358	—	8
	1360	3	—
	1365	—	1
	1391	5	2
Over	1300	—	9
	1301	—	4
	1306	2	1
	1308	—	—
	1316	—	1
	1316?	—	3
	1328	7 (+ ?)	1
	1332	—	—
	1339	—	—
Walsoken	1295	—	1
Chatteris	1271	1	—
	1287	—	3
	1289	2	3
Cranfield	1294	1	—
	1300	4	2
	1306	1	1
	1307	2	3
	1312	4	6
	1316	—	—
	1321	—	3
	1321	—	1
	1322	—	1
	1333	—	3
	1356	2	—
	1358	—	5
	1359	2	8

Manor	Year	Licensed	Unlicensed
Little Stukeley	1290	1	—
	1292	—	3
	1294	—	3
	1301	—	1
	1318	—	—
	1356	—	—
Holywell	1288	—	—
	1294	—	—
	1306	—	—
	1311	2	—
	1313	1	—
	1318	—	1
	1326	2	1
	1328	—	—
	1340	3	1
	1353	1	4
	1356	1	—
	1359	4	—
Gidding	1307	3	—
	1312	4	—
	1313	4	?
	1318	—	1
	1322	—	1
	1342	6	1
	1390	1	—

Where considerable numbers have been licensed to leave the manor (Hemmingford Abbots, Ellsworth and Knapwell, Shillington, Elton, Weston, Warboys, Ellington, Graveley, Houghton, Cranfield) it is at once apparent that we have a cycle very much along the same lines as *opera* employment on the demesne.[54] That is, there was considerable licensing around 1300, at the same time that some customary lands were being let *ad censa* and *opera* were being commuted. As we move into the fourteenth century this licensing declines, especially over the second decade, at the same period of heavier employment of *opera* on the demesne. From the 1320's more licences begin to be granted, although the trend is not as immediate or decisive as earlier cyclical movements, just as a commutation of *opera* only gradually began to be re-introduced in the second quarter of the fourteenth century.

On the whole illegal movements followed the pattern of legal movements until the second quarter of the fourteenth century. In an outstanding fashion upon some manors, as with Over in the late thirteenth century, and for short periods upon others, illegal emigration was predominant. Criminal and civil offence, rather than economic motivation, may have predominated at these times. And these non-economic motives, always influencing the movements of a few on any manor (as we have seen in the first table in this chapter), no doubt explains the lack of a clear cyclical

[54] See *Estates,* Chapter VIII.

movement upon manors where only few were regularly *extra dominium*. But the great majority of men preferred to follow the legal process.[55] Movement beyond the domain was not a question of legal freedom in their minds.[56] In this respect it is significant that even the number of illegal movements declined during the period of fuller employment in the second decade of the fourteenth century. And in the gradual trend from the 1320's the legal process seems to have suited most migrants. The temporary confusion after the Black Death brought considerable illegal exodus from some manors, but even in the 1350's the legal process prevailed in most instances.

Undoubtedly the ease with which villagers moved abroad from their native village, as was the case with the ease of entry by outsiders, owed much to the accepted flexibility in the economy of the whole district. Some of the social pull beyond the village indicated by marriage patterns will be seen below in Chapter VIII. Seasonal labourers were important for the manorial economy, and it seemed to be easy for such labour to receive a temporary acceptance into a village through the pledge of the employer.[57] But land, too, attracted the native to move abroad, just as it might attract the freeman or native of another village to entry, as we saw in Chapter III, above. We shall close this chapter with some illustrations of how emigration became such a movement to land.

ABBOTS RIPTON,[58] 1318: And they say that Margaret Horseman, a naif of the lord, fined with Lord John Morite to enter a cottage where she has brought goods and chattels of the lord. And this Margaret finds pledges to return those goods and chattels, namely Roger Bettes and William Hawelound.

ST. IVES,[59] 1307: And they say that a naif of the lord called Adam Godrych took possession of freehold at Niddingworth. And he comes and pays the lord two shillings to be able to live there. And every year at Easter he will give two capons, and has ( ) as pledge.

UPWOOD,[60] 1311: It is recorded that Alexander Gabon now living on the fee of

[55] There are few recorded claims to freedom from the lord in these rolls, even though such claims do seem to come from villagers on freehold, e.g. John the Barker at Wistow in 1313 (B M, Add. Ch. 34917); at Holywell Richard le Eyr in 1311 (P R O, SC 2, Port. 179, no. 16); Walter the son of Hugh at Over in 1294 (B M, Add. Ch. 39597); Adam Smith of Broughton at Cranfield in 1321 (P R O, SC 2, Port. 179, no. 21).
[56] Legal freedom could of course come as a consequence of these movements, but the causal role of the desire for such freedom is another matter. It may be recalled here that 'exile' was the main coercive weapon of the manorial court, and that poverty in itself does not break community bonds; indeed students of the modern slum find the 'homing' instinct remains strong among the poor.
[57] Perhaps the extensive use of seasonal labour explains why villagers were often not fined upon return for being outside the village for a time without licence. Indeed it may be significant that charges of vagabondage under that title are very rare. I have only been able to note such a charge at Broughton in 1297 (P R O, SC 2, Port. 179, no. 9), Upwood in 1438 (B M, Add. Ch. 34823).
[58] See Appendix XXXIV, no. 1.
[59] See Appendix XXXIV, no. 2.
[60] See Appendix XXXIV, no. 3.

John Clervaux is a naif of the lord, born of a naif of the lord, and yet he acts as a naif of the above John and is disobedient. Therefore? etc. Therefore it is ordered that he be distrained by his goods until, etc.

WARBOYS,[61] 1294: And they say that Ralph Fyne has a half-virgate in Caldecote and yet to the great damage of the lord's property he lives in Warboys, and in addition he has sold a grange. Therefore all his land is taken into the lord's hands.

WISTOW,[62] 1313: Thomas son of Michael the Palmer came to Ramsey and fined with the lord to stay on free land in Wistow, and to deliver two capons every year at Easter; Michael the Palmer is his pledge. And by the same pledge he promises to come to the view of frankpledge. And he will begin to deliver the capons at Easter of next year.

UPWOOD,[63] 1308: And they say that John the son of Simon Bannok lives married beyond the lord's fee at Walton where he has brought his chattels. Afterwards this same John comes and fines for the payment of one capon to be delivered to the lord every year at Easter while he lives beyond the fee. His pledge is his father.

BROUGHTON,[64] 1297: Andrew Onty is the pledge of Simon son of Ralph de Hirst of Broughton to take that half-virgate that John Cok held on the Green of St. Ives, or to satisfy the lord that he may withdraw from his fee.

GIRTON,[65] 1294: Robert the son of Nicholas of Upton gives the lord twenty shillings, of which one-half goes to the chamberlain, for licence to leave the lord's lands and take up land at Hokyton.

SHILLINGTON,[66] 1290: And they say that William de Barthon is a naif of the lord holding an acre and a cottage from the lord, and one-half virgate of villeinage from the lord of Holywell. However, they testify that he is obedient and that (   ) live (   ) on the lord's fee in that cottage. He finds Robert ad Grenam to be his pledge.

ELLINGTON,[67] 1321: Richard Besstesson gives the lord forty pence for a licence to live on free land in Sibthorp, and he will give two capons to the lord every year at Easter, will come to the view, and the reeve is pledge.

HEMMINGFORD ABBOTS,[68] 1278: The whole village testifies that Simon Borol, who is a naif of the lord and lives at Huntingdon, has in the village of Hemmingford chattels worth ten marks. These goods were delivered by the steward to the following, namely to James Anngored who admits to one ring of wheat and three rings of barley, to Saleman one ring of wheat and one ring of peas, to Reginald ate Mare a sheep worth sixteen pence.

OVER,[69] 1308: John the son of Alan is the pledge of Rych' the tailor to have his warranty that he is in a tithing at Dytton' on the fee of the bishop of Ely.

---

[61] See Appendix XXXIV, no. 4.
[62] See Appendix XXXIV, no. 5.
[63] See Appendix XXXIV, no. 6.
[64] See Appendix XXXIV, no. 7.
[65] See Appendix XXXIV, no. 8.
[66] See Appendix XXXIV, no. 9.
[67] See Appendix XXXIV, no. 10. And see further numbers 13 and 14.
[68] See Appendix XXXIV, no. 11.
[69] See Appendix XXXIV, no. 12. This text suggests that the flexibility of the pledge system allowed scope for considerable mobility. An interesting example comes from the court of this same manor in 1316 (P R O, SC 2, Port. 179, no. 18) where John Payn who is away from the manor with licence is cautioned to be 'obedient where he is'. Unfortunately this manuscript is too decayed to merit transcription.

CHAPTER VII

PEASANT MOBILITY IN THE FIFTEENTH CENTURY

IN the 1390's more Ramsey villagers began to leave their native homes with permission of the lord than over previous decades. Upon the court rolls of some manors it also began to be noted in the 1390's that certain natives were abroad without permission. Suddenly, around 1400 on nearly all Ramsey manors, the trickle of emigration burst into a veritable tide. The exodus was largely illegal, and to keep a record of the people involved a special paragraph was added to the foot of the court roll listing those beyond the manor without permission (*extra dominium sine licentia*). The less numerous traditional entries that listed those who were off the domain with permission, and were usually placed immediately after the list of jurors and payments of *capitagium* at the head of the roll, continued over this period.

Since the wave of emigration from Ramsey manors around 1400 was so deliberately recorded, and became a more regular feature of manorial life from this time, an effort is made in this chapter to tabulate the movements of villagers. It is important for the construction of these tables that the court record increased in detail with the decline in effectiveness of traditional manorial influences over the naif. The court rolls of most manors reported no naifs abroad without permission over the 1370's and 80's, although in the normal course of village nonconformity there must have been at least a few aberrations; but if so, these were left unrecorded at this time. Nor does there seem to have been concern about the location of those licensed to be abroad over these decades. As a consequence the manorial courts were not well prepared for the developments around 1400 and the whereabouts of a great many naifs was simply reported to be unknown.

After 1400, however, there was a gradual increase in the detail of the court record of those abroad. Both for those away with and without permission it became regular form to report the present location of the exile, no matter how far away he might be, and to note with whom he or she might be living. When it became evident after the 1420's that most of these exiles were not returning the court records began to note with greater regularity whether women abroad had married with a licence from the lord, and whether men had married, and if so, what children they had.

The degree to which such information could be collected is often extraordinary. But unfortunately none of the Ramsey documents seems to hint just how these polls were taken. The court roll entry merely says that 'the homage reports.' Since there is no evidence for compulsion in the obligation to report, and the lord could do little to force the return of the exile in any case,[1] it may be suggested that even naifs at some distance away usually kept in touch for a time with friends and relatives on the home manor, and these friends and relatives volunteered their information in the lord's court.

It was the obligation of the villager to appear at the annual view of frankpledge, unless he had been properly essoined, so it is the court record for the annual view that must take formal cognisance of all those beyond the manor with or without licence. There are many extant records for the other annual court on Ramsey manors, the 'autumn court.' But even scattered references in the autumn court rolls to those beyond the manor became less regular after 1400, and by the second quarter of the century it is only by exception that there is any mention of those beyond the domain in such rolls. For many manors information upon those *extra dominium* was transcribed *en bloc* from the view of frankpledge court roll to the account roll. However, especially after the farming of the manors,[2] these entries do not seem to be very 'active' in the account rolls.[3] That is to say, the account roll entries do not kept up to the 'view' reports about fines paid or not paid, villagers abroad who have moved again, and so forth. For the above reasons data from the view of frankpledge alone are used in the following tables, although autumn courts and account rolls have often been found useful for the identification of some persons and places.

At first glance the material about natives away from their home manor has pitfalls that would seem to discourage analysis and tabulation. A person's name is often entered long after he has been proclaimed dead. The same name may be found listed twice, that is, as beyond the domain both with and without licence. Several members of a family often migrate together, and at a time of changing orthography for family names, and when in any case a relatively small variety of Christian names was employed, the problems of identification from year to year can be extremely difficult. Upon detailed examination, however, many of these difficulties

---

1 See next chapter, section I.
2 See *Estates,* p. 289 ff.
3 For example, the account rolls for Warboys in 1442, 1443, 1445, and 1447, list from five to eight persons beyond that manor; but in the court view of 1440 there were ten, and in that of 1448, twenty-six beyond the manor.

may be overcome. In general it may be said that with this examination one grows in appreciation of the scribal competence. It becomes clear that a native's name is still entered after his death in an attempt to determine the existence or nonexistence of his issue. For the annual entries below (that is, the first four columns of the following table: those beyond the domain with licence, those on other Ramsey manors, those on other manors, those whose whereabouts is unknown) the dead are simply omitted, and no entry is made for the issue unless these have been specifically numbered. Since we are not informed about the issue of the majority of the natives beyond the manor, this tabulation does not give, therefore, a significant cumulative picture of movements beyond the domain. Over the longer period of several generations, however, annual total figures do indicate how the rate of emigration was being maintained.

Duplicate entries may be traced to uncertainties about the legality of the native's movements for that particular year, or simply to scribal inefficiency. There were many cases of such uncertainty over the first decade of the fourteenth century owing to the fact that the native licensed to be abroad had not appeared at the annual view of frankpledge. But the fact that a native has not appeared at the annual view cannot be taken as an immediate sign that he was deliberately withdrawing from his lord's jurisdiction. A regular entry in the court roll at this period lists several resident on the home manor, in addition to those licensed to be abroad, who owe suit to court and have not appeared at the view. Often many miles from his home manor, the careless or busy man could easily fail to appear at the view of frankpledge set for a specific day only. This failure to appear usually meant too that the annual licence fee to be abroad was not paid. But even after several years of neglect the native sometimes re-appeared and paid his fine. In such instances the native is assumed for the purpose of the following table to have maintained his licensed status throughout. Many of these licensed to be abroad did of course gradually withdraw from their lord. But the manorial courts recognized such withdrawals and after a brief period removed from the list of those abroad with licence the person now illegally absent. So for the following table the court list of those abroad with licence has been taken as it stands until the court itself signifies that the native is considered to have lost his legal status.

While it was usual for natives licensed to be abroad to be listed separately from illegal emigrants at the beginning of the fifteenth century, such manors as Elton and Wistow did not always have the two sets of entries. From the second decade of the fifteenth century the report on those beyond the manor without licence was more and more frequently presented to court without first checking off the names of those licensed to be abroad.

Only after such presentation was it written in above the appropriate names that these had 'fined' to be abroad. It is this procedure that would seem to explain the greater number of duplicate entries. At the same time this interlinear note about the native's fine serves as a very clear recognition of the licensed native who had decided upon illegal departure. That is to say, when the previously licensed native is listed among those without licence for several years without any note to the effect he is still paying a fine, it can be assumed for the following tabulation that he is unlicensed. The mixing of licensed and unlicensed emigrants under one paragraph in the court rolls also has the advantage of telling us more about the whereabouts of licensed natives since it was not the traditional concern of the entries about licensed natives at the head of the roll to note where the native was now resident. But with the one common paragraph the whereabouts of the licensed native, if known, was entered before the fact of this licence.

An apparent duplicate entry may merely refer to two persons with the same name. Such persons can nearly always be distinguished by means of their places of residence over a considerable period of time. Where this distinction cannot be made they are assumed to be duplicate entries for one person in the totals tabulated below. In the same way places of residence make possible the distinction of various members of a family over a series of entries. This method of tabulation inevitably excludes the person with the same name as another naif abroad, when the former is only reported for a short time. But such possibilities are too infrequent to be of any great significance for the total movement. At Wistow, where more than a dozen persons with the family name of Onty (or Owty) were listed beyond the manor over the first half of the fifteenth century, and at Warboys where there were nearly twenty Berongers *extra dominium* over the same period, the problems of identification were very complicated. But there were on the average for the manors of the following table no more than two names possibly referring to one person about which uncertainty as to a distinct identification remained. In other words, the annual totals in the following tables represent an identification of at least ninety-five per cent of the names listed beyond the manor in the court rolls.

A perhaps surprising feature of the exodus from Ramsey manors is the number of natives who simply went to other Ramsey manors. The emigrant did not always enter the lord's service upon the manor where he settled. Sometimes the native settled with another landholder; and at other times we are only told that he was in the village belonging to Ramsey. But frequently as many as one-half of the natives moving from a particular Ramsey manor are reported to be in another village over which the abbot

of Ramsey had the view of frankpledge. An analysis of this type of movement is obviously very important to the understanding of the whole
movement of Ramsey *nativi*. In the following table, therefore, under the
heading 'to Ramsey manors' have been tabulated the numbers of those
who moved to villages where Ramsey had the view of frankpledge, whether
the native entered service of the lord in that village or not.

Despite the possibility of tabulating annual movements from the court
rolls, these annual data were far from being a complete survey of all
former natives away from their home manor. Certain naifs never were
placed on these lists because of a special category of permission.[4] Entries
were not uniformly thorough over the whole period under consideration.
A certain confusion and repetition in the reports for a few years after 1400,
and again from the late 1440's on many manors, accompanied efforts at
longer and more detailed lists. On the other hand the entries remain more
static over the 1420's and '30's and there are doubtless many omissions
from these as the maintenance of the manorial courts on Ramsey villages
suffered a serious decline at this time. By far the most important way in
which the court rolls were incomplete followed from the fact that they
were not (uniformly) cumulative. In the greatest number of cases, after
his death a native's name would gradually be dropped from the roll
together with the names of his children, even when the location of the
latter was known. Names of naifs whose whereabouts was not known were
simply dropped from the reports at certain times. Many whose whereabouts
was not known from the 1390's disappeared from the rolls around 1410;
many of those unknown from around 1400 had their names removed in
the 1420's, and by the 1440's the old list has again been cleared up. Even
when the location of those abroad was known, their names might be
dropped from the court lists in an apparently arbitrary fashion. No doubt
lack of information determined the fact that natives at a distant residence
were dropped, but the policy would seem to vary from manor to manor.
The names of villagers on villages near their home manor might be dropped
according as a legal status was recognized (e.g. a marriage fine for a
woman), but the practice was not uniform.

One fact is quite clear, however, about those withdrawing from Ramsey
manors. Very few natives, even of those licensed to be abroad, returned
to their home manor. This fact prompts some effort to calculate the
cumulative effects of the withdrawals. Since, in the final analysis, nearly
all names are dropped from the rolls in an arbitrary fashion, no adequate
construction of a cumulative figure can be made directly from the materials

---

4 See Chapter VIII, below, pp. 175 ff.

available. The final column in the following table is, therefore, an extrapolation, a suggested estimate only. Men and women remaining away from Ramsey manors are assumed to have merely replaced themselves by natural increase.[5] As men and women died or disappeared away from their home manor they continue to represent one unit in the cumulative total unless, of course, their children do actually remain on the lists.[6]

Something of the construction of this cumulative total may be illustrated

[5] There is evidence for the size of families, however, to suggest that the population was just maintaining itself. The court roll evidence for the size of families is the following. Occasionally there is an entry to the effect that the *nativus* outside the demesne is reported to have a certain number of children. In other instances when children are reported for a native outside the manor without a query whether there are any more children, there seems to be a presumption that the whole family has been accounted for. Thirdly, it would seem possible to assume in some cases that the whole family has moved from the home manor, that is to say, when the scribe lists the father and children leaving without referring to any further relatives remaining on the manor. The 118 entries for these three categories report 242 children, or an average family of 2.05. Since these children would seem nearly always to be reported as adults (that is, of an age to be working away from their parents), this figure suggests a bare maintenance rate of reproduction.

However useful these figures may be as corroborative of other studies (e.g. J. C. Russell, *British Medieval Population,* Albuquerque, New Mexico Press, 1948, p. 245), I must add that I do not feel they are adequately certain in themselves. I suspect that reporting upon the size of families *extra dominium* was not too reliable since, in the absence of evidence for coercion through pledges, etc., the lord's bailiffs must have had to depend upon voluntary information for these reports. The large number of cases in which the size of the family is not known, or at least where there is further query as to whether the reported children represent all the family, lend additional weight to the suspicion that the reports are minimum. Suspicion of the inadequacy of the other two sources for the data on families arises from the fact that we are told very little about transient labour at this period. Nearly all the natives about whose movements we have knowledge after they left the home manor tended to settle in one place. Did none of these become vagabonds, or malefactors, — a noticeable labour category around 1300 as we have seen in Chapter VI? Again therefore, our information seems to be minimum data derived from the more stable sector of the villagers. On the other hand, however, the largest families reported are usually three or four (five at the most, and this only in some half-dozen instances). In short, it is my impression that the bare rate of reproduction is an indicative figure worth our attention, despite the technical imprecisions involved.

[6] The occasional decline in cumulative totals found in the following tables may be explained by the appearance of certain names on the rolls for one year only. Some of these appearing *extra dominium* for one year only returned to their native manor, as we shall see in the following chapter. Some women very likely received a licence to marry after one year abroad, and were dropped from the rolls as a consequence. But where no definite information is available, it has not seemed advisable to include these 'one-entry' persons in the cumulative total.

The high proportion of names appearing only once, and the uneven incidence of court roll survivals for a long period from the late thirteenth century, has made construction of a cumulative table impossible for this early period. However, some of the better series, like that of Elton, suggest an accumulation perhaps not less than that of the fifteenth century. At Elton over 1292-1312 there is evidence for at least 25 persons going abroad, of whom 4 were women: 11 of these went with licence to depart, 14 without licence, and 2 of those leaving without permission later received licence. Of those abroad with licence, at the last report of this series 3 had failed to report at the frankpledge, 1 had died, 2 were ordered to return (no doubt for failing to report), the son of 1 was ordered to return, and son of another had not obtained a licence to be abroad. In summary, the families of 8 of the 11 abroad with licence showed definite signs of remaining away.

from the manor of Wistow. For this manor, as with others, the jurors reported least regularly on those absent from the manor whose place of residence was not known, and eventually such names were dropped altogether from the lists. It was reported in 1408 that the whereabouts of William son of Robert Hyche was unknown, and this is the last record of William. It was reported in 1430 and 1438 that it was not known where Thomas Hyche was, but no further mention is found of this man. The whereabouts of William the son of Thomas Owty was reported unknown in 1400, 1406, and 1408, but then his name disappears. Robert Rede could not be found in 1413, but in 1420 and 1421 he is reported to be at Ramsey; thereafter no further mention is found of his name. With Robert and William Fraunce, whose whereabouts was not known however, the jurors kept the names on the roll from 1406 to 1438 before they were let drop (1406, 1408, 1410, 1411, 1413, 1421, 1430, 1438). Sometimes contact was lost with villeins perhaps because they were in more distant parts and from thence moved on farther. William Catelyn could not be found in 1406 or 1408, but in 1410, 1413, 1420, and 1421, he was reported at Ashton; thereafter his name disappears from the roll. John Taylor, also reported at Ashton for these years, disappears from the rolls from that time. This does not mean that the jurors tended to simply forget the missing. The courts apparently made renewed checks over old lists. For example, Thomas Gowler was noted to be at Toseland in 1410, but in 1413 it was said that his whereabouts was unknown. There was no further reference to this Thomas from 1420 to 1438, but over 1445-56 the jurors checked again and reported that he could not be found. Occasionally this renewed check made it possible to complete the dossier on a particular villein. For example, it was first reported of Stephen Wareyn in 1420 that he could not be found, but then he was reported to be in Peterborough. However the following year Stephen could not be found again, and in 1430, 1438 and 1445 he is not even mentioned; but in 1456 it was reported that Stephen had died. The court entries are more complete where migration to other Ramsey manors is concerned, although occasionally the records will cease once this has become established. Such would seem to be the case with a certain Wylymott who went to St. Ives in 1399, although his family stayed on at Wistow according to the records of that manor. Where there is no suggestion that such residence became permanent, as with John Brunne who was reported to be at Warboys only in 1406, the name has not been added to the cumulative total.

TABLE VII

FIFTEENTH-CENTURY MOVEMENTS BEYOND THE MANOR

BROUGHTON

Year	With lic.	To Ramsey manors	To other manors	Not known	Annual total	Cumulative total
1399	1	2	3	3	8	8
1400	1	2	5	3	10	10
1403	1 ?	2	3	6	11	12
1405	1	2	3	6	11	12
1406	1	2	3	6	11	12
1409	1	3	2	4	9	10
1410	1	3	2	4	9	13
1411	1	3	2	4	9	13
1412	1	3	1	5	9	13
1418	1	3	—	4	7	13
1420	1	1	1	4	6	12
1432	—	8	—	2	10	19
1452	—	9	7	2	18	29
1455	—	9	8	2	19	31
1462	—	8	8	—	16	33
1464	—	6	10	—	16	36
1467	—	9	7	—	16	36
1469	—	5	9	—	14	34
1473	—	7	7	3	17	40
1483	—	7	2	—	9	—

ELTON

Year	With lic.	To Ramsey manors	To other manors	Not known	Annual total	Cumulative total
(1402)	?	1	5	—	6	6
1405	1	1	5	2	8	9
1410	2	1	7	—	8	9
1411	—	1	7	—	8	10
1413	2	1	5	—	6	9
1419	1	1	3	2	6	12
1424	1	2	4	1	7	13
1425	1	2	4	1	7	13
1428	2	2	4	1	7	13
1429	2	2	4	1	7	13
1432	2	4	5	1	10	16
(1434)	2	4	5	3	12	(18)
1437	2	4	4	2	10	16
1440	(2)	2	3	3	8	16
1443	(2)	2	2	2	6	16
1446	3	2	4	1	7	17
1447	3	2	4	1	7	18
1451	(3)	2	8	(2)	12	23
1452	(3)	3	6	(2)	11	23
1453	(3)	2	5	2	9	24
1454	(3)	2	5	2	9	24
1455	(3)	1	6	3	10	25
1458	(3)	2	7	1	10	26

WARBOYS

Year	With lic.	To Ramsey manors	To other manors	Not known	Annual total	Cumulative total
1405	—	5	10	1	16	16
1410	4	4	7	1	12	17
1411	—	4	7	1	12	17
1412	2	3	5	3	11	19
1418	2	5	8	1	14	22
1421	2	6	7	1	14	27
1423	3	7	6	2	15	28
1424	3	7	6	2	15	28
1440	?	5	5	1	10	31
1448	—	11	9	6	26	47
1455	—	4	8	5	17	51
1458	—	4	6	3	13	52
1462	—	4	6	1	11	54
1469	—	2	5	1	8	53
1473	—	4	8	1	13	58

WESTON, BRINGTON & BYTHORN

Year	With lic.	To Ramsey manors	To other manors	Not known	Annual total	Cumulative total
1405	5	11	4	7	22	22
1410	7	12	6	8	26	27
1413	4	12	9	6	27	28
1419	4	10	9	8	27	31
1424	4	9	8	5	22	37
1425	4	8	8	6	22	39
1427-8	3	4	6	9	19	38
1429	3	4	6	9	19	39
1432	3	4	6	9	19	39
1434?	3	4	6	9	19	39
1450	1	2	3	3	8	43
1454	1	2	4	4	10	46
1455	2	4	8	2	14	50
1456	1	2	11	5	18	54
1457	1	2	11	2	15	54
1460	?	3	8	1	12	55
1462	?	4	9	2	15	64
1473	—	2	10	—	12	—

WISTOW

Year	With lic.	To Ramsey manors	To other manors	Not known	Annual total	Cumulative total
1400	3	5	1	3	9	9
1403	—	5	2	4	11	11
1405	—	6	2	5	13	13
1406	4	4	3	5	12	13
1408	4	3	3	6	12	14
1410	4	1	7	3	11	13
1411	—	4	6	3	13	15
1412	—	1	5	3	9	12
1413	4	1	5	5	11	14
1418	—	2	5	3	10	13
1420	2	2	6	3	11	14
1421	2	4	5	3	12	15

WISTOW (continued)

1423	—	5	5	3	13	17
1424	—	5	5	3	13	17
1428	4	1	4	4	9	17
1430	4	1	4	5	10	18
1438	4	1	4	5	10	18
1445	—	3	6	4	13	25
1446	4	10	7	4	21	34
1451	3	12	5	3	20	38
1453	4	12	6	3	21	40
1457	7	11	6	1	18	41
1458	7	8	7	1	17	42

HOUGHTON

Year	With lic.	To Ramsey manors	To other manors	Not known	Annual total	Cumulative total
1403	4+	8	12	4	24	24
1405	9	8	11	8	27	27
1409	8	12	12	1	25	28
1411	5	11	9	1	21	25
1419	5	10	12	1	23	34
1421-2	3	8	10	1	19	31
1428	3	8	7	1	16	30
1429	3	8	10	1	19	33
1432	3	8	10	1	19	33
1433	3	8	10	1	19	33
1455	5	6	4	8	18	44
1458	5	8	5	7	20	51
1461	5	7	3	7	17	49
1462	?	7	2	7	16	49
1464	?	14	4	2	20	55
1473	?	12	9	0	21	—

GRAVELEY[7]

Year	With lic.	To Ramsey manors	To other manors	Not known	Annual total	Cumulative total
1399	1	1	3	7	11	11
1402	1	—	3	4	7	13
1405	1	—	4	4	8	14
1410	2	1	2	5	8	15
1411	2	1	2	5	8	15
1424	2	2	6	6	14	21
1427-8	2	2	6	—	10	24
1433	2	2	7	1	10	24
1446	3	1	6	1	8	27
1448	(1)	1	5	2	8	29
1453	1	1	5	2	8	30
1455	1	2	5	1	8	31
1457	(1)	4	4	2	10	33
1458	(1)	4	3	1	8	33
1465	1	1	3	1	5	35

[7] The only men licensed to be away from this manor between 1400 and 1450, John West, William Rabat, and William the son of William Rabat, withdrew from the lord's jurisdiction so that finally their whereabouts was unknown.

UPWOOD

Year	With lic.	To Ramsey manors	To other manors	Not known	Annual total	Cumulative total
1403	—	1	4	—	—	—
1405	—	1	8	—	9	9
1406	2	1	8	—	9	10
1409	—	1	8	—	9	11
1411	—	1	7	—	8	10
1413	1	1	7	—	8	12
1420	1	—	6	—	6	10
1421	1	—	6	—	6	10
1422	1	—	6	—	6	10
1425	1	—	8	—	8	13
1427	1	—	8	—	8	13
1430	—	—	8	—	8	14
1435	—	—	8	—	8	14
1438	—	—	8	—	8	14
1443	—	3	3	—	6	12
1448	—	1	5	—	6	12
1450	—	2	4	—	6	12
1452	—	2	5	—	7	14
1453	—	2	5	—	7	14
1454	—	2	5	—	7	14
1456	—	—	9*	6	15	14
1457	—	—	4	2	6	18

* Assuming 3 sons of Nicholas Albyn are still at Lynn.

HOLYWELL[8]

Year	With lic.	To Ramsey manors	To other manors	Not known	Annual total	Cumulative total
1391	4	—	1	3	4	4
(1395)	3	—	1	2	3	4
1400	4	4	6	1	11	13
1403	4	2	6	4	12	14
1405	5	3	6	3	12	16
1409	6	4	6	4	14	17
1413	4	5	5	2	12	17
1420	3	4	6	1	11	17
1423	3	4	5	1	10	17
1427	3	4	3	1	8	—
1428	3	5	3	2	10	16
1432	—	2	4	2	8	17
1437	—	1	5	2	8	17
1443	1	2	1	2	5	22
1452	1	2	2	2	6	23
1454	1	2	1	2	5	23
1456	1	2	1	2	5	23

8 The frequent movement of Holywell people to Chatteris has complicated the picture for this manor. For example, on the Holywell roll it was last reported in 1437 that Robert Gere was at Chatteris, the whereabouts of his brother John was reported unknown from this time, and another brother William was last reported at Chatteris in 1428. In Chatteris rolls of 1452-3 we are told that John and William Gere are dead, that their brother Robert is at Chatteris, where there is also the son of the late John, and William the son of the late William is at Cambridge. William the son of Alan Gere reported to be at Wreck in 1403, 1409, and 1413, is likely John the son of Alan Gere reported licensed to be at Wreck during this time, or a duplicate entry for a William said to be at Chatteris.

ABBOTS RIPTON

Year	With lic.	To Ramsey manors	To other manors	Not known	Annual total	Cumulative total
1400	(1)	3	4	8	15	—
1405	2	1	6	11	18	21
1407	1	1	6	8	15	19
1411	—	3	10	9	21	27
1443	1	5	5	—	10	36
1452	1	6	3	1	10	37
1455	1	5	2	2	9	36
1462	—	3	2	1	6	36
1465	—	2	1	1	4	35

THERFIELD

Year	With lic.	To Ramsey manors	To other manors	Not known	Annual total	Cumulative total
1391	4	—	6	2	8	8
1409	6	—	9	2	11	11
1412	5	—	7	5	12	12
1420	3	—	8	6	14	14
1428	2	—	6	3	9	12
(1427)	—	—	10	3	13	—
1439	—	—	10+	2	12+	16
1455	3	—	18	2	20	29
1462	—	1	11	1	12	30
1465	1	2	8	2	12	34

SHILLINGTON

Year	With lic.	To Ramsey manors	To other manors	Not known	Annual total	Cumulative total
1409	7	1	10	6	17	17
1420	4	1	4	6	11	17
1422	—	1	3	4	—	—
1428	1	1	3	5	9	15
1451	1	1	6	2	9	19
1452	1	1	6	2	9	19
1458	1?	1	7	2	10	22
1461	—	—	6	1	7	18

ELLINGTON

Year	With lic.	To Ramsey manors	To other manors	Not known	Annual total	Cumulative total
1391	5	—	3	5	8	—
(1400)	4	7	4	1	12	—
1402	3	6	4	1	11	—
1405	3	7	8	1	16	16
1407	4	7	7	1	15	15
1424-5	6	7	2	2	11	18
1426	6	6	4	3	13	20
1428	6	6	3	3	12	20
1429	4	5	3	2	10	18
1432	2	3	4	1	8	18
1447	2	2	4	2	8	23
1452	2	5	5	1	11	29

ELLINGTON (*continued*)

1453	2	3	6	1	10	26
1455	2	4	6	2	12	28
1459	—	3	9	2	14	31
1460	—	3	10	1	14	31

HEMMINGFORD ABBOTS

Year	With lic.	To Ramsey manors	To other manors	Not known	Annual total	Cumulative total
1391	3	—	—	3	3	—
1395	3	—	—	3	3	—
1399-1400	3	1	—	3	4	—
1403	2	—	1	1	2	—
1405	2	—	2	1	3	—
1409	1	1	4	4	9	10
1411	1	2	3	4	9	10
1419	—	2	7	3	12	14
1423	—	5	4	3	12	17
1428	—	5	2	3	10	18
1429	—	5	2	3	10	18
1432	—	6	3	3	12	20
1433	—	6	3	3	12	20
1454	—	—	—	—	12	25
1458	—	4	5	2	11	27
1462	—	—	—	—	9	28
1465	—	—	—	—	7	27
1469	—	—	—	—	8	29

BARTON

Year	With lic.	To Ramsey manors	To other manors	Not known	Annual total	Cumulative total
1391	3	—	4	4	8	—
1400	2	—	10	6	16	—
1405	9	5	14	7	26	—
1409	7	3	9	4	16	21
1420	7	1	19	6	26	35
1422	8	1	15	7	23	36
1428	7	1	17	3	21	37
1432	5	1	12	4	17	37
1441	2	1	6	4	11	47
1444	3	—	3	6	9	47
1451	3	1	7	6	14	57
1455	4	2	8	2	12	59

ELLSWORTH & KNAPWELL

Year	With lic.	To Ramsey manors	To other manors	Not known	Annual total	Cumulative total
1402	2	—	1	10	11	11
1405	4	2	6	10	18	18
1410	4	2	7	14	23	24
1411	4	3	7	15	25	27
1424	2	9	5	12	26	35
1427	2	6	6	7	21	35
1433	2	2	8	9	19	33
1452	2	5	7	2	14	39
1456	—	2	10	9	21	48
1469	—	2	4	6	—	—

CRANFIELD

Year	With lic.	To Ramsey manors	To other manors	Not known	Annual total	Cumulative total
1399-1400	1	1	8	1	10	—
1405	3	2	7	1	10	—
1410	2	1	7	1	9	—
1420	4	—	11	7	18	20
1422	3	—	10	10	20	23
1429	4	—	10	7	17	26
1430	5	—	13	7	20	29
1432	4	—	13	6	19	29
1455	4	—	11	2	13	34
1458	4	—	11	1	12	36
1461	—	—	13	—	13	43

CHAPTER VIII

THE CAUSES OF PEASANT MOBILITY

WHAT were the decisive influences at work behind the villagers' movements of the fifteenth century? If peasant mobility were a 'new thing' even from the fourteenth century, the answer to this question might be relatively simple. Once it is recalled that peasants moved widely in the thirteenth century, however, no ready explanation for movements in a later period is to be expected. As we shall see in this chapter, mobility involved complicated decisions on the part of villagers, reflected various aspects of the whole economy of the region, and was closely tied to extravillage social intercourse.

I

Mobility and Lordship

It is first necessary to stress that the lord apparently has little place in a description of the causes of peasant mobility. Only one certain instance of control over the movements of naifs by the lord has been found in Ramsey documents. Richard Aleyn of Cranfield, licensed to be abroad in 1405, died sometime around 1420 at Salford and left three sons. By a manorial court order of 1420 John and William Aleyn of Cranfield, brothers of the deceased Richard, were bound over to have the sons of Richard at the next court under penalty of forty shillings. This coercion seems to have had its desired effect. William, the son of Richard Aleyn, returned to Cranfield from Chickely in 1422 and remained on his lord's domain. From 1429 at least, John and Thomas, sons of Richard Aleyn, were licensed to be abroad. There were no doubt other examples of an effective coercive control by the lord of Ramsey over his naifs at this time,[1] but so

---

[1] For example, see below, marriages, p. 182.

On the other hand there is a variety of corroborating evidence that special efforts to re-take villagers failed. For example, Thomas Albyn son of Nicholas of Upwood was licensed to be away from that manor in 1443, and was reported to be at Whittlesey. However, from the Norwich *Register* there is a special order of 1447 to take that Thomas Albyn: Omnibus Christi fidelibus ad quos presens scriptum pervenerit Johannes permissione divina Abbas monasterii de Rameseye salutem. Noveritis nos ordinasse fecisse et constituisse dilectum nobis in Christo Johannem Rikkes de Rameseye fidelem attornatum

far no parallel cases have been discovered. In view of the large amount of data available upon the movement of naifs the case of the Aleyn brothers remains, therefore, an exceptional if not a unique example of movement enforced by coercion.

A few texts are given here to illustrate efforts by the lord to prevent the movement of his villagers. We have no evidence for the success of these proscriptions. But it is clear that such proscriptions are very rare. In other words, usually the lord was able to exert no coercive pressure through the courts for the recovery of a villager.

WESTON,[2] 1402: It was presented that John of Bythorn took his daughter Margaret who is a native of the lord beyond the domain to Tychmarsh and has not yet brought her back.

ELLINGTON,[3] 1432: The jurors say that Richard Mok, a native of the lord, took his son John to Brampton. Therefore it is ordered that he bring back the said John to the lord's domain before the feast of the birth of the Lord under penalty of twenty shillings.

GRAVELEY,[4] 1434: They say that William Marres, tailor, William Marres, labourer, and Godfrey Thirnyng of Toseland assisted in carrying goods and chattels from the lord's manor in Graveley during the night, together with John Smith the former farmer there. Therefore they are in mercy, etc.

nostrum ad capiendum arrestandum et in dominium nostrum reducendum Thomam Albyn filium Nicholai Albyn nativum et villanum nostrum ad manerium nostrum de Upwode in comitate Huntingdoni cum omnibus bonis et catallis suis ubicumque inventum... (pp. 165d.-66). But Thomas Albyn remained outside the manor without permission, and was reported in Upwood court rolls to be at King's Lynn until 1454 when his name disappears from the records.

There is a record of another order by the abbot in 1417: "Thomas permissione divina Abbas monasterii Rameseye Willelmo ballivo manerii de Barton, salutem. Precipimus quod capias Adam Tayllor de Barton, Ricardum Stoneley, Robertum West, Willelmum filium Roberti West, (Johannem) filium Alani Matthew, et Thomam filium Johannis Smyth de eadem, nativos nostros ad manerium nostrum de (Barton) spectantes et pertinentes ubicumque fuerint inventi cum omnibus bonis et catallis suis..." (Norwich *Register*, p. 139). Only three of these men can be certainly identified on the court rolls of Barton, and these three men remained abroad from this time.

Whether special warrants were issued for the arrest of all illegally beyond the lord's domain, it is impossible to say. The court rolls only say that the migrants are to be taken if they return to the domain, so perhaps the above men had occasioned particular harm to the village by their departure so that the lord felt obliged to deputize an attorney to try to take them. There is no evidence that the statute of labourers was of special assistance to the lord of Ramsey in retaining his men. The co-operation of the officers of the abbot with the enforcement of the assize of labourers is indicated in three texts in the Norwich *Register* (p. 103, twice, and p. 171d). But the three men involved in these texts do not seem to have been naifs of Ramsey Abbots, but only to have come under the jurisdiction of their liberty.

2 P R O, SC 2, Port. 179, no. 47.
3 P R O, SC 2, Port. 179, no. 61.
4 P R O, SC 2, Port. 179, no. 62.

HOLYWELL,[5] 1437: And that John Wryghte took Thomas Wryghte, a tenant of the lord, with his chattels outside the domain during the night. Therefore he is in mercy (six shillings, eightpence).

ELTON,[6] 1455: The jurors present that Richard the son of William Attegate, a naif of the lord, left this year with his chattels, his wife and three children to go from the domain to Makesle without licence. Therefore they are ordered to take him.

HEMMINGFORD ABBOTS,[7] 1370: And that Thomas Clarell' a naif of the lord arranged to have his daughter stay beyond the lord's domain at London. And he is ordered to have her brought back before the feast of the Nativity of the Lord, under penalty of twenty shillings (sixpence fine in margin).

SLEPE,[8] 1375: And that Thomas Hogge a naif of the lord arranged to have William his son stay outside the domain, and it is ordered that he have him brought back, under penalty of twenty shillings (twelve pence).

HEMMINGFORD ABBOTS,[9] 1377: And that Simon Duntyng' a naif of the lord lives at Daventry without licence of the lord through arrangement by Agnes Duntyng' and John Hecthe.

Since nearly all naifs, licensed as well as unlicensed, ultimately failed to return to their native manor, it is difficult to understand why any bothered to obtain licences to go abroad. Continuation of the legal permission to be abroad even after the Black Death[10] may have been important for the maintenance of this tradition in the fifteenth century too. But this is not an adequate explanation when so many ignored permission. Certainly the licence was such a nominal amount that in itself it would not have discouraged the proper legal procedure. On the other hand villeins moved without licence to neighbouring Ramsey manors with impunity, so again why pay even a nominal fee for this movement ? It would seem that there was some other motive involved when the villein bothered to obtain licence. Probably in such cases the villein still had chattels on the manor, or had the possibility of considerable inheritance in land or goods, so that it was worth his while to maintain his legal standing with the lord. On the other hand, the villager who stayed abroad without permission obviously was intent upon seeking his whole fortune elsewhere; this latter suggestion is borne out by the fact that practically no chattels of such villeins were found to be confiscated on his home manor over this whole period, even when such men had previously been landholders.

---

5 P R O, SC 2, Port. 179, no. 63.
6 P R O, SC 2, Port. 179, no. 67.
7 P R O, SC 2, Port. 179, no. 38.
8 P R O, SC 2, Port. 179, no. 40.
9 P R O, SC 2, Port. 179, no. 41.
10 See above, Chapter VI.

In the final analysis the inconsequence of the lord's control over the movements of Ramsey serfs is best depicted by the direction of these movements themselves. These movements were singularly indifferent to the necessities or the location of the lord's domain. It was quite clearly the pull of new economic attractions rather than the force of legal jurisdiction that directed the Ramsey naifs along many roads of the Eastern Midlands. While there was previous underemployment of men and lands on all Ramsey manors at this time, Ramsey natives moved in large numbers to neighbouring Ramsey manors to be employed with impunity at the service of any landholder.[11] Ramsey men moved from one manor of the abbey to another roughly according to the proximity of the manors, and of course in proportion to the total numbers who had moved off a particular manor. From manors contiguous to several other Ramsey Abbey manors (Broughton, Warboys, Wistow, Houghton, Holywell, Ellington, Hemmingford Abbots, and Abbots Ripton) Ramsey men whose whereabouts was known tended to move to other Ramsey villages as much as to lands of other lords. At the other extreme, from Ramsey villages remote from other land of the lord (Therfield, Shillington, Barton, and Cranfield) very few moved on to Ramsey lands. Elton, Graveley, Ellsworth, and Weston — less remote from the main group of Ramsey lands — tended to have a high percentage of the migrants move to Ramsey villages, although the proportion was much less than from those villages in the main Huntingdonshire block.[12] From 1400 to 1480 the following Ramsey manors received permanent (that is, at least five years residence) immigrants from other Ramsey manors: Cranfield (1), Wistow (20), Broughton (11), Warboys (15), Upwood (4), Weston (15), Houghton (18), Abbots Ripton (6), Elton (2), Barton (2), Shillington (1), Ellington

---

[11] The movement of villeins was both cause and effect in the collapse of the manorial economy. That is, the increasing indebtedness on the manorial accounts, the disrepair and dilapidation of properties, the undercapitalization of demesne as well as villeinage, reduced opportunities for the villager in his home manor.

[12] On the whole the movement of unknowns complemented the above pattern. That is to say, in those manors of the Huntingdonshire block — Broughton, Warboys, Wistow, Houghton, Upwood, Holywell, Ellington, Hemmingford Abbots, and to a degree Elton and Weston — those whose whereabouts was unknown tended to be fewer in number than those who had moved into other Ramsey villages. However, except for Ellsworth (with Knapwell) and to a lesser degree Shillington, the 'unknown' from the remaining manors were fewer than those known to be on certain non-Ramsey manors. Of course where those whose whereabouts was unknown were dropped from the lists, as at Abbots Ripton after the first decade of the fifteenth century, the relative weight of those known or unknown could be changed dramatically thereby. Upwood is an exception to the overall pattern of migration from the villages. Until the second half of the fifteenth century the whereabouts was known of all away from Upwood but, as the cumulative total indicates, the relatively few who left Upwood reduces the importance of this manor for the explanation of the direction of movements of villagers.

(10), Holywell (8), Ellsworth and Knapwell (3), Graveley (5), Hemming-ford Abbots (6), Therfield (0).[13]

Through the machinery of the manorial courts Ramsey Abbey was technically in a position to obtain knowledge about all persons upon those manors where the abbey held the view of frankpledge. But for only about twenty-five percent of the entries do the court rolls state the nature of the employment, or who the native was with, on these Ramsey manors. Consequently it is impossible to determine with any precision how many men and women re-entered the service of their lord on another of his manors. It seems clear, nevertheless, that licence to leave one's manor was not established by employment upon another Ramsey manor. Some typical examples may be given. William, the son of Walter Newman of Graveley, left his home manor with permission of the court, and ended up in the village of Ramsey as an employee of the lord abbot. Robert Sande left Holywell without a licence, was reported to be in Abbots Ripton in 1443, and several times in the 1450's was reported to be in the service of the farmer of the manor of Slepe. William Hicson, and John the son of William Hicson, left Ellington without licence. William Hicson was in the service of the lord abbot (*cum domino*) at Ramsey and at Bigging over the 1450's. John the son of William Hicson was for a time at Houghton near Brampton in the 1440's, and over the 1450's was at Ramsey in the employ of the subcellarer of the abbey. William Neel, a smith, and Thomas Bonde, both left Broughton without permission of the court. The former was finally reported to be on the lord's fee (*super bondagium domini*) at Ramsey, the latter on the lord's fee at Wistow.

The abbot's villeins employed on Ramsey properties were not necessarily, therefore, legitimate exiles from their native Ramsey manors. On the other hand licensees from Ramsey properties were for the most part employed in villages where Ramsey had no jurisdiction of any kind. This is not surprising in view of the fact that from the court entries giving the conditions for licences in most cases no interest was manifested in a record

---

[13] A study of migration from Huntingsonshire villages from the eighteenth century based upon marriage statistics provides interesting comparisons with fourteenth and fifteenth-century movements, see A. Constant, "The Geographical Background of Inter-Village Population Movements in Northamptonshire and Huntingdonshire, 1754-1943" in *Geography*, XXXIII (1948), pp. 78-88. The author's general remarks about the direction of the flow, the table of contacts within thirty miles (p. 86) and beyond the thirty mile radius (p. 87) are of special interest — as illustrating how much the same type of mobility existed in the eighteenth as in the fifteenth century. However, a detailed comparison of movements in the two periods seems impossible, largely because marriage information provides but a small portion of the total picture of movements in the fifteenth century; and in turn the large number whose whereabouts was unknown in the fifteenth century makes even this information about marriages unsuitable for comparisons with other periods.

of the destination of a naif. Richard the son of Henry Hobson of Elton licensed to be abroad in 1405, went to London. John Harper from the same manor was at Rothwell, and John son of John Grosse of the same manor was in Creeton, Lincolnshire; both without licence. Yet the latter two men obtained a licence to remain in these places in 1446.[14]

To all intents and purposes, therefore, Ramsey manors in the fifteenth century were competing for Ramsey men with each other as well as with non-Ramsey villages. There are a few texts given below to illustrate the competition for labour within some of the villages.

HOUGHTON,[15] 1395: John Bythorn fines for licence to have his daughter Matilda in his service so long as the lord pleases (eighteen pence).
William Taylor of Hirst fines for licence to have John Upton, a naif of the lord, in his service as a tailor for three years (sixpence).
John Upton fines for licence to have Beatrice Upton, a naif of the lord, in his service so long as the lord wishes (twelve pence).

WARBOYS,[16] 1427: William Strug (threepence) raises a charge against Agnes Brouncus' to the effect that she took away Alice the daughter of that William from his service, so that he suffered harm to the amount of six shillings, eightpence. And upon inquisition it is established that the said William should recover nothing, therefore he is in mercy, etc.

WISTOW,[17] 1438: And that Joan Attenok (six shillings, eightpence) took into her house for a long time Walter Hayward the servant and dependent of the farmer, and (so) took him away from the service of the said farmer. Therefore, etc.

II

Men and Mobility

Owing to the number of former Ramsey men and women about whose whereabouts nothing was known it is impossible to estimate the proportion of migrant labour among these people.[18] Only two cases of wandering beggars were reported. From Weston court rolls John of Bythorn was reported to be a beggar (*mendicus*) in the 1420's, and then his name disappears from the lists. John Haukyn of Therfield was reported to that village

[14] Such licences were practically speaking tantamount to the granting of manumissions, see below, Chapter IX, p. 188. And see Appendix XXXII, no. 10, for an example of the lord's knowledge of villein families, and of the location of villeins abroad.
[15] P R O, SC 2, Port. 179, no. 44. These are the first appearances of such licences in the court rolls.
[16] B M, Add. Ch. 34370.
[17] B M, Add. Ch. 34823.
[18] Presumably those whose whereabouts was not known once they left home, had moved to some distance, and were likely to move about with less concern.

to be a beggar over the first two decades of the fifteenth century until his name was dropped. But there were enough reported moving to several villages to suggest that a goodly number were engaged as casual labour.[19]

At Graveley, for example, William the son of William Rabat was reported several times to be at St. Neots around 1430; in 1446 and 1448 he was at Rothwell, Northamptonshire; but his whereabouts was not known in 1453 and then he was reported dead from 1455. John the son of William Smyth from Holywell was at Colne in 1403 and 1405, at Soham in 1409 and 1413, at Ely in 1420 and 1423, at Ramsey in 1427, 1428 and 1432, and last reported at Ely again in 1437. William Hicson of Ellington was at Ramsey in the early 1450's, at Bigging in 1459 and 1460, and at Long Stow in 1465. John the son of John West of Abbots Ripton was at Sutton in 1411, at Walton in 1443, and at Buckworth from 1452. John the son of John Bocher from Weston was at Tychemarsh around 1410, at Raunds over the 1420's, at Trafton in 1450, and was reported dead at Raunds in 1462. William Sande of Warboys was at Houghton in 1448 and 1455, at Hemmingford Abbots in 1458 and 1462, and at Chatteris in 1473.

While about one-third of the emigrants from several manors whose whereabouts was known were reported at more than one place, upon an equal number of manors the reported mobility was negligible, so that deductions about the degree of mobility would be hazardous. If the migrant was young it might be expected that he take employment at several places before he settled down to marry and acquire land. The scattered nature of court roll survivals could easily conceal the major lines of a pattern of mobility, if such a pattern did in fact exist. The court rolls do reveal, however, three basic types of mobility: the return to the native manor, movements of artisans, and social mobility by marriage. The remainder of this chapter will be a descriptive exposition of the nature and degree of these three forms of movement.

Of the hundreds of Ramsey men and women who left their home manors, the court rolls indicate specifically that only twenty-one returned. The usual reference is an interlinear entry (*revenit*); in a few cases there is the expression *modo in villa*. Except for the one instance already mentioned, that of the family of William Aleyn of Cranfield, there is no evidence that legal or economic coercion brought about the return of these natives. Six people were indicated to be away from their village only in the same year that their return is indicated. In 1422 Thomas the son of John

---

[19] Such men had taken land on short-term leases; see Chapter III, above, under subletting.

Godewyn returned to Cranfield from Northampton, while William the son of Richard Aleyn returned to the same village from Chickely. John Gille of Abbots Ripton, at first merely reported away in 1411, was noted to have returned without any indication of where he had been. Agnes Salding of Elton, reported at Dosthorp in 1419, was said to have returned in the same year. John the son of John Priour of Barton was at Ramsey in 1405, but returned the same year to Barton. John Law of Ellsworth was reported to be at St Ives in 1427, but he returned the same year. Apparently these were natives who left their home manor for some seasonal employment only. No doubt there were many others in this category whose names were not entered on the rolls. For example, William Attegate of Elton was living off the lord's fee in that same manor in 1452, but he presumably returned during the year for there was no further mention of him in rolls for 1453 and the following year.

The majority of the men and women who returned to their home manors would seem to have done so only as an accidental step in their wanderings as migrant labour. Thomas, the son of Walter Hacon of Weston, was in Godmanchester in 1455, back in Weston for a time in 1456, and was reported dead at Grasham in 1462. John the son of Alan Mathew of Barton, after being in Stondon in 1420, Flaxstede in 1422, and Cranfield in 1428, returned to Barton in the latter year. John, the son of Richard Mokke of Ellington, in 1432 returned to that manor from Brampton where he had been with his father. But John Mokke moved on and was reported to be at Leighton in 1443. After a few years when his whereabouts was unknown he was reported to be at Tilbury in 1452. Then after his whereabouts was unknown for a few years John Mokke was reported to be somewhere in Essex in 1460, and at Ipswich in 1462. John the son of William Hicson of Ellington was at Houghton near Brampton in 1447, was back in his village in 1452, but at Ramsey from 1454. Richard, the brother of John Boner of Ellsworth, had been at Huntingdon but was back in Ellsworth in 1452. But from 1456 Richard Boner was reported to be in Offord. John, the son of William Smyth of Graveley was at Brampton with William Hare junior in 1446. In 1448 John Smyth returned to Graveley after a period at Offord. He is likely the same John Smyth son of William who was reported to be in Stamford in 1465. John the son of John Bellelond of Hemmingford Abbots returned to that village from a stay at Godmanchester in 1411. But John Bellelond was abroad again, this time at Holywell, in 1419. Robert Marshall returned to Hemmingford Abbots from Godmanchester in 1428, but it is probably the same Robert Marshall who was at Ely from the mid-century.

A multitude of reasons not indicated in the court rolls could of course account for the return of men and women to their old homes. Christina, the daughter of Richard Gernoun of Broughton, had been at Ramsey for more than ten years when she was reported back in her home village in 1410. Her visit may have been for social purposes only, for Christina was back in Ramsey over the next decade, although she was reported in the village of Broughton again in 1420. Henry the son of John Wildefowle, and William the son of Robert Sparrow, both returned to their home manor of Shillington in 1412 after having been licensed to be away. Whether they returned because of the withdrawal of their licence is not indicated, but it was certainly within the lord's jurisdiction to demand their return.

Since a villein must be licensed to be abroad no matter how ignoble or exalted his trade or profession, it might be expected that court roll information about the movement of natives would tell us much about occupations at this time. On the whole, however, such information is irregular. This may be explained in part at least by inconsistencies in court enrollment. School children of natives could be licensed to attend school outside their manor, but the court rolls tell only of some half-dozen so licensed on Ramsey manors in the early fifteenth century. Adam Carter paid a fine of fourpence to put his son at school in 1405, and the boy was to remain a naif.[20] Thomas Poleyard junior of Graveley paid fourpence for his son to attend school 'so long as the lord wishes'.[21] In 1409, and again in 1412, John the son of John Attewode of Shillington payed a fine of fourpence for his son to go to school. Fourpence a year was apparently the normal licence fee, for this amount was also paid at Hemmingford Abbots by William Ingel and William Martyn for their sons. At Barton, however, William Sare (1405, 1410) and others[22] were fined at the annual rate of sixpence to send their sons to school. Violation of the lord's authority occurred in this field of school permissions as well as in others. William Martyn was fined twopence in 1405, and again in 1409, for sending his son to school without a licence. Only in 1411 was it noted that the licence was paid. In 1400 William Smyth was charged in Barton court with having permitted his son Thomas to go to school and to receive all the holy orders without permission of the lord. Thomas Smyth was said to be under the bishop of Norwich.[23] However, the school children are not entered in either the columns of those beyond the demesne with or without

---

20 *Weston*, 1405: Et Ade Cartere nativo domini de fine pro licentia ponendum filium suum ad scholas hoc anno viiid. Et est nativus sicut prius. (P R O, SC 2, Port. 179, no. 50).

21 *Graveley*, 1405: Et Thome Poleyard juniori nativo domini de fine pro licentia ponendum filium suum ad scholas per annum iiiid. quandiu domino placuerit. (P R O, SC 2, Port. 179, no. 50).

22 P R O, SC 2, Port. 179, numbers 50 and 52.

23 P R O, SC 2, Port. 179, no. 45.

licence, so that the above examples may be merely exceptional and hapha-zard.[24]

Apprentices and practitioners of various crafts and professions were listed in the usual categories of persons beyond the manor with or without permission. As a consequence there is much more information about these specialists than was obtainable for school children. At the same time this information is nothing like a complete survey of craftsmen among mobile Ramsey Abbey naifs. In addition to the fact that nothing is known of the whereabouts, and *a fortiori* the occupations, of many of these natives, there were a larger number of persons said only to be 'with someone' than there were persons listed according to professions. No doubt many 'with someone' were servants and unskilled labour, but from the nature of this type of information in the court rolls it would appear probable that many of these were apprentices. Nevertheless, if the information on crafts and trades is too scattered to be a significant picture for the pull of the fifteenth-century textile revolution upon Ramsey men, the wide range of movement and the varied professions throw a useful light on the tradi-tional economy.

Beyond the *famuli* in the lord's employ whose wages were recorded in the account rolls,[25] manorial documents are not concerned to give regular entries about the local tanners, cobblers, smiths, and so forth. There is one exception to this rule. The court rolls usually mention that certain persons have paid a fine to exercise the office of butcher (*bocher* or *carnifex*) for the year. Around 1400 most of the Ramsey villages were noted in the court rolls to be licensing one butcher, a common fee being sixpence or a chicken. For example, John Say of Holywell was licensed in 1395 as butcher for one chicken. Hemmingford Abbots and Cranfield were exceptions in having two or three butchers regularly licensed at this time.

There is just enough incidental information in the court rolls about other crafts to suggest that these could pay licence fees to the lord also. Over the 1390's at Holywell, John the son of Thomas Hunne, paid six-pence to be a smith. In 1405 at Cranfield the court roll lists Thomas Terry, butcher, John Butcher, butcher, John Attemede, cobbler, John Frost, fuller, John Adam Barker, tanner; each fined at the rate of fourpence to practice his trade. In the court rolls of a few years later for this manor, however, only the butchers are entered. At Houghton in 1409, and again in 1411, Nicholas Marshall was paying twopence to the lord as a fine for

---

[24] In only one instance does this type of entry appear among the general category of those beyond the demesne — John the son of John Hunne of Holywell was noted with others beyond the demesne to be at school with permission of the lord in 1409. The 'cleric', 'a son of John Hunne', who was reported at Chatteris in 1413, was likely the same person.

[25] See *Estates,* pp. 205-8.

licence 'to use and to learn the art of smithy with Godfrey Smyth'.[26]
These fees were of course nominal, and it would not be surprising if the
lord waived craft licences in an attempt to keep such specialists upon his
domain. In such an event it may be indicative that of the above licensees
Nicholas Marshall of Houghton was away from the lord's domain (at
Great? Stukeley) by 1419, and John Frost of Cranfield was as far away
as Bentham, Gloucestershire, by this same year.

Licences to practice or to learn various trades beyond the home manor
were also nominal in cost. In 1405 at Houghton John Upton paid one
shilling to 'practice the art of tailor at Hemmingford.' From the same
court roll we learn that John Elyot of the same manor paid only sixpence
per annum to practice the art of tailor at Hemmingford. The most detailed
text of this nature comes from the court of St. Ives (1395 ?):

'At this court the lord Abbot Edward granted and conceded to John Raven his
naif from the manor of Warboys permission to stay for his lifetime in the village of
St. Ives on the lord abbot's fee. And he was granted licence to exercise his craft
there, that is the art of tanner, so long as he lives. And it was granted that henceforth he may not be constrained to take villeinage there or anywhere against his own
wishes for his whole life. For having this concession and such a licence from the lord
abbot, the same John Raven will give annually to the lord for the remainder of his
life three shillings, fourpence, payable to the manor of Warboys as chevage.[27]

The list of those who have left Ramsey villages becomes almost a trades-
man's gazette for many districts in the fifteenth century. In addition to
the above mentioned men, cobblers from Ramsey estates were found at
St. Neots (William the son of William Rabat of Graveley over 1414-33),
and at St. Ives (John the son of Thomas Gotte alias Belman of Houghton,
1409-19). The smithy trade attracted Richard son of John Lawe of Ellsworth to work with Thomas Filhous at Ramsey. In 1455 Thomas Aleyn
of Cranfield was in Salford as smith, and from that time John Leche of the
same village of Cranfield was a smith at Kempston. Tailors were well
represented. At Godmanchester in 1455 as tailor was John the son of
Walter Hacon of Weston. Andrew Roger from Houghton was tailor in
Weston from 1405. In 1409 a son of Richard Aleyn of Upwood was with
a tailor in Upwood. In 1400 John the son of William Justice of Broughton
was a tailor at Ely. For tanners there were John Raven of Warboys whose

26 P R O, SC 2, Port. 179, numbers 52 and 53.
27 Ad istam curiam dominus Edwardus abbas concessit Johanni Raven nativo suo de
manerio de Wardebois et eidem Johanni dedit licenciam ad commorandum ad totam vitam
suam in vico Sancti Ivonis super feodum domini abbatis. Et ad utendum ibidem artem
suam videlicet ars tannatoris tempore quo advixerit. Ita quod de cetero non sit artatus ad
tenendum terram nativam domini ibidem nec alibi contra voluntatem suam propriam
toto tempore vite sue pro qua concessione, et tali licencia de domino abbate habenda
idem Johannes Raven dabit domino annuatim ad terminum vite sue iiis. et iiiid. de
chevagio ad manerium de Wardebois. (P R O, SC 2, Port. 179, no. 44).

original licence was quoted above, and this same John Raven was known to be practising at St. Ives on into the fifteenth century. John Wyllymot of Wistow was another tanner at St. Ives around this time.

Ale consumption was very basic to the economy of Ramsey villages to judge from the number of ale-wives fined on court rolls. But only seldom is the professional brewer mentioned among tradesmen. John, the son of Simon Miller of Weston, was in Ramsey in 1405 and was referred to as the former brewer to the lord abbot. John Carter of Weston was brewer in London in 1450. Robert Godewyn of Cranfield was a brewer in Gloucestershire by 1430.

Skilled carpenters were equally important for building maintenance at the time, and a formal training was apparently required. From 1445 Thomas Attegate of Wistow was in Ramsey to learn carpentry. John the son of William Hicson from Ellington was reported to be in London as a carpenter over 1447-55. John West of Abbots Ripton was in Walton with the carpenter Robert Wryghte in 1443. From 1424 Thomas Saldyng of Elton was a carpenter with John Bardwell of Ramsey. Thomas, the son of Roger Sparrow of Shillington, was a couper in Peryton from 1409.

Other trades are only mentioned once or twice. John Beronger of Warboys was a pewterer in London in 1473. Thomas Hicson of Ellington was a pewterer at Higham Ferrys over at least 1452-73. John, the son of John Smyth of Holywell, was in Orwell, Cambs., as *medicus* from 1443 to 1456. John Benson of Warboys was a haberdasher in London in 1473. Thomas, the son of Thomas Aleyn of Cranfield, was said to be a fuller in Lytlyndon from 1455. As would be expected, Ramsey men were also likely to undertake skilled farm tasks. William Bronnote of Wistow was the lord's pigman at Warboys in 1400. Richard Beronger of Warboys was shepherd in Wisbech in 1473. Thomas Leche of Cranfield was farmer of Wotton from 1455.[28]

III

Women and Mobility

One of the most striking phenomena concerning mobility of Ramsey naifs is the wide range of social intercourse among various villagers implied in the marriage records. By the merchet the lord taxed the marriage of the daughters of his naifs only, and not the sons. However, the manorial court was concerned with whether woman outside their home manor had

---

[28] Occupational aliases, commonly added to surnames of tenants at the end of the fourteenth century, were very rarely retained for those beyond the manor.

paid the merchet. It is, consequently, only about the marriage of women that the view of frankpledge attempts to supply consistent information.[29] In fact the merchet was apparently the sole title for inquiry about the movement of women abroad. If the merchet had been paid manorial jurisdiction was at an end. At first glance it is surprising that only four women, among all those away from their home manor, can be found listed as abroad with licence. Christina Baron of Graveley, at St. Neots with Isabella Grantesden in 1446, was listed as licensed. From Barton, Isabella the daughter of Richard Stonely was licensed to be abroad in the 1420's, Agnes Brock and Agnes Bonne in 1432. At least a dozen or so women abroad *with* someone else, like Christina Baron, were likely employed as servants.[30] But the court rolls only inquire whether women abroad have married, and if so, whether they have paid the licence for so marrying.

Once the daughter of a Ramsey naif had fined to marry abroad she was no longer under the jurisdiction of the lord, and her name was dropped from the court rolls. Occasionally the whole picture can be seen. Joan Cabe of Broughton was listed as at Huntingdon without permission in 1452. But in 1455 the view of frankpledge for Broughton reported that Joan had married John Ridman at Ramsey, with a licence from the lord, and thereafter her name was dropped. Emma Newman of Hemmingford Abbots was at Burwell in 1411. From the Court Book, in an entry under the year 1413, we learn that Emma Newman had paid a fine to marry whomsoever she wished. But apparently she did not marry, or at least did not report to have married, for she continued to be listed upon the Hemmingford court rolls as at Burwell until the 1430's.

While the women illegally absent from Ramsey manors were far outnumbered by the men in the same category,[31] their numbers were still considerable in some manors. In the following table these women have been tabulated. Since it is probable that those classified as simply 'with someone' were servants, these have been tabulated as servants in the following table. Of those whose whereabouts is known, the column of servants is therefore exclusive of those under the column of the married. On the whole women moved shorter distances from their home manor and more is known about the whereabouts of women than of men. This is no doubt partly to be explained by the fact that women would not travel with the ease of men in the society of the time. But at the same time since marriage and domestic service attracted most women away, it may

---

29 Occasionally, in the course of an inquiry as to whether a man beyond the manor has issue, the court will first inquire if he has married.

30 There is little information in the rolls about women servants on Ramsey manors themselves.

31 Contrast the cumulative or yearly totals in table VII of Chapter VII above with the following table.

be expected that personal acquaintances on neighbouring villages would provide the first stopping off places.

This is not to say that many women did not finally get far from their native village. London attracted many: Emma, the daughter of John Robyn of Houghton, Agnes and Margaret Wythe of Houghton, Emma Smyth and Petronilla Stoneley of Barton, Katherine Asplond of Wistow, Emma the daughter of William Benson of Warboys, Joan Godard of Shillington. Joan, the daughter of John Beronger of Warboys, was reported in London in 1440, 'somewhere' in Kent in the 1450's, and at Harrow-on-the-Hill, Surrey (*sic*) by 1462. Dionysia, the daughter of Robert Newman of Graveley, was reported to be in Kent from 1405 to 1427, but to be somewhere in Norfolk in 1433. Alice and Agnes, daughters of Richard Heryng of Upwood went together to Bury St. Edmunds at the beginning of the fifteenth century, and remained there for at least forty years. Joan, the daughter of John Frost, and a daughter of Thomas Aleyn, accompanied their parents from Cranfield to settle in Bentham, Gloucestershire.

TABLE VIII

WOMEN OUTSIDE THE MANOR

Years	Total	Whereabouts known	Married	Servants
Hemmingford Abbots				
1405-69	8	5	4	—
Graveley				
1399-1465	10	10	5	3
Elton				
1405-58	2	2	—	—
Ellington				
1405-59	5	5	5	—
Shillington				
1409-61	5	5	1	—
Holywell				
1400-56	3	3	1	2
Barton				
1405-67	17	10	2	2
Cranfield				
1405-65	8	8	3	1
Ellsworth and Knapwell				
1402-56	13	8	1	3
Therfield				
1409-65	12	10	—	—

Again, however, with marriage as with other social contracts the proper context of movements from the manor is that of a two-way flow. From the rolls of the late thirteenth and early fourteenth centuries it was suggested that at least as many newcomers entered Ramsey manors as there were villeins who departed.[32] How many 'foreign' labourers straggled

---

[32] See Chapter VI, above. Note also that there was no great difference between the early fourteenth and the fifteenth century with respect to the law to be in tithing and its observance.

on to the manors after 1349 it is impossible to determine since prosecution for having received such aliens practically ceases. Probably the extra labour had been so welcome at the busy season that no fuss was made about their not being in a tithing at that time. We do know for the period of the Court Book that considerable numbers from abroad received land on Ramsey manors. Over the first half of the fifteenth century covered by these records, at Abbots Ripton five families settled on land with no indication of marriage to 'natives' or of any other relationship; four settled in the say way at Holywell, five at Wistow, one at Houghton, one at St. Ives, one at Ramsey (Bodesheye), four at Warboys, five at Upwood, two at Woodhurst (Slepe), and one at Weston. The population of the manors was supplemented equally over this period by the marriage of *nativae* of the manors to outsiders who took land through their wives. The data of Table IX, below, are only a sample from this period, but this information does indicate the proportion of married tenants acquired by this means.

This type of entry to a tenure by marriage may have been just as important before 1349. From prosecution of an outsider for marriage to a woman on a Ramsey manor who had failed to pay a *gersuma*, we find one case for Wistow in 1279, two in 1294, one for Shillington in 1288, one for King's Ripton in 1294, one for Houghton in 1306 and another for the same manor in 1308. But before the period covered by the Court Book there is no sufficiently detailed record to establish a table for such entries. In addition, when land was involved the villeins would be more careful to get permission (as we pointed out in Chapter Two, those who left in the thirteenth, and fourteenth centuries are rarely mentioned as former tenants); and at the same time, as some examples show in Chapter Two, there was no problem involved in the heir to a property marrying an outsider — but all these conditions changed from the late fourteenth century.

Occasionally the Court Book makes it possible to trace movements of married villeins. In Weston in 1419 John Wryghte paid a four shilling fine for his daughter Margaret to marry Richard Dycon of Barnwell. Dycon apparently settled at Weston to take over responsibilities inherited by his wife for in 1438 Richard Dycon is mentioned as handing back to the lord, to be held at service by John Foster, one messuage and one virgate of land formerly of John Wryghte. And in the same year Richard Dycon obtained a licence for John Wryghte to stay at Houghton for the remainder of his days. From the records of the same manor we get an idea of the bargaining involved in order to obtain tenants. In 1446 Robert Thommyson of Wenewyk, apparently a labourer at Weston, paid a fine for permission to marry Margaret daughter of John Carter of that manor. But 'if he stays in the village and takes the land formerly held by John Bocher for 20s. the fine will be waived'.[33]

Fines for marriage beyond the manor frequently indicated how employment had attracted the villein to a certain village. For example, in the court of Houghton in 1426 it is reported that John Upton of Hemmingford gives a fine for permission to marry Alice daughter of Robert Upton of Houghton and for permission to keep Alice in his service until their marriage. On the eighteenth day of June, 1446, there came into the manor court of Houghton Anna Gottes, daughter of John Gottes, Cobbler alias Belman, the son of Thomas Gottes who formerly lived in St. Ives. And this Anna, who was servant of Radulphus Kerner of Ramsey and a *nativa* of the lord, paid a fine to marry William Botolf of Ramsey, cutter, for three capons. In the Upwood court of September 1, 1448, Agnes daughter of the late Nicholas Albyn and *nativa* of this manor 'who now lives in the service of the rector of Over,' paid a fine to marry whomsoever she wished. Finally, on the 16th day of April, 1448, John Marshall paid a fine in Hou ghton of which village he was a naif for his daughter Alice to marry William Mabely of Girton, and the fine was reduced since John was a servant of the Prior of St. Ives. The inevitable complications in tracing relationships from these marriages is exemplified in Houghton in 1420 where Richard Payn of that vill paid a fine to marry Alice daughter of William Howe naif of Ripton (Abbots) and widow of William Justice of Broughton. The following table, although far from a complete record, indicates that for many manors nearly fifty per cent of the marriages were with 'outsiders' of the village.

TABLE IX

MARRIAGE DATA FROM COURT BOOK (1400-60)

Manor	Notice of marriage licence only	Notice of licence for marriage on demesne	Licence to marry one from beyond demesne	Total
Abbots Ripton	4	5	4	13
Holywell	3	13	3	19
Wistow	2	19	3	24
Houghton	4	5	4	13
Warboys	3	17	13	33
Broughton	1	7	6	14
Upwood	1	4	3	8
Hemmingford	2	9	3	14
Woodhurst (Slepe)	1	8	4	13
Brington	—	7	—	7
Weston	3	11	11	25
Bythorn	1	12	1	14

[33] Robertus Thommyson nuper de Weneyke dat domino de fine pro licentia disponsare Margaretam (filiam Johannis Carter nativi domini de sanguine hac vice) profert' vi capones, si expectat in villa et teneat terram et tenementum nuper Johannis Bocher habebit favorem financie, solvet xxs. (Court Book, p. 214).

CHAPTER IX

INTERNAL DISSOLUTION OF VILLEINAGE

I

Manumissions

SINCE the movements of naifs from Ramsey manors with or without
permission resulted in nearly all cases in a complete loss for the lord, it
may well be asked whether there was any effort to come to a practical
compromise in the situation. Through commutation of *opera*, *arrentata*
rentals, life rentals, and finally the farming of manors, the lords of Ramsey
had shown a tactical ability to cope with changing situations from the
thirteenth century. But these various forms of commutation, although
they involved the lessening of personal controls, never called for the sacrifice
of the lord's jurisdiction as such. In the fifteenth century, however, the
very fact of the lord's jurisdiction was at stake in the emigration of natives.
If the abbots of Ramsey were to compromise in this situation they had to
be willing to manumit their serfs; they had to be willing to commute
their personal jurisdiction.

From sources for the movements of naifs, information on manumissions
is negligible. The account roll of Upwood notes three maumissions in
1411.[1] In all the court rolls only two manumissions were indicated:
William, the son of Thomas Fete alias Martyn of Little Stukeley, was
manumitted in 1429; John Colle of Therfield was freed in 1459. However,
from fifteenth-century Ramsey cartularies it can be established that
manumissions were much more numerous. Eight manumissions are
recorded in a cartulary now at the British Museum[2]; a cartulary now
preserved in the Norwich Public Library[3] repeats these eight manumissions and adds fifty-three others. Additional members of the family
are added in three instances, so that the total known figure for those
manumitted comes to seventy-nine. The Norwich cartulary includes
manumissions up until the end of the fifteenth century. The concentration

---

1 See *Estates*, pp. 284-5.
2 B M, Add. MS. 33450.
3 *Ramsey Register*, Norwich. The whereabouts of this Register could not be ascertained
at the time of the remarks about the paucity of manumissions in *Estates*, p. 284.

of manumissions around certain dates suggests that there was a policy to manumit that varied from time to time. All manors had one or two villeins manumitted, while there were many more freed at some manors: Walsoken (15), Shillington (5), Baiton (5), Barnwell (4), Graveley (3). These manumissions have been arranged in chronological order for the following table.

TABLE X

FIFTEENTH-CENTURY MANUMISSIONS

1431 — John Grene of Shillington[4]
1431 — James Child of Barton[5]
1432-3 — John Attesan of Barton[6]
1436 — William Buk of Ellington[7]
1436 — Alice, daughter of John Attewode from Shillington, and widow of William Smyth of Arlesey[8]
1437 — Lawrence Attessan, son of William alias Chibbele, of Barton[9]
1438 — John Bateman of Ellington[10]
1438 — Henry son of John Juge, of Barnwell[11]
1437-8 — Richard Hunter, son of John, of Walsoken[12]
1439 — John Mylys of Upwood[13]
1438-9 — John Juge of Barnwell[14]
(1439) — Thomas Gylle and family (five) of Little Stukeley[15]
1441 — Thomas Brendhous, the son of Robert, of Hemmingford Abbots[16]
1443 — Simon Hyche, the son of William, of Barnwell[17]
1443 — Godfrey Swalowe, the son of John, of ?[18]
1444 — Roger Nicholas, the son of Thomas, of Holywell[19]
1444 — John Roger, the son of John, of Houghton[20]
1444 — Richard Curteys, the son of John, of Helgeye[21]
1445 — John Pye of Lyn, of Helgeye[22]

---

4 Add. Ms. 33450, p. 4.
5 *Ibid.*, p. 4.
6 *Ibid.*, p. 4d.
7 *Ibid.*, p. 6.
8 *Ibid.*, p. 6.
9 *Ibid.*, p. 7.
10 *Ibid.*, p. 9.
11 *Ramsey Register*, p. 81d.
12 *Ibid.*, p. 81d.
13 Add. Ms. 33450, p. 13.
14 *Ramsey Register*, p. 88.
15 *Ibid.*, p. 91d.
16 *Ibid.*, p. 93d.
17 *Ibid.*, p. 99d.
18 *ibid.*, p. 99d.
19 *Ibid.*, p. 168d.
20 *Ibid.*, p. 99d.
21 *Ibid.*, p. 101d.
22 *Ibid.*, p. 104d.

1445 — Thomas Brook, the son of John, of Walton[23]
1445 — John Alby, the son of Robert, of Barnwell[24]
1445 — John Attemede, the son of John, of Shillington[25]
1446 — William Stevenesson, the son of ?, of ?[26]
1447 — Thomas Priour, the son of John, of Barton[27]
1447 — John Hunter senior, the son of Robert, of Walsoken[28]
1448 — Thomas Sparngh' of Burwell [29]
1452 — William Wattes, the son of Thomas, of Abbots Ripton[30]
1455-6 — Richard, the son of Adam Hony', of Walsoken[31]
1456 — John Denyell of Knapwell [32]
1456 — Edward Stevenesson, the son of William, of Walsoken[33]
1456 — John Rede senior, the son of Robert, of Wistow[34]
1457 — Walter Pamplyon, the son of Bartholomew, of Walsoken[35]
1457 — Thomas Colman, the son of Richard, of Shillington[36]
1459 — Thomas Colle, the son of John Colle Attewayer, of Therfield[37]
1459 — William Colle, the son of Thomas, of ? [38]
1461 — Thomas Mey, the son of Robert, of Walsoken[39]
1461 — Thomas Aleyn, the son of John, of Cranfield[40]
1462 — William Baron, the son of John senior, of Bythorn[41]
1463 — William Hyche, the son of John, of Abbots Ripton[42]
1463 — William Therry, son of ?, and family (three), of Cranfield[43]
1463 — William Pamplyon, the son of Thomas, of Walsoken[44]
1464 — Thomas Saldyng, the son of Thomas, of Elton[45]
1464 — William, the son of Richard Colman, of Shillington[46]
1465 — Thomas Herde, the son of John, of Hemmingford Abbots[47]
1465 — William Asplond of Wistow[48]
1465 — Everard Frere of Walsoken[49]

23 *Ibid.*, p. 105.
24 *Ibid.*, p. 105.
25 *Ibid.*, p. 105d.
26 *Ibid.*, p. 112.
27 *Ibid.*, p. 109d.
28 *Ibid.*, p. 165d.
29 *Ibid.*, p. 168.
30 *Ibid.*, p. 208.
31 *Ibid.*, p. 216d.
32 *Ibid.*, p. 217d.
33 *Ibid.*, p. 111.
34 *Ibid.*, p. 111d.
35 *Ibid.*, p. 116d.
36 *Ibid.*, p. 116d.
37 *Ibid.*, p. 128.
38 *Ibid.*, p. 128d.
39 *Ibid.*, p. 139.
40 *Ibid.*, p. 139d.
41 *Ibid.*, p. 137.
42 *Ibid.*, p. 144d.
43 *Ibid.*, p. 145d.
44 *Ibid.*, p. 146.
45 *Ibid.*, p. 148d.
46 *Ibid.*, p. 149.
47 *Ibid.*, p. 150.
48 *Ibid.*, p. 152d.
49 *Ibid.*, p. 152d.

1466 — Reginald Stevenesson, the son of Stephen Peter alias Pamplyon, of Walsoken[50]
1468 — William Mey, the son of Lawrence, of Walsoken[51]
1468 — Richard Beronger, the son of William, of Warboys[52]
1468 — John Soule, the son of John, of Walsoken[53]
1468 — John Botiller, the son of Thomas of Ramsey, of Broughton[54]
1469 — John Hunter of Ramsey, the son of John, of Walsoken[55]
1468 — John Hunter, Peyntour, of London, the son of John, of Walsoken[56]
1471 — John Rabat, the son of Thomas, of Graveley[57]
1471 — John Benson, the son of Thomas, of Warboys[58]
1472-3 — James Stevenesson of Walsoken, and sons Stephen and John[59]
1482 — Richard Smyth, the son of John, of Graveley[60]
1483 — Simon Bryghtyeve alias Hede, and family (five) of Lawshall[61]
1485? — John Smyth of Godmanchester, of Graveley[62]
1487 — John Maye, the son of Robert of Townesende, of Walsoken[63]
1492 — William Childe, son of Robert, of Barton[64]

In the majority of cases the cartulary entry is a memorandum only, stating that a certain villein of such and such a manor had been freed on this date, and bound himself under a penalty (usually of forty pounds sterling) not to use his freedom to the disadvantage of the lord. A few detailed manumissions are given, however, and these serve to illustrate the common form:

To all the faithful in Christ who should read this letter greetings from John, by the grace of God abbot of the monastery of Ramsey, and from the convent of the same place. Be it known that by our unanimous assent and will we have manumitted and made free and removed of all yoke of servitude, John Milis, the son of Robert Milis deceased, a naif and villein of ours of our manor of Upwood, both this same John Milis with all his children either now born or yet to be born, and all his goods and chattels everywhere, to be released free and quit and to remain in a free state forever more. Accordingly neither ourselves, nor our successors, nor any other in our name, may make any right or claim on the above John Milis or his descendants now living or yet to be born, or upon the chattels of any of them, under the pretext of any villeinage and servitude charged to the same John Milis nor shall we henceforth be able to compel or sell him. But all actions of right and claim are excluded

50 *Ibid.*, p. 177.
51 *Ibid.*, p. 179d.
52 *Ibid.*, p. 180.
53 *Ibid.*, p. 180d.
54 *Ibid.*, p. 182.
55 *Ibid.*, p. 182d.
56 *Ibid.*, p. 184.
57 *Ibid.*, p. 188d.
58 *Ibid.*, p. 191.
59 *Ibid.*, p. 191d.
60 *Ibid.*, p. 97d.
61 *Ibid.*, p. 218.
62 *Ibid.*, p. 218d.
63 *Ibid.*, p. 227d.
64 *Ibid.*, p. 157d.

by these letters. In witness thereof our seal together with the seal of our chapter are here attached. Given at Ramsey in our chapter house, the twentieth day of April, in the year of our lord, 1439.

(The guarantee made upon manumission). Be it known to all by these presents that I John Milis of King's Ripton hold and strongly oblige myself to the abbot of Ramsey for forty pounds sterling, to be paid to the same abbot or to his successors at Ramsey on the feast of Saint Michael the Archangel next following after the present date without any delay. I oblige myself, my heirs, and my executors through these presents by the seal signed by me to well and truly make and fulfill this same payment. Given at Ramsey on the twenty-sixth day of April, in the seventeenth year of the reign of the King, the sixth Henry after the conquest.

The condition of this guarantee is this: that if the undersigned John Milis shall never henceforth himself perform or have brought about ingratitude or trouble against the abbot of Ramsey and his successors or tenants, or shall never stand against them in any case of plea, unless only in a case of title to a right and to his own reasonable welfare as it bears on himself alone, that then the present guarantee shall be of no value; but if he should do otherwise, it shall remain and stand in its effectiveness.[65]

In addition to this formal deed of manumission, there was an agreement about the actual price to be paid for freedom. Despite the arrangements made for payment in the above guarantee clause, all evidence for actual payments shows that there were payments distinct from the amount of the guarantee or pledge. Only ten manumission fines were recorded in the cartulary memoranda. Richard Hunter and William Stevenesson paid twenty pounds each; John Hunter, twenty marks; Thomas Sparngher and John Rede at ten pounds each; Thomas Colman and William Hythe at twelve marks each; John Bateman, Thomas Brook and Walter Pamplyon at ten marks each.[66] Assuming that all naifs would pay a fine for their freedom, the remarkably short period allowed for payment of the fine may explain the frequent omission of reference to fines in the cartulary entries. The cartulary memoranda did not follow a chronological order, and indeed in some instances entries vary by thirty or forty years from a chronological sequence. On the other hand fines for manumission were to be paid in a few years. Richard Hunter was to pay twenty pounds in two years; Thomas Brook was to pay ten marks in about two years. John Rede of Wistow had eight years to pay his ten pound fine. Thomas Colman paid one-half of his twelve mark redemption fee at the time of manumission, and he was to pay the remainder upon a certain date in the future that the records do not specify. Of his twenty marks John Hunter paid five when he was manumitted on September 12, 1447, another five were to be paid at Michaelmas 1448, another five at Easter

---

[65] See Appendix XXXV, no. 1; and see further this appendix for other examples.
[66] The three men mentioned on the Upwood roll of 1411 were paying £20., £20., and £10. for freedom.

1449, and the final payment at Michaelmas, 1449. Where other fines are mentioned, an interlinear note gives the amount only. From what the records have told us, however, it would appear that the fine would usually be long since paid when the memorandum of manumission was entered in the cartulary, so there was no purpose to a record of the fine even where a more complete memorandum was enrolled.

It still remains to inquire why there was such a wide variety in the amounts paid for manumission. Why should one naif pay twenty pounds for his freedom, but another only ten marks? Was it a question of 'what the traffic would bear'? The variety in periods for payment as well as amounts, and the naif's ability to pay off his fine in a few years, would seem to suggest that barbaining power did not rest solely on the side of the lord. The location of the serf does not provide a simple answer to this question of persuasion. Only in three or four cases do the manumission records mention that the naif was abroad. However, thirty-four of those manumitted came from manors for which good court roll series are extant, and eighteen of these thirty-four names can be found among those listed beyond their home manor. No significant proportion of these eighteen men were abroad with or without permission. In short, the lord and his serf worked out a bargain when and where they could do so. In some instances, no doubt, the lord would have been willing to recoup his losses as best he could from a native already lost to his jurisdiction. In other cases, the wealthy villein would be able to offer a tempting sum that the lord could ill afford to overlook, without weighing the threat of desertion in the bargain. The few details about arrangements for manumission that are reported in the cartulary memoranda suggest a wide variety of bargaining conditions. The Richard Hunter manumitted from Walsoken was farmer of the Ramsey hamlet of Poppenhoe in that village, and his taking the farm contract seems almost to be a condition of manumission. There must have been some discussion about how many of the family were to be manumitted. In some instances sons were manumitted independently of their fathers, no doubt because the former had already arrived at maturity; in the four instances of Gylle, Terry, Stevenesson, and Byghteve, the children are mentioned individually, but usually the manumission merely indicates that all descendants (*sequela*) are freed by the same act. Thomas Colle and William Colle of Therfield were unwilling to sign guarantee statements, the memorandum tells us, although we do not know the reason for their reluctance. The cartulary entry covering the manumission of Thomas Sparngher at Burwell is stroked out at one place with the note 'cancelled since it was not sealed'; and upon another copy there is the note 'cancelled since an agreement could not be reached.' There are two interesting entries about men working in London to pay their manumission fines:

Memorandum that the above William Asplond is a citizen and brewer in London, and lives in Saint John Street, and he left the said manor of Wistow several years ago during which he now works to have his freedom, and he has no children, neither is he married. And he paid to have his licence, etc.[67]

And a memorandum that the above Everard is a citizen and armourer of London living in Wodestrete, and he has married there and does not have any children. He is doing the same for his freedom as the above William. And he pays for this (   ). And let it be noted that this same Everard lives in a hostel in Wodestrete called the 'castle'.[68]

Another type of bargain, that well represents the lord's disadvantage in the land market of the period, was struck by William Wattes at Abbots Ripton:

(If the same William should hold fully from the abbot of Ramsey in lands and tenements of this abbot in his vill of Abbots Ripton, and should continue to live with his goods and chattels in the above tenement and to keep that same land and tenement sufficiently and the buildings in repair, paying the rents at the usual times as well as all other obligations, for the whole life of this William, that then the present obligation may be cancelled,   )
And he takes an oath to stay on the fee of the lord in the same vill for the rest of his life. And if he should leave this holding for another within the vill or beyond the vill he must by this oath find suitable tenants for the lord for the maintenance of this tenement.[69]

For the family of William Wattes the wheel has turned full circle. The villager who originally received land at the price of villeinage, now receives his freedom as the premium for tenure ! While many villagers must have found it difficult, or unattractive, to pay twenty pounds or even ten marks for freedom in the fifteenth century, the enticement of freedom may have kept many men on Ramsey lands from the mid-fifteenth century. From the time that William Wattes gained his independence (1452) there was a decided fall in the number of tenements left unoccupied on Ramsey villages.[70] But the description of the conditions for the freedom of William Wattes is still unique in our sources, so that one can do no more than suggest the probably wide employment of this type of arrangement.

---

[67] *Ramsey Register,* p. 152d.

[68] *Ibid.,* p. 152d.

[69] The portion given here in brackets is stroked out and incomplete in the cartulary transcription. See Appendix XXXV, number 4.

[70] See *Estates,* p. 288. Note that in the manumission grant above, pp. 186-7, the naif freed from Upwood has taken residence in the Ramsey village of King's Ripton.

II

Failure in Land Demand, and Dilapidation

The story of manumissions on Ramsey estates in the fifteenth century lacks the dramatic force of a social revolution partly at least because the manumission was only one of several legal avenues to freedom. Some of these avenues led to a complete legal freedom, others to a *de facto* freedom. When a servile tenement was not at stake lordship was often dispensed with for a small nominal fine. It would be because women were not personally able for work on an agrarian tenement that they were allowed for a licence fee to marry outside the manor, and thereby to withdraw from the jurisdiction of their lord. Clerics and craftsmen were licensed for school and apprenticeship at home or abroad. By the very fact of this licence it was inevitable that many from these occupations would be lost to the lord. But even if he should remain in his home manor, the crafts-man's particular obligations to his lord were covered by a small licence fee. Since crafts and trades predominated in market villages rather than agrarian villages, the old adage 'stadt luft macht frei' had its meaning for market villages and towns under baronial jurisdiction as well as for boroughs enjoying a royal charter. From this point of view the town, even when the town came under the lord abbot of Ramsey, to a certain extent freed Ramsey villeins. The records of St. Ives and Ramsey villages bear this out as a practical step, if not as a legal process.[71] At both St. Ives and Ramsey servile obligations were negligible. Whether free men were allowed to hold the lord's tenements in these villages cannot be determined. But the difference between freedom or naifty was not in any case of great importance, so that it is not surprising to find that no effort was made to keep a record of the lord's men and women who moved out of these market villages.

In the long run the only practical foundation for villein status was the servile tenement. The crisis of villeinage in the fifteenth century centred, therefore, about the villein tenement itself. Villeinage was a workable alternative to slavery because the peasant craved land. This peasant demand gave vitality to customary law; a forceful attraction to land removed the need for personal allocation of tenants by the lord. Court

---

[71] Historians have been far more concerned to contrast the freedom of the town with the restrictions of villeinage, although there is evidence for degrees of freedom in the town also, e.g. S. L. Thrupp, *The Merchant Class of Medieval London* (1300-1500), Chicago, 1948, pp. 2-3, 61-2, 70, 104, 117, 207 n. 23, 215 n. 34, 258.

rolls of Ramsey Abbey estates from the thirteenth to the end of the fourteenth century amply illustrate the adequacy of peasants' demand for
land as a system of allocation. A regular system of inheritance and conveyance fines kept Ramsey tenements occupied, even when many men went
off the manor in the late thirteenth century, or when the population had
been depleted by the Black Death.

It was of revolutionary significance for the system of villeinage, therefore, that in the late fourteenth century villeins refused land. Tenements
were vacated around 1400, and from this time many tenements were left
vacant. However, a falling demand for land is discernible as early as the
Black Death in the increasing failure to maintain properties and in the
declining rate of succession to customary tenements.

Despite the regular spate of fines for carelessness or neglect in work
upon the lord's demesne, references to villein properties in disrepair are
very scattered before the mid-fourteenth century. When notices of dilapidation do occur in this earlier period, the tenant was well pledged to
ensure the improvement. Robert Preston of Upwood was given three
pledges to repair his tenement in the early fourteenth century; two pledges
were required for a repair at Broughton in 1316; at Warboys in 1320 two
pledges were fined one shilling for a repair not done by their principal,
and were warned to have the repair completed before next court under
penalty of one-half mark.

Such rare references to fines for disrepair can only mean that villeins
were scrupulously careful in this respect. For it was a condition of villein
tenure that both buildings and land be maintained at the proper standard.
For example, it was complained in the court of Warboys in 1372 'that
John Fyne took all his corn from his one-half virgate in Warboys to Broughton and does not collect manure to put on his land to the loss of that land
and damage to the lord.' At Abbots Ripton in 1296 Robert the son of
Walter and Roger of Ostend were given as pledges for Alice of Brerhog
that she would build a house on her plot before the next view. Land
was too scarce at this time for the villein to take a chance on losing it by
carelessness in the maintenance of buildings or property.

From the mid-fourteenth century, reference to a property in disrepair
began to become a frequent entry in court rolls. At the court of Weston
in July, 1354, it was presented that William Wenrich had not repaired
his buildings nor had he cultivated the demesne nor his own villein lands
as well as he was able. The court ordered that he be distrained to do so.
However, in the thirty or forty years after the Black Death it was unusual
to find a reference in a court roll to dilapidation on more than one property. The demand for villein tenements apparently still provided an
adequate guarantee for the maintenance of these lands.

A radical change in the strength of villein demand for land becomes evident on the court rolls of the late fourteenth century. At Ellsworth in 1387 it was noted that two tenants had buildings in disrepair; a house had been allowed to collapse at Holywell in the same year. In 1390, three lots were in disrepair at Warboys, in 1391, three at Upwood and three at Weston. Therfield and Warboys noted one dilapidated property each in 1391. From around 1390 it was unusual for a court not to have some record of dilapidation. And the number of decayed properties gradually increased. The five properties in disrepair at Weston in 1370, four at Elton in the same year, and the eight at Warboys in 1372, were exceptional. But by 1400, five or six properties in disrepair became the more common court roll report. At Broughton there were two decayed properties in 1399, seven in 1405, and twelve from the second court of 1405; at Houghton five in 1399, seven in 1400, and seven in 1405; at Abbots Ripton seven in 1402, and three in 1405; at Wistow one in 1402, six in 1403, and eight in 1405; Warboys, seven in 1405, Burwell, six in 1407 and ten in 1411, Shillington, eight in 1402 and two in 1409, Elton, six in 1409 and five in 1413, Slepe, two in 1402 and ten in 1405, Cranfield, three in 1399-1400 and six in 1405, Barton, one in 1400, Ellsworth, six in 1402, Graveley, eight in 1402, Weston, one in 1403, Holywell, two in 1403, Upwood, two in 1403.

On the overall picture more properties were reported from the 1420's to the 1440's, some manors often reporting eight or nine. But it is impossible to draw an accurate statistical estimate of decayed properties. Some court rolls report no dilapidation, or very little. For example, at Wistow in 1424 only one decayed property is noted, and only two for Warboys in the same year. Or at Wistow in 1441 there were only three. There were only three at Upwood that year, but eight in 1443. Wistow had five in 1446, nine in 1451, three in 1453, four in 1457; Warboys, seven in 1448, five in 1455, seven in 1462. A great accuracy is not to be expected from Ramsey court records in the second quarter of the fifteenth century; but there are other explanations for the wide variety in the number of decayed properties.

First of all, when decayed properties were vacated and left in the hands of the lord (a common practice for properties that were not repaired soon after the first court notice),[72] these were regularly reported in the account roll rather than in the court roll. In this way a number of decayed properties were withdrawn from the court roll records while the list of vacated holdings in the lord's hands grew in the account rolls. An exceptional

---

[72] See *Estates*, pp. 288-9.

court roll of Warboys over 1423-4, for example, has listed the properties fallen into the lord's hands. In addition to seven tenants who were fined in that court for dilapidation, ten decayed properties of Warboys were in the hands of the lord that year. A second qualification with respect to court roll data on repair touches agreements upon improvements. Quite often the required repairs were very extensive and could not be carried out in one year with ordinary villein capital resources. From the Court Book it is clear that Ramsey made agreements with villeins that allowed a year or several years for the required property improvements.[73] Such agreements were not noted in the court rolls. Many unimproved properties might in this manner escape mention in the court rolls.

No doubt the thoroughness of the court roll report upon dilapidation was influenced by the fines imposed, and of course by whether any fine were imposed. By the fifteenth century the lords of Ramsey were not in a position to enforce traditional penalties for dilapidation. Well back into the fourteenth century villagers had not hesitated to give up lands when deserting their native village. In 1369 John Attewode of Therfield, who had been a tenant of twenty-four acres, slipped away at night with his whole family (elongavit se extra dominium noctanter cum tota familia sua) so that three acres were left uncultivated and scarcely any crop remained. Before giving up one-half virgate at Slepe in 1377, Christine Bony had to pay one-half mark in fine for dilapidation of the land. John Zutte of Knapwell, who was tenant of a 'three-quarter land,' withdrew from that land and the manor in 1411, and his whereabouts was unknown. In 1391, Thomas Dunwode withdrew from one virgate and John Parkyn from a one-half virgate and one cotland at Cranfield; both men may have remained on the manor since the bailiff was able to collect heriots. Peter Martin also withdrew from one virgate in Barton in 1391, and a heriot was collected.[74] Many of those outside the lord's fee had formerly held tenements, but records do not give enough information as to whether they withdrew illegally from these lands or formally handed these over to the lord. Probably they simply withdrew when they were intent upon leaving the lord's domain without licence.

Next to leaving the tenement and the manor, the villein could harm the lord's villeinage by neglecting his tenement. The villein always gave pledges when he entered a property that he would maintain the conditions of tenure, maintenance being one of these conditions. However, rather

---

[73] These maintenance arrangements can be found much earlier for holdings in St. Ives, see 'Rent and Capital at St. Ives', *Mediaeval Studies*, XX (1958), pp. 87 ff.

[74] Other references abound for this form of withdrawal.

than putting the burden on pledges,[75] or threatening with eviction, an ordinance with a heavy penalty clause emerged as the main legal weapon against dilapidation in the latter half of the fourteenth century. In 1387 a tenant was ordered to repair a building under the penalty of forty pence, another at Therfield in 1391 under the penalty of twenty shillings, three at Cranfield over 1399-1400 under the penalty of twenty shillings. In actual fact, however, the ordinance penalty does not seem to have been imposed. The penalty was really replaced by a petty fine, although the ordinance continued to be enunciated. For example, at Warboys in 1390, three were fined at threepence, eighteen pence and twelve pence respectively for ruinous buildings, although the court went on to decree that all buildings must be kept in repair under the penalty of ten shillings. At Weston in 1391, five were fined at threepence although the ordinance penalty was ten shillings. At Weston in 1370, five had been fined, two at twopence, two at threepence, and one at sixpence. At Warboys in 1372, eight had been fined at threepence and one at sixpence, although the ordinance penalty was ten shillings. At Broughton in 1405, seven were fined at twopence, while the ordinance penalty demanded twenty shillings.

With prospective tenants in short supply, and tenants willing to vacate lands and leave their native manor, the lord and his bailiff were in no position to enforce traditional penalties for dilapidation. It was a long way from those thirteenth-century conditions where women might be obliged to marry or give up a tenement when at Broughton in 1380 two widows, who had according to customary law succeeded to the virgates of their late husbands, were required to find pledges that they would not leave the manor but would maintain their buildings and lands. The bargaining powers of the lord were not great by 1400, so a variety of arrangements were attempted. At Elton in 1405, for example, William Conlid was reported to have buildings still in disrepair although he had found two pledges that he would repair at the last court, and had been ordered to do so under penalty of forty shillings. William was fined twopence and ordered to repair before the next court under penalty of forty pence. At Elton in the same year it was reported that John Wrighte had a decayed property. The court issued a thundering order to seize his

---

[75] An exceptional entry from Chatteris in 1452-3 shows how the pledge could be involved: Et quod Willelmus Pyronn' et Johannes Massely non reparaverunt tenementum Ricardi Broun prout manuceperunt et habuerunt in pena; ideo incurrent penam (iis.). Et quod Richardus Broun fecit vastum super bondagium domini eo quod permisit cadere unam domum et etiam non reparavit alteram domum ad dampnum domini taxatum per inquisitionem xls. quos preceptum est levare de plegiis suis predictis. Et dicunt quod certa bona dicti Ricardi apretiata per inquisitionem ad vs. remanent in custodia Johannis Rede quae preceptum est retinere etc. quousque etc." (Add. Ch. 34827).

goods, chattels, and crops until he did repair. But when it was reported that John had been quitted of repair obligations for a year after he received the tenement, the court merely dismissed the case after pledges were found that repairs would be made. In the same year William Whitewell, rector of the church of Elton, had not repaired a tenement even though he had been allowed forty pence for this purpose when he received the property. Whitewell was ordered to repair under penalty of one hundred shillings.

The lord had everything to lose if the villein would not co-operate. What could prevent a villein from stripping a property bare before his decease, or his flight ? At Broughton in 1399 it was reported that Emma Hale who held a ruinous plot and one quarter of a virgate 'died since the last court and nothing comes as heriot since the tenement has fallen into the lord's hands. And the said Emma wasted that tenement so that it lies unproductive. And Emma had nothing in goods or chattels.' At Weston in 1370, John Abovetoun did not maintain or work his land as he ought, and was fined threepence. In this same year at Weston the messuage and one-half virgate of Richard Moltesson were ordered to be seized because he would not maintain it. At Warboys in 1405 it was reported that Henry Norburgh and Thomas Eyr had let buildings fall and an unknown had carried away the timber. The two men were fined at twopence and their crops seized until they should repair. The court of Wistow presented in 1403 that John Attegate had wasted a capital messuage and allowed the grange to fall down and was unable to maintain the property. Robert Attegate had a dilapidated grange. Both were fined twopence and ordered to repair. On the same manor in this year John Randolf had a ruinous hall, Thomas Onty a ruinous building (*solarium*), Richard Wodecok a ruinous hall and John Salyne a ruinous bakehouse. All were fined at threepence. But most of these men, and others, were fined for the same dilapidations in 1405; and John Okynon and John Clervaux were fined at two and threepence for leaving one-quarter and one-half virgates uncultivated.

No matter how serious the decay, or how large the threatened penalty, fines from the beginning of the fifteenth century were nearly always a nominal two or threepence. By the second quarter of the fifteenth century no fines were imposed in a large number of cases. In such cases the tenants were warned of the traditional penalties, but there is not evidence that these were ever enforced. For example, at Wistow in 1441 three tenants had neglected properties, and in 1446 five tenants were ordered to repair, but in none of these cases were there fines. Nor were there fines to the two tenants at Upwood with dilapidated property in 1441, the five at Warboys in 1455, or the seven at Warboys in 1448.

Towards the mid-fifteenth century the court rolls begin to point out that the lord was donating the timber for repairs. From the court book it may be seen that at the time of conveyance special timber rights for repair were given from early in the century. However, the court rolls only mention special gifts of timber towards the mid-century.[76] For example, at Ellington in 1446 'Hugh Sely had not repaired buildings that are very ruinous. And he has timber given by the lord and has not used it (fourpence).' Eight others had not repaired and were fined (seven at twopence, one at fourpence). The court then ordered that 'each repair his roofing (*in tectura*) before the feast of the purification of Blessed Mary under the penalty of ten shillings, and his woodwork (*in carpentra*) before the feast of the Nativity of Saint John the Baptist under penalty of ten shillings.'

The court of Wistow in 1451 reported that 'Richard Skynner had not repaired the roofing of his house (twopence). John Hiche also had not repaired his roof. Therefore both are in mercy, etc. And William Benet (twopence) had timber from the lord and did not use it to repair, therefore he is in mercy, etc. And William Pyyard (twopence) has not repaired the roof of his bakehouse, etc. And Richard Baker has not utilized the timber given him by the lord for repairs, etc. (twopence). Richard Wryghte has not repaired his tenement with straw (*cum stramine*). Therefore etc. (twopence). And Thomas Croft has not repaired his tenement, formerly held by John Onty. And John Baker (twopence) has a cottage in ruins. Richard Baker (twopence) did not repair his bakehouse with straw. Therefore etc. And all are bound to repair before the feast of the Purification of the Blessed Mary, under the penalty to each of thirteen shillings, fourpence.'

From the mid-fifteenth century there is some evidence for a firmer

---

[76] The account roll record of repairs for buildings cannot usually be distinguished from other expenditures, but for the following three manors the account rolls yield more consistent information upon the lord's expenses in this category:

Items under Custos Domorum in Account Rolls

Holywell				Upwood				Houghton							
1354 —		6s.	3d.	1371 —		5s.	5d.	1364 —	£ 2.	7s.	6d.	1407 —	£ 6.	5s.	5d.
1356 —	£12.	5s.	4d.	1406 —		15s.	4d.	1369 —		12s.	7d.	1408 —		18s.	6d.
1399 —		8s.	4d.	1408 —		18s.	4d.	1371 —		15.15s.	2d.	1411 —		1.13s.	2d.
1401 —		19s.	8d.	(1430)—	£ 5.18s.		3d.	1372 —	4.	2s.	1d.	1418 —		2.	5d.
1405 —		1.16s.	6d.	1446 —	14.		6d.	1379 —		2s.	8d.	1446 —		6.19s.	7d.
1412 —		2.19s.	6d.	1447 —	11.11s.			1383 —		3s.	4d.	1448 —	3.	5s.	3d.
(1440)—		8. 3s.	5d.	1448 —	7.		6d.	1387 —		1.17s.	6d.	1452 —		3.16s.	7d.
1450 —		6.17s.	10d.	1452 —	2. 9s.		10d.	1388 —		1.16s.	2d.	1453 —	5.	3s.	2d.
				1455 —	3. 9s.		6d.	1389 —	2.		5d.	1454 —		11.14s.	1d.
								1393 —	7.		3d.	1455 —		12.11s.	5d.
								1394 —	7.	3s.	8d.	1456 —		5.15s.	
								1396 —	1.		4d.	1460 —		7. 3s.	
								1404 —		17s.	8d.	1462 —		22.19s.	2d.
								1405 —	11. 1s.						

policy with respect to dilapidation on the villeinage. Rather than earlier *ad hoc* arrangements, a common policy for all Ramsey manors is suggested in the common entry for Therfield, Hemmingford Abbots, Houghton, and Warboys in 1462: 'And it is directed that all tenants repair their tenements well and adequately, in straw before the feast of Saint Andrew, and in timber before the feast of the Nativity of Saint John the Baptist next.' The threatened penalties continued to differ among manors, however. In 1487 it was reported from Upwood 'that William Forten, John Rose, Robert Baker junior, John Newlode, all of Upwood, and John Lane and John Smyth of Raveley, had returned to the lord their tenements which were without tenants. And the bailiff is ordered to distrain the above men to make what are adequate repairs on their tenements in the judgment of the homage before they withdraw.' In 1496 the bailiff was curtly ordered to seize tenements at Wistow if these were not repaired. At Holywell in 1487 tenants were threatened with a penalty of forty shillings for dilapidation.

It is difficult to say with any precision how effective were these efforts to prevent dilapidation in the late fifteenth century. Court roll survivals are not as many or as detailed for this period. Certainly there is much evidence for dilapidation well into the sixteenth century. And fines continued to be light in many instances. At Barton over 1490-1 one tenant was bound to repair under a penalty of forty shillings; six other tenants also had properties in disrepair and these were not fined but bound over to repair under a penalty of forty shillings; six other tenants also had properties in disrepair and these were not fined but bound over to repair under a penalty of twelve pence. At Burwell in 1490, six men who had dilapidated properties were not fined but ordered to repair under penalty of three shillings, fourpence. Hemmingford Abbots had six tenements in decay in 1512 that were ordered to be repaired. Three tenants of Holywell were fined at fourpence each for dilapidation in 1494.

The forces that brought about farming of Ramsey manors in the early fifteenth century changed by commutation one of the basic conditions of villeinage, the payment of service. This change was intended to be temporary, but gradually as the decades wore on account rolls deleted ancient references to *opera*. Torn from the age-old obligations to work and services the customary tenement had lost its main economic *raison d'être*. Would the legal form of customary tenure evolve to fit new economic realities?

The village tenement could not simply flee the remaining vestiges of the villeinage system, as the villagers so often did on Ramsey properties. But villein tenure could become impossible without villeins. Scores of village tenements were left in the hands of the lord; easy terms failed to attract tenants to vacant holdings; tenants who actually took tenements exploited the situation by allowing dilapidation of properties and passing some of the burden of repair on to the lord. The real remaining signs of villeinage were customary taxes, but when the demand for land was barely marginal, or often ineffective, customary taxes were lost in the marketing process. The situation came to a significant crisis from the mid-fifteenth century when customary tenants began to neglect what was practically the sole remaining significant customary charge, the entry fine (*gersuma*). The story of this crisis, and of a frustrated evolution from customary tenure to freehold, will be told in the following section.

III

Challenge to Customary Tenure

Since payment of the entry fine (*gersuma*) was the villein's title to seisin in the manorial court, it is not surprising that the lord was seldom if ever vexed with failures to pay this fine in the thirteenth and fourteenth centuries. The penalty for failure to pay a *gersuma* was forfeit of the holding. Even after 1400 it was very rare that an entry fine was left unpaid. There were two lands for which entry fines had not been paid at Abbots Ripton in 1405, one at Broughton in 1409, one at Elton in 1411, and in 1419 two at Chatteris and one at Weston. There was little to be gained at this time by ejecting the villein from his tenement, so fines of one or twopence were usual for failure to pay the *gersuma*, although the threat of forfeiture was invoked. The small fine does not seem to have encouraged carelessness since notices of unpaid entry fines are infrequent over the 1420's and 1430's, at a time when carelessness was so widespread in many other ways. From around 1440, however, a notice of some lands without paid entry fines becomes a regular entry on most manors.[77] Table XI below gives examples for this increased neglect of the entry fine.

We are not told why this neglect was occurring at this particular time. Perhaps the small fine had eventually encouraged carelessness, or the number of entry fines condoned for repairs was leading to decreasing concern for this fine. On the other hand the rapid decline in the size of court rolls from this time, and the few entries in the court book, may point to a legal and clerical incompetence that allowed tenants to escape the fine. In any case, from the scattered nature of the rolls, and the sparse

---

[77] The expression *terra ingersumata* began to be employed after 1440 rather than the earlier *sine gersuma* or *non gersumata*.

entries in court rolls at this time, it is impossible to say more. Only one
entry profers some details. At the view of frankpledge of Broughton in
1455 it was said that Sir Henry, rector of the church in that vill, held a
virgate and a quarter together with one cotland, all without entry fine.
And he had held these properties for eight years. Sir Henry was fined
fourpence, and the bailiff ordered to seize the lands unless, etc.

TABLE XI

UNPAID ENTRY FINES

1424 — Broughton	— 2		1450 — Ellington	— 9
1424 — Shillington	— 2		1450 — Weston	— 1
1430 — Chatteris	— 2		1451 — Barton	— 1
1432 — Weston	— 1		1451 — Wistow	— 2
1433 — Chatteris	— 4		1452 — Shillington	— 1
1434 — Cranfield	— 1		1452 — Knapwell	— 3
1434 — Weston	— 1		1453 — Ellington	— 8
1437 — Hemmingford Abbots	— 6		1454 — Ellington	— 9
1440 — Warboys	— 1		1454 — Brington	— 8
1440 — Ellington	— 32?		1455 — Broughton	— 3
1440 — Barton	— 2		1455 — Cranfield	— 1
1440 — Hemmingford Abbots	— 3		1455 — Therfield	— 4
1440 — Little Stukeley	— 1		1455 — Barton	— 1
1441 — Barton	— 3		1455 — Warboys	— 4
1443 — Cranfield	— 3		1455 — Weston	— 12
1443 — Ellington	— 4		1454 — Bythorn	— 6
1444 — Barton	— 1		1456 — Bythorn	— 8
1446 — Ellington	— 3		1457 — Bythorn	— 7
1447 — Ellington	— 4		1460 — Bythorn	— 4
1446 — Broughton	— 3			

From the 1450's a new term was applied to the unpaid entry fines.
Henceforth court rolls refer to lands held with unpaid entry fines as *sine
copia* rather than *terra ingersumata*. Owing to the scattered nature of court
roll survivals in the latter half of the fifteenth century, it has been impossible
to gauge any possible disciplinary effect of the new term. Certainly there
was substantial neglect at some periods. The unusually detailed court
rolls of 1473, for example, list three tenements of Barton held without
copy (*sine copia*) for which the tenants were fined at twopence. In the
same year Weston had nine tenements *sine copia* (fined at twopence), and
Ellington six tenements *sine copia* (fined at one penny). In 1486 there were
eleven tenements without copies at Ellington, and one at Therfield.

It is an anomoly of history that the word 'copy,' which was to have such
a long history in tenure by copyhold, should first appear in a negative
context in our documents. Indeed the word 'copy' (*copia*) never became

part of the enrollment formula itself, but was added to the margin of the
court roll to designate the entry. Differences in ink sometimes suggest
that this marginal entry was added to the court roll at a later date, perhaps
by an auditor rather than by the court scribe. But as yet nothing definite
can be said on this point. In addition, since the word 'copy' was not
intrinsic to the enrollment formula it is not surprising to find that it has
been omitted in many instances. Once the form of entry *per copiam* had
become accepted the marginal designation was only for the convenience
of those searching the rolls for land titles. However, there is no doubt
that customary tenure became tenure *per copiam* on all Ramsey manors
in the latter half of the fifteenth century. The most consistent evidence
for this comes from the form of entry at the death of a customary tenant.
Such a tenant was explicitly said to have held by copy. At Cranfield in
1497, for example, Thomas Rede who had held *per copiam* was said to have
died and his wife succeeds in the tenement. In the same court John Wryght
handed over the customary tenure of a half virgate to Robert Balle, but
the court has not bothered to designate this as a copy. An agreement from
Girton in 1493 best illustrates how the hereditary customary tenure has
become tenure by copy: 'It is agreed between the lord and his tenants
that if any tenant or farmer of this domain who has customary lands or
tenements at the will of the lord by copy or at farm should harm, indict,
oppose,...'[78] An ordinance for repair at Ellington in 1513 also identifies
customary tenants as copyholders: 'All tenants of the lord by copy of the
court roll are ordered to repair their tenements well and sufficiently
before the feast of Pentecost next of the following year, under penalty oʃ
twenty shillings to each.'[79]

Did copyhold come to mean the issue of a document to the customary
tenant? The charter (*carta*) was symbolic of freehold in Ramsey manorial
courts; customary tenants who held only by the will of the lord held by
no such independent proof of seisin. No evidence has been found in Ramsey
materials that the copy was ever identified as a charter.[80] But there is

---

[78] *Girton*, (P R O, SC 2, Port. 179, no. 75): Concordatum est inter dominum et tenentes
suos quod si aliquis tenens aut firmarius huius dominii qui habet terras seu tenementa
custumaria ad voluntatem domini per copiam aut ad firmam scandalizat, litigat, obsurgat
vel falsat aliquem tenentem de aliquo veredicto seu presentatione aut (pri)vilegio in curia
et lete huius dominii presentato, quod ipse qui inventus fuit in tali defectu per sufficientem et legittimum testimonium aprobatum perdat, amittat et disonerabitur de huius-
modo terris, tenementis, pratis, pasturis que tenet de domino huius manerii tam per copiam
quam ad firmam sine gracia domini fine vel redemptione domino facto, etc.
[79] *Ellington*, (B M, Add. Ch. 34310): Preceptum est omnibus tenentibus domini per
copias rotulorum curie quod repereant tenementa sua bene et sufficienter citra festum
Pentecoste proximo anno sequenti cuilibet tenenti predicto sub pena xxs.
[80] See, however, the Therfield entry for 1486 (P R O, SC 2, Port. 179, no. 73): Et quod
Johannes Lewyn tenet sine copia xiii acras terre ex concessione propria. Ideo in miseri-

repeated evidence, especially by the sixteenth century, that the customary tenant had a document called a copy. Did the copy become a sort of indenture arrangement, whereby the tenant had a charter similar to the entry on the court roll?[81] In the 1473 entries for Shillington the tenants were spoken of as having copies (*habet copiam*). After the dissolution of Ramsey Abbey, tenants of Hemmingford Abbots were gathered together in 1545 to be enfeoffed and to swear fealty to a new lord. Following the names of free tenants, and of tenants by copy, the court roll of this manor for 1545 lists several persons 'who hold by copy and seek a day to exhibit their copies at the next court' (tenent per copiam qui petunt diem ad monstrandum copias ad proximam curiam).[82] A court summons issued in English, apparently for the vill of Bury (near Ramsey) on October 9, 1540, shows a similar form: 'I pray you warne the kyngs courte to be kept at By(ry) Lukes day next and that the tenants have their copyes and their (   ) and all other thyngs register for the same, and that all the tenants (both free ?) and copyeholders be warned to be there to (be) sworn and be they servants to the king...'[83]

While copyhold was concerned with the traditional servile tenure, the position of the customary tenant was far different in 1450 from that of his forbears of the previous centuries, and the formula adopted by the copyhold entry reflected mid-fifteenth-century conditions. A brief formula of entry *per copiam* was adopted on all Ramsey manors that at first glance is difficult to distinguish from the traditional freehold conveyance. Whereas the Court Book spelled out in the ancient formula that customary lands were 'servile tenements held in bondage at the will of the lord for customary services and obligations,'[84] the copyhold entry gradually omitted any reference to servility. In the late fifteenth century references to 'servile' land and to tenure 'in bondage' seems to practically disappear,[85] and by

---

cordia et preceptum est ut prosequatur pro cap'. Et quantum ad messuagium cum quinque acris terre utrum tenet per cartam vel ne ignorant, inde petunt diem ut possunt recurrere ad registrum domini abbatis ad inquerendum, etc.

81 Such would seem to be the case in the text cited in footnote 87 below.

82 P R O, SC 2, Port. 178, no. 88.

83 B M, Add. Ch. 34378.

84 In the Court Book entries for tenements of St. Ives, however, a formula is frequently employed in the second quarter of the fifteenth century that expresses the lord's right to remove the tenant for failure in maintenance or payment of rents 'hac copia non obstante'.

85 Sample texts :

Shillington, 1473 (B M, Add. Ch. 39656): Leefchild habuit copiam de certa terra sibi dimissa et clamata per uxorem suam et quia non reperabit messuagium suum prout habuit in pena diversis vicibus, ideo dominus per Matheum Chaumbre prepositum suum intrabat et inde per se concessit copiam Willelmo Goodman qui quidem Willelmus inde habet copiam tenendum secundum consuetudinem manerii.

Et quod Margareta Toprest in Ecclesia de Shitlyngton coram Matheo Chawmbre ballivo domino et omnibus parochianis ibidem existentibus X° die Novembre anno R Edwardi IIII[to]

the sixteenth century the court rolls frequently have clipped entries of term, rent, and fine only. Obviously, of course, such properties could be as readily let to freemen as to villeins, and there is no evidence from court rolls of the second half of the fifteenth century and later that freemen and outsiders were discouraged from holding customary lands. It is dangerous to emphasize too much the form of court roll entries, since these may often have been abbreviated for convenience whereas fuller entries were made elsewhere. But the court book as it has survived ends about the time copyholds began to be mentioned, and as we shall see below, sixteenth-century lawsuits were interested in searching the court rolls for copyhold entries, so the court rolls appear to have been the final records from the mid-fifteenth century.

The copyhold shaded toward freehold in another way. Whereas custom-ary tenure was traditionally designated as simply 'at the will of the lord and according to the custom of the manor,' the copyholder received land for his heirs and assignees (*heredibus et assignatis suis*).[86] Again the emphasis

---

XII relaxabat quietum clamavit et sursum reddidit ad usum Ricardi Eton totum ius titulum et interesse quod habuit de se in uno messuagio cum X acris terre vocate Matilde Fullers iacentis in Shittlynton predicta, qui quidem Ricardus Eton ex gratia curie inde habet copiam tenendum sibi secundum consuetudinem manerii ibidem.
Upwood, 1534 (B M, Add. Ch. 39661): Ad hanc curiam venit Johannes Leche senior et cepit extra manerium domini unum messuagium cum una virgata terre tribus clausuris et uno pitello modo in tenura Ricardi Wilfey, cui dominus concessit seisinam habendam et tenendam sibi heredibus et assignatis ad voluntatem domini secundum consuetudinem manerii. Reddendo inde domino annuatim ad terminos usuales in xxvis. viiid. et faciat omnia alia onera servitia et consueta inde prius debita et dat de fine ut in capite (finis, vis. viiid.) et fecit fidelitatem, etc. (copia).
Barton, 1493 (B M, Add. Ch. 39731). Thomas Spaldyng sursum reddidit, etc. ad opus Thome Goldsmyth unum cotlandum cum pertinentiis habendum, etc. reddendum, etc. xixd. Et faciat, etc. Et dat domino tam de herietto quam gersuma ii capones et fecit fidelitatem. (copia)
86 The most continuous extant series of conveyance entries over this period is from the chamberlain's book for his Lawshall manor (Add. Ms. 33450, pp. 18-53d.). In these the following periods are found: 1392-3 to 1400-1 thirty-four entries (twenty-six in bondage at the will of the lord; two for ten years; one for life at the will of the lord; remainder not clear); 1402-3 to 1455-6, (139 entries, 119 in heredity, 15 for life, 1 for 2 years, 4 not clear); 1455-6 to 1526-7, (36 entries — all to heirs and assignees).
The abbey chamberlain also had scattered small holdings in Ramsey village, St. Ives and the adjacent manor of Slepe, Wistow, and Walton. From 1392-3 until 1486-7 of the fifty-five conveyances, thirty-three were for life and twenty-three were for terms (usually of around ten years until the 1450's and thereafter around twenty years). It may be recalled that a policy of life or twenty-year lease began to be widely adopted in place of traditional tenure on Ramsey manors from the 1370's, see *Estates*, pp. 259-60. From 1489-90 the entry form 'to heirs and assignees' begins to be found, although the longer term rather than the grant to heirs remained common. The terms for the thirty-seven entries between 1489-90 and 1538-9 show a tendency to lengthen, as we see from the following (in chrono-logical sequence): heirs; life; 40 years; 60 years; 21 years; 40 years; 101 years; 30 years; life; 120 years; life; 105 years; 63 years; 57 years; 42 years; life; 49 years; 42 years; 58 years; heirs; 60 years; 106 years; 106 years; 106 years; heirs (ten entries); 20 years; heirs; life.
The term *copia* is first employed in the above entries in 1450-1, and thereafter occurs

is shifted to the action of the tenant, therefore, and away from the will of
the lord and manorial inheritance customs, although there is no evidence
to suggest that this made any practical difference to the traditional 'right
by blood' of the villager. The implications of the introduction of the word
'assignees' to customary tenure are possibly more revolutionary. In
traditional freehold the right to assign meant the right to sublet. The
complete lack of evidence of fines for the illegal subletting of customary
lands, and the lack of reference to licences to sublet in the second half of
the fifteenth century, would indicate free subletting of customary tenements
also. Once the lord's demesne had been farmed there was no practical
reason to forbid subletting of villeinage, and so customary lands must have
moved freely in the local time lease market.[87]

The evolution of customary tenure over the fifteenth century on Ramsey
estates was dramatically underlined in the second quarter of the sixteenth

frequently. The 1450-1 entry is concerned with the letting of eight and one-half acres of
meadow with one-half acre of arable and concludes (fol. 36d): Et si redditus predictus in parte
vel in toto aretrus fuerit non solutus per sex septimas post aliquod tempus quo solvere
debeat aut si idem Johannes aliquid accomptavit quod aveneat in prejudicium abbatis de
Rameseye confratrum vel tenentium suorum quod tunc liceat camerario predicto qui pro
tempore fuerit in dicto prato et terre remittere et de eisdem disponere pro voluntate sua
hac copia non obstante.
87 The lord would, of course, continue to require a view and nominal licence for
subletting in order to prevent absolute alienation of customary land as freehold. The
most detailled copyhold entry I have been able to obtain is from the Norwich Register,
and well illustrates the above remarks: (p. 126) Hec copia indentata facta decimo die
mensis Maii Anno R. Henrici sexti post conquestum trecesimo septimo et anno domini
Johannis Stowe Abbatis XXIIII°. Johannes Weston cepit de domino rensionem unius tenementi ibidem quod nuper fuit in tenura Radulphi Osborne et unius tenementi nuper
Johannis Michell; que quidem tenementa Ricardus Weston pater eiusdem Johannis et Johanna
uxor eius per copiam ad terminum vite sue ad voluntatem domini secundum consuetudinem manerii habendum et tenendum rensionem tenementorum predictorum, post
decessum predictorum Ricardi et Johanne eidem Johanni Weston et assignatis suis ad
voluntatem domini secundum consuetudinem manerii a die obito predictorum Ricardi et
Johanne uxoris sue usque ad finem et terminum octoginta et nonedecim annorum extunc
proximum et immediate sequentem. Reddendo inde domino per annum pro tenemento
nuper Radulphi Osborne xiid. et pro tenemento nuper Johannis Michell duos solidos ad
terminos manerii usuales et faciendum omnia alia servitia debita et consueta durante dicto
termino. Predictus Johannes Weston et sui assignati dictum tenementum domos et edificia
eorum de anno in annum substentabunt et reperabunt bene et sufficienter eorum propriis
expensis durante dicto termino. Et non licebit dicto Johanni nec suis assignatis dictum
tenementum postquam ius sive titulus eis vel eorum alicui in eisdem accrevere vendere
alienare legare vel assignare sine licentia domini unde petita et obtenta. Ita quod quilibet
tenens post ipsum Johannem successurum ante aliquo eius ingressu in dicto placea
seu tenementa, admittatur per annum et per copiam secundum consuetudinem manerii, et
solvet de certe pro fine sue sex denarios vel duos caponos sub pena amissionis sui statui.
Et si predictus redditus in parte vel in toto aretatus fuit insolutus per quindecim post
aliquod terminum quo solveri debetur aut si idem Johannes vel aliquis alius tenens
deficit in sustentacione ac reparacione domorum tenementorum predictorum ut predictum
est, tunc bene licebit domino et ministris suis in predicto tenemento reintrare ut in pristino
statu suo hac copia non obstante. Et dat domino de fine hac prima vice duos caponos.

century when tenants by copyhold at Abbots Ripton claimed tenure by 'fee simple, fee taile' and full rights to the use of wood on their properties. The counter charge by the new lords of Abbots Ripton, Sir John and his son Oliver Saint John, was basically a claim to traditional rights of the lord over customary tenure. But in his counter charge Oliver Saint John attempted to prove that the copyhold was an innovation of only twenty years standing, and he thereby tacitly admitted that tenure by copy had become more than customary tenure. The meaning of copyhold, not of customary tenure, was the core of the case. Both parties, the one explicitly, the other tacitly, admitted that copyhold had become a form of fee simple. In a way this was to say that tenure by fee simple had arisen under customary law. It is most fortunate that the evidence collected for the ensuing lawsuit between Saint John and his tenants has been preserved. This evidence throws much light upon the confusion concerning the tenure by copy in the 1540's;[88] it also provides an interesting account of conveyance procedure in Ramsey courts by the former steward of the abbey and his assistants. Finally, we get a lively picture of the embittered tactics employed by the lord and stubborn tenants prior to more legal processes. Since the evidence is largely in a clear, forceful English, it is presented in Appendix XXXVI with as little comment as possible.

The lawsuit was resolved at Abbots Ripton in favour of the lord. And the future pattern is clear for former Ramsey properties. From court rolls throughout the remaining years of the sixteenth century it is clear that tenants failed to establish freehold on customary lands. The very few freeholders in the former Ramsey villages of Huntingdonshire in the polls of the early nineteenth century signal the long history that still lay ahead for customary tenure.

---

[88] In his recent book *Copyhold, Equity, and the Common Law* (Cambridge, Mass., 1963), Charles Montgomery Gray gives a valuable description of how the common lawyers gradually came to protect copyhold over the sixteenth century. Not surprisingly, therefore, many matters familiar to the manorial courts began to appear in common law records of the sixteenth century. The early complaints in chancery cited by Gray (*ibid.*, pp. 26-31) are familiar to manorial court rolls of the thirteenth and fourteenth centuries. Or, the one year lease and subletting by licence under the copyholder that were upheld in common law by the 1580's (*ibid.*, pp. 65-6), we have seen flourishing in the late thirteenth century courts of Ramsey manors. But, as Gray points out (*ibid.*, pp. 76-92), the common lawyers failed to reconstruct the status of copyhold upon a historical basis. So the question of first importance for the history of the village remains, not how many pleas were entertained in common law courts from the fifteenth century, but why did the manorial court become insufficient to uphold customary law? No doubt the failure of fifteenth and sixteenth-century lawyers to turn their discussions of copyhold upon the decline and disappearance of villeinage encouraged the too abstract arguments upon the origin of copyhold.

CHAPTER X

THE VILLAGE COMPLEX

THERE were two silent revolutions in the social history of the villager in mediaeval England: the emancipation of the slave, and the emancipation of the serf. No dramatic recognition was given by men of the time to the disappearance of the numerous slaves of Domesday Book by the twelfth century, or to the fact that the fifteenth-century copyholder, who succeeded to the villein long identified as unfree by servile burdens, might be freeman or naif. These revolutions were silent because they developed through the custom of village life itself rather than through the 'public' laws of the age, either common or canon. As mediaeval writers were fond of saying, custom 'is a certain law established by what is done.' It was in the pragmatic decisions of daily life, rather than through ideas, programmes, and reformers, that these silent revolutions found their course.

At first custom appears less than kind to the efforts of the historian to unravel its history. That is to say, a social historian approaches the history of villeinage with difficulty because, in the usual categories of social history, villeinage is a stage of transition. Neither slave, nor freeman, the villein has elusive characteristics: remarkably stable in his rights, yet personally dependent; possessing a secure tenure in land, yet with no real title to property; surprisingly mobile, yet with the most localized of 'citizenships.'

Upon closer examination, however, these apparent paradoxes tend to soften and indeed to disappear. For this closer examination it is an *a priori* requirement that the categories applied to customary life by common lawyers be avoided, and that the mechanism of works and services detailed in manorial surveys be not taken as the sole central framework of village life. Even in the economic ordering of the 'manorial economy' itself there was a balance that set limits to the exploitation of tenants, lands, and capital. More works and services from a villager implied a larger tenement with more numerous livestock. The lord's labour requirements for his demesne were resolved through the peasants' demand for land. It was the peasants' demand for land that made possible the substitution of serf for slave labour, and that made possible the great continuity of the demesne economy. Until the fifteenth century, every change in manorial organization is a tribute to the vital persistence of the peasants' demand for land:

the direct management of his demesne by the lord, or the indirect management through his villagers; the payment of villein services, or their commutation; the clearing or draining of new smallholds, and its enclosure into the large fields; the concentration of lands among villagers, or the scattering of smallholdings from demesne and villeinage among many villagers.

Undoubtedly the peasants' love for land remained so strongly directed towards the villeinage because customary tenure was built into the family community. Villeins on Ramsey villages in the thirteenth century were far removed from those eleventh-century slaves and smallholders in England who received land and stock from the lord but gave up the same upon their decease.[1] At least by the thirteenth century,[2] customary tenure allowed that the villager in many manors should bequeath his chattels by will, and that various persons in every village had a right by blood to their tenements. The anomalies in the legal formula of customary tenure by 'will of the lord' can only be properly perceived in the wide variety of family claims by blood to the tenement, and in the wide variety of rights instituted in the tenement by the villager himself through maintenance arrangements, life leases, and subletting.

In fact by many of these arrangements the family community shaded into the village society. The open field system brought villagers together in a system of co-operative agriculture. While villein services required work on the demesne, all the villagers — free and unfree — must work together to repair roads and ditches. In the enactment and enforcement of local byelaws free and unfree were *de facto* peers. These villagers were capable of adapting all types of institutions to their own use: reeve and beadle were not merely officials of the lord, but servants of their fellow villagers; the pledge was not just a legal extension of the kinship bond, but became a legal tool for cohesion in the village; the *villata* was not only a village unit responsible under the public law of frankpledge, but the *villata* was adapted to their own purposes by customaries. It is small wonder that no status barriers to marriage existed among free and unfree in the local community. The picture was further complicated by the desire and capacity of the villein to buy freehold, and the desire and capacity of the freeman to hold villeinage.

---

[1] See *Rectitudines Singularum Personarum, English Historical Documents* (London, 1953; editors, D. C. Douglas, and G. W. Greenaway), pp. 813-14.

[2] While the traditional view associating alienability and heredibility with the social movements from the Black Death (e.g. Plucknett, *Year Books*, 13 Richard II, *op. cit.*, pp. XXXV-VI) is untenable, it is no more possible to prove that these rights of villeins began with the thirteenth century. Contractual rights are clear for villeins from the thirteenth century, but what was prior to the written survey? The twelfth-century villager may have depended more upon the will of the lord for practical decisions, but at the same time the community spirit of the villagers themselves may very easily have been much more vital in the twelfth century than later.

Our sources are not inclined to show the interaction among the legal, social, and economic segments of the village community. Through rights of inheritance and maintenance arrangements we see only one level of activity in the kinship complex; through ordinances governing common rights we see administrative arrangements of the manorial economy, but little of the 'community spirit' invigorating co-operative activity. Between kinship ties and economic co-operation comes neighbourliness, of which we know very little. It is even difficult to isolate priorities of law. The lord, like the king in his system of law, had a final jurisdiction; and it was the lord's officials (reeve, beadle, court steward, etc.) who provided much of the administrative arm for village law. But in the actual daily practice of the village the lord was one landholder among many whose rights must be protected. Works and services owed to the lord's demesne were only one type of the many contractual obligations in the village that must be enforced. If there was a law demanding conveyance of land through the lord's court, and a law demanding payment of services to the lord, there were also laws governing family rights of inheritance to property, and rights of maintenance from property. A continued study of village byelaws reveals increasingly how the dynamism of these regulations was from below rather than imposed from above by the lord.[3]

In part our knowledge of social relations in the village has been limited by the nature of the sources available. In particular, if the most detailed court rolls of the late thirteenth and early fourteenth centuries had come at the same time as the detailed extents of the mid-thirteenth century, or had even been contemporary to the account rolls of the early fifteenth century, then tenurial structure (Chapter One) could have been compared more closely with familial (Chapter Two) and commercial relations (Chapter Three).[4] On the other hand, the various village activities, studied in Chapter Four for example, fail to reveal a fixed formula of activities, or a tendency to formalism in decisions. So the very limitations of the court rolls tend to reveal the highly developed complexity of the village social order. Whether it be in the lack of explicit dependence of the village ordinance upon the lord's decision, or in the failure of the court record to show a dependence of the ordinance upon neighbourhood or kinship ties, a well-developed social organization is implied. It was this development

---

[3] From the multiple resolution of personal, familial, and property rights, much could be said for a description of the manorial court as a court of equity. After the decline of the manorial court, perhaps it was no accident that 'equity rather than chancery was more liable, and in the long run did come to the relief of the customary tenant' (Plucknett, *op. cit.*, p. XL).

[4] In more sophisticated terms these three divisions approximate the ecological, ethnological, and economic.

and great complexity that permitted multiple change in village life without destruction.

*
* *

What acquaintance have the court rolls thus far given us with the persons of the villagers ? The history of the movement of villagers serves to emphasize how villein condition turned so essentially about tenure in villeinage. Once the peasant was detached from the local customary tenement, he (or she) became for practical purposes a part of a wider social economy. The failure to have a customary tenement was not in itself an adequate reason for the villager to leave his native home, since there is no evidence that able-bodied persons willing to work were 'prohibited the vill', and various welfare services tended to the needs of non-able-bodied. However, all evidence seems to indicate that the villagers did not consider their native village a closed social and economic unit. One would hesitate to say that there were more marriages beyond the manor after 1400 than around 1300; one would hesitate to say that the villager moved beyond the manor with more reticence in the thirteenth century than in the fifteenth. If each person manumitted in the fifteenth century represented a family of four, there may have been some three hundred persons freed over this time. But the more important point is the relative insignificance of this figure (most easily seen on an annual basis), not only against the data for periods of heaviest exodus from the village in the late thirteenth or early fifteenth century, but against the regular movements from the village from the thirteenth century for marriage, holy orders, crafts, or misdemeanors. Tenure, rather than a static village, was the core of villeinage.

Did tenure in villeinage create in turn a nuclear family in the village ? That is to say, did not hereditary tenure by blood form 'stable, typical, and accepted' foci of unity in the village as against the outside family — 'mobile, unsettled, and unpropertied' ? Pilot samplings in an effort to isolate nuclear families from several villages have so far been unsuccessful. This may be largely owing to the fact that the clipped account-roll entries are inadequate to trace blood ties of new tenants in the late thirteenth and in the fourteenth centuries. A full tabulation of the thousands of villagers' names over the fourteenth and fifteenth centuries may eventually reveal important nuclear groupings.[5] At the same time it is clear that sons of tenants were not the last to leave their native manors under the pressure of

---

[5] It is hoped that such an exhaustive demographic analysis may be completed in the future.

economic conditions in the late thirteenth century. In so far as we have evidence, the concentration of lands on the manor from this time was by individuals, or groups of individual customaries, rather than through an extension of family ties. The willingness of customary tenants to hire for labour men or women off the road at this period also suggests that the villager may have looked more to the open village labour market than to blood relatives in the use of his greater freedom of disposition of labour once the lord began a regular policy of commuting work owed on the demesne. It is the small modern family — man, wife, and children — that appears uniquely in village documents of the fifteenth century. Economic individualism may have penetrated as deeply into the village community family as into the lord's economic organization from the thirteenth century !

Further observations may be made along these lines with respect to the organized village community. The *villata* that appears in fourteenth-century documents was less and less the whole village communal body that had been represented in the view of frankpledge or as a vital unit of the lord's jurisdiction in the thirteenth century. Equally significant, the *villata* that was a commercial confraternity gradually became displaced by smaller groups of customary tenants in the fourteenth century. Far more startling for the social historian than the commutation of villein services in the fourteenth century, is the fact that the *villata* failed to replace the lord in the management of the manorial economy from the fourteenth century as they had done in earlier times. When the remnants of the village demesnes were finally farmed in the fifteenth century, they were in all instances farmed to one or two men rather than to groups of villagers.

It is important for our understanding of village history over this time to stress that the villagers first deliberately deserted villages before the problem of deserted villages was to arise. While there were no deserted villages on Ramsey properties, a vital village economy failed to develop in place of the manorial economy. This is most clearly seen in the problem of waste and dilapidation in the village. The most easily established charge against the tenants of Abbots Ripton by Sir John Saint John in 1544 was the charge of dilapidation. This problem of waste had persisted for one hundred and fifty years, but it could not remain in the new economic spirit of the sixteenth century. The charge of inefficiency that would finally bring to an end the open field system itself weakened the customary tenants in the face of the new commercial spirit of their lords.

Can we extend the question further: what type of man was the villager whose life we have been studying ? Upon the basis of the classical historical

concept of the mediaeval villager, certain social psychologists find that he
was 'chained to his role in the social order'.[6] At the centre of this classical
concept is 'the immobility of land and labour.'[7] While it seems indisputable
that, 'The origin of this fixity of factor combinations lay in the vested
interest which every peasant had in the conforming behaviour of his
fellows',[8] the exact meaning of conforming behaviour is still far from clear.
Certainly from the history of Ramsey villages immobility of resources does
not in itself require conformity, in view of the presence of a new agricultural
frontier until the thirteenth century, and the tradition of peasant mobility
from the thirteenth century.

Perhaps more important than structural determinants, however, is
that *lack* of an anxiety complex that more subtle investigations are now
able to attribute to the mediaeval peasant.[9] The court rolls of the villages
studied in this volume lend support to such investigations. The outstanding
feature of the villagers appearing in their records is the very few 'rebels'
as against the many non-conformists. The truculent and instransigent
social rebel who dislikes co-operation occurs only infrequently: that Godfrey
Puskere and Richard Long 'who falsely and maliciously contradicted their
comrades in the taking of the oath' at Wistow in 1301; that Ralph of
Houghton who did not wish to be at scot and lot with his neighbours at
Slepe in 1305; that Robert Jurdon at Abbots Ripton in 1405, 'rebellious
and contrary in court, who contradicted the jurors in this court by his
oath in contempt of the lord and of the court'.

Non-conformity appears through the large number of fines on the court
rolls every year, especially in the detailed records of the thirteenth and
fourteenth centuries. Furthermore, comparison of villagers' names from
year to year on these rolls indicates that non-conformity was of a wide
incidence rather than the repeated performance of the few. The failure to
increase small regular fines must have been an important condition for this
attitude towards the law. Aberrations from the law appear as strongly with
respect to obligations for work on the lord's demesne, or against the assize
of ale, as in the easy encroachment on lands of a neighbour or of the
common, or in civil and criminal violence in personal lives. The very fact
that non-conformity should move against the family, neighbourhood,

---

6 E.g. Erich Fromm, *Escape From Freedom* (New York, 1941), pp. 40 ff.
7 E.g. Walter Firey, *Man, Mind and Land* (The Free Press of Glencoe, Illinois, 1960),
p. 97: "another limitation on the substitutability of productive factors in the open field
complex was the immobility of land and labor. To understand this fixity, we shall have
to consider a feature of the medieval social order that has thus far gone unnoticed. This
is the manor." Firey has, however, made some intersting advances upon our thinking in
this area by the very fact that he started with the village rather than the manor.
8 *Ibid.*, p. 96.
9 E.g. Rollo May, *The Meaning of Anxiety* (New York, 1950), p. 111, note 62.

customaries, as well as against the lord, defies rationalization. The failure of a villager to work on the lord's lands may have been due to the fact that the son of this customary tenant left the domain without the consent of either parent or lord. The carelessness of the alewife certainly redounded most frequently to the expense of her husband who was her pledge. The individuality of the villager escapes easy historical formulation.[10]

[10] At the same time there are many possibilities for biographical studies of villagers after the court rolls have been completely exploited. It may be recalled at this point that the above study has only investigated village life in the two areas of tenure and mobility. But these court rolls provide materials for the study of at least a dozen such major areas of investigation!

APPENDICES

SINCE the following texts are properly considered as excerpts from the court rolls, no attempt has been made to establish complete information on the persons and places mentioned in these texts. Nor has an attempt been made to indicate the wide variety in form of entries. We have tried throughout the volume to capture something of this variety by rather free translations, especially as the excerpts are often merely phrases or lists. However, only by the use of brackets in the following texts have we indicated words or phrases that seem to be understood, or to be doubtful owing to a decayed manuscript, or appear in the margin. In general the endings of formulae have been standardized, as in *sursum reddidit*, or *in manu domini*, although varied forms of even such basic expressions do occasionally appear throughout the rolls. For phrases that are less frequent, the sometimes unusual not to say inconsistent readings have been retained, as long as the meaning is clear. The Latin endings are not usually extended for place names, especially when these are for familiar Ramsey villages. However, an effort has been made to retain Latin and English surnames, and to distinguish descriptive titles (e.g. *prepositus*) from surnames.

APPENDIX I

DIVISION OF THE WASTE AT UPWOOD AND RAVELEY, 1448-9

UPWODE Quedam percella vasti de marisco iacens iuxta le Snapemede anno R.H. VI^{to} XXVII° inclusa (est) pro prato ex assensu domini Abbatis de Rameseye qui est dominus feodi Nicholai Styvecle militis ac Johannis Hore armigeri tenentes dicti Abbatis, que quedam percella mensurata (est) per perticam longitudinis xvi pedes et continet in primo capite versus Ravele lii perticas, in alio capite versus Botnale lxii perticas, in latere versus Walton xi^{xx}. xviii perticas, in alio latere versus Upvale xi^{xx}. ii perticas que faciunt iiii^{xx}. i acras iii rodas dimidiam et x perticas. Quod quidem pratum divisum est in percellis per metas et bundas ut sequitur.

In primis predictus Johannes Hore habebit pro se et tenentibus suis vesturam percelle dicti prati in principio vasti versus Ravele latitudinis in utroque capite xxx perticas per perticas predictas.

Et iuxta predictum Johannem Hore Elemosinarius Rameseye nomine decime habebit iii perticas latitudinis in utroque capite.

Et iuxta predictum Elemosinarium predictus Nicholaus Styvecle miles pro se

et tenentibus suis habebit vesturam alterius percelle latitudinis in utroque capite
xxxiii perticas tam pro manerio quam pro tenemento nuper Johannis de Ravele.

Et iuxta predictum Nicholaum Styvecle Elemosinarius predictus nomine decime
habebit iii perticas et quartam partem unius pertice latitudinis in utroque capite.

Et iuxta predictum Elemosinarium dominus Abbas qui est dominus feodi et solus
ville de Upwode et Ravele cum pertinentiis habebit xiii perticas latitudinis in utroque
capite et non plus quia ex gratia sua remisit et assignavit totum residuum dicti prati
dividendi tenentibus suis ad voluntatem de Upwode et Ravele et eorum sequelis ut
sequitur.

Thomas Newman tenet i virgatam, Johannes Freeston i virgatam, Ricardus
Genge i virgatam, Robertus Newman i virgatam et i quartam, Ricardus Aleyn i
virgatam et i quartam, Johannes Hendesson i virgatam et i quartam, Henricus Skynner dimidiam virgatam, Johannes Aleyn i virgatam, Johannes Bukeworth i virgatam
dimidiam, Johannes Edward i virgatam, Johannes Leche iii quartas, Johannes
Hurre i virgatam, Thomas Peny i virgatam i quartam, Thomas Goular i virgatam,
Willelmus Edward iii quartas, Ricardus Wrghte i quartam, et Ricardus Sewar iii
quartas. Quorum quilibet habebit et singillatim prout stat in ordine pro qualibet
virgata terre ii perticas in utroque capite et sic pro rata si tenet plus plus si minus
minus habebit. (xvi virgatae dimidia)

Et Elemosinarius predictus pro decime de tenentibus nihil habebit de feno sed
nomine fan' de quolibet tenente qui tenet i virgatam terre iid. et de quolibet tenente
qui tenet cotagium inferius id.

RAVELEY Et ex tunc tenentes domini ad voluntatem in Ravele videlicet Willelmus
Cusse i virgatam dimidiam, Walterus Baldok ii virgatas et i quartam, Johannes
Bretham ii virgatas, Johannes Wrghte i virgatam, Thomas Penyman i virgatam
dimidiam, Ricardus Baron i virgatam dimidiam, Willelmus Colleson dimidiam
virgatam, Willelmus Skynner dimidiam virgatam, in manu (domini) quondam
Ricardi Skynner i quartam, et in manu quondam Willelmi Alcok i virgatam. Quorum quilibet habebit singillatim prout stat in ordine pro qualibet virgata ii perticas ut supra.

Et ex tunc quilibet predictorum tenentium domini tam de Upwode quam de
Ravele habebit singillatim prout stat supra in ordine pro qualibet virgate ii perticas in utroque capite et secundum ratam ut superius dictum est.

Et ex tunc tenentes cotagiorum domini ad voluntatem tam de Upwode quam de
Ravele quilibet eorum prout stat in ordine habebit pro quolibet cotagio i perticam
latitudinis in utroque capite et sic pro rata si teneat plus plus si minus minus etc.
videlicet Rogerus Bryne iii cotagia, Johannes Ray ii, Johannes Broronote i, Henricus
Baker i, Johannes Jerken i, Willelmus Love ii, Thomas Newman i, Johannes Hendesson dimidium, Henricus Skynner dimidium, Ricardus Erle i, Thomas Peny dimidium, Johannes Leche i, Johannes Bukworth i, Willelmus Skynner i, Johannes
Bretham i. Et in manu domini quondam Cristine Wilde dimidium, Willelmi
Baylyesman i, Ricardi Fraunceys i, Willelmi Dycon i, Ricardi Attewelle i, Ricardi
Skynner dimidium. Et includuntur in pastura apud Ravele iiii pro quibus iiii cota-
giis nihil de feno assignatur.

Et ex tunc remanet quedam percella in fine dicti vasti versus borean iuxta fossatum
que continet in latitudine in capite versus boscum xviii perticas et in alio capite
versus Walton xvi perticas.

                    (*Ramsey Register*, Norwich Central Library, pp. 126d.-127).

APPENDIX II

APPENDIX II

PROCLAMATION TO THOSE WITH RIGHT TO A TENEMENT

1. WISTOW, (B M, Add. Ch. 39853): Alice Kabe venit in plena curia et reddidit sursum in manu domini dimidium cotlandum quod de eo tenuit in bondagium. Et proclamatum est in curia si quis sit de sanguine qui dictum cotlandum debet tenere, et nullus apparuit. Ideo consideratum est per totam curiam quod totus sanguinis ipsius Alice inde sit exclusus. Et super hoc venit Robertus Molendinarius et gersumat dimidium cotlandum tenendum secundum consuetudinem manerii.

2. ELLSWORTH, (P R O, SC 2, Port. 179, no. 12): Juratores dicunt quod Adam Gravele propinquior heres est Juliane (Segrave). Et quod maius ius habet in crofto quondam dicte Juliane secundum consuetudinem manerii. Qui quidem Adam in plena curie (   ) vocatus est ut dictum croftum habeat. Et non venit. Ideo traditum est dictum croftum Murielle Cane qui dat domino in gersuma pro dicto crofto quatuor solidos ut patet per rotulum gersumarum Ramesiae, plegii, Robertus Russel, (   ) Porter.

3. WARBOYS, (B M, Add. Ch. 39856): Juratores presentant quod Robertus Berenger' qui tenuit i messuagium et i quartum terre et i peciam prati iuxta Boylescroft pro servitiis et consuetudinibus contentis in libro custumario obiit, et quod Johannes filius eius est proximus de sanguine secundum consuetudinem manerii, qui postea venit et gersumavit et fecit fidelitatem.

4. HOUGHTON, (P R O, SC 2, Port. 179, no. 11): Andreas filius Emme electus est ad tenendum et defendendum croftum que fuit Margarete le Hyrde defuncte, qui non venit. Ideo preceptum est quod distringatur cum venerit, etc.

5. ABBOTS RIPTON, (P R O, SC 2, Port. 179, no. 10): Andreas West electus est per juratores ad gersumandum illam dimidiam virgatam terre quam Robertus Sabyn quondam tenuit.

6. CRANFIELD, (P R O, SC 2, Port. 179, no. 32): (Inquisitio de terris in manu domini capiendis). Walterus Rideler, Robertus Wodehall, Simon Coleman, Radulphus Catelin, Johannes Basel, Willelmus Aleyn, qui dicunt super sacramentum suum quod Walterus le Erb abilis et sufficiens est ad capiendum i messuagium, i virgatam terre que quondam fuit Alicie Katelon, sustentabit, etc. secundum consuetudinem manerii etc. Et dat in gersuma (xid., in margin, and stroked out). Fecit fidelitatem.

7. BURWELL, (P R O, SC 2, Port. 179, no. 33): Et quod Robertus Rolf abilis et sufficiens est ad capiendum dimidiam virgatam terre.

8. SHILLINGTON, (P R O, SC 2, Port. 179, no. 7): Et dicunt quod terra Roberti West est in manu domini. Ideo preceptum est preposito prevenire proximam ad illam terram gersumandam citra proximam curiam.

9. HOLYWELL, (P R O, SC 2, Port. 179, no. 10): Dictum est per iuratores quod croftum quondam Willelmi Haconn est in manu domini. Et Robertus Mariot electus est ad illum croftum gersumandum, plegii Willelmus Haconn et Absalonis Gunne.

10. BARTON, (P R O, SC 2, Port. 179, no. 39): Ad istam curiam venit filia et heres

Nicholai Adam et petit se admitti ad hereditatem suam, videlicet ad unum messuagium et unam virgatam terre quod Johannes Richard tenet, quod quidem messuagium et terra sibi defendere debet jure hereditario post decessum Nicholai Adam
patris sui. Et super hoc venit dictus Johannes Richard et dicit quod ad dicta tenementa predicta filia nullum habet ius et petit quod inquiratur per curiam et predicta filia similiter. Et super hoc inquisitio capta in eadem curia qui dicunt
super sacramentum suum quod predictus Nicholaus fuit seisitus de tenementis
predictis, et de servitiis eisdem dictis tenementis pertinentibus per magnum tempus
cessavit, et tenementa predicta reliquit, et sic seisita fuerunt in manu domini pro
servitiis et consuetudinibus per predictum Nicholaum (sic) retractis, unde proclamatione facta in eadem curia, etc. Et sic dimissa fuerunt tenementa predicta predicto
Johanni Richard, tenendum sibi ad voluntatem domini, etc. Et super hoc consideratum est quod predictus Johannes habeat et teneat tenementa predicta sibi secundum
consuetudinem manerii, etc.

11. BURWELL, (P R O, SC 2, Port. 179, no. 52): Adhuc preceptum est seisire in
manu domini xii acras terre quas Johannes Paule nuper tenuit ad terminum vite
sue, quo humato, nullus venit ad calumpniandum eas de etc. Et rendere domino
de exitibus, etc. Et provideret de tenente etc. citra proximam curiam etc.

12. LAWSHALL, (B M, Add. Ms. 33450 p. 21d.): Robertus Jotee in propria persona
sua ad eandem curiam venit et sursum reddidit in manu domini i quartum terre
native cum (mes ?), quondam Johannis Godyng, ad opus Willelmi Godyng, tenendum sibi et sequele sue in bondagium ad voluntatem domini, reddendo domino
annuatim omnia servitia et consuetudines inde debita et consueta secundum consuetudinem manerii. Et custodit et manutenebit idem tenementum sine vasto. Et
fecit domino fidelitatem servitii, et dat domino de gersuma vs. Et sciendum quod
ad curiam tentam apud Lawshall' die (   ) festum Sancte Mathei Apostoli
anno quinto Regis supradicti, proclamatione facta tribus curiis precedentibus,
Johannes filius et heres predicti Johannis Godyng vocatus non venit ad recipien-
dum hereditatem suam, in perpetuum amisit per iudicationem predictam, et super
hoc predictus Robertus Jotee in eadem curia cepit de domino dictum tenementum,
tenendum sibi et heredibus suis secundum consuetudinem manerii prout per rotulos
curie plenius patet.

13. ABBOTS RIPTON, (B M, Add. Ch. 39477) 1405: Et quod unum messuagium
et una virgata terre nuper Willelmi Thedwar sunt in manu domini. Et dictum
messuagium devastatur et terra iacet frisca et inculta etc. Et dicunt quod Johannes
Howlond et Johannes West sunt potentes ad dictum messuagium et terra tenendum.
Et postea dictus Johannes (the entry stops here, and in the margin is the remark
'in manu domini').

14. HOLYWELL, (P R O, SC 2, Port. 179, no. 30) 1340: Totum homagium elegit
Willelmum Bryon ad tenendum illud croftlandum quod Robertus de Riptone quon-
dam tenuit (quod) defectu tenentis fuit in manu domini usque nunc. Et dictus
Robertus nichil dat pro ingressu quia (   ).

APPENDIX III

SUCCESSION BY THE WIDOW

1. SHILLINGTON, (P R O, SC 2, Port. 179, no. 33): Et quod Adam Attewell mortuus est et tenuit i messuagium et ii virgatas terre et pro eo venit i vaccam pretii iiis. nomine herietti. Et dicunt quod Alicia uxor eius prima tenebit predictum tenementum secundum consuetudinem manerii sine gersuma.

2. GRAVELEY, (P R O, SC 2, Port. 179, no. 30): Curia juratorum presentant quod Johannes Underbur' qui de domino tenuit in bondagium dimidiam virgatam terre diem clausit extremum. Et quod Katerina relicta eiusdem tenebit dictam terram ad terminum vite secundum consuetudinem manerii. Et postea Ricardus Lake fecit finem cum domino pro dicta Katerina ducenda in uxorem.

3. SLEPE, (P R O, SC 2, Port. 179, no. 35): Juratores presentant quod Johannes Asplon qui de domino tenuit i virgatam terre in villenagium domini obiit post ultimam curiam. Et Margareta uxor eius que tenet dictam virgatam terre secundum consuetudinem manerii, dat domino de herietto (vs.).

4. HOUGHTON, (P R O, SC 2, Port. 179, no. 35): Et quod Johannes Wald nativus domini qui de domino tenuit i virgatam terre in villenagium, obiit praeter ultimam curiam. Et Margareta uxor eius que tenens vitans dictam terram, dat domino in herietto (viis. vid.).

5. BROUGHTON, (B M, Add. Ch. 39473): Juratores presentant quod Willelmus Abbot qui de domino tenuit unum messuagium et dimidiam virgatam terre native, obiit praeter ultimam (curiam) et Matilda (uxor) tenebit dictam terram secundum consuetudinem manerii. Et dat de herietto ut supra (iis. vid.).

6. OVER, (P R O, SC 2, Port. 179, no. 25): Et dicunt quod Johannes atte Grene qui de domino tenuit in bondagium unum messuagium et unam virgatam terre, diem clausit extremum pro quo venit nomine herietti vs. secundum consuetudinem manerii. Et super hoc venit Agnes uxor eius et tenebit predictum tenementum ad terminum vite sue et fecit fidelitatem. Et invenit plegium videlicet totum homagium ad reparandos et sustentandos domos et tenementum et ad facienda servitia et consuetudines pertinentes ad dictum tenementum.

7. WYTON, (B M, Add. Ch. 34370): Juratores presentant quod quidam Johannes Plombe qui tenuit de domino unum messuagium et ii virgatas et dimidiam terre et prati secundum consuetudinem manerii, obiit post ultimam curiam et dat domino de herietto vs. et uxor sua tenebit dictam tenuram dum vivit sola.

8. BARTON, (B M, Add. Ch. 34370): Et quod Johannes Grene qui tenuit de domino i messuagium et unam virgatam terre cum forlando obiit post ultimam (curiam) et dat domino de herietto unum bovem quem (potest?) quod mittitur usque Rameseye. Et quod Etheldreda uxor eius habebit dotem suam de predicto tenemento.

9. BARTON, (B M, Add. Ch. 34370): Et quod Johannes Hexton qui tenuit de domino unum messuagium bene edificatum et unam virgatam et dimidiam terre obiit post ultimam curiam et dat domino de herietto unum equum quod potest mitti usque Rameseye. Et quod Matilda nuper uxor predicti Johannis habebit dotem de predicto tenemento secundum consuetudinem manerii. Et quod Johanna

Forster est proxima heres ipsius Johannis Hexton ad predictum tenementum. (ideo intret?)

10. BARTON, (B M, Add. Ch. 39473): Et quod Emma (est) uxor Willelmi Roger qui de domino tenuit unum croftlandum continens unam acram (et) obiit praeter ultimam curiam (   ). Emma gersumavit dictam terram et unam acram prati, viiis. provenient de herietto ut vendebitur ad proficuum.

11. BARTON, (P R O, SC 2, Port. 179, no. 59): Juratores dicunt quod Matilda nuper uxor Johannis Roger habebit in dote tres rodas terre de uno messuagio et dimidiam virgatam terre sed nihil habebit de met'. Item eadem Matilda habebit dotem de uno cotagio cum crofto vocato Lynewyk. Item eadem Matilda dimittet Johanni Forster ibidem de principalibus unam ollam emam, unam petellam, i hayre, i fan,' unum bussellum, unam carectam cum rotis, unum aratrum cum ferris propriis, sicut est consuetudo huius ville. Et sic habuerunt Thomas Wylymote, Simon Fraunces, Willelmus Prour, Edwardus Childe, Ricardus Childe, Johannes Prour, Thomas Stoucle, Johannes Prour junior et Hugo Hale et multi alii. Et quia terra non fuit warectata habebit fabas crescentes super le falowe.

12. UPWOOD, (B M, Add. Ch. 34811): Et quod Robertus del Hill qui de domino tenuit in bondagium unum croftlandum, continens ii acras, diem clausit, etc. Et quod Elena relicta eiusdem tenebit eandem terram ad terminum vite sue secundum consuetudinem etc. sine herietto. Et faciet consuetudines, etc.

13. UPWOOD, (B M, Add. Ch. 34810): Per iuratores presentatum est (quod) Stephanus le Wrce nativus domini qui de domino tenuit i messuagium et ii terras in bondagium diem clausit extremum. Et super hoc venit Agnes relicta eiusdem Stephani et clamat dictam terram esse suam ad terminum vite sue secundum consuetudinem manerii. Et concessum est ei. Et facit fidelitatem, etc.

14. GRAVELEY, (P R O, SC 2, Port. 179, no. 11): Willelmus Barun et Walterus ad Portam sunt plegii Alicie uxoris Walteri Barun de decem solidis solvendis domino medietatem ad Natalem Domini proximo futurum et residuum ad Pascham sequentem pro terra sua tenenda usque festum Sancti Michaelis proximum futurum. Quia quedam terra capta fuit in manu domini pro eo quod Walterus vir eius predictus iter cepit ad terram Jerosalymam sine licentia domini. Et quod (   ) interim servitia inde debita et consueta in omnibus.

15. WARBOYS, (B M, Add. Ch. 34342): Et dicunt quod Agnes Faber vidua que tenet de domino dimidiam virgatam terre convicta est in capitulo super fornicationem cum Ricardo Ingram. Ideo capiatur terra sua in manu domini et de exitibus domino respondeatur donec, etc. Et postea fecit finem pro xxs. plegius Willelmus prepositus.

16. GIRTON, (P R O, SC 2, Port. 179, no. 7): Et dicunt quod Matilda Warewyk relicta Roberti Warewyk convicta est in capitulo super fornicationem cum Roberto Corebes et ibidem perdidit catalla domini. Ideo capiatur terra in manu domini. Et respondeatur de exitibus. Fecit finem pro iiis. cum camerario ut dicit prepositus. (This last sentence is added later).

17. ABBOTS RIPTON, (P R O, SC 2, Port. 179, no. 10): De Margarete Balle quia retraxit arruram domini de sex sellionis. Misericordia condonatur quia terra sua capta est in manu domini. (preceptum est)
Et dicunt quod Alicia atte Dam tenet dimidiam virgatam terre nec facit servitia

predicte terre debita nec sustinet domos. Et postmodum invenit plegios ad omnia predicta facta videlicet Johannem le Bonde et Willelmum filium Johannis prepositi.

Andreas Bonde et Johannes de Hyrst fuerunt plegii Alicie atte Dam quod intraret et teneret illam placeam quam gersumavit de Fratre Reginaldo de Castro in Wenyngton' pro ii solidis annui redditus, et nichil inde solvit nec residens fuit in illa placea. Ideo preceptum est quod dicti denarii leventur de supradictis plegiis. Et sic de anno in annum donec, etc.

18. Houghton, 1402 (P R O, SC 2, Port. 179, no. 47): Item presentatum quod Johannes Aylmar qui de domino tenuit i messuagium et i virgatam terre servilis obiit post ultimam curiam. Et super hoc venit Juliana que fuit uxor predicti Johannis et clamat tenere tenementa predicta per servicia et consuetudines ad terminum vite sue secundum consuetudinem manerii. Et admissa est salvo iure cuiuslibet. Et dat domino de herietto vs.

APPENDIX IV

Entry to Property by Marriage to a Woman

1. Wistow, (B M, Add. Ch. 39856): Juratores presentant quod Willelmus Sabyn ingressus est ad Matildam relictam Andree Sabyn virgatarii, et gersumavit et fecit fidelitatem.

2. Girton, (P R O, SC 2, Port. 179, no. 16): Testatum fuit in ultimo visu quod quidam Willelmus de Ten'esham extraneus intravit in uno messuagio et x acris terre servilis per gersumam ad Julianem que fuit uxor Roberti de Warewyk nativi et quia dictus Willelmus liber et extraneus est preceptum fuit capere predictum messuagium cum terra in manu domini et respondere de exitibus. Ideo preceptum est Galfrido preposito respondere domino de uno quartero et dimidio frumenti uno quartero et dimidio ordei et de duobus quarteris fabarum et pisarum de exitibus dicte terre provenientibus. Et adhuc teneatur dicta terra ut supra donec etc.

3. King's Ripton, (B M, Add. Ch. 34336): Compertum est quod Katerina que fuit uxor Johannis de Ramesia tenentis de domino tria quarteria terre et unum messuagium in Ryptone Regis, maritavit se cuidam Rogero de Kenlawe extraneo sine licentia domini. Ideo preceptum est quod tota terra predicta capiatur in manu domini nisi idem Rogerus de domino abbate citra festum Sancta Martini possit licenciari.

4. Gidding, (P R O, SC 2, Port. 179, no. 7): Et dicunt quod Sarra le Monek tenuit unum cotagium de domino abbate ad quod cepit virum de homagio domini Reginaldi le Grey. Ideo dictum cotagium fuit captum in manu domini per prepositum de Gyddinge qui super boscum domi eiusdem Sarre pendidit i seruram et dicta Sarra venit et fregit dictam seruram cum i lapide et fecit hamsoken. Ideo in misericordia, plegius Johannes Monek. Et quia maritavit se sine licentia domini, ideo distringatur ad faciendum finem pro gersuma. Et nichilominus capiatur dictum messuagium in manu domini et de exitibus respondeatur. Et predicta Sarra in misericordia vid.

5. Burwell, (P R O, SC 2, Port. 179, no. 16): Willelmus Swyn et Hugo Edward sunt plegii Elene filie Willelmi Prime que tenet de domino unum messuagium cum crofto et tres acras terre, quod non maritabit se alicui nisi de feodo domini.

6. CRANFIELD, (P R O, SC 2, Port. 179, no. 32): Ricardus Taillour et Ricardus Milneward se fidelitatem (faciunt) et cognoscunt se tenere de domino ad terminum vite uxorum suarum ii messuagia dimidiam acram terre de iure uxorum suarum, et dant domino pro ingressu xid.

Laurentius de Bartone dat domino pro ingressu habendo in uno messuagio et dimidia virgate terre ad Isabellam Aleyn. Dat gersumam (iis.).

Willelmus Attehurst dat domino pro ingressu habendo in uno messuagio et i acre de penilondo ad Margaretam quondam uxorem Simonis Attecros, et dat in gersumam (xld.).

Willelmus Aleyn cepit de domino i messuagium, i quartam terre quondam Roberti Godhale. Dat in gersumam (xld.).

Rogerus Longe dat domino pro ingressu habendo ad Ceciliam Attefeld in uno messuagio et iii quarteria terre quondam Willelmi Wykyng. Et dat in gersumam (Ls. cancelled, with remark 'quia nichil gersumat'). Tenendum secundum consuetudinem manerii etc., fecit fidelitatem, plegius Willelmus Heryng.

7. HEMMINGFORD ABBOTS, (P R O, SC 2, Port. 179, no. 32): Juratores presentant quod Willelmus Warde ingressus est ad Christinam Carter virgatariam, et gersumat.

Et quod Alanus Syer ingressus est ad Matildam White virgatariam, et gersumat. Preceptum est distringere pro fidelitate.

Et quod Willelmus Trappe virgatarius obiit et Matilda relicta eiusdem tenebit etc. et villata habebit heriettum.

8. HOUGHTON, (P R O, SC 2, Port. 179, no. 33): De Johanne Whryghte pro ingressu habendo ad Emmam Bedill in i messuagium et i virgatam terre, et dat in gersuma iiid.

APPENDIX V

MAINTENANCE ARRANGEMENTS

1. WISTOW, (B M, Add. Ch. 39757): Convictum est per juratores quod Johannes Catelyn evicit Elenam Martyn de quadam domo quam tenuit ad terminum vite sue secundum consuetudinem manerii, et illam domum postea prostravit. Ideo ipse in misericordia xiid., plegii Henricus Thedwar et Johannes Whyte. Et per eosdem plegios reedificabit dictam domum competenter citra festum Paschae proximo futurum. Et interim inveniet ei congruum hospicium in quo possit manere usque dictum terminum Paschae.

2. UPWOOD, (B M, Add. Ch. 34802): Galfridus Hales reddidit sursum etc. unum messuagium et duas acras terre ad opus Thome filii sui sicut patet per rotulos gersumarum etc. in anno preterito, habendum et tenendum post mortem predicti Galfridi, ita tamen quod idem Thomas interim habeat unam cameram in predicta terra ad libitum suum vivente dicto Galfrido, etc.

3. UPWOOD, (B M, Add. Ch. 34802): Nicholaus filius Ade similiter reddidit sursum, etc. unam virgatam terre ad opus Johannis filii sui sicut patet per rotulos gersumarum, etc. Ita quod dictus Nicholaus habeat in predicta terra hospicium rationabilium ad terminum vite sue. Et predictus Johannes concessit solvere eidem Nicholao annuatim ad terminum vite sue unam ringam frumenti, unam ringam ordei ad Natalicium, unam ringam frumenti, et unam ringam avenae, etc.

4. WARBOYS, (B M, Add. Ch. 39762): Et quod Stephanus le Smyth non sustinet matrem suam secundum conventionem inter eos factam, ideo ipse in misericordia vid. Et postea predicti juratores ordinaverunt quod dicta terra retro datur matri sue et quod illam teneat ad terminum vite sue. Ita quod dictus Stephanus non se incrementeat de dicta terra per totam vitam matris sue.

5. WARBOYS, (P R O, SC 2, Port. 179, no. 31): Placitum inter Bochardum Rolf petentem et Willelmum le Loonge tenentem de una virgata terre servilis in Caldecote quondam Willelmi Rolf patris dicti Bochardi, in hac forma conquiescitur, videlicet, quod predictus Bochardus percipiet annuatim ad totam vitam suam de predicto Willelmo le Loonge i ringam frumenti, ii bussellos drageti et ii bussellos pisarum. Habebit et idem Bochardus ad totam vitam suam unam acram terre de dicta virgata unde dimidia acra iacet in Harewele nunc inbladata cum frumento. Habebit et idem Bochardus vesturas dicte acre terre hoc anno, allocando eidem Willelmo le Loonge semine super eandem acram seminantem per considerationem vicinorum. Et preterea predictus Bochardus habebit ad terminum vite sue post mortem matris sue illud messuagium cum domo super edificata quod mater sua nunc inhabitat. Et licet idem Bochardus uxorem ducat, nichilominus dicta quartum bladi, acra terre, et messuagium ad totam vitam suam optinebit. Et post mortem eiusdem Bochardi omnia predicta quartum bladi, acra terre, et messuagium, prefato Willelmo et successoribus suis integre revertantur, ita quod uxor nec filii eiusdem Bochardi nichil inde percipiant. Et pro predictis, quarto bladi, una acra terre, et messuagio ut premittitur ei optinendo, idem Bochardus sursum reddidit et quietum clamavit eidem Willelmo le Loonge et heredibus suis totum ius et clamium quod in dicta virgata terre quovismodo eidem Bochardo peterit contingere in futurum.

6. ELLINGTON, (P R O, SC 2, Port. 179, no. 4): Willelmus Koc recognoscit quod de blado patri suo debito fuit in arreragium de anno (   ) frumenti, i busellum ordei et i busellum fabarum et pisarum. Et de anno presenti de termino Sancti Michaelis ultimo preterito (   ) frumenti, iii bussellos ordei, et iii bussellos fabarum et pisarum. Ideo Johannes Faber et Ricardus prepositus plegii ad dictum bladum solvendum, in misericordia finis Johanni vid., finis Ricardo vid., plegius alter alterius. Et dictus Willelmus venit et concordatus est cum dicto Waltero patre suo qui dictus Walterus ex gratia sua (arreragium) ad instanciam annorum relaxat eidem Willelmo cum arreragio anni preteriti. Ita quod de termino Sancti Michaelis ultimo preterito solvat dicto Waltero patri suo nunc vi bussellos frumenti, ii bussellos ordei, et ii bussellos fabarum et pisarum. Et tantum ad Purificationem beate Marie et sic de anno in annum quamdiu dictus Walterus vixerit, per plegios Ricardum le Hunter et Ricardum in Hale. Et predictus Willelmus pro iniusta detentione in misericordia, condonatur, plegii supradicti. Et prefatus Walterus sub hac forma concessit eidem Willelmo totam terram suam de Elyngtone. Et ipse Walterus pro predicta conventione tenenda et ut possit recedere extra villam cum suis catallis dabit domino abbati annuatim de predicto blado iis. per plegium Ricardi prepositi.

7. OVER, (P R O, SC 2, Port. 179, no. 10): Rogerus Syward et Alanus Syward sunt plegii Margarete Syward de ii solidis solvendis domino celerario ut habeat considerationem curie de porcione que ei pertinet dum vixerit sine marito de una virgata terre servilis quondam patris sui modo mortui. Et villata venit et dicit quod dicta Margareta et Amicia soror eius secundum consuetudinem manerii habebunt hospicium et unam ringam bladi, videlicet medietatem de frumento et aliam medietatem de pisis. Unde Rogerus Syward frater earum satisfacit eis de medietate et

Alanus alius frater earum de alia medietate ratione quod terra perticipata est modo inter dictos fratres.

8. Wistow, (B M, Add. Ch. 39562): Thomas Palmerus adhuc convictus est per juratores quod fregit pactum Johanne et Sarre filiis Mariote Martini, quam Mariotam duxisse debuerat in uxorem ut patet in rotulo ultimi visus. Et quia invenitur quod Johanna maritata est de conventione ipsius Johanne quietus est. Et versus Sarram sororem dicte Johanne pro conventione prius facta teneatur dictus Thomas a tempore ultimi visus usque in hodiernum diem in sumptibus suis necessariis in una ringa frumenti, una ringa ordei et una ringa fabarum et pisarum. Et quod de cetero dicte Sarre victu et vestitu et omnibus aliis necessariis competenter satisfacit, et pro conventione fracta Alexander Frere et Michael Palmerus plegii predicti Thome fuerunt in misericordia xiid. Et per eosdem plegios dicta Sarra sicut predictum est habeat sua necessaria.

9. Abbots Ripton, (B M, Add. Ch. 39597): Agnes Hubert recognovit se teneri Alicie Martino ratione maritagii filie dicte Agnetis in uno equo pretii vis., uno porco pretii xiid., iiii bussellis frumenti, et iii capriis solvendis dicte Alice citra Pascham, et pro iniusta detentione est in misericordia vid., plegii utriusque Willelmus Haulound et Willelmus Olyver.

10. Upwood, (P R O, SC 2, Port. 179, no. 9): Juliana relicta Ade filii Johannis dat domino vid. pro consideratione curie habenda super portionem unius virgate terre quondam mariti sui, plegius Nicholaus filius suus. Et xii juratores dicunt quod secundum consuetudinem ville deberet habere unam domum cum quadam parva curtilagia de messuagio et annuatim dum vixerit unam ringam frumenti, i ringam fabarum et pisarum, et i ringam avenae.

11. Upwood, (B M. Harleian Ms. 445, Ramsey Court Book, 7 d.): Ad letam cum curia ibidem tentam xxii^{do} die octobre anno supradicto (1399), Willelmus Hauconn venit in propria persona et sursum reddidit in manu domini omnia terra et tenementa sua in Upwode ad opus Nicholao Hendesson de Hemyngford' Grey et Johanne uxori eius. Tenendum etc. ad terminum vite eorum. Reddendo et faciendo in omnibus sicut predictus Willelmus inde facere consuevit. Et dant domino de gersuma i caponum. Et non plus quia tenementum ruinosum (est). Reservata vero dicto Willelmo Hauconn et Cristine uxori eius ad totam vitam eorundem una camera infra mansum tenementi predicti vocatur le Schopp,' reservata etiam eisdem Willelmo et Cristine in forma predicta una acra terre arabilis in duobus campis.

APPENDIX VI

Chattels and the Tenement

1. Upwood, (B M, Add. Ch. 34371): Et quod Johannes Gouler nativus domini qui tenuit de domino i messuagium et iii quartas terre obiit intestans post ultimam curiam. Ideo preceptum est seisire bona et catalla in manu domini.

2. Wistow, (B M, Add. Ch. 39597): Radulphus Keyse citra festum Sancti Michaelis proximum futurum solveret ii ringas ii bussellos frumenti et ii ringas ii bussellos ordei Andree Gylemle et Thome Keyse executoribus Sarre Keyse ad opus puerorum eiusdem Sarre et pro iniusta detentione est in misericordia vid., plegii utriusque Robertus Bronnenote et Simon le Bonere.

3. WISTOW, (B M, Add. Ch. 39755): Robertus Bronnenote et Simon le Bonere fuerunt plegii Radulphi Keyse ad ultimum visum quod idem Radulphus citra festum Sancti Michaelis ultimum preteritum solveret Andree Gilemyle et Thome Keyse executoribus Sarre Keyse ii ringas ii bussellos frumenti et ii ringas ii bussellos ordei ad opus puerorum eiusdem Sarre quod quidem bladum non est adhuc solutum. Ideo dicti Robertus et Simon in misericordia vid., plegii Nicholaus Palmerus et Johannes Andrew. Et preceptum est levare dictum bladum de Radulpho Keyse principali debitore si habeat unde, si nec autem de primis plegiis suis levetur.

4. WARBOYS, (B M, Add. Ch. 39783): Ad hanc curiam preceptum fuit homagio ad inquirandum de certa consuetudine infra maneria predicta. Qui onerati et jurati dicunt super sacramentum suum quod est in villa de Warboys talis — consuetum si aliquis custumarius tenens domini terram tenens obierit sine herede inter se et uxorem suam quod tunc dominus manerii predicti participaret omnia bona mobilia et immobilia tam ex parte dicti defuncti quam ex parte relicte sine die quo obiit inventa, et tercia pars dictorum bonorum secundum consuetudinem predictam penes dictum dominum equaliter et integre remaneat; et est ista consuetudo tam post obitum uxoris quam viri cum contigerit eos dies suos claudere extremos sine herede inter eos legittime procreato sicut predictum est. Et ideo consideratum est et concessum per homagium predictum quod predictam consuetudinem integre in omnibus sicut predictum est de cetero observetur in villa de Warboys predicta. Et ulterius juratores presentant quod Robertus Pankerell alias Benson et Robertus West alias Borowe quorum unus tenuit unam virgatam terre custumarii et alter sex quarterios terre custumarii sine herede inter se et uxores suas obierunt et post ultimam curiam. Et quod Johannes Pankerell alias Benson frater et executor dicti Roberti Pankerell et Jacobus West alias Borowe nepos et administrator bonorum predicti Roberti West alias Borowe fecerunt domino finem pro tertia parte predictorum bonorum predicti Roberti Pankerell et Jacobi West pro consuetudine predicta.

APPENDIX VII

DIRECT DESCENT OF PROPERTY

1. WISTOW, (B M, Add. Ch. 39853): Juratores presentant quod Robertus Haukyn qui de domino tenuit dimidiam virgatam terre in bondagium diem clausit extremum. Et quod Thomas filius eius gersumare eandem terram non venit nec fecit sacramentum hoc die quia infirmus (est). (Then is added in another hand: Postea fecit sacramentum).

2. WESTON, (P R O, SC 2, Port. 179, no. 36): Et quod Johannes Baroun qui de domino tenuit in villenagio dimidiam virgatam terre obiit post ultimam (curiam). Et Rogerus filius eius nativus domini est proprior heres et dicunt quod dominus nihil habebit per mortem ipsius Johannis salvo quod heres dabit gersumam ad voluntatem domini. Ideo distringatur ad faciendum etc.

3. SHILLINGTON, (P R O, SC 2, Port. 179, no. 30): Juratores presentant quod Agnes in le Slade que de domino tenuit in bondagium i virgatam terre in Stondon diem clausit extremum pro qua (mittitur) i vacca pretii vs. pro herietto. Et quod Walterus filius eius gersumavit eandem terram et fecit sacramentum.

Et quod Matilda atte Grene que de domino tenuit i virgatam terre in Shitlyndon in bondagium diem clausit extremum pro qua venit pro herietto i vaccam pretii vs. Et quod Walterus filius eius plene etatis gersumavit dictam terram et fecit sacramentum.

Galfridus filius et heres Isabelle Okolt venit in ista curia et probavit plenitudinem etatis sue petens se admitti ad i acram quondam de hereditate dicte Isabelle et que fuit in manu domini post decessum eiusdem Isabelle (conditione?) minoris etatis eiusdem Galfridi et concessa est ei inde seisina. Et fecit fidelitatem.

4. HEMMINGFORD ABBOTS, (P R O, SC 2, Port. 179, no. 7): Et dicunt quod messuagium cum crofto adiciente que Thomas Thykene quondam tenuit est in manu domini. Et senescallus ex officio suo illud messuagium cum crofto tradidit Emmam Ange. Et eadem Emma in (persona) in plena curia per assensum Ange mariti sui reddidit sursum totum jus suum ad opus Johannis filii eiusdem immo quod prius gersumandum est illud messuagium cum crofto pro sexdecim solidis de domino abbate.

5. SHILLINGTON, (P R O, SC 2, Port. 179, no. 36): Compertum est per juratores quod Henricus Lewyne iniuste deforciavit Johanni filio Walteri (Pechat) tertiam partem unius virgate terre quam predictus Walterus pater ipsius Johannis nuper tenuit et de qua ipse obiit seisitus. Ideo consideratum (est) ad recuperendum etc.

6. WARBOYS, (B M, Add. Ch. 34324): Nicholaus Oseborne dat domino iis., plegius prepositus, ad inquirendum de una terra que vocatur Sixxepennywurthlond quam Ricardus Godwyne modo tenet. Et dicit predictus Nicholaus ius habet, etc. Et iurati dicunt quod quidam Ricardus Oseborne pater predicti Nicholai tenuit dictam terram ut ius suum et predictus reddidit sursum illam ad opus Cristine sororis sue et dicta Cristina eam de domino gersumavit. Et predicta illam terram sursum reddidit ad opus predicti Godewyne qui illam de domino gersumavit et adhuc tenet. Et ponitur in respectu coram domino. Et predictus dominus abbas ex sua gratia speciali concessit et tradidit predictam terram predicto Nicholao Oseborne qui dat domino in gersuma xiid. de quibus prepositus oneratur rotulo accomptere, et solvet per annum viiid. ad terminos usuales. Et inveniet unum hominem ad precariam domini in autumpno et alium ad Lovebones et ad fenum levandum et solvet (v?) gallinos et ova et omnia alia servitia faciet et consuetudines quas prius dicta terra facere est consueta.

7. KNAPWELL, (P R O, SC 2, Port. 179, no. 18): Nicholaus Isabel dat domino xii denarios pro consideratione curie habenda de una dimidia virgate terre versus Annam relictam Willelmi Alred, predictam terram modo tenentem per decessum viri sui. Quam quidem dimidiam virgatam terre predictus Nicholaus precat et clamat ut (iuris) et hereditatis sue eo quod quidam Robertus Isabel pater suus dictam terram tenuit qui in vita sua illam sursum reddidit ad opus dicti Willelmi Alred tenendum ad terminum vite sue. Unde predictus Nicholaus dicit quod secundum consuetudinem manerii predicta terra post decessum dicti Willelmi Alred sibi debet resortiri. Et quod ita sic ponat se in Rotulo gersumarum Rameseiae. Et dictum est ei quod petat dictos rotulos citra proximam curiam.

8. HEMMINGFORD ABBOTS, (P R O, SC 2, Port. 179, no. 11): Compertum est per juratores quod Henricus Trappe per unam cartam emit de Alicia Hering unam rodam et dimidiam terre. Et per aliam cartam de Matilda Hering dimidiam acram terre. Et super hoc venit Thomas filius Simonis de Styvekle qui duxit uxorem dicti Henrici monstrans duas cartas et fecit fidelitatem.

Preceptum est capere in manu domini illam rodam et dimidiam terre quam

Henricus Trappe emit de Alicia Heryng per unam cartam. Et etiam illam dimidiam acram terre quam idem Henricus emit de Matilda Heryng donec Johannes filius et heres dicti Henrici venerit ad calumpniandam illam terram. Et quod levari faciant de Emma Iugel relicta predicti Henrici xviiid. de vestura illius terre anni presentis seminante drageto, et comorant' cum eadem Emme. Et memorandum quod carte de predicte terre tradite sunt Thome Marescallo tunc preposito ad custodiendum donec, etc. Et postea venit dictus Johannes et dat domino in gersuma pro dicta terra tenenda ad voluntatem domini (iis.). Et faciet servicia inde debita et consueta. Et preterea dabit domino quolibet anno i caponum ad Pascham de incremento.

Memorandum quod Adam Hog et Thomas le Marescal sunt plegii Johannis filius Henrici Trappe quod erit obediens domino et faciet servitia debita et communia pro terra illa quam gersumavit ut patet plenius in rotulo superius. Et quod respondeat de duabus cartis de dicta terra sibi in plena curia traditis quando exigantur ab eo.

9. HEMMINGFORD ABBOTS, (P R O, SC 2, Port. 179, no. 17): (   ) Ricardus le Fyssher tenuit predictam terram de domino praeter cuius mortem descendit ius predicte terre Cristine filie et heredi ipsius Ricardi secundum consuetudinem, etc. Ad quam quidem Cristinam (maritus fuit) quidam Johannes Trappe in predicta terra sine gersuma et genuit de eadem Cristina Willelmum le Fyssher patrem predicti (Johannis) qui nunc petit et predictus Willelmus tenuit et habuit unam virgatam terre. Mortuo vero predicto Johanne Trappe, prefata Cristina superstes reddidit sursum predictam terram in manu firmarii ville ad opus predicti Johannis le Fyssher filius predicti Willelmi le Fyssher. Ideo consideratum est quod predictus Thomas nihil capit de predicta terra et quod predictus Johannes predictam terram recuperet. Et dat domino in gersuma ii marcas. (Several lines are obliterated at the beginning of this entry.)

10. WARBOYS, (P R O, SC 2, Port. 179, no. 11): Illa virgata terre que fuit Roberti filii Mabile de Caldecote qui arripuit iter in pertibus transmarinis sine licentia domini capta fuit in manu domini cum catallis. Et modo tradita est quattuor hominibus scilicet Johanni Segely, Roberto Harsyne, Simoni filius Roberti, Ricardo filius Roberti qui respondent domino de omnibus serviciis et consuetudinibus ad dictam terram spectantibus donec, etc.

11. BROUGHTON, (P R O, SC 2, Port. 179, no. 30): Et quod Cristina Everard que de domino tenuit unam virgatam terre in bondagium diem clausit extremum, et Johannes filius eius gersumavit dictam terram tenendum secundum consuetudinem manerii, et fecit fidelitatem.

12. LAWSHALL, (B M, Add. Ms. 33450): Johannes Bedford de London carpentarius et Sabina uxor eius filia Alicie Coupere veniunt et clamant iuris et hereditarionis post mortem prefate Alicie matris eiusdem Sabine i tenementum de x acris quod Galfridus Walter iam tenet ex dimissione Willelmi Togood et petunt se admitti ad tenementum predictum. Et super hoc inquisitio capta fuit per xii iuratos huius curie qui dicunt super sacramentum suum quod predicta Sabina proxima heres est prefate Alicie et quod predicta Alicia mater eiusdem Sabine obiit seisita de tenemento predicto secundum consuetudinem manerii et quod prefata Sabina ius habet ad tenementum predictum. Ideo consideratum est quod predicta Sabina recuperet tenementum predictum. Tenendum de domino per servitia et consuetudines inde debita et consueta secundum consuetudinem manerii. Solvendo per considerationem totius curie pro expensis et reperationibus factis per predictum Willelmum

Togood centum solidos per manutenentem et plegium Simonis ballivi domini. Et dat domino de fine pro ingressu habendo iiis. iiiid., plegium predictum.

13. SHILLINGTON, (P R O, SC 2, Port. 179, no. 12): Hugo Waryn et Alicia uxor eius veniunt et dant domino pro consideratione curie habenda xiid., plegius (Walterus?) Lamb, ad inquirendum de tribus acris terre quas Rogerus le Carter modo tenet, quas quidem tres acras predicti Hugo et Alicia petunt ut ius dicte Alicie ratione quod predicta terra fuit cuidam Ricardo le Bole patri predicte Alicie nunc petentis cuius heres ipsa est. Et quam terram prefatus Ricardus in vita sua dimisit (ipso) Rogero ad terminum annorum. Et hac petunt quod inquiratur. Et predictus Rogerus venit et dicit quod (gersumavit) predictam terram de domino Willelmo Abbate Rameseiae. Et ad hoc vocat Rotulum Gersumarum Rameseiae ad (inquirandum). Ideo dictum est ei quod querat predictos Rotulos citra proximam curiam.

14. CRANFIELD, (B M, Cotton., Vesp. XVIII, pp. 89-90): Omnibus Christi fidelibus presens scriptum visuris vel audituris Johannes dei gratia Abbas Rameseiae salutem in domino. Noveritis nos quod per finem xx marcas quem dilectus noster Galfridus de Craule fecit nobiscum concessimus eidem quod super terram nostram censuariam apud Cranfeld ex licencia nostra speciali habeat ingressum ad Aliciam filiam Cristiane de la Burne et eam ducat in uxorem cum toto illo messuagio in Cranfeld cum terris, pratis, et bosco adiacentibus quod quidem messuagium cum terra et bosco ipsa Alicia filia Cristiane de la Burne de nobis gersumavit post decessum prefate Cristiane matris sue. Ita scilicet quod predictus Galfridus integre teneat toto tempore vite sue dictum tenementum cum omnibus pertinentiis suis et in eodem cum catallis suis tenemento continue resideat. Faciendo nobis et ecclesie nostre singulis annis arruras, herciaturas, precarias, carriagia, talliagia, et omnia alia servicia inde debita et consueta excepto officio prepositure quod quidem servicium eidem Galfrido suo perpetuo presenti scripto relaxamus. Preterea dictus Galfridus domos dicti tenementi, muros, et hayas in eodem statu seu meliori quo eas recepit sustinebit et conservet et omnes fructus terre predicte super tenementum illud apponet. Nec licebit eidem Galfrido aliquid de bosco dicti tenementi vel de vinis hayis alicui vendere vel conferre vel extra feodum cariare, vel vastum facere vel ad opus proprium sumere nec tantum pro rationabili sustentatione domi sue ad hayas et focale et pro domibus ruinosis relevandis et erigendis sine licentia nostra speciali. In cuius rei testimonium etc. hiis testibus.

15. KING'S RIPTON, (P R O, SC 2, Port. 179, no. 6): Johannes Pege dat domino vid. pro habenda consideratione curie de una grangia cum quadam placea quondam in manu Cristine Umfrey soror eius nuper obiit etc. Johannes le Malker et socii sui xii iurati dicunt quod Willelmus Umfrey quondam adquisivit dictas placeam et grangiam et dictas legavit in morte sue dicte Cristine ad terminum vite sue et praeter decessum dicte Cristine quod reverterent dicto Johanni filio suo. Ideo consideratum est quod habeat inde seisinam etc.

16. ELLINGTON, (B M, Add. Ch. 34320): (   ) dat domino dimidium marcum, plegii Walterus Faber et Henricus Attebrok, pro consideratione curie (   ) terre versus Nicholaum Burgeys qui predictam terram tenet, dicens se maius ius (   ) secundum consuetudinem ville sicut petens quam prefatus Nicholaus sicut tenens eo quod quidam Hugo (   ) Ricardi cuius heres ipse est propinquior predictam virgatam terre tenuit ut ius suum secundum predictam (   ) et inde obiit seisitus post cuius mortem (dicta?) terra ei descendere debet tamquam filius et heres propinquior dicti Hugonis secundum consuetudinem etc. Et quod tale sit ius suum petit quod inquiratur. Capta inde inquisitio per assensum? videlicet per

Ricardum le Hayward, Bartholomeum in Lyneland, Simonem filius Johannis filius Walteri, Willelmum Aldych, Thomam Godman, Willelmum Burneys, Rogerum Aldych, Galfridum Buk, Johannem filius Sarre, Willelmum filius Walt', Willelmum Lennard, et Adam prepositum. Qui dicunt per sacramentum quod quidam Hugo in Estate tenuit predictam virgatam terre ut ius suum et inde obiit seisitus. Et dicunt quod predictus Hugo habuit tres filios videlicet Thomam, Adam, et Ricardum qui modo petit. Predictus Adam disponsavit quamdam Julianem que tenuit unam virgatam terre et predictus Thomas filius predicti Hugonis (   ) disponsavit Agnetem filiam dicte Juliane (conventionem?) inter eos factam quod predicti Thomas et Agnes haberent predictam virgatam terre post obitum dicti Hugonis. Et sic predictus Hugo (   ) in eadem terra per tempora longa vixit mortuo vero predicto Thoma prefatus Hugo adhuc superstes (   ) predicta terra dum postea remansit et vixit, mortuo vero predicto Hugone predicta Agnes predictam terram (   ) ville et per octo annos et amplius p'mnd' illam tenuit. Requisiti predicti iurati si prefatus Hugo in (   ) predictorum Thome vel Agnetis sursum reddidit nec ne, dicunt quod non. Et quia compertum (   ) dimisit predicta Agnete predictam terram contra consuetudinem prohibentem intrare et in qua nihil (   ) ponat eo quod prefatus Thomas vir suus in vita sua numquam inde fuerat seisitus nec in (   ) in illa optinuit, in misericordia xxs. Requisiti postea iurati si predictus Ricardus post mortem dicti Hugonis patris sui ut filius et heres petebat predictam terram nec ne, dicunt quod non. Sed dicunt expresse quod de bonis propriis et catallis patris sui? gersumavit predictus Ricardus tria quarteria terre abbatis infra predictam villam ne amplius in predicta virgata terre clamium apponeret nec iuris aliquid exigeret. Ideo consideratum est quod predictus Ricardus nihil capiat de predicta terra, que postea per licentiam et gratiam domini comitatur predicto Nicholao Burgeys qui prius eam tenuit et dat domino pro gersuma xls.

17. SHILLINGTON, (P R O, SC 2, Port. 179, no. 36): Memorandum est quod Walterus Pechat ad ultimam curiam gersumavit unam virgatam terre quam Adam le Wyne prius tenuit ad opus Johanni filio predicti (Walteri) et Margerete filie et heredi predicti Ade tenendum secundum consuetudinem manerii. Super quod ad istam curiam venit Walterus atte Wode et terram predictam (clamat) ut heres et consanguineus cuiusdam Alicie atte Wode mater Walteri atte Wode pater predicti Walteri eo quod predicta Alicia (inde tenuit) secundum consuetudinem manerii ut dicit. Et modo veniunt tam predicti Johannes filius Walteri Pechat quam Margareta filia predicte Ade (ut   ) Johannis et defendant (   ) etc. ut ius ipsius Walteri et dicunt quod predicta Alicia atte Wode per quam ipse clamat impotens erat ad tenementum predictum sustendendum (   ) per assensum ipsius Alicie senescallus domini qui tunc temporis fuerat (ordinavit quemdam?) Silvester Lewyne nativum domini de (   ) in uxorem capiendam et terram illam gersumandam et tenendam sibi et heredibus suis per consuetudinem manerii. Et Silvester et Alicia defendaverunt sust'? ? Henricus ut filius et heres eorundem de? Henricus defendebat ius predictorum? tenentium, cuidam Ade? ut filius et heres predicti Henrici et de Ade distring'? feodum et ius preterite Margarete ut filie et herede predicti Ade qui modo est tenens (   ). Et quod tale sit eorum ius predicti Johannes et (   ) et predictus Walterus dicit ius inde habet et petit similiter ad juramentum. Ideo (   ) insuper (   ) per sequentes xii juratores. Compertum est quod quedam Alicia Atte Wode nuper tenens, tenendum secundum consuetudinem manerii, impotens erat ad tenementa predicta sustenenda quia impotens etc. per assensum ipsius Alicie et senescalli illius manerii qui pro tempore fuerat ordinavit quemdam Silvester Lewyne (   ) ad predictam Aliciam (   ) uxorem capiendam et terram illam

gersumandam, tenendum secundum consuetudinem manerii sibi et heredibus suis
etc. Et quod de Silvester (et Alicie) descend' feodum et ius cuidam Henrico filio
et heredi eorum, de Henrico descend' ius Ade ut filio et heredi predicti Henrici et
de Ade descend' feodum et ius Margarete filie et heredi predicti (et ordinatum est
quod ius ten'). Compat' predictis Johanni et Margarete uxori eius et non Waltero
et ideo considerant quod predictus Walterus nihil caperet pro (querel') in misericordia pro falso clamore, et quod predicti Johannes et Margareta tenebunt in pace.

18. SHILLINGTON, 1306 (P R O, SC 2, Port. 179, no. 12): De Waltero Cobbe pro
consideratione curie habenda ad inquirendum de iure suo quod clamat habere in
uno messuagio et una virgata terre quondam Hugonis le Carter xiid., plegius Willelmus le Hauscomp. De Roberto Gill' pro eodem xiid., plegius Adam Richard.
De Hugone le Carter pro eodem xiid., plegius Willelmus le Faycour.

Mortuo Hugone Cartarius qui tenuit de domino unum mesuagium et unam
virgatam terre. Et venit quidam Walterus Cobbe et petit dictum tenementum ut
ius suum tenendum per licentiam domini. Et dicit quod dicta Juliana obiit sine
herede de se. Et (sic?) tenementum sibi competit tamquam proximo heredi. Et
super hoc venit quidam Hugo filius predicti Hugonis (et clamat) predictum tenementum ut ius suum ratione quod predictus Hugo pater suus supervixit dictam Julianam. Et predictus Hugo sponsavit Johannam matrem dicti Hugonis et in predicto
tenemento ingenuit predictum Hugonem qui modo petit (ius suum?), tam predictus
Walterus quam predictus Hugo petunt ut inquiratur quis eorum maius ius habet.
Et (   ) facta per xxiiiior bonos et legales homines de villa predicta qui dicunt
per sacramentum suum quod (invenitur?) secundum consuetudinem manerii
aliquod ius habet in predicto tenemento eo quod quidam Robertus Cobbe (pater?)
predicte Juliane post cuius decessum dicta Juliana que obiit sine herede de se intravit
dictum (tenementum?), habuit tres sorores videlicet Agnetem, Matildam, et Johannam. Et per consuetudinem manerii talis hered (   ) competit primogenite
filie Agneti tamquam heredi. Et de predicta Agnete descendebat dictum ius cuidam
(Ricardo) ut filio et heredi. Et de predicto Ricardo cuidam Nicholao ut filio et
heredi propinquiori, qui predictus (Nicholaus) compertus et presens est. Et dictum
est ei quod sequatur ad dictam terram gersumandam.

19. KING'S RIPTON, (B M, Add. Ch. 39775): Dicunt quod Willelmus Hrech obiit
post ultimam curiam intestatus et sine exitu de corpore suo exeunte, sed dicunt quod
habuit duas sorores unam Julianam nomine sponsam Ricardi Baker de Holme et
aliam Agnetem maritam Roberti Fabyon istius villate. Que quidem Juliana habuit
exitum unum Johannem Baker qui clamat ut proximus heres ius dictam mediam
partem cuius terre et tenementorum nuper in tenura predicti Willelmi Hrech avun-
culi sui in villa predicta. Et petit sic admitti his in plena curia secundum communem
legem Anglie et secundum consuetudinem huius curie. Et altera soror predicta
Agnes uxor prefati Roberti Fabyon clamat solita habere omnia partita terre et
tenementorum nuper predicti Willelmi Hrech fratris sui sola ut proxima heres
secundum (consuetudinem?) in predictis terris et pertinentiis. Et prefatus Robertus
Fabyon vir suus tenementorum ut a iure uxoris sue secundum consuetudinem (   )
(huius sic plene admissat et curia in misericordia).

20. WOODHURST, (B M, Add. Ms. 33450, p. 20): Anno XIX° Regis Ricardi secundi
et anno domini Edwardi abbatis XVII° videlicet XXIIII^to die julii. Johannes in le
Wroo cepit de Fratre Ricardo de Schenyngdon custode ibidem unum messuagium et
unam virgatam terre et unam vacuam placeam et dimidiam virgatam terre que pater
suus prius tenuit et que Thomas frater suus junior habere et tenere secundum consue-

tudinem manerii totaliter refusavit. Tenendum eidem Johanni in bondagio ad voluntatem domini ad terminum vite sue. Reddendo inde domino annuatim xxxixs. ter-
minis Sancti Andree, Anuntiationis, Sancti Benedicti et Nativitatis beate Marie equa-
libus portionibus. Et faciendo preterea annuatim precaria carucarum et autumpna-
lium et alia servicia et consuetudines debita et consueta ut ceteri pares sui secundum consuetudinem manerii. Et omnes domos et inclausturos dicti tenementi predictus Johannes durante toto termino suo predicto sumptibus suis propriis in omnibus
bene et competenter sustentabit reperabit et manutenebit. Et non licebit dicto
Johanni predicta tenementa infra terminum suum predictum relinquere nec alicui
dimittere in parte vel in toto sine licentia dicti custodis qui pro tempore fuerit. Et
dat domino de gersuma vis. viiid.

21. ELLINGTON, (B M, Add. Ch. 34320): Et Willelmus de Cotenham dat domino
(iiiis.), plegii Ricardus filius Alicie et Simon Peverel pro (   ) habendum de
uno messuagio cum una virgata terre in Elyngtone et uno messuagio (   )
supradictam virgatam terre versus Walterum de Cotenham qui predicta messuagia
et terra tenet (   ) habere in predictis messuagiis et terris secundum consuetudinem ville sicut petens quam predictus Walterus (   ) tenens, eo quod Willelmus
Faber pater ipsius Willelmi cuius heres iste est propinquior tenuit predicta duo
messuagia et predictam terram ut ius suum et inde obiit seisitus, post cuius mortem
predicta messuagia et terra eidem Willelmo tamquam heredi propinquiori de prima
uxore patris sui genito ut ius suum secundum consuetudinem predictam defendere
debet et (retinere). Et quod tale sit ius suum petit quod inquiratur. Et prefatus
Walterus qui predicta messuagia et terram integre tenet dicit quod maius habet
ius in predictis messuagiis et terris secundum consuetudinem predictam sicut tenens
quam predictus Willelmus sicut petens ratione quod disponsavit Isabellam filiam
prefati Willelmi Faber (secunda) uxore ipsius genita que maius habet ius in predictis messuagiis et terra secundum predictam consuetudinem quam prefatum
Willelmum (   ) uxore genita et hoc similiter petit quod inquiratur. Capiatur
inde inquisitio per (... twelve names given, some obliterated) (qui dicunt) quod
quidam Willelmus Faber a tempore quo non stat memoria tenuit predicta duo
messuagia (terre) integre ut ius suum que nunquam a predicta tempore nequaquam
fuerunt seperata qui quidem (Willelmus) sponsavit quandam Cristinam de qua
genuit predictum Willelmum qui modo petit. Mortua vero predicta Cristina idem
Willelmus Faber postmodum duxit quandam Emmam in uxorem de qua genuit
Isabellam uxorem priorati Walteri qui predicta duo messuagia et virgate terre
modo tenet. Et dicunt quod filii et filie de secunda uxore geniti sicut predictum
est maius habent ius secundum consuetudinem predictam ad terram patris eorum
optinendam quam filii vel filie de prima uxore geniti. Quare consideratum est quod
predictus Willelmus filius Willelmi Faber nihil de predictis duobus messuagiis et
virgata terre capiat, et quod predictus Walterus in pace ea optineat. Et dat predictus
Walterus domino ut bene irrotuletur iis.

22. HEMMINGFORD ABBOTS, (P R O, SC 2, Port. 179, no. 4): De Henrico filio
Galfridi pro custodia curie habenda de ii rodis terre quas Henricus filius Rogeri et
Agatha vidua tenent, vid., plegius Simon filius Galfridi. Et juratores veniunt et
dicunt quod numquam viderunt aliquam antecessorem dicti Henrici illas ii rodas
terre tenentem L annis preteritis. Ideo dictus Henricus nihil recuperet pro suum
clamium et predicti Rogerus et Agatha tenent, etc.

23. HEMMINGFORD ABBOTS, (P R O, SC 2, Port. 179, no. 9): Simon de Benelond
dat domino vid. pro consideratione curie habenda de dimidia roda terre inter ipsum

et Thomam filium Henrici. Et datus est dies Ranulpho ad capud ville, Willelmo le Warde, Ade Hog, Thome Maresch, Simoni de Styvecle, Nicholao le Fermer, Reginaldo filio Fabri, Ade Almar et Willelmo filio Petri, Nicholao de Elysworth, Willelmo Selede, Jordano Tuppe, Reginaldo filio Petri, Willelmo ate Style, et Simoni filio Galfridi atte Mare usque ad Pascham ad inquirendum quis eorum de predictis Simone et Henrico maius ius habet in predicta dimidia roda terre. Qui dicunt quod dictus Thomas totum ius habet in eadem. Ideo preceptum est quod ponatur in seisinam.

24. ELLINGTON, (P R O, SC 2, Port. 179, no. 12): Willelmus Brun venit et dat domino pro consideratione curie habenda xiid., plegius Ricardus West, ad inquirendum de una roda terre quam Rogerus Aldych per longum tempus ei iniuste detinuit, et adhuc detinet. Capta inquisitione per supradictos iuratos qui dicunt per sacramentum suum quod prefatus Willelmus Brun maius ius habet in predicta roda terre secundum consuetudinem ville quam prefatus Rogerus. Ideo consideratum est quod predictus Willelmus recuperet predictam rodam terre. Et quod dictus Rogerus pro iniusta detentione sit in misericordia vid., plegius Ricardus West, prepositus.

25. HEMMINGFORD ABBOTS, (P R O, SC 2, Port. 179, no. 17): Agnes filia Nicholai le Hunne venit et petit admitti ad unum croftum gersumandum quod fuit patris sui praeter mortem dicti patris sui. Et compertum est quod dicta Agnes maritata est cuidam libero. Ideo teneatur dictum croftum in manu domini et respondetur de exitibus. Et dicta Agnes nihil inde capiet. Postea testatum est quod gersumandum fuit altero.

26. WESTON, (P R O, SC 2, Port. 179, no. 10): Adam de Goseholm qui tenet de domino illam dimidiam virgatam terre quam Henricus Randolf quondam tenuit, de qua quidem terra quedam Mariota filia predicti Henrici secundum consuetudinem manerii habuit ii rodas terre post decessum eiusdem Henrici antecessoris sui, donec, etc., que quidem Mariota terram eandem tradidit ad firmam per plures annos cuidam Ade Buncy. Et quia dicta Mariota fuit residens in longinquis pertibus nec ad pertes de Weston noluit accedere, dictum fuit prefato Ade Buncy quod faceret dictam Mariotam venire ad ostendendam personam suam ad terminum diem sub pena perdendi dictam terram. Ad quem diem dictus Adam Buncy non habuit ipsam, inde dicte ii rode capte fuerunt in manu domini de quibus dominus cepit exitus et expleta per duos annos. Modo venit dictus Adam de Goseholm et dat domino iis., plegii Willelmus de Bytherne, Adam filius Rogeri, Galfridus Cartarius et Simon Buncy ut habeat bonam inquisitionem utrum dicte ii rode sunt pertinentes ad suam dimidiam virgatam terre nec ne. Et inquisitio venit et dicunt quod predicte ii rode terre sunt pertinentes ad dimidiam virgatam terre prefati Ade de Goseholm sed quia ignoratur utrum dicta Mariota fuit superstes vel alicui maritata tradite sunt predicte ii rode terre prefato Ade de Goseholm ad colendum et seisandum et ut inde respondeat prefate Mariote si venerit. Plegii supradictorum.

27. BURWELL, (P R O, SC 2, Port. 179, no. 15): Laurentius de Borewell et Henricus le Wyse sunt plegii Agnetis le Fisschere et Matilde sororis sue venire apud Rameseiam citra Natale domini ad scrutandum ibidem rotulum si Agnes que fuit uxor Henrici le Fysscher mater predictarum Agnetis et Matilde gersumavit quoddam cotagium quondam Roberti filio Emme (   ) heredibus suis vel ad terminum vite.

28. ELLINGTON, (B M, Add. Ch. 39468): Agnes (Alet) dat domino iiid. pro con-

sideratione curie habenda de quedam placea in gardino quondam patris sui, plegius prepositus.

29. SHILLINGTON, (P R O, SC 2, Port. 179, no. 7): Adam Richard dat domino xiid. per plegium Reginaldi de Hamscomb ad inquirendum utrum ipse maius ius habet in una roda prati sicut petit quam Matilda matertera sua sicut tenens.

30. WISTOW, 1349 (B M, Add. Ch. 39763): Johanna Baronn cepit de domino i messuagium dimidiae virgatae terre quondam Nicholai Baronn patris sui, que dat domino pro ingressu (gersuma iis. is stroked out with remark 'pro in libro gersumarum'), plegius Willelmus Baronn.

31. WARBOYS, 1339 (B M, Add. Ch. 39853): Nicholaus Plumbe qui de domino tenuit in bondagium dimidiam virgatam terre diem clausit extremum. Et Alicia uxor eius cepit dictam terram per heriettum xxxd. Et tenebit dictam terram secundum consuetudinem manerii.

Cristina Harsine que de domino tenuit dimidiam virgatam terre in bondagium diem clausit extremum. Et Johannes filius eius gersumavit dictam terram et fecit fidelitatem.

32. CRANFIELD, 1347 (P R O, SC 2, Port. 179, no. 32): Concessum est in curia domini Johanni de Wassyngle quod habeat ii acras dimidiam terre quondam deveniunt in manu domini ratione minoris etatis Thome filii et heredis Willelmi Haym nativi, et dictus Johannes sustentabit puerum ad plenam etatem et dat de ingressu.

Idem Johannes cepit de domino custodiam terre et Johannis heredis Roberti Whrite, videlicet xvi acras terre dimidiam cum prato et bosco quondam dicti Roberti que deveniunt in manu domini ratione minoris etatis dicti Johannis heredis dicti Roberti, et dictus Johannes de Wassingle sustentabit puerum usque ad plenam etatem, et terram et boscum sine vasto. Dat gersumam (dimidiam marcam).

APPENDIX VIII

CONVEYANCE WITHIN THE FAMILY

1. HEMMINGFORD ABBOYS, (P R O, SC 2, Port. 179, no. 18): Willelmus filius Simonis Koc venit et reddidit sursum in manu domini unam virgatam terre quondam patris sui ad opus Laurentii Koc fratris sui qui dat villate pro ingressu habendo quamdam vomeram sicut patet in rotulo gersumarum de Rameseia. Et faciet servitia et consuetudines.

2. SHILLINGTON, (P R O, SC 2, Port. 179, no. 33): Robertus Sammer dat domino ut possit morari extra dominium ad terminum vite sue unam marcam unde invenit plegios; videlicet Robertus West, Nicholaus Attemede, Henricus del Abbey, Walterus Attewode. Et dictus Robertus Sammer reddit sursum in manu domini i messuagium ii virgatas terre ad opus Willelmi filii sui qui dat domino in gersuma etc. unde venit unam jumentam pro herietto per consuetudinem manerii. Presentatus (per) plegios predictos quod dictus Willelmus reperatia domos faciet, consuetudines, servitia, etc.

Robertus Attegrene junior reddidit sursum in manu domini i messuagium i virgatam terre ad opus Johannis filii sui et dat herietto unam (jumentam) et dictus Johannes gersumat et fecit fidelitatem, datur domino ingressum? tenendum secundum consuetudinem manerii sibi et sequelis suis. Faciendo servitia et consuetudines.

Lucia Waryn reddidit sursum in manu domini i messuagium et i virgatam terre ad opus Henrici Waryn filii sui (qui dat) domino in gersuma etc. Unde venit pro herietto per consuetudinem manerii i ovem.

3. BURWELL, (P R O, SC 2, Port. 179, no. 33): Johannes Edrich cepit de domino i messuagium xv acras terre quondam Thome patris sui, et dat in gersuma iis. Idem Johannes cepit de domino unam placeam edificatam ad opus Johannis filii sui que reddit per annum xviiid., quam idem Thomas Rolf quondam tenuit, et dat in gersuma iiid.

4. CRANFIELD, (P R O, SC 2, Port. 179, no. 16): Rogerus filius Willelmi Faber gersumat unum cotagium cum crofto quod quondam fuit Emmo Muriel, pro iiiis. ad opus Willelmi filii sui.

5. HOUGHTON, (P R O, SC 2, Port. 179, no. 32): Et quod Willelmus Froyl sursum reddidit dimidiam virgatam terre servilis ad opus Rogeri filii sui qui gersumat et fecit fidelitatem.

6. ABBOTS RIPTON, (B M, Add. Ch. 39586): Radulphus Attehyl fecit vastum in uno messuagio quod Hugo Attehyl modo tenet (   ) predictus Hugo dictum messuagium et terram gersumavit amputando et asportando arbores (   ). Ideo est in misericordia iis.; plegius bedellus. Simon filius Thome, Ricardus Gerold et Johannes le Vernoun sunt plegii Radulphi Atehyl (   ) domino de hoc quod se subtrahit de feodo domini et residet super terram Philipi de Aula uxoratus cum catallis suis, ubi edificavit et plant vit unam domum de arboribus quas amputavit et asportavit de feodo domini que crescebant in predicta dimidia virgata terre quam Hugo Attehyl modo tenet ut supra dictum est. Et postea fecit finem pro ii caponis solvendis ad pascham per annum, plegius Thomas Onty, et pro xld. quos dedit per manus ut licite posset manere super terram predicti Philipi. Et veniet ad visum franciplegii semel per annum per plegium predictum.
Convictum est per juratores quod Radulphus Attehyl elongavit unum langsetel extra domum Hugonis Attehyl. Ideo consideratum quod retornat et satisfacit ei de dicto langsetel. Et pro trangressione in misericordia iiid. plegius Nicholaus bedellus.
Convictum est per juratores quod Hugo Attehyl tenetur Radulpho Attehyl in undecim denarios et quadrantem quos idem Radulphus pro eo solvit domino pro redditu terre sue. Ideo satisfacit ei. Et pro iniusta detentione in misericordia vid.; plegius bedellus.
Convictum est per juratores quod Hugo Attehyl tenetur Radulpho Attehyl fratri suo in viginti solidos quos ab eo (   ) quod idem Hugo redderet sursum ad opus dicti Radulphi totum ius suum de una dimidia virgata (   ) patris sui quando sibi accideret, et etiam tenetur ei in quatuor solidos (   ) quam pro eadem conventione ab eo recepit quam vero conventionem idem (   ) Radulpho postea fregit. Ideo consideratum est quod dictus Radulphus recuperet versus Hugonem predictos viginti solidos et quatuor solidos et pro iniusta detentione predictus Hugo in misericordia iis., plegii Johannes de Hurst, Willelmus Haulond et Nicholaus Hubert et Nicholaus bedellus.

7. UPWOOD, 1344 (B M, Add. Ch. 39854): Et quod idem Robertus sursum reddidit ante obitum suum videlicet filio suo i cotagium quod gersumavit.

8. SHILLINGTON, ca. 1400 (P R O, SC 2, Port. 179, no. 46): Et quod Alicia Attewell Pekesdone (Pegsdon) sursum reddidit in manu domini i messuagium et i virgatam terre servilis ad opus Johannis Attewell filii sui. Et dicta Alicia dat domino de herietto i vomerem venditum per ballivum ad (viiis.).

9. Barton, 1409 (P R O, SC 2, Port. 179, no. 52): Et quod Emma Smyth sursum reddidit in manu domini unum messuagium et dimidiam virgatam terre ad opus Johannis Smyth. Et dat domino de herietto unum bidentem pretii viiid.

APPENDIX IX

Conveyance Beyond the Family

1. Graveley, (P R O, SC 2, Port. 179, no. 15): Willelmus Bercarius qui reddidit sursum in manu domini duodecim annis elapsis unum messuagium et (qu') acras terre ad opus Willelmi filii Dyke venit et uxor eius et petunt gratiam domini ut possunt reintrare ad predictum messuagium et terram. Et quia dictus Abbas precepit inquirere quotquot custagia et superexpensa prefatus Willelmus Dyke posuit et expendidit in predictis messuagio et terris postquam eos gersumavit ut in emendacione tam domorum quam terre. Iurati super hoc clerici requisici dicunt quod predictum messuagium et terra modo? in omnimodis custagiis et misis factis per prefatum Willelmum probus valet per sexaginta solidos quam valuit tempore quo eos gersumavit extra gersumam suam dimidie marce quam contulit domino pro ingressu habendo in predictis messuagio et terra etc.

2. Graveley, (P R O, SC 2, Port. 179, no. 19): Et dicunt quod Walterus ad Portam nativus domini dimisit messuagium suum cum dimidia virgata terre servilis cuidam Johanni Onty nativo domini ad terminum annorum sine licentia domini. Qui quidem Walterus recessit de feodo et manet in extraneis pertibus sine licentia. Ideo preceptum est capere in manu domini totum predictum tenementum et de exitibus inde provenientibus respondere quousque etc. Postea venit et fecit finem cum domino.

3. Wistow, (B M, Add. Ch. 39763): Andreas Maunger reddidit sursum in manu domini i hidlandum quondam Johannis Maunger ad opus Roberti Barker. Tenendum secundum consuetudinem manerii etc. qui dat domino pro ingressu habendo, plegius Willelmus Waryn (gersuma iis.— this is stroked out with the remark, quia in libro gersumarum).

4. Weston, (P R O, SC 2, Port. 179, no. 38): Ad istam curiam venit Ricardus Moltisson et sursum reddidit in manu domini unum messuagium et dimidiam virgatam terre ad opus Johannis Moltisson filii predicti Ricardi salvo jure Ricardi fratris predicti Johannis. Tenendum ad terminum vite sue ad voluntatem domini, faciendo servitia et consuetudines que ad dictum tenementum pertinent et dat in gersuma vis. viiid.
Ad istam curiam venit Galfridus Godeford et dat domino de gersuma vs. pro licentia habenda tenere unum messuagium et dimidiam virgatam terre in commune cum Waltero Penyell' ad voluntatem domini ad terminum vite ipsius Walteri. Et post decessum dicti Walteri predictus Galfridus habebit et tenebit predictum tenementum sibi et heredibus suis ad voluntatem domini secundum consuetudinem ibidem usitatam (vs.).

5. Weston, (P R O, SC 2, Port. 179, no. 40): Ad istam curiam veniunt Robertus Smyht de Bitherne et Maragreta uxor eius et sursum reddidit in manu domini medietatem unius messuagii et dimidie virgate terre ad opus Ricardi filii Ricardi Makynesson.' Tenendum sibi ab isto tempore usque ad terminum vite sue sub ista

conditione quod predictus Ricardus deserviet predictis Roberto et Margarete ad terminum vite eorum et post decessum dictorum Roberti et Margarete predictus Ricardus habebit alteram medietatem illius messuagii et dimidie virgate terre. Tenendum sibi et heredibus suis ad voluntatem domini faciendo domino per annum in omnibus sicut predictus Robertus facit, et gersuma pertinet ville per firmam illorum quia est nativus ville predicte et non extraneus.

6. WARBOYS, (P R O, SC 2, Port. 179, no. 20): Nicholaus Palmer reddidit sursum in manu domini unam acram terre ad opus Johanni Wariner, unam rodam iacentem apud Hotel,' unam rodam iacentem super Waterlondum et unam rodam iacentem super Longelondum et unam rodam iacentem apud tres quercus. Et dictus Johannes dat domino iiiid. pro gersuma et fecit fidelitatem.

7. ELLSWORTH, (P R O, SC 2, Port. 179, no. 18): Et Johanna filia Johannis Broun pro quadem parte cuiusdem placeae Henrici Notte habenda ad terminum vite sue, i caponus annuatim ad Pascham. Et nihilominus dabit annuatim quandum vixerit predicto Henrico aut successoribus suis pro eadem placea xiid., plegius Johannes Broun pater suus.

8. THERFIELD, (P R O, SC 2, Port. 179, no. 21): Radulphus de Crishale venit in plena curia et dat domino xs. pro Dionysia uxore sua ut possit tenere totam illam terram ipsa tenet de domino ad terminum vite sue si supervixerit dictum Radulphum, solvendo annuatim pro eodem tenemento (xvis.) terminos usuales.

9. THERFIELD, (P R O, SC 2, Port. 179, no. 12): Thomas de Bramcestre venit et fecit fidelitatem pro tota terra que quondam fuit Johannis de Harpefeld ad tenendum ad terminum vite.

10. THERFIELD, (P R O, SC 2, Port. 179, no. 21): Johannes de Bramcestre venit in plena curia et dat domino xiiis. iiiid. pro ingressu habendo in duodecim acras terre tenendum ad terminum vite sue. Reddendo annuatim decem solidos ad terminos usuales.

11. CRANFIELD, (P R O, SC 2, Port. 179, no. 10): Johanna filia Ricardi de Campo venit et dat domino in gersuma xx solidos pro xi acris terre quas Elyas Hog' quondam tenuit et pro iii acris terre quas dictus Ricardus tenuit de domino solvendo ad Nativitatem beate Marie. Et faciat domino singulis annis omnia servitia inde debita et consueta, plegius Ricardus de Campo.

12. ST. IVES, (B M, Add. Ch. 34774): Et dicunt quod Robertus le Taylour allocavit de Roberto Parys unam rodam terre ad termnium vite sue, iacentem ate Lane versus Ocle ad quam quidem rodam terre idem Robertus le Taylour arrando appropriavit sibi de communa ad quantitatem unius percitate in longitudine et idem in latitudine. Ideo preceptum quod distringatur ad respondendum.

13. SHILLINGTON, 1410 (P R O, SC 2, Port. 179, no. 52): Et quod Isabella Hughson alienavit unum messuagium et unam virgatam terre Johanni Warde. Et Isabella dabit heriotum videlicet optimum animalium suum quod quidem animal est vitulus etatis i anni pretii iiiis. (Note: an entry similar to this may be found for Cranfield in 1420, Port. 179, no. 56).

14. BARTON, 1455 (P R O, SC 2, Port. 179, no. 67): Et quod Willelmus Chylde sursum reddidit in manu domini unum messuagium cum una virgata terre ac cum forlando ad opus Ricardi Gregory filii Johannis Gregory senioris ut patet in libro gersumarum, pro qua quidem sursum redditione dat domino de herietto secundum consuetudinem manerii unum ovem pretii etc.

APPENDIX X

APPENDIX X

LIMITATIONS TO CONVEYANCE BEYOND THE MANORIAL COURT

1. SLEPE, (P R O, SC 2, Port. 129, no. 17): Preceptum est preposito et bedello repondere domino de lviiis. iid. de xvi ringis frumenti xvi ringis drageti et xii ringis pisarum de vestura totius terre Johannis West capte in manu domini ratione quod predictus Johannis nativus gratis permisit Adamo filio Willelmi filii Hugone liberi appropriare? terre sue libere de terra servili quam dictus Johannes tenet de domino in villenagio ad exhereditarionem domini etc. Et preceptum est adhuc tenere predictam terram in manu domini donec etc. Et postea testatum est quod predicta terra emendatur in statu suo pristino. Et predictus Johannes fecit finem cum domino pro xiid. ut habeat et tenet terram predictam.

2. SLEPE, (P R O, SC 2, Port. 179, no. 16): Preceptum est retinere in manu domini medietatem unius messuagii cum pertica quam Willelmus de Gillynge prius habuit de dono Alicie filie Johannis Pak' per cartam eo quod predicta medietas messuagii non fuit reddita sursum in manu domini in curia sua sicut preceptum fuit in ultimo visu.

SLEPE, (P R O, SC 2, Port. 179, no. 17): Adhuc preceptum est retinere in manu domini medietatem unius messuagii cum pertica quam Willelmus de Gillynge habuit de dono et feoffamento Alicie filie Johannis Pak' per cartam eo quod predicta medietas non fuit sursum reddita in manu domini in curia sicut preceptum fuit in ultimo visu. Et testatum est quod predictus Willelmus occupat predictam medietatem contra voluntatem ballivi domini et predictus Willelmus in plena curia dicit quod predicta medietas sibi propria velut domino abbati nec ne et nihilominus senescallo enormiter contempsit. Ideo pro contemptu dimidiam marcam.

3. BURWELL, (P R O, SC 2, Port. 179, no. 16): Et dicunt quod Goderobus nativus domini vendidit Radulpho le Ber nativo unum messuagium censuarium. Ideo capiatur in manu domini et respondetur ei fideliter de exitibus inde provenientibus.

4. ELLSWORTH, (P R O, SC 2, Port. 179, no. 23): Et dicunt quod Henricus Fynch nativus domini vendidit per cartam Thome Leg' et Willelmo filio suo unum messuagium cum crofto adiacente. Et postea compertum est quod pater predicti Henrici qui fuit nativus domini et omnes antecessores sui perquisivit predictum tenementum de feodo de Bokeswurth. Et dominus abbas qui pro tempore fuit predictum messuagium cum crofto tamquam suum villenagium arentavit pro quinque solidis annuatim redditis. Et illud tradidit patri predicti Henrici tenendum in villenagium per predictum redditum et alia servicia inde debita et pro gersuma etc., qui modo predictam terram per cartam vendidit predictis Thome Leg' et Willelmo filio suo qui ostenderunt cartam inde hoc eodem testante que quidem carta in plena curia cassatur. Et ideo preceptum est seisire in manu domini predictam terram et respondere de exitibus donec etc.

5. HEMMINGFORD ABBOTS, (P R O, SC 2, Port. 179, no. 15): Et dicunt per iuratos quod quidam Willelmus Gapup tenuit de domino unum messuagium et duas virgatas terre in predicta villa tempore Regis Henrici sine carta et per gersumam ad voluntatem domini Abbatis qui pro tempore fuit et fuit pro predicta terra ad scot et lot in omnibus cum predicta villa sicuti aliquis alius qui terram servilem in eadem villa tenet. Et dicunt etiam quod dictus Willelmus genuit quandam Agnetem filiam

suam modo superstitem de Lyna uxore sua que disponsata fuit cuidam Thome de
Ocolt fratri domini Willelmi de Ocolt Abbatis de qua dictus Thomas genuit Thomam Onnpron et Agnetem sororem suam omnes superstites defuncto vero dicto
Thome de Ocolt, obiit dictus Willelmus Gapup, post cuius decessum dicta Agnes
filia sua dictam terram gersumavit ad voluntatem domini W. de Gomecestre Abbatis. Et postea venit quidam Simon Byle Whyt nativus domini et dedit domino
in gersuma ad intrandum in dicta terra ad disponsandam predictam Agnetem
duas marcas argenti. Ita quod teneret dictam terram per talia servicia sicuti alii
serviles de predicta villa. Et dicunt quod dicti Simon et Agnes modo per cartam
suam feoffaverunt dictum Thomam Opron de medietate dicti messuagi et predicte
terre quam cartam idem Thomas profert et hic testatur. Et dicunt quod postea
dictus Thomas feoffavit dictam Agnetem sororem suam per quandam cartam quam
dicta Agnes profert de quadam perticula predicti messuagii. Et dictum est eis quod
fuit in gratia domini de predictis (terris tenendis) ad voluntatem domini et reddant
cartas suas qui sponte ad idem in plena curia (   ). Et ideo preceptum est capere
totam predictam terram in manu domini tam illam quam predictam (Simoni et
Agneti in) eo quod feoffaverunt per cartam suam ad exhereditationem domini
dictum Thomam de terra servile (que abbatis te? idem Thomas habuit per eorum
feoffamentum etc.).

6. WESTON, (P R O, SC 2, Port. 179, no. 40): Et Jacobo Piteman extraneo de
gersuma pro uno messuagio et una quarta terre quondam Thome Bacheler faciendo
per annum in omnibus sicut predictus Thomas fecit (vs.).

APPENDIX XI

CONDITIONS OF LAND SALE AMONG VILLAGERS

1. ELLSWORTH, (P R O, SC 2, Port. 179, no. 10): Convictum est per iuratores
quod Henricus de Wardebois est in aretro versus Alanum filium Philipi, qui solvit
sursum terram suam ad opus eidem Henrico, de v ringis frumenti, ii ringis ordei et
ii ringis drageti et i ringa pisarum ex quibus dictus Alanus relaxat i ringam frumenti
et i ringam ordei. Et sic remanent viii ringae quas solvet ad terminos subscriptos,
plegii Willelmus Simond, Willelmus Baldewyne, Henricus filius Eustachii et Simon
Brun, videlicet ad Purificationem Beate Marie i ringam frumenti et i ringam ordei,
et ad festum Sancti Michaelis totum residuum. Et pro iniusta detentione est in
misericordia vid., plegii supradicti.

2. GRAVELEY, (P R O, SC 2, Port. 179, no. 7): Robertus Beneyt queritur de
Johanne Herneys seniori quod idem Johannes iniuste ei detinet dimidiam marcam
argenti ex una parte et duodecim denarios ex altera parte et tres ringas frumenti,
tres ringas ordei et ii ringas et iii bussellos drageti de conventione sua quam fecit
secum pro filia sua disponsanda, et petit quod inquiratur et dictus Johannes similiter.
Et vicini iuratores veniunt et dicunt quod conventio talis erat inter ipsos quod dictus
Johannes daret predicto Roberto dimidiam marcam eodem die quo gersumaret
terram suam ad quem diem dictam dimidiam marcam ei non solvit. Et duodecim
denarios daret eidem eodem die quo emerit sibi unam ollam eneam qui quidem dies
non dum venit. Sed de predicto blado dicunt quod dies solutionis positus non erat
nisi ad voluntatem et secundum posse predicti Johannis. Ideo consideratum est quod
idem Johannes solvat predicto Roberto de predicta dimidia marca xvd. ad Purifica-

tionem beate Marie et xld. ad Pascham, et predictos duodecim denarios ad unam ollam insimul et predictum bladum secundum quod conventio eorum supra notatur. Et predictus Johannes pro iniusta detentione sit in misericordia vid.; nullus plegius quia pauper. Et predictus Robertus similiter in misericordia pro falso clamore suo vid. Plegii Willelmus Ko et Robertus ad Puten.

3. GIRTON, (P R O, SC 2, Port. 179, no. 7): Margareta ad Grenam dat domino xiid. pro conventione inter ipsam et Thomam Rodbaund facta rotulanda secundum recognitionem eiusdem Thome quam fecit in plena curia et obligavit se tenendum. Et est conventio talis, videlicet, quod dictus Thomas pro quaddam dimidia virgata terre quam tenet ex dimissione eiusdem Margarete solvet annuatim eidem Margarete ii quarteria frumenti, ii quarteria ordei, et iis. argenti ad quattuor anni terminos per equales portiones. Et inveniat eidem Margarete hospitationem in quaddam solaria infra curiam suam. Et in eadem domo quo dictus Thomas et familia sua comedebunt permitet dictam Margaretam commedere sumptibus eidem Margarete. Excepitur ad predictum Thomam in vasis suis propriis et sumptibus suis, providentiam dicte Margarete providebit sicut providentiam suam propriam. Et pistabit panem eidem Margarete quando furnabit panem suum proprium. Et etiam unam vaccam habebit dicta Margareta in curia dicti Thome? vicelicet in estate sumptibus eidem Margarete et in hyeme sumptibus dicto Thome. Et eadem Margareta habebit unum porcum, unum gallum et quinque gallinarum per totum annum in curia eiusdem Thome sumptibus ipsius Margarete. Et quia idem Thomas recognovit se detinuisse iiid. argenti et i ringam ordei de conventione supradicta de anno preterito, et quia postea convictum est per vicinos iuratos quod ultra eosdem tres denarios et dictam ringam ordei predictus Thomas detinuit alios tres denarios, idem Thomas est in misericordia vid., plegii Petrus filius Rogeri et Willelmus Sbyrrene. Et taxata sunt dampna dicte Margarete ad sex denarios qui dantur clericis.

4. LITTLE RAVELEY, (B M, Harleian Manuscript 445, Ramsey Court Book, 134d.): Ad eandem letam tentam apud Wystowe venit Johannes Walgate et sursum reddidit in manu domini i messuagium et i virgatam terre nuper Ricardi Catelyne ad opus Johanni Owty filio Johannis Owty junioris. Tenendum eidem Johanni ad terminum vite sue ad voluntatem domini secundum consuetudinem manerii. Reddendo et faciendo inde in omnibus sicut predictus Johannes Owty nuper fecit. Et gersuma ii caponi. Preterea dictus Johannes Walgate concessit eidem Johanni Owty mensam suam isto anno proximo sequente et frumentum ad seminandas iii dimidias acras terre, iii quarteria vi bussellos ordei ad seminandum et iii equos videlicet Bayard,' Balle et don' et post annum completum concessit ei unum aratrum cum apparatu ad tres equos. Concessit eidem Johanni Owty sustentacionem pro iii equis hoc anno proximo sequente. Item predictus Johannes Owty concessit eidem Johanni Walgate i cameram ad portam et unum carthous et aisamentum in gardino et le Foryard et unam virgatam terre.

5. WARBOYS, (B M, Add. Ch. 39856): Acceptum est per testimonium vicinorum examinatorum quod Willelmus Cowherde sursum reddidit i messuagium et ix acras ad opus Thome Gerold sub istis condicionibus quod idem Willelmus et uxor eius habebunt ad terminum vite eorum i porcionem messuagii ut sapibus cum includebantur et ii acras terre arabilis de tenementis predictis, et reddent eidem Thome quolibet anno in festo Sancti Michaelis iis. Et predictus Thomas arabit et herciabit quolibet anno predictas ii acras terre debitis seisonis sicut et quoties terra parum suorum aratur. Et si idem Thomas predictas duas acras terre debitis temporibus

arare noluerit, liceat dicto Willelmo et uxori sue dictos ii solidos per annum retinere, et de arura dictarum ii acrarum terre alibi providere. Acceptum est etiam per eosdem vicinos quod predicta portio messuagii non fuit assignata per numerum pedum in latitudine et longtitudine sed per sepes includentes. Et quod invenerint in libro gersumarum certitudine pedum latitudinis et longitudinis non per mensuram communem sed per estimationem.

6. LAWSHALL, (B M,Add. Ms.33450, p. 21): Willelmus Togood venit ad eandem curiam et sursum reddidit in manu domini i tenementum de x acris cum pertinentiis vocatur Auncelles quod Johannes Kyng quondam tenuit, ad opus Johanni Underwode et Johanne uxoris eius post terminum Roberti Peek qui dictum tenementum iam tenet ad terminum certorum annorum ex dimissione dicti Willelmi. Tenendum eisdem Johanni et Johanne uxoris eius et sequele sue in bondagium ad voluntatem domini completo termino antedicto. Reddendo et faciendo domino annuatim omnia servitia et consuetudines inde debita et consueta secundum consuetudinem manerii. Et custodiat et manutenebit dictum tenementum sine nocumento. Et si aliquis heres calumpniare voluerit dictum tenementum (inde ?) omnia costagia et expensae restaurabit predictis Johanni et Johanne et eorum sequelis per considerationem curiae et tenentium domini ad hoc juratorum. Et predictus Johannes fecerit domino fidelitatem servilem. Et dant domino de gersuma xs. Solvendo infra proximam letam sequentem.

7. OVER, (P R O, SC 2, Port. 179, no. 15): Convictum est quod Willelmus filius Willelmi Ive et Margareta uxor eius tenentur Roberto Ive in octodecim solidos pro custibus quos idem Robertus posuit in terra que fuit Johannis Lauwe tamquam illam tenuit ad firmam et quam terram predictus Willelmus Ive modo tenet. Ideo satisfaciet eidem Roberto de dictis denariis videlicet medietatem ad Pascham et aliam medietatem ad festum Sancti Laurentii, plegius Willelmus Ive prepositus.

8. ELLINGTON, (P R O, SC 2, Port. 179, no. 10): Ricardus le Beaumeys est plegius Emme filie Henrici le Bok quod citra proximam curiam plantabit unam domum super placeam quondam Henrici Bok patris sui pro qua domo cepit dimidiam marcam de Willelmo filio Bate.

9. ABBOTS RIPTON, (P R O, SC 2, Port. 179, no. 9): Robertus Sabyn venit et petit versus Agnetem Sabyn vi ringas frumenti, vi ringas ordei et vi ringas fabarum et pisarum quas debuit ei solvisse de arreragio sex annorum predictorum et in uno anno ii ulnas et dimidiam bludi et russeti et in alio anno iii ulnas linei panni et sic continue per predictos sex annorum, et hospicium super terram. Et petit quod inquiratur per totam villatam. Et omnes de villate veniunt et dicunt quod non intendunt quod dicta Agnes teneatur eidem Roberto in blado predicto ratione quod ad ultimum visum franciplegii concordati fuerunt super omnibus contentionibus sub hac forma quod dicta Agnes solveret infuturum predicto Roberto i ringam frumenti ad Purificationem beate Marie, i ringam fabarum ad Pascham et i ringam ordei ad Gulam Augusti et quolibet (   ) ulnis et dimidie panni lanei et pro iii ulnis linei panni iiis. xd. quos solverit ad quodlibet festum Sancti Michaelis xxd. (   ) quod dicta Agnes (haberet) terram suam pacifice et solvat annuatim dicto Roberto ut supra per plegium Ricardi Messoris et Andree Onty.

APPENDIX XII

SUBLETTING ON THE CUSTOMARY TENEMENT

1. WARBOYS, (B M , Add. Ch. 39756): Godefridus Scut venit et recognovit se fregisse conventionem Amitie Bugge de uno selione terre quem allocavit eidem Amitie per quattuor annos in partem solutionis debiti sui de una vacca. Ideo est in misericordia vid. Et quia compertum est quod nullus custumarius potest aliquam partem terre sue servilis dimittere vel locare alicui nisi ad terminum duorum annorum secundum consuetudinem manerii, preceptum est quod predictus selio terre capiatur in manu domini donec etc.

Godefridus Scut recognovit se fregisse conventionem Amitie Bugge de uno selione terre quem sibi locavit in partem solutionis debiti sui ad dampnum suum taxatum ad (   ) quos solvit ei. Et quia conventione fracta in misericordia vid., plegius. Et preceptum est quod dicta Amitia habeat dictam terram usque ad duas vesturas, inde preceptum (vacat quia inferius).

2. SHILLINGTON, (B M, Add. Ch. 39774): Et preceptum ballivo seisire in manu domini unum messuagium cum xvi acris terre nuper Johannis Waryn eo quod presentatum est per totum homagium quod dictus Johannes in vita sua dimisit dictum messuagium cum dictis xvi acris terre ultra terminum unius anni contra consuetudinem manerii, etc. Et domino de exitibus rendere etc.

3. ABBOTS RIPTON, (P R O, SC 2, Port. 179, no. 12): Convictum est per iuratores quod Johannes le Carpenter fregit conventionem Martino Onty de una roda terre quam sibi allocavit ad duas vesturas inde percipiendas cuius non habuit inde nisi unam vesturam inde ad dampnum dicti Martini xviiid. quos solvet ei. Et pro transgressione est in misericordia iiid., plegii utriusque Willelmus Elynn et Olyver atte Dam. Et solvet ei dictam pecuniam citra Nativitatem beate Marie.

4. HEMMINGFORD ABBOTS, (P R O, SC 2, Port. 179, no. 16): Convictum est per iuratores quod Agnes le (Geminn) fregit conventionem Radulpho Bischop de tribus vesturis terre quas ei locavit ad dampnum suum trium solidorum et trium denariorum. Ideo satisfacit. Et pro iniusta detencione in misericordia iiid., plegius Radulphus Vernoun.

5. SHILLINGTON, (P R O, SC 2, Port. 179, no. 17): Johannes Hamond qui tenet de domino dimidiam virgatam terre dimisit predictam terram per percellas aliis diversis per quod dominus perdit aruras suas et alia servitia eo quod predictus Johannes pro inopia illa facere non potest nec alii qui terram suam tenent illa faciunt. Ideo preceptum est capere dictam terram in manu domini et respondere de exitibus. Fecerunt aruras.

6. WESTON, (P R O, SC 2, Port. 179, no. 16): Et dicunt quod Willelmus Prat nativus locavit unum quarterum terre Rogero Attehill ulterius quam debuit per consuetudinem ville. Ideo capiatur in manu domini. Et respondetur de exitibus donec etc.

7. ELLSWORTH, (P R O, SC 2, Port. 179, no. 4): De Roberto filio Johannis quia locavit Willelmo Elene hoc' praeter ii selliones ad unam vesturam, pauper.

8. ELLSWORTH, (P R O, SC, 2, Port. 179, no. 7): Preceptum est preposito res-

pondere de exitibus unius crofti capti in manu domini quod cum domo adiacente Robertus le Gage locavit Alano Dylle juniori ad quatuor vesturas.

9. GRAVELEY, (P R O, SC 2, Port. 179, no. 7): Walterus Barun, Willelmus Barun et Robertus Algar executores Roberti Berkarii veniunt et petunt iiiis. versus Simonem Halyday seniorem qui quidem venit et dicit se in nichilo teneri quia dictus Robertus habuit dimidiam acram terre sue ad iiiior vesturas super quas habuit durante termino suo ii bussellos frumenti et iiii ringas, ii bussellos drageti pro dictis denariis. Et quod ita sit promptus est facere legem cum tertia manu sua, plegii legis Willelmus Hulot et Ricardus Danyel.

10. WARBOYS, (B M, Add. Ch. 39754): Et dicunt quod Willelmus Lucas dimisit quamdam peciam messuagii sui Radulpho Wrench ad terminum vite dicti Willelmi et dimidiam rodam in crofto suo. Ideo pro transgressione in misericordia vid., et dictum tenementum capiatur in manu domini.

Et dicunt quod idem Willelmus dimisit quamdam peciam messuagii sui Johanni le Pondere et preceptum est ut supra.

11. WARBOYS, (B M, Add. Ch. 39755): Et idem Johannes (le Pondere) dat i caponum ut possit tenere illud messuagium per duos annos quod conduxit de Willelmo Lucas solvendo eidem Willelmo per annum illos sex denarios quos prius solvit domino abbati.

12. WARBOYS, (B M, Add. Ch. 39597): De parte messuagii quod Margareta de Hawegate dimisit Ricardo Derward ad unam fabricam construendam iiid. per annum.

De Johanne le Pondere singulis annis i caponem tm' ut possit tenere illud dimidium messuagium per iii annos quod conduxit de Willelmo Lucas solvendo eidem per annum illos viii denarios quos prius solvit domino abbati.

13. HOUGHTON, (B M, Add. Ch. 34897): De Roberto Trappe quia dimisit domum suam vacuam et non premunivit ballivos, vid., plegius Ricardus Plumbe.

De Ricardo filio Agnetis quia dimisit domum suam Roberto Trappe, xiid., plegius Alexander filius Agnete.

14. WISTOW, (B M, Add. Ch. 39562): Ranulphus filius Andree convictus est per juratores quod fregit pactum Johanni Gernun de una vestura unius acre terre pro quo satisfacit ei pro xiid., et pro transgressione in misericordia vid., plegius Ricardus Long.'

15. ABBOTS RIPTON, (B M, Add. Ch. 39597): Et dicunt quod Johannes filius Johannis dimisit quamdam partem curie sue Stephano Bercario ad terminum x annorum. Ideo idem Johannes in misericordia vid. Et preceptum est capere illam partem curie in manu domini donec, etc.

16. ABBOTS RIPTON, (P R O, SC 2, Port. 179, no. 10): Et Willelmo Huwelot quia asportavit vesturam unius dimidie acre terre frumento seminato per Nicholaum le Dyneker, quam quidem terram idem Nicholaus seminavit tempore quo Willelmus Palmerus terram illam tenuit priusquam dictus Willelmus Huwelot illam terram gersumavit, vid., plegius Johannes de Hyrst. Et preceptum etc.

APPENDIX XIII

Subletting to Freemen and Outsiders

1. WESTON, (P R O, SC 2, Port. 179, no. 18): Et dicunt quod Thomas Randolf dimisit (   ) terre cuidam Ricardo le Carter libero. Ideo preceptum est quod capiatur in manu domini et de exitibus respondetur.

2. SHILLINGTON, (P R O, SC 2, Port. 179, no. 26): (Prepositus ?) inde respondit de vestura dimidiae acre frumenti quam Edytha Hammond nativa domini dimisit Simoni Bercario libero sine licentia.

3. SLEPE, (P R O, SC 2, Port. 179, no. 11): Et preposito et bedello quia non ceperunt in manu domini prout precipiebatur eisdem vesturam unius acre terre seminato de drageto, quam Robertus Baldewyne locavit Johanni Moring' libero, que appreciatur ad quattuor solidos quos solvit (   ), plegii alter alterius.

4. HOLYWELL, (P R O, SC 2, Port. 179, no. 18): Et dicunt quod Johannes de Upwode nativus tenet de domino dimidiam virgatam terre servilis. Et de celerario unam virgatam terre servilis preterquam unum croftum. Dimisit inde Johanni de Hermingo libero duas acras et dimidiam ad terminum trium annorum. Et Johanni le Clerk duas acras ad eundem terminum. Et totum residuum dicte terre preterquam tres acras quas retinet penes sex dimisit eisdem Johanni et Johanni ad serviandum hoc anno pro medietate vesture inde provenientis. Ideo preceptum est quod tota predicta terra capiatur in manu domini. Et de exitibus inde provenientibus domino respondeantur.

5. SHILLINGTON, (P R O, SC 2, Port. 179, no. 52): Et Petro Cook de fine pro licentia dimittendi terram suam nativam ad firmam cuidam extraneo per annum, iiiid.

6. BARTON, (P R O, SC 2, Port. 179, no. 56): Et Agnes Sare de fine pro licentia dimittendi terram suam ad firmam dum manet extra dominium, per annum iiiid. Et ultra hoc invenit plegios, videlicet Ricardum Wodward et Walterum Wodward pro herietto suo pretii vis. viiid. restituendo si obierit extra dominium.

7. HEMMINGFORD ABBOTS, (P R O, SC 2, Port. 179, no. 18): Et Nicholaus D(enmeys ?) pro una virgata terre Nicholai Pate tenenda per tres annos ex dimissione dicti Nicholai, iis., plegius prepositus.

8. BURWELL, (P R O, SC 2, Port. 179, no. 20): (   ) Johannes Hukyn venit in visu isto et dat domino pro xxiii acris terre servilis tenendis a festo Sancti Michaelis anno domini Simonis abbatis sexto per quinque annos proximos sequentes iis. Et faciet domino servicia et consuetudines que ad dictam terram pertinent.

9. WESTON, (P R O, SC 2, Port. 179, no. 10): Willelmus le Newebonde convictus est quod ex seductione ad decipiendum dominum locavit Waltero filio Johannis (   ) unam rodam terre ad opus Johanni filio Laurentii libero, qui quidem Johannes tradidit pecuniam dicto Waltero ad (hoc faciend'). Preceptum est ambo in misericordia, finis Willelmi xiid., plegius Simon Bacheler, finis Walteri xiid., plegius Bartholomaeus (Curteys ?).

10. HEMMINGFORD ABBOTS, (P R O, SC 2, Port. 179, no. 10): Dicunt et presentant quod Nicholaus (Laurentius) dimisit Willelmo filio Martini le Longe de homagio

domini Reginaldi de Grey duas acras terre de siligo (   ) seminato. Et quod combussit quamdam grangiam suam et vendidit meremium de eadem. Et quod vendidit arbores (crescentes) in curiam suam. Ideo est in misericordia xiid. Et quia customarii hoc permiserunt facere sunt in misericordia dimidiam marcam.

11. ELLINGTON, (P R O, SC 2, Port. 179, no. 12): Et dicunt quod Willelmus Aldych nativus domini dimisit duas rodas terre servilis cuidam Thome le Skynnere libero. Ideo capiatur dicta terra in manu domini. Et quod prepositus respondit de exitibus inde provenientibus.

Et dicunt quod Julyana Le Neweman nativa domini dimisit Matilde Kannt dimidiam acram terre servilis ad firmam extra feodum domini. Ideo capiatur in manu domini. Et quod respondetur de exitibus.

12. ELLSWORTH, (P R O, SC 2, Port. 179, no. 16): Et dicunt per iuratores quod Cristina que fuit uxor Thome Faber que est de hommagio persone locavit duobus capellanis unum messuagium quod predictus Thomas vir suus tenuit de domino. Ideo capiatur in manu domini, et respondetur de exitibus donec, etc.

13. WARBOYS, (B M, 39470): Preceptum est preposito respondere de vestura i rode terre seminatis cum pisis quam Willelmus Semar dimisit cuidam libero sine licentia.

14. LAWSHALL, (B M, Add. Ms. 33450, p. 21d.): Ad visum francipleggii cum curia ibidem tenta die sabati proxime post festum Exaltationis Sancte Cruce anno xxmo Regis Ricardi secundi et anno domini Edwardi abbatis xviii° tempore Ricardi de Schenyngdon camerarii Rameseiae. Simon Wrghte, Johannes Carpidhook et Nicholaus Stothoo per licentiam domini dimiserunt Willelmo Smyth de (Hawstede) duas acras terre sue native prout iacent in quodam crofto vocatur sokkescroft iuxta Smaleweye. Tenendum eidem Willelmo a festo sancti Michaelis ultimo preterito usque ad finem et terminum viginti annorum extunc proxime sequentium et plenarie completorum. Reddendo inde annuatim prefato Simoni et aliis sociis suis provenientibus xiid. ad festum sancti Petri advinculi pro omnibus aliis servitiis. Et dant domino de fine pro (   ) i caponum.

15. OVER, 1316 (P R O, SC 2, Port. 179, no. 18): Et Johannes Dereman (   ) vendidit Willelmo Tryle unam placeam servilem continentem in longitudinem (   ) vid., plegius Alanus filius fabri. Et preceptum est ballivis capere dictam placeam in manu domini.

16. WISTOW, 1328-9 (B M, Add. Ch. 39852): Et dicunt quod Robertus (Brunne) nativus domini dimisit cuidam libero terram suam ad semandum per unam vesturam sine licentia. Ideo ipse etc. iiid. Et preceptum est capere in manu domini dictam terram donec, etc.

APPENDIX XIV

LEGAL ENFORCEMENT OF PROPERTY CONTRACTS AMONG VILLAGERS

1. HEMMINGFORD ABBOTS, (P R O, SC 2, Port. 179, no. 18): Preceptum est ballivo et preposito videre quamdam peciam prati de quo conventio est inter Adam Cademan nativum domini et Johannem Porthos. Et inter Thomam Oremund' nativum domini et predictum Johannem. Ita quod (   ).

2. OVER, (P R O, SC 2, Port. 179, no. 18): Convictum est per juratores quod Rogerus Molle iniuste fregit conventionem Murielle Linene de una roda terre ad dampnum suum octodecim denarios quos ei solvit. Et pro transgressione, etc. iiid., plegii Eudo Kylle, Robertus prepositus, Johannes Ine. Et per eosdem plegios predicta Muriella habebit predictam rodam ad unam vesturam autumpnam.

3. HOUGHTON, (P R O, SC 2, Port. 179, no. 20): Convictum est per iuratores quod Johannes filius Brayerson contradixit conventionem quam fecit cum Johanne Child de una acra et dimidia terre quas cepit de eodem Johanne ad terminum quinque annorum (terminatio fuerit in quadragesima proximo sequente). Et quod iniuste detinet eidem Johanni dimidium bussellum frumenti appreciati ad septimos denarios quos ei solvit. Et pro transgressione etc. vid., plegius Reginaldus Gomesson.'

4. OVER, (P R O, SC 2, Port. 179, no. 25): Convictum est per sex iuratores quod Agnes Garyn fregit conventionem versus Willelmum Garyn de dimissione unius grangie ad dampnum predicti Willelmi taxatum ad duos solidos. Et pro transgressione etc. vid., plegius utriusque bedellus.

5. CRANFIELD, (P R O, SC 2, Port. 179, no. 16): Hugo filius Cecilie recognovit se fregisse conventionem Willelmo le Coupere de terra quam sibi vendidit ad dampnum suum taxatum ad xviiid. quos solvit ei. Et pro transgressione est in misericordia xiid., plegii Johannes de Bretenden' et Rogerus de Pyro.

6. GIDDING, (P R O, SC 2, Port. 179, no. 16): Convictum est per iuratores quod Johannes Bynethetoun tenet Johanni Le Monek in xiiiid. ex mutuo, et xviiid. de quodam crofto et uno bussello fabarum, et fregit ei nichilominus conventionem de quadam pecia prati ad dampnum suum sex denarios quos ei solvet. Et pro iniusta detentione in misericordia vid., plegius Willelmus Graunt. Et inde clerico vid.

7. WARBOYS, (B M, Add. Ch. 39597): Vicini jurati liberi et alii dicunt quod Johannes de Hygen' fregit conventionem Reginaldo de Suton de i domo ad dampnum suum xiid. Ideo in misericordia xiid. plegius Alexander Camberlanus.

8. WARBOYS, (B M, Add. Ch. 39759): Convictum est per juratores quod Thomas Puttok iniuste detinet Ricardo Puttok quamdam partem cuiusdam messuagii, sex ringas frumenti, duas ringas ordei, unam ringam fabarum, et duodecim denarios de quadam conventione inter eos prius facta ut patet in curia manerii. Quos ei solvet per plegios Hugonem Beneyt et Radulphum Semar, simul cum dampno taxato ad decem denarios. Et pro iniusta detentione etc. vid., plegii supradicti.

9. ABBOTS RIPTON, (P R O, SC 2, Port. 179, no. 18): Convictum est per iuratores quod Alicia filia Stephani de Burcestr' fregit conventionem Johanni filio Roberti de una domo quam de eo locavit ad dampnum suum trium denariorum quos ei solvet. Ideo in misericordia iiid., plegius utriusque Rogerus filius Bartholomei.

APPENDIX XV

TENURE OF FREEHOLD BY A VILLEIN

1. ELLINGTON, (P R O, SC 2, Port. 179, no. 16): Robertus filius Ricardi prepositi, Rogerus in le Hale, Johannes le Wodeward, Ricardus de Coten' et Simon filius Johannis adhuc sunt plegii Alicie filie Bartholomei in Inlond' que tenet de domino unum messuagium, x acras, i rodam terre et amplius libere quod predictam terram

in parte vel in toto non alienabit nec se maritabit alicui sine licentia domini et hoc nemini nisi nativo domini. Postea dominus Abbas in septimam Pascham ad instanciam domini Roberti de Hereford concessit eidem Alicie ut possit maritari cuidam Galfrido Unterhyl libero pro quadraginta solidis sicut patet per rotulos gersumarum de anno eiusdem Abbatis xxvi. Et quod habeat predictam terram in pace sine calumpnia aliquali etc.

2. LITTLE STUKELEY, (P R O, SC 2, Port. 179, no. 18): Et dicunt quod Henricus Houlot adquisivit de Willelmo Brekespere duas acras terre. Et de Johanne Wale tres rodas et dimidiam terre qui quidem Henricus venit et invenit plegium quod non alienabit dictam terram scilicet Robertum Ben'eth.

Et dicunt quod Willelmus le Daye nativus domini adquisivit de eodem Willelmo unam acram et dimidiam terre. Et Johannes filius Roberti Clerici est eius plegius quod dictam terram non elongabit.

Willelmus Rolf est plegius Roberti Ben'eth quod non alienabit unam rodam terre quam adquisivit de Willelmo Brekespere.

Et dicunt quod Rycherus Ben'eth adquisivit de predicto Willelmo Brekespere unam acram terre. Et de Johanne Wale (duas?) acras terre. Et de Matilda Sutor dimidiam acram et dimidiam rodam terre qui quidem Richerus invenit plegios scilicet Hugonem, Thomam, et Robertum Ben'eth quod dictam terram non alienabit.

3. CRANFIELD, (P R O, SC 2, Port. 179, no. 20): Johannes Catelyne nativus domini venit et ostendit cartam suam de dimidia acra terre que adquisivit de Nicholao Clerici et invenit plegios Simonem Catelyne et Robertum Catelyne quod non dictam terram alienabit.

Laurentius Hayn venit in plena curia et ostendit cartam suam per quam Johannes Capellanus feofavit ipsum de una acra terre et invenit plegium quod non alienabit, plegius videlicet Simon de Barton, carta?

Et dicunt quod Laurentius Hayn adquisivit dimidiam acram terre de domino Johanne Capellano et invenit plegios videlicet Robertum Gardiner et Petrum Aleyn quod dictam terram non alienabit et cartam suam ad proximam curiam ostendebit.

4. HEMMINGFORD ABBOTS, (P R O, SC 2, Port. 179, no. 20): Et dicunt quod Willelmus Plumbe nativus domini adquisivit ii acras i rodam et dimidiam terre de Radulpho Bischop libero sine licentia domini ideo ipse etc. xld., plegius Simon ate style. Et per eundem plegium dictam terram non alienabit.

Et dicunt quod Petrus Sley nativus domini adquisivit unam acram terre de Radulpho Byschop libero ideo ipse etc. iis., plegius Johannes Roger. Et per eundem plegium dictam terram non alienabit.

5. GIRTON, (P R O, SC 2, Port. 179, no. 20): Et dicunt quod Radulphus Faber nativus emit duas acras terre libere ideo ipse etc. vid., plegius Johannes in salicibus. Et per eundem plegium dictam terram non alienabit sine licentia domini, venit et ostendit cartam.

6. OVER, (P R O, SC 2, Port. 179, no. 18): Robertus le Baxster et Henricus Walt' plegii Willelmi de Temesford ad ostendendam cartam suam de uno messuagio, iii acris dimidie, i roda terre et iii rodis prati que adquisivit de Thoma Aylward sicut presentatum fuit, et hoc citra festum beati Johannis.

Johannes adquisivit unam acram terre de Thoma Gilbous. Ideo distringatur ad ostendendam cartam suam ad proximum visum.

7. ABBOTS RIPTON, (P R O, SC 2, Port. 179, no. 18): Philipus de aula est plegius

Willelmi le Bateman ad ostendendam cartam suam de uno messuagio adquisivit ab Stephano de Northfolk.'

8. LITTLE STUKELEY, (P R O, SC 2, Port. 179, no. 18): Et dicunt quod quidam de Bramptone cuius nomen ignorant adquisivit de predicto Willelmo Brekespere unam acram et unam rodam prati. Ideo distringatur ad ostendendam cartam suam ad proximum visum.

9. WESTON, (P R O, SC 2, Port. 179, no. 18): Et dicunt quod Rogerus filius Michaelis adquisivit dimidiam acram terre de Hugone filio Walteri Gautron qui ostendebit cartam (suam ad) proximam curiam per plegium Willelmi Fabri. Postea fecit homagium.

Et dicunt quod Willelmus le Hayward adquisivit de Ricardo le Chamberlyn unum cotagium qui venit et ostendit cartam suam. Et inventa fuit dicta carta defecta et invenit plegium scilicet Johannem Baronn ad dictam cartam emendandam.

10. OVER, (P R O, SC 2, Port. 179, no. 26): Et dicunt quod Johannes filius Egidii de Holywell' adquisivit unam acram terre de Thome Gon de feodo domini. Ideo distringatur ad ostendendam cartam suam.

11. OVER, (P R O, SC 2, Port. 179, no. 7): Ricardus filius Serbini dixit se non esse nativus domini. Et convictum est per duodecim quod est servilis conditionis. Ideo invenit plegium, Willelmum Bonde, quod decetero erit obediens domino et suis ballivis. Et quia idem Ricardus emerit de feodo domini duas acras terre quarum una acra seminata fuit de frumento que taxatur ad iis. de quibus onerando preposito, invenit plegium, Alanum Maynor, ad faciendum finem pro dicta terra tenenda, xiid.

12. ELLINGTON, (P R O, SC 2, Port. 179, no. 16): Simon Pen'el et Willelmus le Hunter sunt plegii Walteri Burgeys quod non alienabit tres acras terre libere sive plus sive minus habeat sine licentia domini quas perquisivit.

13. HEMMINGFORD ABBOTS, (P R O, SC 2, Port. 179, no. 18): Et tota villata quia permiserunt Willelmo atte Grundehous intrare in unam acram prati liberi praeter mortem patris sui sine gersuma. Faciant inde domino xld. Postea gersumat dictam acram prati prout continetur in Rotulo gersumarum de Rameseye.

14. LITTLE STUKELEY, (P R O, SC 2, Port. 179, no. 20): Adhuc preceptum est plegiis distringere Willelmum filium Roberti le firmarius ad faciendum domino homagium et fidelitatem de una acra et una roda prati quod adquisivit de Willelmo Brekespere.

15. KNAPWELL, (P R O, SC 2, Port. 179, no. 18): De preposito de Knapwelle quia non distrinxit Radulphum filium Willelmi et Elianorem uxorem suam ad faciendum domino homagium relevium et fidelitatem pro terre (que tenent) de domino in Knapwell, iiid. Et preceptum est adhuc quod distringantur ad hoc faciendum.

16. OVER, (P R O, SC 2, Port. 179, no. 18): Et Johanni de Overe et Willelmo Fabro plegiis Johannis Bycardun de Stanton quia ipsum non habuerunt ad faciendum domino homagium et fidelitatem pro una acra terre que adquisivit de Thome de Ellesworth, condonatur. Et presentatum est adhuc quod distringatur ut prius. Et present' compert' quod non tenetur de domino nisi per (   ). Inde nihil inde.

Johannes de Overe est adhuc plegius Johannis Freysel ad faciendum domino homagium pro sex cotagiis et sex acris terre que adquisivit de Mariota Fynor, citra festum Nativitatis Beati Johannis Baptiste.

17. BURWELL, (P R O, SC 2, Port. 179, no. 20): Et preposito et bedello quia non distrinxerunt Thomam filium Paukn de Halt' ad faciendum domino homagium relevium et fidelitatem de tenemento quondam Thome de Beyvelle in Burwell, xiid. Et preceptum est quod distringant.

18. WESTON, (P R O, SC 2, Port. 179, no. 18): Iuratores dicunt quod Willelmus filius Johannis Adekoc adquisivit de Johanne filio Rogeri le Schephirde unum cotagium. Et invenit plegium quod dictum cotagium non elongabit, scilicet Rogerum prepositum.

19. WESTON, (P R O, SC 2, Port. 179, no. 10): Et dicunt quod Johannes filius Wylke nativus domini emit dimidiam acram terre de Johanne de Elyngton. Et compertum est quod tenet de domino in capite. Et fecit domino feodalitatem.

Et dicunt quod Walterus filius Juliane emit de eodem Johanne unam rodam et dimidiam terre. Et compertum est quod tenet de domino in capite. Et fecit feodalitatem.

20. OVER, (P R O, SC 2, Port. 179, no. 14): Et dicunt quod Willelmus Howe unior liber emit tres acras terre de Johanne Payn. Ideo distringatur.

Et dicunt quod Willelmus Lord nativus emit libere unum messuagium de Waltero Fynor quod Willelmus dat domino (   ) pro eodem messuagio pacifice tenendo.

Et dicunt quod Robertus Syleby emit libere unam acram terre de Waltero Fynor. Et dat domino xiid. pro eadem pacifice tenenda, plegius bedellus.

Et dicunt quod Ricardus Wylle homo episcopi emit duas acras terre de Johanne Payn. Ideo distringatur ad faciendum (   ) quare ingressus est feodum domini.

Et dicunt quod Rogerus Crane nativus domini libere emit unum messuagium de Roberto Fynor et dat domino pro eodem tenendo xiid.

Et dicunt quod Willelmus filius Howe junior liber emit unam acram terre de Ricardo Baudre. Ideo distringatur pro ingressu feodum.

Et dicunt quod Willelmus Taby junior nativus domini emit unam rodam edificatam de Ricardo le (Parn'or), et unam terre de Ricardo Baudre, et unam acram terre de Johanne filio Letitie. Et predictus Willelmus dat domino pro dictis terris pacifice tenendis, xiid.

21. CRANFIELD, (P R O, SC 2, Port. 179, no. 19): (   ) quod dominus Johannes Morite adquisivit de Thome Fychyer nativo domini unam placeam quinque acrarum terre, unam acram prati et unam acram bosci de feodo domini. Ideo distringatur ad faciendum domino omnia que de iure facere debet.

22. CRANFIELD, (P R O, SC 2, Port. 179, no. 21): De Waltero le Wodeward nativo domini quia adquisivit unam rodam terre libere sine licentia de Ricardo le Marshal vid., plegius Henricus atte Wod.'

Et dicunt quod Thomas Terri nativus domini adquisivit duas acras terre de Radulpho Dumbely sine licentia. Ideo ipse in misericordia iis., plegius (Hugo   ). Et preceptum est distringere dictum Thomam ad ostendendam cartam suam citra proximam (curiam).

Et dicunt quod Willelmus le Fauken' nativus * domini * adquisivit unam dimidiam acram terre et unum cotagium de Johanne Atteburne Capellano. Et invenit plegium ad ostendendam cartam suam ad proximam (curiam). * These two words are stroked out.

23. HEMMINGFORD ABBOTS, (P R O, SC 2, Port. 179, no. 21): Et dicunt quod Thomas filius Thome Marescalli nativus domini adquisivit dimidiam rodam terre libere de Thome Jordon et venit et ostendit cartam suam. Ideo ipse etc. xxs., plegius prepositus. Et per eundem plegium dictam terram non alienabit.

Johannes filius Thome de Stivecle dat domino xld. pro ingressu habendo in tribus rodis terre libere quas pater eius adquisivit, plegius prepositus.

24. ELLINGTON, (B M, Add. Ch. 34336): Et prepositus et Ricardus West sunt plegii Willelmi Brun quod satisfaciet domino abbati ut (Cristiana) filia sua libere possit tenere illam dimidiam virgatam terre libere quam idem Willelmus emit de Abbate de (   ) prefate Cristiane quam ( ) ducet apud Rameseyem coram predicto domino abbati.

25. SHILLINGTON, (P R O, SC 2, Port. 179, no. 7): Radulphus Faber nativus qui emit libere unam acram terre de Galfrido de Aldebyry dat domino annuatim de incremento redditus i denarium.

26. ABBOTS RIPTON, (P R O, SC 2, Port. 179, no. 18): Johanna que fuit uxor Clementis de Eltyslo nativa domini venit et ostendit cartam suam de quamdam peciam unius (gardini ?) quam ipsa simul cum Clemente quondam viro suo perquisivit de Thoma le Ladde et Mariota uxore eius. Et invenit plegios videlicet Willelmum le Hawelound et Johannem le Veronn quod dictam peciam terre non elongabit.

27. UPWOOD, 1332 (B M, Add. Ch. 39582): Et dicunt quod Ricardus Swon nativus domini adquisivit duas acras et dimidiam rodam terre de Willelmo Clervaux libero sine licentia. Ideo ipse etc. xld., plegius Willelmus Heryng.

28. WARBOYS, 1325 (B M, Add. Ch. 34898): Et dicunt quod Thomas Raven junior cepit cum uxore sua unum messuagium tres acras terre libere in liberum maritagium, prout carta sua testata, et ostendit cartam suam in plena curia. Et invenit plegios quod dictam terram non alienabit videlicet Thomam patrem suum et Galfridum bedellum. Et predictus Thomas dat domino pro predicta adquisitione, xiid.

29. WARBOYS, 1390 (B M, Add. Ch. 34814): Et quod Johannes de Holywell est nativus domini et habet infra dominium de Wardebois unum messuagium et tres acras terre libere, et ignorant de quo tenet dictum tenementum. Ideo preceptum est distringere ipsum ad demonstrandum qualiter et de quo tenet illud, et modo tempore preceptum est seisire quousque, etc.

Et seisire in manu domini unum messuagium liberum quod Johannes Raven de Sancti Ivone tenet quousque monstraverit qualiter et de quo, etc.

APPENDICE XVI

LAND EXCHANGE AMONG THE VILLAGERS

1. SHILLINGTON, (P R O, SC 2, Port. 179, no. 12): Compertum est per iuratores quod Robertus de Ocolt tenuit de domino in Schytlyndon unam virgatam terre per servitium quinque solidorum et octo denariorum. Et illam terram vendidit diversis tenentibus. Et super hoc venit Radulphus de (   ) qui est unus tenentium eiusdem terre. Et petit quod portiona sua aportionetur scilicet pro xviiid. De Matilda de Stondon pro portione sua de xid. De Alicia de Stondon (viiid.). De Johanne Pistor pro iid. De Roberto Capellano pro id. De Johanne de Barton pro obolo.

De Radulpho Chapman pro obolo. De Radulpho Faber pro obolo. De Willelmo de Hamescompe pro iid. De (Magistro) Johanne de Schytlyndon pro iiid. ob. q. De Willelmo filio vidue pro iiiid. De Alicia ( ) pro xiiid. ob. q.

NOTE: The rents were apparently first entered in capons, and then these were rubbed out to enter the above amounts.

2. KING'S RIPTON, (P R O, SC 2, Port. 179, no. 12): Compertum est per totam curiam quod Stephanus Rabat in vita sua perquisivit in villa de Ryptone Regis tres acras i rodam terre quarum dimidiam acram iacet apud Rameseyweye et dimidiam acram apud Mortelande, dimidiam acram apud Langelond iuxta Johannem le Stalker et dimidiam acram apud Watlondum iuxta Johannem Wyllyam, i rodam apud Lange(bred) iuxta Johannem filium Simonis et i rodam versus pratum iuxta Henricum Hanetok, dimidiam rodam apud Hyhyl, i rodam iuxta Hugonem in Angulo, i rodam apud Lytlemer' iuxta Nicholaum le Neuman, i rodam versus pratum iuxta Nicholaum Carpentarium. Quam quidem terram prefatus Stephanus legavit Johanni filio Johannis le Palmer prout continetur in testamento dicti Stephani. Ideo consideratum est quod dictam terram in pace optineat.

3. WESTON, (P R O, SC 2, Port. 179, no. 15): Convictum est per juratores quod Reginaldus filius Andree Le Freman tenuit de domino W. de Gomecestre Abbate Rameseiae unum messuagium et xxxti acras terre et prati, qui quidem Reginaldus obiit seisitus de predicta terra infra etatem in custodia dicti domini Abbatis post cuius decessum Petronilla, Letitia et Alicia sorores dicti Reginaldi successerunt in predicta terra et tamquam participes dictam terram tenuerunt donec dicta Petronilla pro? partem suam dedit Simoni filio Willelmi de Elyngton qui de p'parte predicta feoffavit Johannem fratrem suum et predictam Petronillam die qua ipsam disponsavit sibi et heredibus de se legitime procreatis. Et postea predicta Alicia p'pertem suam dedit dictis Johanni et Petronille similiter sibi et heredibus legitime de se procreatis. Qui quidem Johannes et Petronilla totum predictum tenementum alienaverunt diversis tenentibus excepto messuagio predicto et una acra tribus rodis terre de qua dicta Petronilla post mortem dicti Johannis viri sui obiit seisita, post cuius decessum Thomas filius eius venit et petit dictum tenementum de quo dicta Petronilla mater sua obiit seisita secundum formam donationis predicti, et concessum est ei. Et quia totum predictum tenementum de quo dictus Rogerus obiit seisitus tenetur de domino Abbate per servitium militaris et per homagium et fidelitatem et per servitium faciendi per annum duas sectas ad curiam de Broughton et unam sectam ad curiam manerii de Weston et quicumque tenens fuit de predicta terra per predictum servitium venerit in propria persona ad precariam domini in autumpno cum uno homine operante. Et preceptum est distringere dictum Thomam tenentem de uno messuagio continente unam acram terre et de una acra tribus rodis terre in campis de Bythern. Et Philipum filium Laurentii de Bytherne tenentem quartem partem messuagii et duas acras terre. Et Johannem filium Laurentii tenentem duas acras et dimidiam et unam rodam terre, et Michaelem de Bytherne tenentem unam acram (et) Henricum de Millesworth quinque acras et dimidiam, Johannem filium Emme unam acram, Matildam le Plouwryte unam acram dimidiam, unam rodam et dimidiam, Walterum Bercarium unam rodam et dimidiam, Willelmum Faukes i acram, i rodam, Simonem Secour unam acram, unam (rodam), Ricardum Fabrum unam acram et dimidiam, Reginaldum delbyrg unam rodam et dimidiam, Willelmum Fabrum dimidiam acram, Willelmum Fabrum et Letitiam uxorem suam coheredes dicti Reginaldi tenentes tertiam partem unius messuagii et decem acras terre de predicto tenemento, ad facienda omnia servicia predicta.

4. HEMMINGFORD ABBOTS, (P R O, SC 2, Port. 179, no. 11): Petrus molendarius dat domino iis. pro inquisitione habenda de tribus rodis terre quas Thomas filius Henrici tenet iniuste ut dicit pro eo quod spectant ad illam virgatam terre quam idem Petrus gersumavit de domino Abbate. Et juratores super hoc examinati dicunt per sacramentum suum quod predicta terra quondam excambita fuit per quemdam tenentem illius terre cum antecessore predicti Thome tempore quo non existat memoria, de nominibus tam (?) excambiatorum nihil inquirere possunt propter elapsum temporis. Ideo dictum est predicto Petro quod petat dominum Abbatem si sibi viderit expedire, vel quod conveniant inter se.

5. WARBOYS, (B M, Add. Ch. 39851): Et Roberto Bronnote, Stephano Aubyns et Roberto Atebrok pro licentia excambiandi terram prout continetur in Rotuli, manerii xiid., plegii alter alterius.

6. WISTOW, (B M, Add. Ch. 39856): Et quod Thomas del Halle qui tenuit i placeam de messuagio Johannis Boonde cotmani in Ravele Parva in escambium pro i acra terre domini ad firmam super le Osshes de manerio de Upwode obiit et quod Sarra relicta eiusdem tenebit ad terminum vite etc. et fecit fidelitatem.

7. WISTOW, (B M, Add. Ch. 34915): Thomas Onty dat domino xiid. ut licite possit tenere per escambium unam rodam terre subter curiam suam quam escambiavit cum Mariota Gernon tempore Willelmi Abbatis sine licentia pro una roda terre super Lytlehyl. Et Nicholaus Ger'non dat domino in escambium xiid. pro predicta terra dicte Mariote licite tenenda, plegii alter alterius.

APPENDIX XVII

THE ACTIVE LOCAL LAND MARKET

1. KING'S RIPTON, 1322 (P R O, SC 2, Port. 179, no. 20): Ricardus de Bernewell reddidit sursum in manu domini unam dimidiam acram terre ad opus Johannis Waryn iacentem super Langelondum. Et idem Johannes dat domino iid. pro gersuma et fecit fidelitatem.

Ivo in Angulo reddidit sursum in manu domini unam dimidiam acram terre iacentem super Flytlondum ad opus Johannis Waryn. Et dictus Johannes dat domino iid. pro gersuma et fecit fidelitatem.

Nicholaus Ballard reddidit sursum in manu domini duas rodas terre ad opus Johannis filii Nicholai Atehalle quarum una roda iacet ate polys et alia roda iacet ate goldsmithlond. Et dat domino iid. pro gersuma et fecit fidelitatem.

Margareta Atehalle reddidit sursum in manu domini ad opus Johannis filii Nicholai Atehalle unam rodam terre iacentem apud le polys. Et predictus Johannes dat domino id. pro gersuma et fecit fidelitatem.

Johannes Brytwold reddidit sursum in manu domini ad opus Johannis filii Nicholai unam rodam terre iacentem in lyllondum. Et idem Johannes dat domino id. pro gersuma et fecit fidelitatem.

Margareta Atehalle reddidit sursum in manu domini ad opus Michaelis Atehalle unam dimidiam acram terre iacentem apud Enslade. Et idem Michael dat domino iid. pro gersuma et fecit fidelitatem.

Ivo in le Hirne reddidit sursum in manu domini ad opus Walteri de Shenyngdon unam acram terre iacentem ate yondenhaye. Et idem Walterus dat domino iiiid. pro gersuma et fecit fidelitatem.

Ivo in le Hirne reddidit sursum in manu domini ad opus Walteri de Shenyngdon unam dimidiam acram terre iacentem super lepytfurlong. Et idem Walterus dat domino iid. pro gersuma et fecit fidelitatem.

Ivo in le Hirne reddidit sursum in manu domini ad opus Walteri de Shenyngdon unam rodam terre iacentem super sexperis. Et idem Walterus dat domino id. pro gersuma et fecit fidelitatem.

Ricardus de Bernewell reddidit sursum in manu domini ad opus Walteri de Shenyngdon et Johanne uxoris sue dimidiam acram terre iacentem in le Groneslade. Et iidem Walterus et Johanna dant domino iid. pro gersuma et fecerunt fidelitatem.

Ivo in le Hirne reddidit sursum in manu domini ad opus Willelmi filii Hugonis Palmer unam rodam terre iacentem apud Brodheed. Et idem Willelmus dat domino id. pro gersuma et fecit fidelitatem.

Ricardus de Bernewell reddidit sursum in manu domini ad opus Henrici filii Simonis unam partem cotagii quod continet quartam partem unius rode. Et idem Henricus dat domino id. pro gersuma et fecit fidelitatem.

Ivo in le Hirne reddidit sursum in manu domini ad opus Ivonis filii Henrici unam dimidiam acram terre apud Smalthorn. Et idem Ivo dat domino iid. pro gersuma et fecit fidelitatem.

Nicholaus filius Hugonis legavit Ivoni filio Henrici unam dimidiam acram terre apud Rameseyweye prout patet per testamentum ipsius in curia exhibitum. Et idem Ivo dat domino iid. pro gersuma et fecit fidelitatem.

Nicholaus filius Hugonis legavit Johanni filio Thome Coupere unum messuagium iacens iuxta messuagium Ade filii Ricardi tenendum ad terminum vite Margarete sororis dicti Johannis. Et similiter legavit eidem Johanni dimidiam acram terre super Longlondum, et unam rodam et dimidiam super Grone tenendum in feodum ut patet per testamentum dicti Nicholai. Et predictus Johannes dat domino iiiid. pro gersuma et fecit fidelitatem.

Nicholaus filius Hugonis legavit Margarete sorori sue unum messuagium iacens iuxta manerium domini abbatis tenendum ad terminum vite ipsius Margarete. Et praeter decessum dicte Margarete dictum messuagium remaneat Johanni filio Thome le Coupere, tenendum in feodum. Et dicta Margareta dat domino iid. pro gersuma et fecit fidelitatem.

2. THERFIELD, 1347 (P R O, SC 2, Port. 179, no. 33): Robertus Per'onn qui de domino tenuit vii acras dimidiam terre libere pro servicio iis. vid. per annum et i dimidiam acram terre servilis pro servitio ad metendum i dimidiam acram terre frumenti in autumpno diem suum clausit extremum, et super hoc venit Robertus Per'on frater et heres dicti Roberti et cepit de domino predictam terram, tenenda per servicia predicta, fecit fidelitatem, dat relevium (iis. vid.).

Willelmus Waryn cepit de domino i messuagium dimidiam virgatam terre quondam Stephani patris sui, et dat domino in gersuma (dimidiam marcam, in hierietto i equum).

Johanna Attewode reddidit sursum in manu domini i messuagium xv acras terre ad opus Johannis Atewode qui dat pro gersuma (vs.). Memorandum quod predicta Johanna habebit iii acras terre ad terminum vite sue de predictis xv acris sine servitio (utrum resid?).

Juratores presentant quod Thomas Rous sufficiens est etc. capere i messuagium et dimidiam virgatam terre quondam Roberti Sterling usque ad plenam (etatem) Henrici filii dicti Roberti et fecit fidelitatem. De gersuma nihil quia minoritas. Unde venit i jumentum pro herietto.

Et quod Robertus Steven' etc. i messuagium dimidiam virgatam terre quondam Roberti Bradenach, tenendum ad voluntatem domini, etc.

Et quod Johannes Waryn etc. i messuagium (x?) v acras terre quondam Roberti Watte ad opus Willelmi filii predicti Roberti (in die?) pervenit et venit domino in herietto i boviculum.

Et quod Thomas Andrew etc. i messuagium dimidiam virgatam terre quondam Johannis Bedell junioris, tenendum ad voluntatem domini (heriettum? i vacca).

Et quod Johannes Rolf etc. i messuagium xv acras de cotlando quondam Johannis Bedell (heriettum i vacca).

Et quod Johannes filius Lucis Rolf etc. i messuagium xv acras de cotlando quondam dicti Lucis (patris) in herietto venit (i vacca).

Et quod Robertus Waryn etc. i messuagium et x acras terre quondam Johannis Waryn usque ad plenam etatem heredis dicti Johannis (heriettum i vacca).

Et quod Sabina uxor Simonis Gilbert (decessi?) tenebit i messuagium x acras terre et heriettum (i vacca).

Et quod Johannes Wynegor alius Robertus etc. i messuagium x acras terre cotlandi quondam Willelmi Wynegor etc., i vitulus pro herietto.

Et quod Willelmus Attewode etc. i messuagium dimidiam virgatam terre quondam Rogeri Duk' etc., heriettum i vacca.

Thomas Rous cepit de domino dimidiam virgatam terre quondam Roberti Renisson et dabit per annum (   ) Roberti iib. frumenti, iib. pisarum, etc. Tenendum etc., et dat domino in gersuma (iis.)

APPENDIX XVIII

Activities of the Reeve and Beadle

1. Burwell, (P R O, SC 2, Port. 179, no. 20): Et preposito et bedello quia non distrinxerunt Thomam filium Panham de Halt' ad faciendum domino homagium relevium et fidelitatem de tenemento quondam Thome de Beyville in? Burwell, xiid. Et preceptum (est) quod distringatur.

Johannes Ideyne et Henricus le Drynere sunt plegii Willelmi le Oryner ad repertanda bona et catalla sua que subtraxit de feodo domini et predictus Willelmus presentatus traditus fuit in custodia prepositi et bedelli et quia ipsum non habuerunt ideo etc. vid. Et preceptum est distringere dictum Willelmum ad respondendum ad proximum.

Et preposito et bedello quia non distrinxerunt Nicholaum Arfick ad faciendum domino homagium pro una acra terre que adquisivit de Bartholomeo filio Barthotomei sicut preceptum fuit in ultimo visu, iiid. Et preceptum est quod distringatur ad idem faciendum citra proximum visum.

Et preposito quia non arestavit Nicholaum Clericum sicut ei preceptum fuit in curia autumpna pro eo quod se subtraxit de feodo domini cum catallis suis sine licentia domini, iiid. Et preceptum est quod distringatur ad respondendum apud proximum de eo quod se subtraxit.

Et preposito et bedello quia non arestaverunt Goderobbe de eo quod falcando abduxit marischum domini iiid. Et preceptum (est) quod arestetur ad respondendum ad proximum ad faciendum domino etc.

2. Hemmingford Abbots, (P R O, SC 2, Port. 179, no. 18): Et prepositis quia non

arestaverunt Thomam Neel ad respondendum de hoc quod se subtraxit etc. vid. Et preceptum est quod arestetur etc.

Et prepositis quia non levaverunt de Thoma le Marescal xxiid. ad opus Thome filio Ade quos recuperaverunt nec ipse (   ) iiid. Et preceptum adhuc quod leventur.

Et prepositis quia non habuerunt Matildam Eduard ad respondendum de hoc quod male glenavit in autumpno (   ).

Preceptum ballivo et preposito videre quamdam peciam prati de quo conventio est inter Adam Cademan nativum domini et Johannem Porthos. Et inter Thomam Oremund' nativum domini et predictum Johannem. Ita quod etc.

Et prepositis quia non distrinxerunt Johannem de Hagenham ad respondendum Willelmo Plumbe de placito transgressionis iiid. Et preceptum est adhuc quod distringatur ad respondendum ut prius.

3. HEMMINGFORD ABBOTS, (B M, Add. Ch. 39582): Et dicunt quod Thomas Jordan arrando appropriavit sibi de quarentena vocato Watelondo in longitudine xl perticatarum et in latitudine unius pedis ad nocumentum etc. Ideo ipse etc. vid., plegius prepositus. Et preceptum (est) quod emendetur.

Et dicunt quod idem Thomas arrando appropriavit sibi de communa apud Langemerch in longitudine iiiior pedum et latitudine iii perticatarum ad nocumentum. Ideo ipse etc. vid., plegius propositus. Et preceptum (est) quod emendetur.

Et dicunt quod idem Thomas fodiendo deterioravit pratum domini ad caput crofti dicti Thome. Ideo ipse etc. xld., plegius prepositus. Et preceptum (est quod emendetur).

Et dicunt quod idem Thomas et manupastus sui continuatim metent prata vicinorum suorum ad dampnum totius homagii. Ideo etc. xiid.

Et dicunt quod idem Thomas procuravit capitalis taxatoribus quintidecimo denario hoc anno se admitti pro vicinis suis et ibidem ostendit dictis taxatoribus secreta vicinorum suorum per quod tota villata taxata fuit ad maiorem summam per procurationem dicti Thome, ad quadraginta solidos. Ideo pro transgressione in misericordia xxs.

Et dicunt quod idem Thomas dedit ballivis domini Regis et aliis magnatibus ad procurandum quod esset unus de taxatoribus pro vicinis suis guarantum, et sic expendit catalla domini ad dampnum etc. Et quod est communis adulator contra proficium totius homagii ad dampnum etc., xld., plegius Willelmus Trappe.

Et dicunt quod idem Thomas detinet iiiior s. de tota villata. Ideo preceptum (est) prepositis levare dictos iiiior s. ad opus totius ville, vid.

APPENDIX XIX

GROUP RESPONSIBILITIES OF CUSTOMARY TENANTS

1. WISTOW, (B M, Add. Ch. 39562): Omnes custumarii de Wystowe et Parva Ravele petiierunt ad ultimum visum respitum usque ad Natale domini pro registro querendo insimul cum gratia domini super consuetudinem habere recipiendi et asportandi extra pratum domini die falcationis et hoc sub pena xxs. domino solvendorum. Et ab illo tempore usque nunc inde nihil fecerunt, nec in registro secundum calumpnium ipsorum nihil inventum est pro eisdem. Ideo pena predicta de eisdem levetur.

Omnes custumarii de Wystowe et Parva Ravele in contemptu domini remanerunt et contra dixerunt falcare in prato apud Thurnbrugg uno die pro proximo die operabili eisdem recompensando ad instantiam Willelmi de Beaumeys tunc servientis exparte domini factam. Ideo sunt in misericordia iis.

2. Wistow, (P R O, SC 2, Port. 179, no. 10): Quia omnes custumarii de Parva Ravele nondum procuraverunt? dominum abbatem ad superonerandam separabilem pasturam dicti domini apud Assedyche quam quidem pasturam dicti custumarii bestiis suis pascebant duobus annis elapsis pro quibus bestiis debuerunt domino satisfecisse sub pena xxs. et nihil inde fecerunt. Ideo preceptum est quod dicti denarii leventur de eisdem vel quod inde a domino impetrent remedium.

3. Wistow, (B M, Add. Ch. 39850): Et de tota villata de Parva Ravele quia non veniunt ad cariandum fenum domini apud Rameseye quando sumoniti fuerunt exceptis Willelmo Marger et Thoma Beneyt, iiiis. Et de predictis Willelmo et Thoma xiid. Plegii alter alterius.

Et tota villata de Wystowe cum Parva Ravele quia contradixerunt collegere nuces in bosco prout de iure debent que estimantur ad sex busellos pretii xxxd. Et pro transgressione in misericordia vis.

Preceptum est preposito levare de omnibus custumariis de Parva Ravele xxs. ad opus domini pro eo quod pascebant separabilem pasturam domini apud Assedyche per tres annos prout compertum fuit ad ultimam curiam.

4. Wistow, (B M, Add. Ch. 39755): De omnibus custumariis de Wystowe et Ravele quia supercedebant arrare domino in septima proxima praeter Nativitatem beate Marie, anno regni Regis Edwardi xxi°. Et posuerunt se in registro quod dictam arruram non deberent sicut patet in proximo visu precedente in quo visu dictum fuit eis quod facerent scrutare per dictum registrum quod quidem non fecerunt. Ideo in misericordia iis., plegii alter alterius.

5. Abbots Ripton, (P R O, SC 2, Port. 179, no. 12): Omnes custumarii de villata de Ryptone qui cariare debent averagium in misericordia eo quod cum summoniti sunt sepissime ultra manerium ad faciendum averagium suum in crastino versus Rameseiam sacci eorum perimpleti sunt. Et sic commorantur dicti sacci impleti usque in crastinum usque ad horam primam et horam tertiam antequam dicti custumarii veniunt ad cariandum dictum averagium apud Rameseiam ad magnum dampnum domino et conventui, dimidia marca, plegii alter alterius.

6. Bury, (B M, Add. Ch. 39562): Omnes custumarii de Byri subtrahunt et non faciunt nec dum facerent arare aruras domino suo debitas et consuetas scilicet qualibet septimana per diem veneris vel mercurie unam aruram. Dum tamen ipsi arant super terram propriam vel etiam super terram alienam pro qua quidem arura terre aliene capiunt pecuniam. Sed dicunt expresse se non teneri eidem domino in aliqua arura postquam terra sua propria penitus sit arata. Prefixus est eis dies ad discuciendum istud negotium coram domino abbate et senescallis suis ad diem dominicam proximam post festum Sancte Lucie virginis apud Rameseiam, ita quod quilibet eorum ad tunc veniat ibidem sub pena dimidie marce.

7. Houghton, (B M, Add. Ch. 39586): Omnes custumarii de Houghton et Wytton videlicet lxix virgatarii et semivirgatarii calumpniati sunt in ista curia per senescallum de hoc quod irierunt ad cervisiam ad denarium emendum apud Huntyngdon et Sanctum Ivonem et aliis diebus quam diebus fori contra permissionem et ordinationem factas per abbatem Willelmum de Gomecestre sicut continetur in rotulis curie autumne anno dicti abbatis quinto et per dominum Johannem abbatem nunc

adhuc continuatas sicut continetur in curia autumpna tenta die sabbati in crastino Sancte Margarete anno dicti domini abbatis x°: quod si quis custumarius predictorum inde fuit convictus conferret domino duodecim denarios nomine pene. Qui veniunt (et dicunt) quod nullus eorum se sane potest acquietare nec dedicere quam contra permissionem et ordinationem predictas deliquerit (   ) est quod predicta pena videlicet lxixs. levetur de predictis custumariis videlicet de quolibet eorum xiid.

8. GRAVELEY, (P R O, SC 2, Port. 179, no. 7): Preceptum fuit toti villate querere unum lapidem molarem apud Sanctum Ivonem sicut ex consuetudine deberent ut creditur. Et hoc contra dicunt facere. Sed dicunt quod ad cariandum illum lapidem adiuvare tenentur et non omnino sumptibus eorum propriis illum cariare. Ideo preceptum est querere registrum de consuetudinibus et servitiis eorum.

APPENDIX XX

BYELAWS DERIVING FROM THE WHOLE VILLAGE

1. HEMMINGFORD ABBOTS, (P R O, SC 2, Port. 179, no. 10): Quia ex assensu omnium custumariorum statutum fuit in curia visus quattuor annis elapsis quod si aliquis de predictis custumariis convictus fuerit quod emit cervisiam caram quam ad obolum daret domino xii denarios de pena. Et compertum est per inquisitionem quod omnes emerunt cervisiam ad denarium praeter Willelmus Dargon, unde summa custumariis lxiiiis. Et ad presentiam fecerunt finem pro xxs.

2. WARBOYS, (B M, Add. Ch. 39760): Totum homagium de Wardebois tam liberi quam alii petunt in plena curia quod non liceat decetero alicui de comitate vendere vel dare aliquem roscum barbatum vel tassatum in marisco de Wardebois quousque illum roscum vel (   ) in mansis suis propriis cariaverunt et tassaverunt sub pena dimidie marce domino solvendo quotienscumque aliquis eorum contra dictam ordinationem deliquerit aliquo modo. Et concessum est in plena curia etc. in forma predicta.

3. BROUGHTON, (B M, Add. Ch. 39477): Ordinatus tam per dominum quam per totum homagium quod nullus se intromittat in campo ad falcandum metendum seu aliquum bladum carectandum decetero per totum autumpnum neque sero neque mane dummodo nox est sub pena cuilibet xld. Et quod nullus conculcabit stipulam alienam cum aliquibus bestiis durante toto autumpno usque festum Sancti Michaelis nisi unusquisque super terram propriam sub pena predicta. Et quod nullus pasturabit cum aliquibus bestiis inter aliquum bladum in campis donec ubi blada amoveantur plenarie per spatium unius stadii sub pena predicta.

4. WARBOYS, 1301 (B M, Add. Ch. 39850): Ex assensu omnium custumariorum de Wardebois et de Caldecote concessum est quod si quis eorum fuit convictus quod emit carius cervisiam quam lagenam ad obolum infra manerium predictum dabit domino sex denarios de pena. Et ideo inquirendum est, etc.

5. WISTOW, 1294 (B M, Add. Ch. 39755): Preceptum est quod de cetero nullus intret mariscum de Wystowe ad falcandum roscum donec omnes simul et semel intrent ad falcandum sicut dudum ordinatum fuit per communem assensum totius villate sub pena ii solidorum quod potest invenire in curia tenta apud Wystowe die lune proxime post Translationem Sancti Benedicti anno Willelmi Abbatis xviii°.

APPENDIX XXI

Enclosure for the Common Good

1. Abbots Ripton, (B M Add. Ch. 34370): Et quod Catsherdgap obstupetur citra festum Sancti Laurentii sub pena iiiid.

2. Little Raveley (Wistow): (B M, Add. Ch. 34823): Ponitur in pena quod omnes gappes de Ontyescroft corel usque Rowdich claudantur citra festum Anunciationis Beate Marie cuilibet sub pena predicta, vid. domino et vid. ecclesie.

3. Upwood, (B M, Add. Ch. 39661): Et pena omnibus tenentibus tam de Upwode quam de Raveley quod faciunt sepes et fossata erga neumedowe ante festum Sancti Hugonis proximum sub pena cuilibet iiis. iiiid.

Et quod nullus ponat aliquam bestiam in dicto neumedowe a festo Sancti Laurentii usque festum Sancti Michaelis sub pena vis. viiid.

4. Wistow, (B M, Add. Ch. 34822): Ponitur in pena quod quilibet faciat clausuram suam inter le Hathe et campum citra festum Sancti Martini sub pena xiid. domino et xiid. ecclesie.

5. Warboys, (B M, Add. Ch. 39775): Et quod sub pena (quilibet) de villata quod faciat unusquisque (claudere?) gappes suas ad latus silve de Wardeboys predicta citra festum Martini Episcopi et Confessoris in hieme proxime futura sub pena (xiid.).

6. Upwood, (B M, Add. Ch. 39775): Et quod sub pena omnia fossata emundentur istius villate et omnes gappes sepem (emse?) obstuperentur citra festum Nativitatis domini proximo futurum sub pena cuilibet xld.

7. Hemmingford Abbots, (B M, Add. Ch. 34323): Et pena quod quilibet faciat clausuram suam propriam ad finem orti sui bene et sufficienter a hoxtensday usque festum ad vincula Sancti Petri proximo futurum, quilibet sub pena vis. viiid.

8. Ellington, (B M, Add. Ch. 34825): Et preceptum est cuilibet quod faciat clausuram circa dimidiam virgultam infra octavum Martini proximum etc. sub pena de xld.

9. Upwood, (B M, Add. Ch. 34827): Et quod quilibet tenens terre erga Nesthaledyche et Bochnalesyde faciat clausuram inter campum et mariscum citra festum Sancti Martini proximo futurum quilibet sub pena xiid.

10. Chatteris, (B M, Add. Ch. 34827): Et ponitur in pena quod quilibet tenens repereat partem suam de clausura manerii citra festum Sancti Petri Advincula sub pena iis.

11. Little Raveley, (B M, Add. Ch. 39870): Et pena quod quilibet faciat clausuram a crofto Willelmi Onty usque Huntyngdonweyena citra festum Omnium Sanctorum sub pena vid. domino.

12. Great Raveley, (Upwood), (B M, Add. Ch. 34829): Et preceptum est cuilibet quod faciat clausuram propriam inter mariscum et highmadefeld infra xv^a cuilibet sub pena (   ).

Et preceptum est cuilibet de Ravele quod non permittat aliquem ire ultra ortos suos neque pedestres neque equestres cuilibet sub pena (   ).

13. Warboys, (B M, Add. Ch. 39774): Et quod quilibet faciat clausuram a Goodmanstile usque Burywodeend citra dictum festum et sub pena predicta etc.

APPENDIX XXII

Byelaws Governing Re-entry to Pasture

1. Upwood, (B M, Add. Ch. 34819): Et quod nullus mittat animalia sua in campum neque iuxta latus le Fen citra festum Sancti Martini sub pena xxs.

2. Wistow, (B M, Add. Ch. 34819): Et quod nullus reintrat in prato citra festum Sancti Benedicti sub pena xiid.

3. Upwood, (B M, Add. Ch. 34370): Et quod nullus veniet in le Frith quousque fenum amovetur sub pena xld.

4. Warboys, (B M, Add. Ch. 34370): Ponitur in pena quod nullus porcus veniet in pascam inter le Logehill et Wolfhay citra fextum Inventionis Sancti Crucis sub pena cuilibet delinqueti vis. viiid.

5. Shillington, (B M, Add. Ch. 39656): Et pena xiid. quod nullus custodiat oves in Stokkynge citra festum Omnium Sanctorum.

6. Brington, (B M, Add. Ch. 39656): Et quod nullus de cetero imponat aliqua animalia in Martyn Slade nisi sic solet (   ) ab antiquo videlicet usque festum Nativitatis Sancti Johannis ( ) sub pena (vid. ?).

7. Upwood, (B M, Add. Ch. 39656): Et quod nullus custodiat aliqua animalia in pratum comitatis post Purificationem sub pena iiis. iiiid. similiter.

8. Little Stukeley, (B M, Add. Ch. 39780): Et ordinatum est quod nullus ponat agnos vel oves nec aliqua alia animalia in tres garse pasturam nisi cum assensu omnium tenentium sub pena cuilibet xxs.

9. Chatteris, (B M, Add. Ch. 39656): Et quod nullus custodiat aliqua animalia in Elehalf de cetero sub pena viiid. domino et viiid. ecclesie videlicet etc.

10. Abbots Ripton, (B M, Add. Ch.34370): Ponitur in pena quod nullus depascat infra dominium nisi mansit infra dominium sub pena xld. domino et xld. ecclesie.

11. Great Raveley, (B M, Add. Ch. 39656): Et quod quilibet exponat porcos suos extra pratum comitatis de cetero sub pena iiis. iiiid.

12. Little Raveley, (B M, Add. Ch. 39661): Et ordinatum est quod nullus ponat aliqua animalia vocantur y est bullock super dominium a festo Sancte Elene usque festum Sancti Michaelis sub pena iiis. iiiid.

13. Upwood, (B M, Add. Ch.39661): Et quod nullus tenens ponat aliqua animalia in Higham Feld nisi equos et vitulos vocantur Wenelyng Calffe a fine autumni usque omnes tenentes concordati sunt et etiam nullus habens nisi cotagium ponat aliqua animalia in dicto campo sub pena cuilibet iiis. iiiid.

14. Warboys, (B M ,Add. Ch. 39771): Et quod nullus ligat nec custodiat animalia sua in le leyes de Caldecote cuilibet sub pena xxd.

15. Warboys, (B M, Add. Ch. 39775): Et quod sub pena nullus commorans dicte villate ligat pullanos suos equos nec equas super communes vias ibidem usque (   ) festum Ascensionis Domini proximo futurum sub pena cuilibet xiid.

16. Weston, (B M, Add. Ch. 39870): Et pena omnibus tenentibus quod nullus fugat equos in tempore estate absque hoc quod sunt ligati sub pena vid.

17. Wistow, (B M, Add. Ch. 39869): Et pena omnibus tenentibus quod nullus permitat animalium neque bidentem intrat infra campum vocatur Wodefeld a festo Sancti Petri advincula usque festum Sancti Michaelis Archangelis, quilibet sub pena xiid. domino et xiid ecclesie.

APPENDIX XXIII

The Byelaw and Pasture Responsibilities

1. Upwood, (B M, Add. Ch. 34823): Ponitur in pena quod nullus teneat pullos neque bestias circa Botnale a festo Purificationis usque festum Sancti Michaelis sine custode cuilibet sub pena xld.

2. Shillington, (B M, Add. Ch. 39656): Et pena iiis. iiiid. quod quilibet tenens i n Stondon custodiat pasturam propriam usque autumpn (   )
Et pena iiis. iiiid. quod quilibet eorum bene exerceat et custodiat officium pro videlicet qualibet dicta custodia.

3. Brington, (B M, Add. Ch. 39656): Et quod nullus custodiat aliqua animalia nec aliqua volatilia in (   ) coram custode ordinato pro custodia eorumdem sub pena iiis. iiiid.

4. Warboys, (B M, Add. Ch. 39775): Et quod sub pena similiter vis. viiid. nullus dicte villate ponat porcos suos (   ) le Herth nisi sunt anulati.

5. Upwood, (B M, Add. Ch. 34831): Et preceptum est omnibus tenentibus quod nullus tenet porcos nisi sunt anulati decetero, cuilibet sub pena xxd.

6. Wistow, (B M, Add. Ch. 34817): Ordinatum est per assensum domini quod nullus depascat cum averiis suis in stipulam comitatis citra festum Nativitatis Beate Marie sub pena xiid.
Et quod nullus depascat cum bidentibus vel boviculis in Chanereth usque idem festum et similiter quod quilibet tenens ligare facit equos suos supra pratum suum proprium et non alibi sub eadem pena.

7. Wistow, (B M, Add. Ch. 39775): Et quod Johannes Randolf f(   ) in ultimo visu edictum quod nullus ponat vaccas suas in campos ibidem nisi sub custodia (   ) ipse fecit contra ordinationem istam, ideo in misericordia.

8. Warboys, (B M, Add. Ch. 39762): Preceptum est quod nullus bercarius nec nullus custos bestiarum amodo teneat nec ducet canes in mariscum, sub pena xiid.

9. Wistow, (B M, Add. Ch. 39856): Et quod Robertus Milner habuit (xx) porcos suos in custodia unius pueri insufficientis in bladum vicinorum ad nocumentum, iiid.

10. Wistow, (B M, Add. Ch. 39878): Et ordinatum est quod quilibet fugabit ligatos pullos suos equinos euntes in campis seminatis post etatem iiii^{or} septimanorum sub eodem forisfacto pro quolibet pullano xxd.

11. Broughton, (B M, Add. Ch. 39484): Et quod nullus custodiat equum in communibus campis inter equos vicini aliquo anno in perpetuum cuilibet sub pena iiis. iiiid.

12. Brington, (B M, Add. Ch. 34909): Et preceptum est quod nullus ligat nulla animalia per capita in commune nisi assensu tenentium cuilibet sub pena iiis. iiiid. domino et iiis. iiiid. ecclesie.

APPENDIX XXIV

BYELAWS CONTINUED: STUBBLE PASTURE, etc.

1. WISTOW, (B M, Add. Ch. 39775): Et quod sub pena nullus commorans istius villate ponat aliquos porcos in campos comitatis citra istum diem per eorumdem communem assensum perficum sub pena vis. viiid., xld. inde solvendo domino et xld. inde ecclesie.

2. GIRTON, (P R O, SC 2, Port. 179, no. 75): Ordinatum est ad hunc diem quod nullus huius villate permittet porcos porcellos equos vaccas bouwnok (   ) in campis seminatis quousque publicalem proclamationem de le hokey sit proclamata per rectorem huius villate publice in ecclesia sub pena cuilibet sit in defectu iid. totiens quotiens defecerit etc.

3. UPWOOD, (B M, Add. Ch. 34828): Et quod nullus custodiat nulla bestia in le falowfeld pro dampno faciunt in frumento cuilibet sub pena xiid. domino et xiid. ecclesie.

4. BROUGHTON, (B M, Add. Ch. 39484): Et pena quod nullus ligat equos in stipulo frumenti a festo Sancti Petri ad vincula usque festum Sancti Michaelis Archangeli de anno in anno cuilibet sub pena pro quolibet defectu vis. viiid.

5. UPWOOD, (B M, Add. Ch. 39765): Ordinatum est per assensum domini et totius comitatis quod nullus homo habeat averia sua euntes in stipulam de tempore quo (   ) blada usque in tres septimas proximas sequentes et ulterius si dominus consenserit nisi sint equi carectarii et adhuc ligati, quilibet sub pena xld. scilicet domino.

6. WISTOW, (B M, Add. Ch. 39857): Ordinatum est per assensum domini et comitatis quod nullus habeat pullos suos euntes in campis quousque omnia blada fuerunt inhorreata sub pena xld.
Et quod nullus permitat averia sua venire inter schokkes sub pena xld. Et quod nullus depascat cum equis in prato de Chenereth citra festum Sancti Michaelis sub pena xld.

7. WISTOW, (B M, Add. Ch. 39860): Ordinatum est per assensum domini et comitatis quod nullus habeat pullanos euntes in bladum domini et comitatis a gula Augusti usque blada fuerunt inhorreata sub pena iis. solvendo domino.

8. ELLSWORTH, (P R O, SC 2, Port. 179, no. 36): Ordinatum est per assensum totius comitatis quod nullus depascat inter blada vicinorum nec in stipula cum bovibus bestiis suis sub pena iis. solvendo domino.

9. BROUGHTON, (B M, Add. Ch. 34819): Et quod nullus mittat animalia sua praeter animalia caruce in stipula frumenti sub pena xiid. citra festum Sancti Michaelis.

10. WYTTON, (B M, Add. Ch. 39656): Et quod nullus decetero pascabit equos in le Schirefeld post bladum asportatum absque communi consensu totius villate cuilibet sub pena xiid.

11. UPWOOD, (B M, Add. Ch. 39661): Et quod nullus tenens de Upwode neque de Rameseye ponat aliqua animalia in campo frumenti vel in campo pisarum praeter (   ) per spatium treize septimas post finem autumni sub pena cuilibet vis, viiid.

12. KING's RIPTON, (B M, Add. Ch. 39775): Et quod sub pena nullus istius villate ponat oves boves seu equos vel equas in campos comitatis infra quindecim dies post quam rector ecclesie ibidem plene cariavit pisas suas extra campos eiusdem villate sub pena cuilibet ( ) quotiens xiid.

13. LITTLE RAVELEY, (B M, Add. Ch. 39662): Et quod nullus ponat porcos suos in campis seminatis ante finem autumpni sine assensu omnium tenentium sub pena cuilibet iiis. iiiid.

14. UPWOOD, (B M, Add. Ch. 34819): Et quod nullus mittat pullanos in stipulam priusquam blada domini cariantur sub pena cuilibet xiid.

15. WISTOW, (B M, Add. Ch. 34819): Et quod nullus numellabit jumenta sua super terram vicini sui antequam blada abinde cariantur sub pena vid.
Ordinatum est quod nullus (mittat) pullanos suos solutos in bladis a festo Sancti Petri advincula usque Michaelis sub pena ( ).

16. ABBOTS RIPTON, (B M, Add. Ch. 34819): Et quod nullus depascat in stipulam cum animaliis suis citra festum Nativitatis Beate Marie sub pena xiid.

17. UPWOOD, (B M, Add. Ch. 34370): Et quod nulli porci neque bidentes venient in campum sine licentia prepositorum autumpnalis sub pena xiid.
Et quod nulla bestia veniet in stipulam frumenti citra festum Nativitatis Beate Marie sub pena xiid.
Ponitur in pena quod nullus ligabit equos in campo cum pullanis solutis sub pena xiid.

18. WISTOW, (B M, Add. Ch. 34370): Et quod nullus depascat in stipulam frumenti citra festum Nativitatis Beate Marie sub pena ( ).

19. ABBOTS RIPTON, (B M, Add. Ch. 34370): Ponitur in pena quod nullus depascat in stipulam frumenti citra festum Sancti Michaelis sub pena xiid. domino et xiid. ecclesie.

20. BROUGHTON, (B M, Add. Ch. 39484): Et pena quod nullus custodiat porcos in autumpno in stipula frumenti donec cariaverunt totum granum restens super suum forlongum de anno in anno cuilibet sub pena xxd.
Et pena quod nullus ponat faldum suum in campis pisarum quousque pisae fuerunt cariatae de anno in anno cuilibet sub pena xiid.

21. WARBOYS, (B M, Add. Ch. 39765): Ordinatum est per assensum domini et comitatis quod nullus homo depascat infra Schokkis cum averiis suis quousque omnia blada unum stadium sunt plenarie inhorreata sub pena xld.

22. ELTON, (B M, Add. Ch. 34819): Et quod nullus mittat pullanos suos inter tassa in autumpno sub pena xiid.

23. UPWOOD, (B M, Add. Ch. 34832): Et ponitur in pena quod nullus ligat equos suos in campo seminato inter grana cum pullo soluto ( ) fine autumpno sub pena xiid.

24. WISTOW, (B M, Add. Ch. 34819): Et quod nullus mittat animalia sua soluta in stipulam quousque stadium reservetur ex una perte sub pena xiid.

25. BROUGHTON, (B M, Add. Ch. 34819): Ordinatum est quod nullus mittat animalia sua in campum priusquam blada i stadium inde cariantur sub pena xxd. domino et xxd. ecclesie.

26. ABBOTS RIPTON, (B M, Add. Ch. 34819): Et quod nullus inducat nec numellat

animalia in stipulam antequam rastetur sub pena vid. solvendo ecclesie et vid. domino.

27. UPWOOD, (B M, Add. Ch. 34370): Et quod nulli pullani sequantur carectas in campum in autumpno sub pena xiid.

28. LITTLE RAVELEY, (B M, Add. Ch. 34370): Et quod nullus depascat in campo quousque rastetur sub pena xiid.

29. GRAVELEY, (B M, Add. Ch. 34817): Et quod nullus ligare faciet equos suos noctenter in campis et infra bladum comitatis in autumpno sub pena xld.

APPENDIX XXV

BYELAWS CONTINUED: DITCHING AND DRAINING

1. ABBOTS RIPTON, (B M, Add. Ch. 34370): Et quod omnia fossata infra dominium mundentur citra festum Sancti Michaelis sub pena cuilibet iiiid.

2. BRINGTON, (B M, Add. Ch. 39656): Et quod fossata in manu domini iuxta Eston Place mundentur et omnia alia fossata ad nocumentum alibi mundentur citra festum Sancti Andree cuilibet sub pena xiid.

3. UPWOOD, (B M, Add. Ch. 39656): Et quod omnes habentes fossata erga Nerthalfdich et Neumede emendentur citra festum Purificationis Beate Marie sub pena iiis. iiiid.

4. GREAT RAVELEY, (B M, Add. Ch. 39661): Ordinatum est quod quilibet tenens estuvabit fossata sua ante festum Sancti Michaelis sub pena cuilibet iiis. iiiid.

5. GREAT RAVELEY, (B M, Add. Ch. 39775): Et pena omnibus ibidem quod omnia fossata eiusdem villate emundentur citra festum Inventionis Sancte Crucis proximum futurum sub pena cuilibet iiiid.

6. KING's RIPTON, (B M, Add. Ch. 39775): Et pena omnibus similiter ibidem quod omnia fossata non mundata emundentur citra festum Sancti Thome Apostoli proximum futurum sub pena cuilibet iis.

7. WARBOYS, (P R O, SC 2, Port. 179, no. 34): Preceptum est toti homagio quod aciat fossata sua debita apud Wodemer et Stokkyng sub pena xld.

APPENDIX XXVI

BYELAWS CONTINUED: ROADS

1. WISTOW, (B M, Add. Ch. 34823): Ponitur in pena quod quilibet tenens erga tenementum suum faciat viam regiam cum lapidis, et quod mundantur fossata sua proprie vie citra festum Michaelis cuilibet sub pena vid.

Et quod firmarius (iid.) manerii non mundavit cursum aquae nec fecit pontem vocat Paddokbrgge per quod aqua amittitur extra rectum cursum suum, ideo preceptum est reparare sub pena xiid.

2. WISTOW, (B M, Add. Ch. 39661): Et ordinatum est quod quilibet tenens per

partem suam (   ) viam in lapidem (   ) ante festum Sancti Michaelis proximum et quod Johannes Syd' et Silvester Campyon' erunt supervisores dicte vie et quod quilibet perm' ordinationes suas in dicta via sub pena cuilibet vis. viiid.

3. Wistow, (B M, Add. Ch. 39478): Ordinatum est per totum homagium quod quilibet homo de Ravele qui habet terram et tenementum colliget ii carectas petri et ponent eos in Waer iuxta portam Johannis Cleryvaux in regia via sub pena cuilibet xiid.

4. Upwood, (B M, Add. Ch. 34826): Et quod nullus faciat viam super terram Thome Newman erga Richewewroke sub pena xiid.

5. Upwood, (B M, Add. Ch. 34832): Et quod nullus faciat viam ultra Longewong neque (   ) sub pena vid.

6. Warboys, (B M, Add. Ch. 39780) : Et quod nullus de Wistowe veniet per agros de Wardeboys cum carrucis suis nisi per stratam vici sub pena cuilibet xls.

Et quod nullus venit super dictum le Bauke cum carrucis suis de aliqua alia villa sub pena xxs.

7. Ellington, (P R O, SC 2, Port. 179, no. 40): Ordinatum est per assensum domini et totius comitatis quod quilibet tenens sit p(   ) ad preceptum prepositi ad faciendam et emendendam regiam viam apud Thornhill citra festum Sancti Martini sub pena xld.

8. Hemmingford Abbots, (P R O, SC 2, Port. 179, no. 18): Preceptum est omnibus custumariis emendare viam versus molendinum citra proximum visum sub pena viginta solidorum domino solvendorum.

9. Warboys, (P R O, SC 2, Port. 179, no. 20): Preceptum est villate quod mundare faciat ripariam iuxta pontem quia obscurata est ita quod regia via submergitur. Et quod hoc faciant citra festum Sancti Michaelis sub pena dimidie marce.

APPENDIX XXVII

Control of the Use of Reeds in the Marsh

1. Upwood, (B M, Add. Ch. 39478): Ordinatum est per totum homagium quod nullus tenens qui manet infra dominium domini falcabit neque mete' sirpos crescentes per litera marisci neque in marisco a die Paschae usque festum Nativitatis Beate Marie sub pena cuilibet de vis. viiid.

2. Upwood, (B M, Add. Ch. 34820): Et quod Robertus Jurdan (iiid.) de Wenyngton, Robertus Juell' (iiid.) de eodem, Willelmus Wattes (iiid.), Johannes in the Hirne (iiid.), Willelmus White (iiid.), Walterus Schepherd (iiid.), s(   ) sirpos in marisco et superoneraverunt communem pasturam et non sunt communari ideo cuilibet eorum per se in misericordia.

3. Wistow, (B M, Add. Ch. 39775): Et quod pena omnibus eiusdem villate nullus succedat aliquas ornos crescentes in le communes balkes ibidem sub pena iis.

4. Ramsey, (B M, Add. Ch. 39662): Et quod dictus Johannes Astone (iiiid.) succidit salices super Newlodebanke in misericordia. Et pena ei ne amodo sic succidat sub pena xls.

5. Wistow, (B M, Add. Ch. 34820): Et quod Johannes Plombe (vid.) de Caldecote venit in marisco et falcavit roscum et cariavit usque Caldecote. Et quod Ricardus persona ecclesie de Wistowe vendidit roscum extra villam videlicet mille Laurentio Merton. Et quod Willelmus Derworth vendidit iiiixx de rosco extra villam. Ordinatum est quod nullus falcet roscum in marisco a festo Sancti Petri advincula usque Pascham sub pena dimidiam marcam. Et quod nullus extraneus falcet in marisco sub pena dimidiam marcam domino et dimidiam marcam ecclesie.

6. Warboys, (P R O, SC 2, Port. 179, no. 34): Tota comitas ordinaverunt quod nemo metat vel falcat in marisco de hoc die usque festum Paschae et a festo Pentecoste usque festum Assumptionis Beate Marie sub pena xxs. et si aliquis habeat plus quam Vᶜ rosci non ligati ultra aliqu (   ).

7. Warboys, (B M, Add. Ch. 39762): Et dicunt quod tota comitas de Broughtone tam liberi quam nativi noctanter cum carectis et operariis suis in mariscum de Wardeboys intrant et per noctem falcant et cariant tam roscum de Wardebois falcatum et ligatum quam roscum proprium ad dampnum domini et totius comitatis. Preceptum est ne amodo hoc faciatur sub pena dimidiam marcam.

8. Warboys, (B M, Add. Ch. 39769): Et quod nullus falcet roscum in marisco a festo Sancti Martini usque festum Inventionis Sancti Crucis sub pena dimidiam marcam.

9. Wistow, (B M, Add. Ch. 39860): Ordinatum est per assensum domini et comitatis quod nullus habeat pullanos euntes in bladum domini et comitatis a gula Augusti usque blada fuerunt inhorreata sub pena iis. solvendo domino. Et quod nullus falcere faciat roscum nisi de assensu del Fenreves sub pena xs.

10. Wistow, (B M, Add. Ch. 39768): Ordinatum est per dominum et totum homagium quod nullus falcabit in marisco de novo rosco priusquam totum vetus roscum falcetur sub pena xs. Et quod nullus falcet roscum in marisco a festo Sancti Petri advincula usque festum Pasche sub pena xs. solvendo domino.

11. Wistow, (B M, Add. Ch. 39755): Preceptum est quod de cetero nullus intret mariscum de Wystowe ad falcandum roscum donec omnes simul et semel intrent ad falcandum, sicut dudum ordinatum fuit per communem assensum totius villate sub pena ii solidos, quod potest invenire in curia tenta apud Wystowe die Lune proximo post translationem Sancti Benedicti anno W. Abbatis XVIIIᵒ.

APPENDIX XXVIII

Community Control of the Use of Turf

1. Great Raveley (Upwood), (B M, Add. Ch. 39656): Et quod nullus de cetero fodiat seu fodere faciat turbas in marisco nisi secundum antiquam ordinationem cuilibet sub pena xxs.

2. Upwood, (B M, Add. Ch. 34820): Ordinatum est quod nullus fodiat turbas super lelakelonde super Fayway sub pena xld.

3. Upwood, (B M, Add. Ch. 34828): Et preceptum est quod quilibet fodit hassocum per totum mariscum et non schotunzeldyng nisi per licentiam custodis marisci, quilibet sub pena xiid.

4. WARBOYS, (B M, Add. Ch. 39766): Et quod nullus de cetero fodit turbas inter Newlode et Cateslyrne sub pena xxs.

5. WISTOW, (B M, Add. Ch. 39861): Ordinatum est per dominum et totum homagium quod nullus de cetero falcabit neque fodiat in marisco inter bundes de Wystowe et Wardeboys per spatium xl pedes in latitudinem iuxta bundes predictos sub pena cuilibet xld.

6. WISTOW, (B M, Add. Ch. 39856): Et ordinatum est quod nullus ducat nec portet turbas extra manerium nisi in cartis sub pena xld.

7. UPWOOD, (B M, Add. Ch. 39863): Item juratores dicunt quod diversi tenentes de Rameseye hoc anno ultimo venerunt in marsicum de Upwode vocatum Up-wodturffen et foderunt et fecerunt diversa fossata vocata lodes ad gravum nocumentum tenentium de Upwode. Ita quod non possunt ire nec fugare animalia sua ultra mariscum predictum sicut debent. Et quod diversi tenentes de Bury et Hetmon-grove venerunt in mariscum predictum et foderunt turbas ex parte occidentali de le Fenbrg ubi communem ad fodendum habere non debent.

8. UPWOOD, (B M, Add. Ch. 34370): Memorandum est quod Johannes Abbas concessit quod quilibet virgatarius de Upwode et Ravele foderet x millia turbarum et semivirgatarius vii millia, i cotarius et tenens iii acras terre iiii millia, et tenens ii acras terre iii millia, et tenens i acram terre ii millia, i cotarius sine terra in campo nulla. Ista licentia inventa fuit in antiquo libro senescalli.

9. UPWOOD, (B M, Add. Ch. 39746): Et quod nullus operarius sive laborarius non fodet turbas in nullo loco in marisco nisi per visum magistri cui opus approba-bitur per diem et hoc per visum custodis marisci neque aliquis laborarius non vendit aliquas turbas in (   ). Et illi qui tenent tenementa non vendent turbas quousque turbas venerunt usque ad (   ) sub pena xs. domino, xs. ecclesie. Et per visum iiiior hominum cum preposito marysci quod quilibet etc.

Et (   ) non dabit licentiam alicui de Rameseye sive de aliis villis venire infra mariscum fodere turbas etc.

Et (   ) Tollesson potuit marisci ducere homines fodere turbas in marisco ad opus extraneorum, ideo ipse etc.

Et quod (   ) fodit ultra Upvale nec Shoteneldyng de cetero post bundes possit per inquisitionem, quilibet sub pena iiis. iiiid. domino et iiis. iiiid. ecclesie.

Et pena quod nullus de Rameseye fodit turbas citra Sheggelode sub pena xxs.

Et quod Johannes Sewer de Bury fodit in mariscum turbas et eas apportavit. Ideo ipse etc. (iid.).

Ordinatio de novo. Et quod quilibet qui tenet unum messuagium et i virgatam terre fodet xvi millia turbarum, medietatem inde percipiet per terram et aliam per aquam et non plura. Et quod quilibet tenet dimidiam virgatam fodet viii millia turbarum et non plura. Et quilibet tenet cotagium v millia turbarum et non plura sub pena xxs.

Et pena quod nullus tenens conducet aliquos forineos ad fodiendum turbas infra dominium sub pena iiis. iiiid.

APPENDIX XXIX

Varied Byelaws

1. Elton, (B M, Add. Ch. 39656): Et quod nullus dicte ville custodiat aliquos ad tabernam vel alio loco illicito post horam octavam in nocte cuilibet sub pena xxs.

2. Ellington, (P R O, SC 2, Port. 179, no. 21): Ordinatum est et inhibitum per senescallum domini et per assensum omnium liberorum et custumariorum quod nullus predictorum custumariorum iacet decetero ad tabernam de denario nec cervisam carius emat quam lagena ad obulum infra villam de Elyngtone. Et si aliquis predictorum custumariorum inde fuerit convictus dabit domino sex denarios nomine pene. Et super hoc preceptum est tastatoribus quod si inveniant aliquam braciaticem que sic nativo domini carius vendit cervisam quam lagena ad obulum quod illa cervisa per eosdem tastatores capiatur attachietur et vendatur. Et de pecunia inde sumpta domino fideliter respondeatur. Inhibitum est etiam quod nulla braciatrix que sit libera vendat infra villam predictam cervisam carius quam lagena ad obulum. Et si aliqua inde fuerit convicta conferat domino quadraginta denarios nomine pene quotiens inde fuit convicta.

3. Broughton, (P R O, SC 2, Port. 179, no. 70): Et pena cuilibet brasiatrici quod nulla earum teneat tabernam suam apertam post octavam orlogii noctis cuilibet sub pena xxs.
Et pena (consideratum est) quod si aliquis fuit inventus sedens in tabernam post octavam orlogii quod attachiet eos et ponantur in coppis ibidem sub bona custodia quousque etc. sub pena vis. viiid.

4. Hemmingford Abbots, (B M, Add. Ch. 34323): Et presentatum est quod nulla braciatrix brasiat de cetero nisi brasiabit per totum annum sub pena vis. viiid.

5. Elton, (B M, Add. Ch. 34323): Et presentatum est quod nulla brasiatrix brasiabit nisi brasiaverit dimidium quarterum brasei ad quamlibet, cuilibet sub pena xld. domino, xld. ecclesie.
Et presentatum est quod quilibet qui brasiabit quod mittet pro tastatoribus sine antequam venditio emitur, quilibet sub pena predicta.

6. Upwood, (B M, Add. Ch. 34828): Et preceptum est cuilibet brasiatrici quod postquam incipiet brasiare quod brasiabit per totum annum cuilibet sub pena iiis. iiiid. domino, iiis. iiiid. ecclesie.

7. Little Ravley, (B M, Add. Ch. 34913): Et quia omnes custumarii de Parva Ravele concesserunt quod nullus eorum emerit cervisam in eadem villa carius quam lagena ad obolum, id. inquirendum est etc. (sub) pena vid.

8. Abbots Ripton, (P R O, SC 2, Port. 178, no. 91): Iterim ordinatum et provisum est per totam curiam quod deinceps omnes pandoxatores communes si fuerunt plures in una aliqua villa per totum hundredum (Abbots Ripton) non pandoxisant similiter et semel una die nisi necesse fuerit set colloquum habeant de qui pandoxat' et pandoxisant. Ita quod vicini non careant aliquo tempore potum sicut antea caruerunt ad nocumentum et quoddam dampnum ligeorum domini Regis. Et quod omnes communes pandoxatores infra hundredum istum deinceps provideant de tempore in tempus serviciam sufficientem ad serviendum specialiter vicinis suis et

aliis ligeis dicti domini Regis sub pena cuilibet in ea parte delinquente vis. viiid. totiens quotiens hunc provisum contrafecerit.

Et quod deinceps nullus pandoxator aut tappeler seu venditor s(   ) vendat quibuscumque ligeis domini Regis per ollas, ciphos, discos seu bolles sed soloni per mensuram rasuratam et signo autentico munitam prout lex requiret et hoc sub pena xiid. totiens quotiens contrafecit eorum aliquid.

9. Wistow, (B M, Add. Ch. 34370): Et quod nullus operabitur in campis in diebus festinalibus sub pena vid. domino et vid. ecclesie.

10. Broughton, (B M, Add. Ch. 34819): Et quod nullus carabit blada sua noctanter sub pena xxd. ecclesie et xxd. domino.

11. Upwood, (B M, Add. Ch. 39775): Et quod Johannes Genge forisfecit pena ultimo viso edicta quod nullus comorans istius villate emerit ellas suas extra villam sub pena cuilibet tenenti quotiens vis. viiid.

12. Broughton, (B M, Add. Ch. 39662): Et ordinatum est quod nullus tenens huius manerii arabit cum aratris suis plures terras arabiles quam sibi limitate fuerunt per homagium domini sub pena cuilibet xs.

13. Broughton, (B M, Add. Ch. 39489): Et quod nullus incrochiat super le communem balk nec in commune bras' sub pena iiis. iiiid. cuilibet. Et quod qui inchroochiavit ibidem seperte iac' sic soluto (   ) debet' sub eadem pena citra proximam curiam.

14. Hemmingford Abbots, (B M, Add. Ch. 39584): Et pena omnibus tenentibus quod quilibet compereat citra oram nonam cuilibet sub pena xiid.

15. Barton, (B M, Add. Ch. 39731): Et pena quod nullus amodo capiat pisces nec iacet aliquas rekas nec aliquas res ad capiendum pisces in le Myllebroke sub pena iiis. iiiid.

16. Warboys, (B M, Add. Ch. 39769): Et quod nullus mittat carectas ad ostia vicinorum nec moveat alestakes sub pena xxs.

Et quod nullus impediet aliquem tenentem de communa sua in croftes in straytyme sub pena dimidiam marcam.

17. Wistow, (B M, Add. Ch. 39868): Et quod nullus ligat nulla animalia in campo sic possit fugare vel ire ad mariscum sub pena xxd. domino, xxd. ecclesie.

Et pena ut in anno precedente quod nullus vertat aratrum in pratum de cetero sub pena xiid. domino, xiid. ecclesie.

18. Wistow, 1294 (B M, Add. Ch. 39755): Et dicunt quod Willelmus molendarius habet quemdam garconum nominem Radulphum in molendino qui est inutilis domino et villate. Ideo est in misericordia (supra), plegii prepositus et bedellus. Et preceptum est quod dictus Radulphus amoveatur.

19. Cranfield, 1300 (P R O, SC 2, Port. 179, no. 10): Convictum est per juratores quod Ricardus de Campo senior de iure et consuetudine antiqua non debet habere viam ad croftum suum que vocatur Denehale per medietatem curie Agnetis de Campo sicut clamat, sed subter curiam eiusdem Agnetis et sic ad quamdam maram eiusdem Agnetis et deinde ad quamdam maram domini Abbatis que ducit ad dictum croftum eiusdem Ricardi, quia idem Ricardus non habuit viam per medietatem curie dicte Agnetis numquam dumodo tenuit illud tenementum ad firmam xxxto annis elapsis. Et idem dictus Ricardus pro falso clameo in misericordiam vid., **plegius** Simon de Barton.

19. Upwood, 1297 (B M, Add. Ch. 34798): Et dicunt quod homines totius villate de Upwode cum Magna Ravele sunt obscurati per unum fossatum ne possunt intrare le Fryth cum bestiis suis. Ideo preceptum est etc. quod emendetur.

20. Ellsworth, 1290 (P R O, SC 2, Port. 179, no. 7): Et dicunt quod Johannes Pykot levavit unum murum per quem ocupat unam viam communem ad latitudinem trium pedorum. Ideo in misericordia vid. Et preceptum est quod per visum juratorum emendetur.

21. Houghton, 1308 (P R O, SC 2, Port. 179, no. 15): Juratores presentant et dicunt quod Ricardus le Porter habet arbores suas crescentes in curia sua quarum ramiculi minus se crescendo extendunt ultra murum suum super Regiam viam ad nocumentum carectariorum ibidem (currunt) de feno et blado cartato. Ideo est in misericordia iiid., plegius Johannes Porter. Et preceptum est quod dicti ramiculi amputentur et emendentur.

22. Holywell, 1306 (P R O, SC 2, Port. 179, no. 12): Et dicunt quod Prior de Sancto Ivone faciendo unum fossatum inclusit quandam peciam de communa apud Onscote, appropriando sibi duas acras et dimidiam in longitudinem et in latitudinem duas perticatas, plantando ibidem plantulavit per quod lada estupatur ad magnum nocumentum communarii et per aquam transeuntem. Ideo distringatur ad respondendum. (Note : The men of Little Stukeley make the same kind of complaint against Robert Mariath of Great Raveley in 1308, P R O, SC 2, Port. 179, no. 15)

APPENDIX XXX

Membership in a Tithing and Pledges

1. Warboys, (P R O, SC 2, Port. 179, no. 10): Quia presentabatur in ultimo visu quod Nicholaus Kannt fuit inutilis et inobediens Nicholao Lone capitali plegio suo. Et Nicholaus Kannt est plegius suus ad habendum ipsum ad proximam curiam.
Presentatum est Nicholao Lone sub pena xiid. quod habeat Nicholaum Kannt existentem in decenna sua super quam presentatum est in visu de Broctone quod idem Nicholaus erat vagabundus noctanter astultando sub perietes vicinorum et quod noctanter piscabatur in piscaria vicinorum.

2. Shillington, (P R O, SC 2, Port. 179, no. 17): Et Johanni de Barton plegio Ade de Batelesden quia non habuit ipsum ad ponendum se in decenna. Et preceptum est quod distringatur ad ponendum se in decenna. Postea venit et posuit se in decenna.

3. Upwood, (P R O, SC 2, Port. 179, no. 9): Et dicunt quod Robertus de Wenyton' manet uxoratus apud Rammeseiam. Ideo preceptum est Johanni de Wenyton capitali plegio suo habere ipsum ad proximam curiam.

4. Ellsworth, (P R O, SC 2, Port. 179, no. 7): Et adhuc dicunt quod Robertus filius Roberti ad boscum manet apud Trumpeton',nihil facit domino. Ideo Matheus ad boscum capitalis plegius est in misericordia quia non habuit ipsum sicut preceptum fuit ei ad ultimum visum, plegius propositus. Et preterea ut alias postea venit et fecit finem pro uno capono, plegii Thomas ad boscum et Willelmus Baldewyne.

5. Wistow, (B M, Add. Ch. 34918): Juratores presentant quod Willelmus Coppyng

residet infra precinctum lete et non est in decenna. Ideo preceptum est quod atta-chietur ad ponendum se in decenna ad proximum visum.

6. Upwood, (B M, Add. Ch. 34769): De Johanne Curteys capitali plegio quia non habuit Johannem Eldman, Johannem Wodekoc, Johannem Cocum, Henricum Coquonum, Johannem Coquonum seniorem, vid., plegius Robertus Alkoc. Et prohi-beatur villa Henrico Coquono quia est extra decennam.

7. Holywell, (P R O, SC 2, Port. 179, no. 5): Et dicunt quod Robertus le Ster manet super terram Ricardi Fraunceys et non est in decenna. Ideo in misericordia vid. Et preceptum est quod prohibeatur ei villa nisi se ponat in decenna.

8. Hemmingford Abbots, (P R O, SC 2, Port. 179, no. 9): Et Thomas filius Henrici Clerici quia non habuit Willelmum fratrem suum existentem in decenna sua qui manet apud Blackerwyk, iiid. Et preceptum est quod arestetur si venerit super feodum.

9. Abbots Ripton, (P R O, SC 2, Port. 179, no. 11): Preceptum est attachiare Willelmum filium Johannis ad Grenam, Andream fratrem suum et Petrum Molen-darium si venerint qui (se) ponuntur extra decennam Philippi de Aula.
Preceptum est Ricardo le Hayward capitali plegio quod habeat Willelmum filium Thome manentem uxoratum apud Heytmundgrove ad proximam curiam.

10. St. Ives, (P R O, SC 2, Port. 179, no. 12): Juratores de Grena dicunt quod Ricardus frater vicarii est residens super feodum domini et non est extra assisam. Ideo preceptum est quod distringatur ad ponendum se in decenna.

11. St. Ives, (P R O, SC 2, Port. 179, no. 10): Preceptum est quod nullus de cetero recepit Bartholomeum coopertorem quia est inobediens capitali plegio suo.
Willelmus de Gilling est plegius Emme Wygar et Johannis filii sui quod bene se habebunt dum fuerunt residentes in villa.

12. Holywell, (P R O, SC 2, Port. 179, no. 10): Adhuc preceptum est distrin-gere Willelmum Bogge et Johannem de Gravele quia sunt inobedientes et nolunt dare ad capitagium.

13. Ellsworth, (P R O, SC 2, Port. 179, no. 10): Juratores de Elysworth dicunt quod Willelmus filius Simonis, Aspelon Gag' et Walterus Gag' subtrahunt se contra adventum justicii et contra diem visus. Et testatur quod utlagii (sunt). Ideo ca-piantur etc.

14. Upwood, 1278 (P R O, SC 2, Port. 179, no. 4): Et dicunt quod Adam le Co nativus domini retraxit se et manet apud Bernewell. Ideo preceptum est Johanni de Wenyton capitali plegio suo ut habeat coram senescallo ad proximum adventum suum, sub pena dimidie marce.

15. Abbots Ripton, 1294 (B M, Add. Ch. 39597): Et dicunt quod Andreas filius Ricardi filius Philipi manet apud Huntingdon et est inobediens Johanni Will' capi-tali plegio suo. Ideo arestetur si venerit super feodum domini (preceptum est).

16. Ellsworth, 1290 (P R O, SC 2, Port. 179, no. 7): Et dicunt quod Stephanus ad boscum manet apud London et nichil facit domino. Sed Mathaeus (   ) manucepit habere ipsum ad proximam curiam sicut prius sepius unde nichil (facit). Preceptum est.

17. Weston, 1300 (P R O, SC 2, Port. 179, no. 10): Willelmo filio Rogeri et Johanni filio (Crane) quia non habuerunt Walterum filium Johannis le Bacheler qui substrahit se cum bonis suis de feodo domini et manet uxoratus apud Walton,

xiid., plegii alter alterius. Et preceptum est ponere dictum Walterum per meliores plegios.

Hugo Akry est nativus et manet apud Drayton Passelewe. Ideo preceptum est Galfrido Renheved capitali plegio suo et eius decenna quod habeant ipsum ad proximam curiam.

APPENDIX XXXI

EXPATRIATION, RECEPTION AND REFUSAL OF OUTSIDERS, CRIMINALS, etc.

1. ELLSWORTH, (P R O, SC 2, Port. 179, no. 12): Et Johannes Gang' capitalis plegius quia non habuit Henricum filium Willelmi Mercator nec Willelmum filium Radulphi extra feodum in decenna sua (vid.). Et preceptum est quod nullus eos recepit.

2. OVER, (P R O, SC 2, Port. 179, no. 11): Preceptum est quod nullus de cetero recepit Alanum filium Roberti Galewey nec Johannem fratrem suum qui positi sunt extra decennam.

Preceptum est quod nullus recepit Henricum Fengers qui positus est extra decennam Walteri Ode donec etc.

Et dicunt quod Donte Goldyene recepit Johannem Cissor extra assisam. Ideo in misericordia iiid., plegius Willelmus Sue. Et preceptum est quod nullus ipsum recepit donec etc.

Preceptum est quod nullus recepit Ricardum de Caxton de cetero cui prohibita fuit villa.

3. ELLSWORTH, (P R O, SC 2, Port. 179, no. 11): Preceptum est quod nullus de cetero recepit Johannem Alderman qui ponitur extra decennam Roberti Kyng pro eo quod est inobediens capitali plegio suo, nec Radulphum Pyk qui ponitur extra decennam Radulphi ad Fontem pro eodem.

4. KING'S RIPTON, 1299 (P R O, SC 2, Port. 179, no. 10): Walterus de Den est plegius Willelmi Russel quod decetero bene et fideliter se habebit dum fuerit residens in ville de Ryptone.

5. ST. IVES, 1306 (P R O, SC 2, Port. 179, no. 12): Et dicunt quod Agnes uxor Moryte et Emma de Erhyth ceperunt stall' Willelmi le Spycer et illas noctanter in domo sua combuss'. Et nihilominus dicta Emma non est valida ad residendum in villa. Ideo preceptum quod eiciantur de domo sua nisi inveniantur sufficientem securitatem quod bene decetero se versus quoscumque habebunt et honeste.

6. THERFIELD, (P R O, SC 2, Port. 179, no. 15): Preceptum est quod nullus recepit Johannem Ateberne, Johannem le Ber, Johannem le Fermer, Reginaldum filium Hotepayn, Henricum Pyg', Ricardum filium Alexandri, Laurentium filium Alexandri le Fuller, Willelmum Sparhauk nec Benedictum filium Johannis Le Fernne qui positi sunt extra decennam Sampsonis filii Reginaldi.

Preceptum quod nullus recepit Johannem Wynter nec Johannem Sutor qui ponuntur extra decennam Roberti filii Willelmi Roger.

7. WARBOYS, (B M, Add. Ch. 34910): Et dicunt quod Agnes Malitras non est digna commorandi infra villam eo quod est mala glenatrix capiendo garbas et ceteras minutias. Ideo prohibeatur ei villa. Et Alanus Haugate ipsam recepit. Ideo etc., iiid., plegius Radulphus Haugate.

Et dicunt quod Elena Baroun talis est. Ideo prohibeatur villa ut supra. Et Ivo de Hurst ipsam recepit. Ideo etc. iiid.

Et dicunt quod Matilda filia Willelmi Pylche male glenavit in autumpno. Ideo etc. iiid., plegius Reginaldus Beneyt.

Et dicunt quod Nicholaus Kannt recepit predictam Matildam. Ideo etc. iiid., plegius Ricardus Puttok.

8. Wistow, (B M, Add. Ch. 39562): Et dicunt quod Walterus Pellipar est inutilis et infidelis. Ideo preceptum est ne aliquis ipsum decetero recepit.

Et dicunt quod Johannes Crane est vagabondus noctanter astultans sub perietes vicinorum. Ideo est in misericordia iiid., plegii Johannes Crane et Robertus Crane. Et per eosdem plegios de cetero bene se geret.

9. Wistow, (B M, Add. Ch. 39757): Et dicunt quod Matilda Crane consueta est capere gallinas vicinorum et alias minutias et non est digna residere inter vicinos etc. Et preceptum est quod nullus eam de cetero recepit sub grave pena quousque etc.

10. Wistow, (B M, Add. Ch. 39853): Et preceptum est per totum homagium domini quod nullus eorum receptet Robertum Michel virum contumeliosum minus nec domos ei dimittet ad inhabitandum sub pena xld.

11. Warboys, (B M, Add. Ch. 34897): Et dicunt quod Ricardus Neel et Agnes uxor eius sint inutiles et malefactores et non digni residere in villam. Et super hoc venit Willelmus prepositus et devenit plegius eorum quod de cetero bene se habebunt. Misericordia condonatur quia pauperes.

Et dicunt quod Margareta Fyne recepit quemdam Thomam Gabyon contra assisam. Nec est dignus residere in villam. Ideo etc. iiid., plegius Willelmus Fyne. Et prohibeatur villa predicto Thome Gabyon.

12. Warboys, (B M, Add. Ch. 39758): Et dicunt quod Beatrix Puttok est communis malefactrix et furata fuit plures minutias. Ideo prohibita est ei villa ne quis eam amodo receptet sub pena xxs. Postea venit et invenit plegios videlicet J. Deward et J. Caton quod bene etc.

13. Wistow, 1326 (B M, Add. Ch. 39760): Et dicunt quod Ricardus Longe recepit Christianam Hobbe cui sepius fuit villa prohibita. Ideo etc. vid., plegii Johannes Baroun et Nicholaus Baroun. Et preceptum est quod nullus eam amodo recepit sub pena dimidiam marcam domino solvendo.

14. Gidding, 1300 (P R O, SC 2, Port. 179, no. 10): Et dicunt quod Adam filius presbyteri et Willelmus filius Emme de aula sunt inutiles eo quod furabantur tres aucas Elene Boyloun. Ideo preceptum est etc. Et postmodo veniunt Willelmus Abovetoun et Johannes le Neweman capitales plegii eorum et manuceperunt pro eis quod de cetero bene se habebunt.

15. Niddingworth 1306 (Holywell), (P R O, SC 2, Port. 179, no. 12): Preceptum est quod nullus receptet Juettam Brabon nec Custanciam filiam suam que sunt communes meretrices et sepius receperunt extraneos ad terrorem vicinorum. Et postea inveniunt plegios scilicet Ricardum Fraunkelyn et Robertum Thurkyl quod decetero bene se habebunt et honeste inter vicinos suos.

De Willelmo filio Ade le Eyr capitali plegio quia non habuit Simonem le Bocwyrte, Simonem de Den existentes in decenna sua vid. Et preceptum est quod nullus eos receptet.

16. Weston, 1312 (P R O, SC 2, Port. 179, no. 16): Juratores de Weston presentant et dicunt quod Alicia le Sonter recepit Margaretam de Tychenis que non

est utilis residendi infra villam. Ideo etc. iiid., plegius Johannes de Hotoft. Et preceptum est quod nullus eam receptet.

17. Wistow, 1347 (B M, Add. Ch. 39856): Et quod Thomas Sutor hospitatur
leprosum contra assisam. Et preceptum est ne de cetero hospitatur sub pena xiid.

18. Wistow, 1334 (B M, Add. Ch. 34809): Et quod Robertus Palmer recepit
Willelmum Fabrum qui est ʾleprosum. Ideo ipse, etc. Et preceptum est non ipsum
amplius. (Preceptum est quod amoveatur).

19. Hemmingford Abbots, 1313 (P R O, SC 2, Port. 179, no. 17): Et dicunt quod
Petrus Molendinarius est minus rebellus vicinis suis et communis malefactor nec est
dignus residere (   ) infra villam predictam, quare omnes petunt ex gratia
speciali ut amoveatur extra villam. Ideo (   ) villa ei prohibeatur et terra sua
capiatur in manu domini et respondetur inde de exitibus donec etc.

20. Little Stukeley, 1318 (P R O, SC 2, Port. 179, no. 18): Et dicunt quod
Robertus Tedbolt recepit Thomam Tedbolt fratrem suum qui est communis malefactor. Ideo ipse etc. iiid., plegius Willelmus Felyce. Et preceptum est quod nullus
eum amodo recepit sub pena xxs.

21. Over, 1301 (P R O, SC 2, Port. 179, no. 11): De Roberto Galewey quia
recepit Willelmum Galewey filium suum extra decennam, iiid., plegius Willelmus
Ive. Et preceptum est quod nullus ipsum de cetero recepit etc.

22. Over, 1308 (P R O, SC 2, Port. 179, no. 15): Juratores presentant quod
Robertus Aylward receptavit quandam mulierem de Drayton que non est utilis
(   ), in misericordia vid., plegius Robertus Pygge. Et preceptum est quod nullus
eam de cetero recepit.
Et dicunt quod Johannes filius Alani recepit duos sutores extraneos extra decennam. Ideo est in misericordia vid., plegius Petrus Demeys. Et preceptum est
quod distringantur ad ponendum se etc. vel quod nullus eos recepit.

23. Weston, 1318 (P R O, SC 2, Port. 179, no. 18): Et dicunt quod Ricardus
Hauuylle mendicus percussit alium extraneum mendicantem per quod iuste levavit
uthesium super eum. Ideo etc. plegius Simon ate Grene.

24. Graveley, 1312 (P R O, SC 2, Port. 179, no. 16): Et dicunt quod Walterus
de Essex hospitatur quemdam extraneum qui circa mediam noctem ipsum Walterum
insultavit et vulneravit per quod iuste levavit uthesium super eundem extraneum,
qui non venit nec uthesium presentatum fuit. Ideo tota villata in misericorda.
Noctanter ideo nichil. Et preceptum est distringere dictum extraneum ad respondendum.

25. Girton, 1321 (P R O, SC 2, Port. 179, no. 20): Et dicunt quod Willelmus
Scherreve recepit Henricum Perys et Ceciliam uxorem suam quibus prohibita fuit
villa. Ideo ipse etc. pauperes, plegius prepositus, et preceptum est quod amodo eos
non recepit.

26. Cranfield, 1306 (P R O, SC 2, Port. 179, no. 12): De Gilberto Carpentario
capitali plegio quia non habuit Reginaldum le Waleys existen temin decenna sua.
Et preceptum est quod nullus eum recepit.

APPENDIX XXXII

Licence to live Beyond the Village

1. Upwood, (B M, Add. Ch. 34917): Impositum est Alexandro Gallon qui residet super feodum Johannis Clervaus quod ipse est nativus domini qui in plena curia hoc dedixit dicendo se esse hominem nativum Johannis de Clervaus. Et preterea compertum est per bonam inquisitionem predictorum juratorum quod ipse Alexander genitus est de nativo domini et ipse et pater eius antecessor suus nativi domini Abbatis fuerunt. Et ideo datur ei die dominico ut veniat coram domino apud Rameseiam respondere de premissis, plegius prepositus. Et postea predictus Alexander fecit finem cum domino pro xiid. modo solvendo et pro ii caponis quolibet anno ad Pascham solvendo, plegius (Johannes) Bygge dum manet super feodum predicti Johannis. Et veniet ad visum franciplegii.

2. Shillington, (P R O, SC 2, Port. 179, no. 5): Juliana Hakel quia sexdecim annis elapsis maritavit se cuidam Rythemundo sine licentia et quia retraxit se super terram Rectoris et fecit se liberam. Condonatur quia paupera. Et de cetero erit obediens, plegii Reginaldus de Hauescomb et Willelmus de Thywell.

3. Ellsworth, (P R O, SC 2, Port. 179, no. 16): Et preposito et bedello quia non arestaverunt Walterum filium Johannis Faber ad respondendum de hoc quod se subtrahit de feodo domini et manet apud Pappewurth, vid. Et preceptum est adhuc quod arestetur. Et de Ade le Typper fratre dicti Walteri quia ipsum Walterum receptat sepissime nec de adventu ipsius ballivis vult premunire. Et postea venit predictus Walterus et est in custodia prepositi et bedelli. Et postea fecit finem pro ii caponis quolibet anno ad Pascham dum manet extra feodum, plegii Johannes Attegrene et Adam le Typper. Et veniet ad visum franciplegii per eundem plegium.

4. Hemmingford Abbots, (P R O, SC 2, Port. 179, no. 17): Et dicunt quod Thomas Canoun manet apud Erhyth extra feodum domini qui postea venit et fecit finem pro xiid. modo solvendo et ad Pascham proximam futuram ii caponis et in posteris per annum i capono ad Pascham, plegii prepositorum, scilicet Nicholaus Buntyng et Johannes, ut licite possit ibidem manere. Et veniet ad visum franciplegii per annum semel.

5. Over, (P R O, SC 2, Port. 179, no. 11): Nicholaus Faber villanus domini fecit finem cum domino Johanne Abbate Rammeseie pro quadraginta solidis argenti ut possit morari et manere super feodum Episcopi Elyensis in villa de Overe ad terminum vite dicti domini Johannis Abbatis. Ita quod sit intendens et obediens sibi et celerariis dicti domini et ballivis eorum tamquam alii villani in eadem villa et ad veniendum adminus semel per annum ad visum franciplegii tentum per dictum dominum Abbatem. Et ad solvendum per annum ad festum Pasche duos caponos, plegii Willelmus Atefen, Willelmus Thurston, Johannes Derman et Willelmus Felipe.

6. Gidding, (P R O, SC 2, Port. 179, no. 15): De Johanne filio Stephani le Graunt ii caponos ad Pascham dum manet extra feodum domini cum catallis suis, plegii Johannes le Bonde et Johannes Monek. Et preceptum est levare de predicto Johanne ii caponos de anno preterito.

Nicholaus filius Johannis le Lathe de Gyddyng dat domino xs. premanibus, et ii caponos per annum ad Pascham dum manet extra feodum cum catallis suis, plegius Johannes le Lathe.

7. HOLYWELL, (P R O, SC 2, Port. 179, no. 16): Nicholaus Laweman dat domino quolibet anno ad Pascham ii caponos, plegii Ricardus filius Radulphi et Willelmus Gray. Et per eundem plegium veniet semel per annum ad visum franciplegii dum manet apud Cotten', et dedit premanibus xiiis. iiiid. sicut patet per rotulos gersumarum.

8. WESTON, (P R O, SC 2, Port. 179, no. 16): Reginaldus filius Willelmi Hakun dat domino premanibus dimidiam marcam et quolibet anno i caponum ad Pascham, plegii Galfridus Hakun et Hugo Hakun, ut licite possit manere extra feodum domini. Et per eundem plegium veniet quolibet anno semel ad visum franciplegii.

Walterus filius Galfridi Bacheler fecit finem cum domino apud Rameseiam pro vs. sicut patet per rotulos gersumarum ut licite possit manere extra feodum domini, et quolibet anno ad Pascham ii caponos et veniet semel in anno ad visum franciplegii, plegii Willelmus filius Walteri et Galfridus Bacheler.

9. ELLINGTON, 1311 (P R O, SC 2, Port. 179, no. 16): Inhibitum est per dominum Johannem Abbatem omnibus custumariis de Elyngton qui habent predictam villam ad firmam quod decetero non permittant aliquem hominem aut mulierem de nativis domini recedere extra feodum domini super alienum feodum comorandum nec aliquem extraneum infra predictam villam recipere residendum sine licentia domini speciali et fine coram predicto domino faciendo, et etiam inhibitum est eisdem quod nulle gersume nec fines decetero fiant nisi coram dicto domino Abbate. Et si predicti custumarii contra predictam formam videlicet in perte vel in tota fuerunt convicti facientes erunt in grave misericordia ad voluntatem domini taxata.

10. ELLSWORTH, (Ramsey Register, p. 30d.): Memorandum est quod Thomas Attewode manens in Stanton' est nativus Abbatis, conventui, et ecclesie, et omnes sui progenitores de tempore cuius non extat memoria. Et nati fuerunt de manerio de Ellesworth in una hameletta vocata la Grave que est sub bosco dicti Abbatis spectante ad dictum manerium. Et sic ex antiquo tempore habent nomen attewode pro eo quod ipsi fuerunt omnes nati et morantes iuxta dictum boscum dicti Abbatis, videlicet Robertus Attewode genuit Henricum Attewode, Henricus Attewode genuit Matheum Attewode tenentem predictum tenementum Attewode cum tota sequela sua et Willelmum Attewode fratrem predicti Mathei morantem in Hilton de licencia Abbatis qui tempore fuit. Willelmus Attewode frater predicti Mathei genuit Johannem Attewode in Hilton. Johannes Attewode postea genuit in Stanton Thomam Attewode qui nunc est.

APPENDIX XXXIII

BEYOND THE VILLAGE WITHOUT LICENCE

1. UPWOOD, (P R O, SC 2, Port. 179, no. 10): Et Johanni de Wenyton et Roberto Crane quia Robertus de Wenyton manens apud Rameseiam nondum satisfecit domino ut possit cum catallis suis licite manere apud Rameseiam vid., plegius alter alterius. Et preceptum est distringere dictum Robertum donec, etc.

2. UPWOOD, (P R O, SC 2, Port. 179, no. 12): Preceptum est distringere Robertum

de Wenyngton nativum domini qui manet uxoratus apud Rameseiam ubi traxit catalla domini sine licentia.

3. ELLINGTON, (P R O, SC 2, Port. 179, no. 18): Et dicunt quod Johannes filius Philippi West manet apud Waltham cum catallis suis. Ideo preceptum est proposito facere de Willelmo West fratre suo duas marcas argenti de bonis predicti Johannis existentibus (in manu) dicti Willelmi. Postea venit et fecit finem ut patet in rotulos gersumarum.

4. WARBOYS, (*Ramsey Register*, Norwich, p. 41d): Johannes Capellanus de Warde-boys invenit plegios Robertum filium Henrici ballivi filii Simonis et totam decen-nam suam quod veniet ad festum Sancti Michaelis et catalla sua ducet super terram domini abbatis.

5. ELTON, (P R O, SC 2, Port. 179, no. 15): De Roberto Gamel et Johanne Dun-nyng plegiis Walteri filii Henrici le Marescal quia idem Walterus non dum solvet domino i caponum quem ei solvere tenetur quolibet anno ad Pascham dum manet extra feodum dicti domini cum catallis suis. Et quia aretro sunt per quatuor annos elapsos in misericordia vid. Et preceptum est levare dictos caponos de plegiis aretro existentes. De eisdem Roberto et Johanne plegiis Simonis fratris dicti Walteri pro eodem per tantum tempus, vid. Et preceptum est ut supra quod arreragium levetur de dictis plegiis.

6. HEMMINGFORD ABBOTS, (P R O, SC 2, Port. 179, no. 19): Et Willelmo de Mol-lesworth et Ricardo Boyken plegiis Thome Neel quia ipsum non habuerunt ad faciendum finem cum domino ad hoc quod se subtrahit cum catallis suis manens uxoratus apud Offord. Condonatur. Et preceptum est ponere dictum Thomam per meliores plegios ad proximum.

7. HEMMINGFORD ABBOTS, (P R O, SC 2, Port. 179, no. 19): Adhuc preceptum est sicut pluries arestare Thomam Neel nativum domini si venerit super feodum ad respondendum de hoc quod se subtrahit cum catallis suis manens apud Offord.

8. SHILLINGTON, (P R O, SC 2, Port. 179, no. 10): Willelmus Byrd maritavit se apud Osseleye ubi traxit bona sua sine licentia. Et preterea invenitur quod decepit dominum in fine sua facta per quinque solidos ut creditur et testatur per aliquos in presentiam curie. Ideo arestetur si venerit super feodum donec etc.

9. BYTHORN (Weston), (P R O, SC 2, Port. 179, no. 12): De Thome Randolf quia non premunivit prepositum de Bytherne de Waltero filio Reginaldi le Bacheler noctanter hospitato in domo sua latitanter. Et quia debuit arrestare sicut preceptum fuit in ultimo visu eo quod subtrahit se cum catallis suis de feodo domini, vid., plegius Willelmus filius Walteri. Et preceptum est adhuc quod arrestetur. Ita quod sit ad proximam curiam, plegius dictus Thomas.

10. ELTON, (P R O, SC 2, Port. 179, no. 12): Preceptum est arrestare Johannem filium Johannis Jolly si venerit qui se subtrahit cum catallis suis. Et postea Michael in Angulo et Johannes de Pappele sunt plegii dicti Johannis ad habendum ipsum ad proximam curiam ad respondendum super sibi in premissis obediendo.

11. ELTON, 1312 (P R O, SC 2, Port. 179, no. 16): Robertus Frere arrestatus est in custodia ballivi eo quod se subtrahit de feodo domini. Et postea Ricardus Keman et Johannes le Wulmonger sunt plegii sui ad faciendam decetero corpora-lem residentiam super feodum domini cum catallis suis. Et quod reducet catalla sua si que habeat extra feodum super feodum domini de die in diem.

12. Abbots Ripton, 1299 (P R O, SC 2, Port. 179, no. 10): Prepositus et bedellus non distrinxerunt Andream filium Stephani Benestrate qui subtrahit cum catallis suis et est uxoratus. Ideo sunt in misericordia, vid. Et preceptum est adhuc quod distringatur donec etc.

Preceptum est Ricardo le Hayward plegio Willelmi filii Thome qui manet uxoratus apud Heytmondegrove quod habeat ipsum ad proximam curiam ad respondendum etc.

Adhuc preceptum est distringere Nicholaum filium Cristine si venerit super feodum qui manet uxoratus apud Chatteris cum catallis suis.

13. Holywell, 1313 (P R O, SC 2, Port. 179, no. 17): Johanna filia Thome Curteys maritata est extra feodum sine licentia domini cuidam de nativis domini in Sancto Ivone. Ideo preceptum est arrestare dictam Johannam ad respondendum et satisfaciendum etc. Et quia compertum est per juratores quod predicta Johanna maritata fuit per assensum Beatrice matris sue et de bonis suis et quod predicta Beatrica solveret eidem Johanne filie sue quatuor ringas bladi per annum, et quia predicta Beatrica non curavit facere finem cum domino pro predicta filia sua maritanda. Ideo capiatur terra sua in manu domini. Et respondeatur ei de exitibus donec, etc. Et quia Robertus filius Elene prepositus, inde premunitam ipsam antequam maritatam fuit, non arestavit, in misericordia vid. Et postea satisfecit domino sicut patet in rotulum gersumarum.

APPENDIX XXXIV

Ramsey Villagers Taking Land Beyond the Village

1. Abbots Ripton, (P R O, SC 2, Port. 179, no. 18): Et dicunt quod Margareta Horseman nativa domini gersumavit de domino Johanne Morite unum cotagium ubi trahit bona et catalla domini, que quidem Margareta invenit plegios ad reportanda predicta bona et catalla, scilicet Rogerum Bettes et Willelmum Hawelound.

2. St. Ives, (B M, Add. Ch. 34774): Et dicunt quod Adam Godrych nativus domini ingreditur liberum tenementum apud Nyddingworth, qui venit et dat domino in gersuma ut ibi possit residere iis. Et quolibet anno ad Pascham ii caponos, plegius (de Brunne).

3. Upwood, (B M, Add. Ch. 34802): Memorandum quod Alexander Gabon manens super feodum Johannis Clervaus est nativus domini et genitus a nativo dicti domini et se gerit tamquam nativus predicti Johannis et est rebellus. Ideo loquendum ? est etc. Ideo preceptum quod distringatur per omnia bona sua donec etc.

4. Warboys, (B M, Add. Ch. 39597): Et dicunt quod Radulphus Fyne tenet unam dimidiam virgatam terre in Caldekote et manet in Wardeboy (ad maximum dampnum ?) terre domini, et quod vendidit unam grangiam. Ideo capiatur tota terra in manu domini.

5. Wistow, (B M, Add. Ch. 34910): Thomas filius Michaelis le Palmer venit apud Rameseiam coram domino et fecit finem ut licite possit manere super liberam terram in Wistowe, quolibet anno ad Pascham ii caponos, plegius Michael le Palmer. Et per eundem plegium veniret ad visum franciplegii. Et incipiet solvere caponos ad Pascham in anno futuro (vacat).

6. Upwood, (B M, Add. Ch. 34801): Et dicunt quod Johannes filius Simonis Bannok manet uxoratus apud Walton extra feodum domini ubi trahit catalla sua. Qui venit postea et fecit finem pro uno capono quolibet anno ad Pascham domino solvendo dum manet extra feodum, plegius pater eius.

7. Broughton, (P R O, SC 2, Port. 179, no. 9): Andreas Onty est plegius Simonis filii Radulphi de Hirst de Broctone ad capiendam illam virgatam terre quam Johannes Cok tenuit super Grenam Sancti Ivonis, vel ad satisfaciendum domino ut possit recedere extra feodum domini.

8. Girton, (B M, Add. Ch. 39597): Robertus filius Nicholai de Upetoun dat domino abbati xxs. ex quibus camerarius habet medietatem, ut licite possit recedere de terra domini et capere terram apud Hokyton.

9. Shillington, (P R O, SC 2, Port. 179, no. 7): Et dicunt quod Willelmus de Barthon est nativus domini tenens de domino unam acram terre cum uno cotagio et de domino de Holewelle dimidiam virgatam terre servilis. Sed testatur quod est obediens et quod (   ) residere (   ) feodum domini in dicto cotagio. Invenit plegium Robertum ad Grenam.

10. Ellington, (P R O, SC 2, Port. 179, no. 21): Ricardus Besstesson dat domino xld. pro licentia residendi super liberum tenementum in Sibthorp, et dabit domino annuatim ad Pascham ii caponos, plegius prepositus, et veniet ad visum.

11. Hemmingford Abbots, (P R O, SC 2, Port. 179, no. 4): Testificatum est per totam villatam quod Simon Borol qui est nativus domini et manet apud Huntingdon habet in villa de Hemmingford catalla ad valenciam x marcarum que quidem bona tradita sunt per senescallum istis subscriptis, videlicet, Jacobo Anngored qui habet bene recognovit i ringam frumenti et iii ringas ordei, Salemanno i ringam frumenti et i ringam pisarum, Reginaldo ate Mare i bidentem pretii xvid.

Et dicunt quod Willelmus filius Simonis est nativus domini et manet in alio homagio nec est in decenna. Ideo capiatur si venerit super feodum domini. Postea venit et est in decenna.

12. Over, 1308 (P R O, SC 2, Port. 179, no. 15): Johannes filius Alani est plegius Rych' Sutoris ad habendum warrantum suum quod est in decenna apud Dytton' super feodum Episcopi Elyensis.

13. Weston, 1307 (P R O, SC 2, Port. 179, no. 15): Et dicunt quod Willelmus filius Thome manet apud Thrapston uxoratus. Et sine licentiatu a domino. Ideo distringatur etc. Postea invenitur in compotu quod fecit pro una marca.

14. Ellington, ca. 1335 (B M, Add. Ch. 34320): (   ) quod Willelmus filius Tebbe subtrahit se de feodo domini et manet super liberam terram Ranulphi Trym cum catallis suis qui venit et fecit finem cum domino pro ii caponis per annum solvendum ad Pascham dum manet super terram predicti Ranulphi, plegii Johannes Bedellus et Adam Prepositus. Et per eundem plegium veniret semel in anno ad visum franciplegii.

APPENDIX XXXV

1. UPWOOD, (B M, Add. Ms. 33450, p. 13): Omnibus Christi fidelibus ad quos presens scriptum pervenerit. Johannes permissione divina Abbas Monasterii de Rameseye et eiusdem loci conventus salutem. Noveritis nos unanimi assensu et voluntate manumisisse ac liberum fecisse et ab omni iugo servitutis liberasse Johannem Milis filium Roberti Milys defuncti, nativum et villanum nostrum de manerio nostro de Upwode, ut ipse idem Johannes Mylys cum tota sequela sua tam procreata quam procreanda et cum omnibus bonis et catallis suis ubicumque se dimitat liber et quietus ac libere conditionis permaneat infuturum. Ita quod nec nos nec successores nostri nec aliquis alius nomine nostro aliquid iuris seu clamei in predicto Johanne Mylys vel sequela sua tam procreata quam procreanda aut eorum catallis pretextu alicuius villenagii et servitutis in ipso Johanne Mylys prehabito decetero exigere vel vendicare poterimus infuturum. Sed ab omni actione iuris et clamei sunt exclusi per presentes. In cuius rei testimonium sigillum nostrum una cum sigillo capituli nostri fecimus hiis apponi. Datum apud Rameseye in domo nostra capitularia vicesimo die Aprilis. Anno domino millesimo CCCCmo XXXIXo.

(Obligatio super manumissionem) Noveritis universi per presentes me Johannem Milys de Ripton Regis teneri et firmiter obligari Abbati de Rameseye in quadraginta libris sterlingorum. Solvendo eidem abbati vel successoribus suis apud Rameseye in festo Sancti Michaelis Archangeli proximo futuro post datum presentum sine ulteriori dilatione. Ad quam quidem solucionem bene et fideliter faciendam et perimplendam obligo me heredes et executores meos per presentes sigillo meo signato. Datum apud Rameseye vicesimo sexto die Aprilis. Anno regni Regis Henrici sexti post conquestum decimo septimo.

Condicio istius obligationis talis est quod si infrascriptus Johannes Milys nullam decetero fecerit neque procuraverit ingratitudinem vel vexacionem versus Abbatem de Rameseye et successores suos neque tenentes, neque steterit contra eos in aliquo casu vel placito nisi tamen in casu titulum ius et statum proprium rationabilem sibi concernentem sive spectantem, quod tunc presens obligatio pro nullo habeatur; sinautem in suo robore permaneat et effectu.

2. RAMSEY REGISTER, p. 91d: Omnibus Christi fidelibus ad quos presens scriptum pervenerit Johannes permissione divina Abbas monasterii de Rameseye et eiusdem loci conventus salutem in domino sempiternam. Noveritis nos unanimi assensu et voluntate manumisisse ac liberum fecisse et ab omni iugo servitutis liberasse Thomam Gylle et Elenam uxorem eius, Thomam Gylle, Radulphum Gylle, filios eiusdem Thome et Aliciam Gylle filiam dicti Thome nativos et villanos nostros manerio nostro de Parva Styvecle spectantes. Ut ipsi iidem Thomas, Elena, Thomas, Radulphus, et Alicia cum tota sequela sua tam procreata quam procreanda (a membrane is apparently missing from the book at this point).

3. RAMSEY REGISTER, p. 105: Thomas Brook de Walton filius Johannis Brook nativus habet manumissionem suam pro eo et sequela sua tam procreata quam procreanda. Datum cuius manumissionis est vi die Octobris anno Regis Henrici VI, XXIIIIo pro X marcis ad rogatum Johannis Solvyle junioris militis et uxoris sue. Et idem Thomas et Robertus Bygge obligati sunt in decem libris pro dictis decem marcis solvendo in proximis festis Natalis domini, Sancti Michaelis Archangeli,

Natalis domini et Sancti Michaelis Archangeli ad quodlibet festum xxxiiis. iiiid. Et ultra idem Thomas obligatus est domino abbati in xl£, datum cuius obligationis est VIIIo die mensis Octobris anno predicto sub conditione quod non stabit nec vexabit abbatem de Rameseye, confratres, tenentes, servientes nec eorum successores.

4. RAMSEY REGISTER, p. 208: Willelmus Wattes filius Thome Wattes nativi domini habet manumissionem suam pro se et pro sequela sua procreata et procreanda, datum cuius manumissionis est IIo die julii anno Regis Henrici VI post conquestum tricesimo.

Idem Willelmus obligatus est abbati de Rameseye in quadraginta libris sterlingorum cum conditione ut sequitur. Conditio istius obligationis talis est quod si infra obligatus Willelmus nullo decetero fecerit neque procuraverit ingratitudinem vel vexacionem versus abbatem de Rameseye et eiusdem loci conventum nec eorum successores servientes et tenentes, neque steterit (contra dictos) aliquo casu vel placito nisi tam in casu titulum ius et statum proprium ipsius Willelmi rationabiliter sibi concernente sive spectante, quod ex tunc etc. sinautem in suo robore permaneat et effectu.

Si idem Willelmus teneat integre de Abbate de Rameseye de terra et tenemento suo ipsius abbatis in villa sua de Ripton Abbatis et personaliter cum bonis et catallis suis resideat in tenemento predicto ac sufficienter eadem terra et tenemento annuatim sustineat in reperatione domorum, solutione redditui ad terminos usuales, et omnibus aliis consuetudinibus durante tota vita ipsius Willelmi, quod ex tunc presens obligatio pro nulla habeatur; sinautem in suo robore permaneat et effectu. (This paragraph has been stroked out.)

Et pro residentia sua super feodum domini in eadem villa facienda durante vita sua, fecit sacramentum, et si exeat a tenemento predicto ad aliud infra villam vel extra villam inveniet domino sufficientem tenentem ad dictum tenementum sufficienter manutenendum per sacramentum suum.

APPENDIX XXXVI

A SIXTEENTH-CENTURY LAWSUIT CONCERNING CUSTOMARY LAND

A. Note.

The bundle of documents in the Court of Requests (P R O, Court of Requests, Bundle 7, number 10) from which we derive the material for this case has been edited by I. S. Leadam (*Select Cases in the Court of Requests*, 1497-1569, Selden Society, 12, 1898, 64-101). For a complete transcription, as well as for a discussion of the function of the Court of Requests, the reader is referred to Leadam's study. However, we woud like to suggest a slightly different order of the documents for this suit. Also, since we raise here the question of the antiquity of copyhold in the sense of customary tenure, a question not apparently of major concern to Leadam, it has been thought useful to make some of the actual text available again.

From internal evidence the sequence of events suggests the following ordering. 1) The lawsuit was apparently originated by a bill of complaint from Simon Kent and fellow tenants at Abbots Ripton (folio 26). These tenants claim copyhold by fee simple against the efforts of Oliver Saint John to replace the copies by indentures for years. This is a personal appeal to the king over lower courts from which the tenants have no hope for justice. 2) Oliver Saint John answered by an explanation of his right as lord to evict, and counter charged that the tenants had unlawfully taken wood (fol. 25). Tenants at Abbots Ripton have not held by copyhold for a sufficient legal period (time out of mind), Saint John claims, hence tenements may be seized at the will of the lord and let by term leases. 3) In a replication Simon Kent and his associates disclaim the adequacy of the answer of Saint John (fol. 24). The tenants' definition of copyhold tenure is broader than in their earlier statement, now reading, 'to them and their heirs in fee simple fee taile for term of life or lives or years at the will of the lord of the manor.' They deny that most copyholds are recent, and claim that even if this were so, it is immaterial to their case. Other charges are simply denied. 4) A royal commission of inquiry was apparently established upon the basis of the complaint of the tenants against eviction. In a counter appeal (fol. 22) Oliver Saint John asked for letters under the privy seal that those who had cut down more than eighty trees should refrain from cutting more until a royal inquiry be made, and that the same tenants be arraigned before the king's council to answer for cutting down trees. 5) A royal order to investigate the case was issued in February, 1544 (fol. 27). The remaining material consists of evidence taken for this inquiry. 6) Letters of interrogation were presented concerning the nature of copyhold (fol. 10-11). 7) Depositions were taken upon these letters on the part of the tenants (fol. 12-12d., 14-14d.). 8) Depositions were taken upon these letters on the part of the lord of the manor (fol. 19-21). 9) An order was issued to search the court rolls (fol. 1), and considerable evidence was collected from this search (fol. 1-9). 10) Letters of interrogation were issued upon the counter charges of Oliver Saint John (fol. 19). 11) Witnesses were called to answer to these questions (fol. 16-19). For the judgement against the tenants, because they had not established copyhold, see Leadam, *op. cit.*, pp. 99-101.

B. Texts.

7) (fol. 12-12d., 14-14d.) Deposycions takyn at Westminster the vii daye of maye of the behalf of Symond Kent and others tenants of Abbots Rypton ageynste Sir John Saynte John and others.

John Sewster of Steple Morden in the countie of Cambridge gentilman of the age of xlii yeres or there abowte sworen and examined the vii daye of maye in the xxxvi yere of the reign of his moste dradd Soverayn lord king henry the viiith by the grace of god king of England France and Ireland defendor of the faythe and in Erthe of the Cyrche of England and also of Ireland the supreme hedd. To the first of the Interrogatoris to hym mynistered deposithe and saythe that by the tyme and space of iii or iiii yeres before the dissolucion of the late monasterye of Ramsey in the countie of huntingdon and for the tyme and space of ii or iii yeres next after the dissolucion of the sayd late monastry the sayde deponent saythe that he was steward and keper of the courte of all the manors and possessyons of the saide late monasterye within the Realme of Englande. And by reason of that office this sayd deponent dyd kepe dyvers and sondry courts at the manor of Abbots Ripton. And there this deponent did see and peruse as he had cawse many of the copyes of the tenants of that manor and many of them were made to theym and to theyr heyres and many for terms of lyffe, and some of theym as dyd not concerne any lands that was appoyntyt to any of the monks being officers of the sayd late abbey were made but for terms of yeres or lyves. And the sayde deponent saythe that he by occasions of serches made for the determynacion of titles of copye holdys that dependyd in that courte in suyte before

hym often tymes betwenne partys he fownde and dyd see as yt wyll appere by the
serche of the olde courte rolles of the saide manor dyvers copies made in his prede-
cessors tymes, being stewardys in the office before this deponent was steward of the
seid abbey, as in viz with Rowlleys tyme with John Wyndes tyme and as in one
Breaes tyme. He fownde many copyes made to diverse tenants there to theym and
to theyr heyres and some for terme of lyffes. And as many commenly as dyd chaunche
to fall and to be graunted in this deponents tyme he being steward, there this deponent
made the copies to theym and to theyr heyres to holde after the custome of the sid
manor at the wyll of the lord and so had Maister Rowlet that was last steward of the
same possessions before this deponents tyme made copies also to dyvers of the saide
tenants to theym and to theyr heyres as this deponent perceyvyd by the president
courte rolles that he had made and ware delyveryd to this deponents hands at his
firste comynge to the sayde offyce and appon lyke tenures by copies in a maner all
the possessions of the saide late abbey in the countey of huntingdon were latt in this
deponents tyme and as well in the late abbots tyme as in the tyme the possessions
therof remayned in the kings majesties hands. And more this deponent rememberyth
not.[1]   (signed John Sewester)

Deposicione takyn at Westminster the xxiii daye of Januarii anno xxxvi R viii
on the behalf of Symond Kent and others ageynst Sir John Seynt John Knight and
others.

William Warwyk of Upwood in the countie of Huntington, husbondman, of the
age of lxiiii yeres or there abowte sworen upon his oathe sayth that he was borne in
Abbots Rypton and dwellyd there all his lyff tyme tyll yt was withe in this fyve
yeres. And his father dwellyd in the same towne lxvi yeres and sayth that the abbots
of Ramsey dyd alwayes graunte for the copies to dyvers of his tenants to theym and to
theire heyres for ever after the custome of the manor, wherof this deponents mothers
father callyd John Wodkocke had one. And one William Lynsey of Abbots Rypton
had another. And John his sone enioyed yt after his deathe and the said John solde
his copye to one Nicholas Aberye who was clercke of the same towne. And this
deponent rememberythe that dyverse other had copyes to theym and theyr heyres
for ever after the custome of the manor as the Westons, Plomes, and of the styles, with
manye others. And further saythe that nowe in hys tyme the abbot did graunte
copies to one William Adams and another to one John Pelle, and to their heyres
after the custome of the manor. And after that there came plentie of tenants and
ther they were dryven to take copies of the abbot for feare of puttyng forthe.[2] And
further examined saithe that he hathe hard hys father saye, that before the batayle
whiche was callyd Ester daye feld, all the tenants of Abbotts Rypton were copie
holders and held of the Abbot of Ramsey. And the nothern men laye there so long
before the feld was fowghten that they impoverished the countrey. And the tenants
were fayne to yeld up theyre copye holdes, for that they were not hable to repayre
theym. And then came other tenants and occupayed theym as tenants at wyll and

---

1 The above statement is the most complete and authoritative deposition, and seems
to leave no doubt that customary tenure was considered to be copyhold by abbey officials
from the fifteenth century.

2 This would seem to confirm that term leases were not considered to be tenure
by copyhold, and that the efforts of the villagers to obtain land for fixed terms in order
to avoid customary dues — so widely employed from the fourteenth century — could no
longer be forced upon the lord.

they had the rents abatyd.[3] And further saythe that duryng the tyme that the lands were in the kings maiesties hands the tenants were never vext nor trowbelyd. And sythens the tyme that the landes came to Sir John Saynt John hands, the said Sir John Saynt John hathe raysed the rents of as many of theym as hathe takyn theyr lands by lease of hym, and will not suffer the tenants to fell and enioye the woods and trees abowte theyre yardes, and theyr woods in the comen hethe, whiche this deponent hathe always knowen to be comen to the tenants and never denyed theym by anny officers tyll nowe. And further saythe that he hathe knowen his father and dyverse other of the tenants that hathe feld some yeres xxti lodys of wood a pece of theym in the comyn hethe, and solde yt to whome that would bye ytt and he that would paye for the fellyngs shuld have yt and they were never denyed nor rebukyd for they so doyng. And further he knowethe not as he sayth. (signed by mark)

(fol. 21) The deposicyons of certayn wytnesses takyn at Abbots Rypton within the countye of Hunt byfore Thomas Hutton and Thomas Hall Esquyers the xviith daye of Aprill the yere of the reign of our soveraign lord Henry the Eight by the grace of god etc. ... by vertue of a comission to thaym direct from the kyngs maiestye for the parte of Simon Kent and other complaynauntes.

John Pakey of Old Hurst clerk of the age of lxxv yeres sworne and examyned upon his oyth sayth that he hayth knowen the manor of Abbot Rypton by the space of fyftye yeres and that he was rydyng steward of the lands that belongyd to the layt monasterye of Ramsey and many tymes by reason of therof he was present with the steward that keapt courts asweall in this shyre of Hunt as Bedford shyre Hertforth shyre and others wher as any lands belongyd to the said monastrye, and therupon examined of the fyrst article and interrogaterye directly sayth, that he knew that the comen usage and custome was ther at that tyme that some and many of the tenants of Rypton tooke dyvers lands videlicet thayr holds by copye of court rolls some for terme of lyff some for terme of yeres and some to thaym and to thayr heyres and assignes and payd thayr fynes rentts and other costomes as yt was agreyed betwyn the lord and tenant and therupon occcupyed thayr lands accordyngly, and all such wood as greywe upon thayr copy holds they dyd and myght fell and have thaym without lett or interupcyon of the abbot or of his offycers.

And to the iid article he sayth that he never knewe any man trobelyd for thayr copye holdland in Rypton, nether whyles the manor was in the kings maiestyes hands nor whyles yt was in the abbotes hands.

To the iiid, iiiid, vth, vith, viith, viiith and ixth articles this deponent can nothyng saye of his knowledge.

William Silke of Benwyke in the countye of Cambridge clerk being of the age of lx yeres and more sayth the he was rydyng steward of Ramsey by the space of xvi yeres, sworn and examyned upon his oythe sayth to the fyrst article of interrogatoryes as the fyrst deponent hayth said concernyng the holdyng and takyng of copy hold lands. And moreover he sayth that he hayth seayn bokks and records maid in kynge Edward dayes the thyrde at suche tyme as Shedyngton, Butterwyk, and Stowe were abbots of Ramsey, that the tenements and land in Rypton byforesaid wer lettyn by copye of court rolle as is byforesaid and deposyd.

---

3 While this account of the repercussions of the Battle of Barnet, 1471, is unique, it should be noted that the general process of tenants giving up hereditary lands because of poverty and the lord having to abate rents in order to obtain new tenants, was typical of fifteenth-century conditions,

To the second article he sayth as the fyrst deponent hayth said and to all the other articles he can nothing saye.

Richard Button of Steple Gyddyng in the said countye of Hunt gent of the age of fyftye yeres sworn and examined to the fyrst interogatorye sayth that he was audytor clerk to the courts at Ramesey and the lands and tenements in Rypton not being no parcell of the demeans hayth beyng lettyn by copye of court rolle to the tenants for terms of yerys and in his tyme about xiii or xiiii yeres sythens he knewe certayn of the copye holders ther that they dyd renewe thayr copyes, that is wher they wer maid to thaym for terme of yeres,[4] they renewyd thaym to be maid to thaym and to thayr heyres and assignes for ever after the custome. And further he sayth that ther was a blak bokk of the Regester callyd a Garseyn Bokk and in that Bokk is regestryd and enteryd maney copyes that belongyd to the said monasterye of Ramsey.

To all the other articles the said deponent can nothyng saye.

Maister John Faunt of Burwell in the countye of Cambridge clerk of the age of xli yeres sworn and examyned sayth to the fyrst article that he hayth knowyn for hys tyme lands letten by copy hold in Rypton after dyvers sorts and costomes as the fyrst deponent hayth said and he hayth sean dyvers old Bokks from the dayes and reign of Kyng Richard the second and so hetherto Bokks wher in was regestryd dyvers copye holdland lying in Rypton beyforesaid and in other places wher the abbot hadd lands and some for terme of lyffe, some for terme of yeres, and some to thaym and to thayr heyres which Bokks were callyd Bokks of Garseyns and fynes to the which Bokks this deponent hadd accesse and hadd thaym in his keaping by reason he was rydyng steward of the lands belonging to Ramesey.

And to the other articles this deponent can nothyng say. But to the viiith article concernyng fellyng of woods he sayth that the tenants by copye ther were accostomyd in his tyme to kytt fell and sell wood growyng upon thayr copye holds to thayr own use without any interrupcyon.

John Martyn of Saynet Ives husb(andman) of the age of xlvii yeres sworn and examinyd upon his oyth he being Baylyf of Rypton xv yeres sythens by the space of vii yeres sayth that all the tenements in Rypton and Wenyngton savyng iii or iiii tenements wer lettyn by copye to the tenants after dyvers sorts as is byforesaid.

And to the viiith article this deponent sayth that the copye holders dyd kytt fell and sell the tymber and wood growyng upon thayr copye hold land so that they dyd and shold imploy the said wood or some other tymber or wood upon the buyldings of his or thayr own houses.

Thomas Danyell of Litle Raveley husbondman of the age of lxviii yeres sworn and examyned sayth to the fyrst article that for the tyme and space of xxti yeres past ther hayth beyn accostomeably lands lettyn to the tenants of Rypton by copye hold as is byforesaid and byfore that tyme some was lettyn by copye and some not as this deponent sayth. And to the seconde article he sayth there was noo interrupcyon in the kyngs tyme nor in the abbotts tyme neyther for thayr holds ne for thayr woods and to all the other articles he canne nothyng saye.

---

4 This is further evidence to support the above (note 2) that the abbots of Ramsey were replacing time leases by copyhold before the dissolution. This may be seen as another step in the trend to longer terms from the late fifteenth century (see note 86, Chapter IX). The court rolls confirm this increased grant of the copyhold in the 1530's. Whereas on an average one copy might be found on a roll before 1530, and then the designation *copia* is not always employed, for the five years or so before the dissolution there are an average of five or six *copia* entries *per* manor *per annum* (see especially, B M, Add. Ch. 39661, and P R O, SC 2, Port. 179, no. 89).

Robert Danyell of the age of lxii yeres sworn and examyned sayth that he hath knowen dyvers copye holds in Rypton this xl yeres sythens and more as John Pell, John Byrt of the Greyn, and others many moo and some he hath knowen to hold at wyll.

To the second article this deponent sayth that in harvest last he sawe oon William Smyth Baylif of Rypton and Wylliam Andrewe houshold servant to Sir John Seynt John knyght loodyng of Wylliam Stokeleys corn that grewe upon his copye holdland and intendyd to cary yt away, and there upon came Stokeley and his wyffe and sonne with hym and seing thaym lodyng his corne sayd they shold cary no corne of his off of that ground and pullyd of the sheyffs of barley of the cart sweryng a great oythe that he wold rather dye then they shold carye any corne off of that ground and so by persuasion of Sir John Danyell chaplyn the said Andrewe said 'Smyth we wyll goo hens for I se weall I cannot fulfyll my maisters commandment onles murder shold ensewe which I wyll not doo lett my maistre do with me what he wyll.'

Item, to the interrogatorys concernyng compulsion and thretts by Sir John Saynt John his offycers and servants as by his steward Maistre Spenser requyred the tenants to delyver in such copyes they hadd or ells bidd thaym avoide out of the court fore they shold here noyne of the secretts of this court without they will so doo, and they shold sowe thayr land but they shold not mowe yt with maney other threttyng and unfyttyng words.

John Walgayt of Raveley of the age of lvi yeres sworn and examyned sayth that he was present at Rypton when Sir John Saynt John sent ii of his servants whos name this deponent knowyth not and discharged William Stokeley from aryng of perte of his copye holdland lyng in the Est feld and this was doyn by the commandment of Sir John Saynt John thayn maister as the said servants said. And Thomas Danyell byfore sworn deposyth the same.

Wylliam Folbeck of Rypton of the age of lxviii yers sworn and examyned sayth that he hayth knowen dyvers copyes takyn within this xxii yeres but as for older copyes he knewe but iii or iiii. And as for the compulsion he sayth as Robert Danyell hayth said in all thyngs.

Wylliam Lucey of Rypton of the age of fyftye yeres and Wylliam Yong of the age of xxii sworn and examyned sayth that the Baylyff of Sir John Saynt John arestyd certayn pease of Wylliam Baksters and afterward by indifferent persones they wer layd in an indifferent place to such tyme as the pertye myght be agreyd but after that the said Baylyf causyd the same pease to be tressyd and sold perte of thaym, that is a bushel or ther about.

They sayd Wylliam Lucey and Wylliam Yonge sayth that the said William Bakster maid and cokkyd certayn haye upon his own ground and after that the said Smyth being baylyff to maistere Saynt John caryed yt away agaynst right and conscience.

The whiche all and single the premisses wee the above namyd Thomas Hutton and Thomas Hall Esquyers the kyngs maiestyes commissioners certyfyeth to the kyngs honorable counsell of his maiestyes court holden in the whyt hall at Westminster. Gevyn undre their sealls and subscribed with their hands accordyngly.

(signed by Thomas Sutton and Thomas Hall)

8) (fol. 20) The deposicyons of certayn wytnessys (of the manor) of Abbots Rypton within the countye of Hunt byfore Thomas Sutton and Thomas Hall Esquires of the xviith daye of Aprill the yere of the reign of our soveraign Lord Henry the Eythe... by vertue of a comishion to thaym direct from the kyngs maiestye for the parte of Syr John Saynt John Knyght and Olyver Saynt John Esquyer defendauntes.

William Byrde of Abbot Rypton byforesaid of the age of iiii^{xx} yeres sworen and examined upon his oyth sayth concerning the first article that he hayth maid his abode in Rypton by the space of xxxth yeres and about xxiiiith yeres sythens a certayn woman callyd mother Greyn desyred this deponent to have his councell howe she might doo to renewe her old copie that she hadd of the abbot of Ramsey. And he said he would aske councell of the copye holders and she said that she knewe no moo copyes in this town but that of thyrs only and this deponent knewe no moo copye hoolders at that tyme.[5] And further after the tyme the abbot sent his offycers to keep court at Rypton and at that tyme the offycers persuadyd the tenants to take thayr holds by copyes of court rolles or else the abbot shold make other provision for the said land and more this deponent cannot saye.

Robert Boston of Rypton of the age of iiii^{xx} yeres sworen and examyned sayth that about xxiiiiti yeres sythens at which tyme he came fyrst to Rypton he knewe but as William Byrde hayth deposyd concernyng mother Greyn copye. But he sayth that Symon Kent bought his copye about xiiii sythens upon oon' Stowoke and William Bakester bought his copye about v yeres sythens. And to the seconde article he cannot anything saye.

Thomas Goslyn of Rypton of the age of lv yers sworen and examyned sayth that he tooke a copye about xiiii or xv yeres sythens and held the said land by the space of iii yers byfore he tooke yt by copye which copye he surrenderyd into the hands of Sir John Saynt John and he knowyth of no moo copyes and as concernyng Simon Kents copye he saythe as Boston hayth deposyd.

Thomas Bell of Rypton of the age of lv yeres sworen and examined who hayth beyn in this parish of Rypton by the space of xl yeres and he never knewe no moo copyes in Rypton at that tyme he came thether but mother Greyns copye wyff to Wylliam Pell. But within this xvi yere he hayth knowen many moo copyes to have beyn takyn of the lord of Rypton and this deponent took oon copy himself to hym and his heyres which he surrenderyd to the Baylyf to the use of the lorde at the desyr of the baylyff rather then he wold goo to the lawe with the lorde and therupon he delyveryd his said copye whereupon the lord promised him a lease by his baylyf of his said copye holdland and as concernyng Simon Kents copy hold be saythe as the other deponents hayth said.

Thomas Bulleyn of Rypton husbondman of the age of lxii yeres sworen and examyned sayth that he haith beyn at Rypton by the space of fyftye yeres and at that tyme he knewe but v copye holds in Rypton, that is, John Pell, Wylliam Adam, Richard Weston, Richard Plume and John Lyndsey which wer maid long sythens but within this xxti yeres this deponent knewe many tenements to be lettyn by copye and this deponent hadd ii copyes hym self oon of xs. rent by yere, (and the other) of xxxvs. rent by yere, which ii copyes the Baylif persuadyd this deponent to delyver to the lords use or else he wold not have receyved his rent and therfore this deponent threw or kast the said copyes to the Baylyf and hadd hym take thaym and the devyll with all.

Item, he sayth that the copye holders have always kytt down wood growyng upon thayr copy holds without interruccyon and caryed away the same wood and inyoyed yt to thayr own use.

5 The impression of this and some of the following witnesses that there were few copyholds a generation before this time, complements the evidence (note 4, above) that may copies were given just before the dissolution. Such evidence also gives credence to the claim of Sir John Saint John (section 2, above) that copyholds were only recently granted. But it is an interesting paradox that the abbot of Ramsey was attemping to recover his jurisdiction over land by imposing the copyhold, whereas Sir John Saint John found the copyhold a challenge to his rights in tenants' lands!

John Bagley of Wenyngton of the age of liiii yeres sworen and examynyd sayth he never knewe no copyes but within this xxti yeres savyng Pelles copye and Adams copye.

John Adleyn of Rypton of the age of xlvii yeres sworen and examyned sayth that he hayth knewe that ther hayth beyn copye holders in Rypton by the space of xl yeres and within this xxti yeres verey maney copye holds letten.

Item, to the seconde article he sayth he never knewe no man troblyd nor interruptyd of thayr copye holds nor for thayr wood but nowe of layt sythens the manor of Rypton came to the hands and possession of Sir John Saynt John.

Item, to the iiid. article he sayth that maney wer compellyd to surrender and gyve up thayr copyes by thretts and many thyngs of Sir John Saynt Johns offycers for they wer thretynyd that yf they sew they shold not mowe thayr grayn.

Item, to the iiiith article he sayth that dyvers rentts be inhawnsyd some to xld., some to vs. some to xiiis. iiiid. and some more or lesse, but what value yt amountyth to in the hoille he knowyth not.

Item, to the vth article he sayth that the servants of Sir John Saynt John dyd dryve Stokeleys horse and his servants of and from Wylliam Stokeleys land, but that the said Stokeleys horse dyd regresse agayn to the same land and occupie the said land for the which Olyver Seynt John Esquyer hayth Stokeley in sewt at the present time.

Item, to the vith article he sayth that Sir John Saynt John his servants dyd tedre and stayk thar horses upon vi hawyns of Stokeleys being his severall copy hold ground and distroyd the (grass) growyng upon the same.

William Botryche of Rypton of the age of li yeres or ther about and hayth dwelt in Rypton by space of xviii yeres and knewe many copye holds takyn in that tyme.

To the second article he never knewe no interrupcyon of the copy holds in Rypton but nowe in Sir John Saynt John tyme and he sayth that dyvers of the tenants hayth gevyn up thayr copies but the nombre he knowyth not.

Robert Queue of Rypton of the age of xlv yeres sworen and examynyd sayth that he knewe divers copy holds (as) Pelle and Yonges about xxxti yeres sythens, and he hayth knowen divers copies takyn within this xx yers.

Item, he sayth that Wylliam Stokeley, William Lucey, William Folbech, John Brown, John Jordayn, John Reid, William Osey, Laurence Carter, John Goslyn in the name of Thomas Bell, Wylliam Tomkyn, William Botryche, Edmond Tomkyn, Robert Queyn, John Hygden, William Dawe, Thomas Bulleyn and other dyd surrendre thayr copyes upon this consideracyon that Sir John Saynt John dyd promyse thaym to make theym leases by indenture yf they wold take thaym for the terme of xl yeres.

Item, to the iiiith article he sayth he paith more rent by xiid. in the rent of xxxs. for that he hadd rather paye xiid. more rent yerely thayn to pay a great fynne and to all the other articles he can nothyng saye.

The whyche all and single the premisses wee the above namyd Thomas Hutton and Thomas Hall Esquyers the kyngs maiestyes commissioners certyfyeth to the kyngs honorable counsell of his maiestyes court holden in the whyt hall at Westminster yevyn undre our sealls and subscribed with our hands accordingly.

(signed by Thomas Hutton and Thomas Hall)

9) The certificat of Nicholas Luke one of the barons of the kyngs Eschequer and Thomas Hutton Esquire to the kings most honorable cownsayll by vertue of a commaundement from the seid cownsayll to us the seid Nicholas and Thomas made and dyrectyd for to vue serche and oversee certayn courte Rollis belongynge and pertaynynge to the manor of Abbatts Rypton in the cowntie of Huntyngdon and

to certifye and make report of all suche mater as we shall see and perceave in the seid courte Rollis consernynge the custom of the seid manor for the contynuans of the copyhold tenure within the seid manor by vertue wherof we the seid Nicholas and Thomas have serched and overseen certayn courte Rollis by one Sir Olyvere Seynt John Esquyer to us exhibeted the true effects wherof perticulerlye herafter folowythe. In wytnesse wherof we the seid Nicholas and Thomas to this present boke have sett owre hands.

Tempore Regis Ricardi Secundi.

Abbotts Rypton Memorandum, at a court holden at Abbotts Rypton Sabbato proximo post festum Sancte Luce Evangeliste primo Ricardo secundi and ther ys no maner of mencon made of the deathe of any copyholder nor of any takynge of any copyhold tenure surrender nor any other thynge for any suche purpos (four similar entries follow).

(fol. 1d.) Sorte and words videlicet quod Willelmus Smythe and Willelmus Martyn amerciantur ad ixd. pro eo quod dicti Willelmus et Willelmus non venerunt ad arandum terram domini quum summoniti fuerunt. Et quod Johannes Atchurche and Johannes Bauke amerciantur ad iiiid. pro eo quod non venerunt ad opus domini quum summoniti fuerunt. Et quod Andrew Colyar, Johannes Sotland, et Johannes Pryche fecerunt vastum super bondagium domini de domibus ruinosis. Ideo quilibet in misericordia iiid. Notandum, Buke is a bondman as apperithe ad curiam tentam apud Rypton predictam anno quarto Henrici quarti post etc. Nota, Johannes Prycke est nativus in sanguine ut apparet ad curiam tentam apud Rypton anno viiiº Henrici quarti proxime sequenti (about a dozen paragraphs follow taking this same kind of evidence for bondage from a dozen different court sessions).

(fol. 3) Tempore Regis Henrici VII.

(After mentioning courts searched for six years of this reign) ther is nothynge presentyd or mencionyd concernynge eny copyhold tenure but only this presentment followynge in theis words. Ad hanc curiam tentam apud Rypton predictam in festo Sancti Dionisii predicti anno XVIImo predicto venit Willelmus Hobson et sursum reddidit in manus domini per virgam dua messuagia cum duabus virgatis terre ut dominus faceret voluntatem. Ideo preceptum ballivo respicere in quo statu predicta messuagia stant. (and another entry of the same form follows).

Tempore domini Regis Henrici Octavi.

(Courts searched for seven years revealed nothing). Abbatts Rypton Memorandum ad curiam ibidem tentam octavo die Octobre anno domini Regis Henrici Octavi XXIIdo ther is presentyd as herafter folowythe. Scilicet ad hanc curiam venit Johannes Jurden et cepit de domino unum tenementum cum terra et prato eidem pertinentibus nuper in tenura Henrici Mallor habend' etc. eidem Johanni hereditatibus etc. Reddendo inde per annum xvis. Ideo etc. meremium de proprio percipiendum etc. iiis. iiiid.

Ad hanc curiam venit Johannes Roger et cepit de domino unum cotagium cum pertinentiis nuper in tenura Johannis Wygyn tenendum sibi etc. Reddendo inde per annum iis. And no more thynge concernyng eny copyhold tenure.

Memorandum ad curiam tentam die jovis proxime ante festum Sancti Michaelis archangeli anno dicti domini Regis Henrici octavi XXIIIto ther is presentyd theys thynges folowynge in theis words videlicet quod Johannes Smythe tenens per copiam obiit post ultimam curiam. Ideo preceptum est ballivo seisire quousque etc. Scilicet ad hanc curiam Johannes Blunte cepit de domino duas clausuras in Estthorpe vocatas le Burshe close et altera the mote close cui dominus concessit etc. habendum sibi etc. sicut placet domino reddendo inde domino per annum xs.

Ad hanc curiam Richardus Smyth et Alicia uxor eius cepit de domino unum mesuagium cum crofto adiacente et octo acras terre iacentes in Callowe croft quibus dominus concessit etc. habendum iisdem et assignatis suis pro termino vite eorundem
et alterius eorum diutius vivent ad voluntatem domini secundum etc. Reddendo
inde annuatim domino xs. etc.

(Tempore Regis Henrici VIII).

Memorandum ad curiam tentam ibidem in die Sancti Simonis et Jude anno Regis
Henrici XXVto et anno domini Johannis Wardeboys Abbas XXVII ther is mencionyd theis thynges folowynge in theys words, videlicet Willelmus Warwyke cepit
extra manus domini unum messuagium cum una virgata terre et dimidia terre et
prati cum pertinentiis cui dominus concessit inde seisinam habendum etc. sibi heredibus et assignatis suis ad voluntatem domini secundum consuetudinem manerii.
Reddendo inde domino per annum etc. xxiiis. iiiid. et faciendo omnia alia onera
consueta etc. et dat domino de garsuma etc.[6]

(extracts and notes from the court rolls conclude with eleven entries of the same
form as this for William Warwyke).

10) (fol. 19) Inprimis what nombre of trees the said Simon Kent hathe fellede or
cutt downe within the manor of Abbotts Rypton aforsaid syns the xxviiith daye of
Januarie in the xxxvth yere of the raigne of our soveraigne Lorde Henry the VIIIth
by the grace of god kynge of Englande Fraunce and Irelande defendor of the faithe
and in erthe of the churche of England and Irelande the supreme hedd, and in what
place the said trees dyd growe.

Item, of what age and valewe the said trees so fellede or cutt downe were of and
after what manner the said Simon dyd occupie or bestowe the said trees.

Item, what nombre of trees the said William Byrde hathe fellede or cutt downe
within the manner of Abbotts Rypton aforsaid syns the said xxviiith day of Januarie
in the said xxxvth yere of the Raigne of our said soveraigne Lorde kynge Henry the
VIIIth and in what place the said trees dyd growe.

Item, of what age and valewe the said trees so fellede or cutt downe were of and
after what manner the said William dyd occupie or bestowe the said trees (the same
queries are repeated for William Stokeley and William Baxter).

11) (fol. 16-17d.) Depositions takyn at Westminster the xxvi daye of Januarie
anno R. H. VIII, xxxvii etc. on the behalf of Oliver Saynt John Esquyer agaynst
Simon Kent, William Birde and others of Abbots Ripton.

Robert Boston of Abbots Rypton in the countie of Hunt husbondman of the age of
lxxxii yeres or there abowte sworen and examined sayth upon his othe deposithe
and saythe that Symon Kent hathe felld and cut downe upon the Thursdaye before
candlemas daye last past within the manor of Abbots Rypton in a close callyd
Pottars close xviii trees some ashes and some elmes beinge of xxxti yeres growyng

---

6 It is significant for the evolution of the customary tenure that no argument is raised
in this lawsuit (contrary to similar cases in the late thirteenth century, for example)
as to whether tenants were not simply villeins. Nor is anything made of traditional
payments of heriots and *gersumae*. Indeed, from the 1540's the traditional *gersuma* remained
the same but another fine under a separate designation (*fina*) began to be added to
conveyances on former Ramsey manors. The whole paraphernalia of customary rents was
inadequate to the new economic organization !

It may be noted here that from 1548 the time of legal memory became the limit for
tenure, that is, the only copyholds were those already based on immemorial custom (cf.
Plucknett, Year Books, 13 Richard II, *op. cit.*, p. XLI).

within all other kindes of wood growynge there in the hedge rowes and othere groves and dyd carye the same wood the space of iiii dayes to kents owne grownde and bestowed no perte therof on Olyver Saynt John grownde, but what valor the wood was of this deponent knowithe nott. And further saythe that after candlemas last past the sayd Symon Kent fellyd xiii trees more the first weke in lent last past in the same grownde as ii or iii of the xii men dyd informe this deponent, but what valor they were of this deponent knows nott. And further he saythe that Symon Kent dothe waste upon the sayd Olyver Saynt Johns grownde and hathe lett fall downe in decaye a bakhowse a maulte howse and the kechyn, whiche the xii men hathe diverse tymes presentyd and yet yt ys nott amendyd. And mor he saythe that he hathe warnyd William Byrd and his servaunt also that they sulde fell no more wood in Olyver Saynt John grownd, whiche William Byrd hathe diverse tymes syns candlemas last past feld diverse kyndes of trees and before candlemas, but to what number or valor he knowithe not but the xii men hathe fownde hym to doo wast and spoyle the grownde. And further examined this deponent saythe that William Stokeley hathe fellyd certeyn young ockes and other woods but to what valor or number he knowithe not but he saythe that they were fellyd syns Whytsontyd last past. And further examined saythe that William Baxter hathe felled myche wood bothe young and olde of the lords next a close callyd harpps to the nomber of lx or more small and great and hathe lett fall downe and decayed a hawle, howse, and a chymyney and two chambers withe loftes over theym, whiche hathe bene fownde by xii men. And he hathe bene warenyd by the xii men to repayer theym but hetherto he would not so that nowe they be downe to the hard grownd. And further this deponent knowith not towching the interrogatoris.

Wyllyam Butterege of Welington in the countie aforesayd husbondman of the age of li yeres sworen and examined saythe that in hillary terme last past before this, Symon Kents wyf comandyd certayn laborers dwelings there in the towne and other of her servaunts to fell woode in an abowte a close callyd pottars closse of xxti yeres growthe but what nomber or valor they were of he knowithe nott but they caryed yt off of Olyver Saynt Johns grownd and on Maister Bolles grownd and there burnyd yt. And further examyned saythe that William Byrd fellyd and causid to be fellyd xii or xiiii trees of a small valor whiche did growe in a close callyd Eastroppe which this deponent estymethe were worthe xvid. And further saythe that towchyng William Stokley he knowithe nothyng nor towching William Baxter, and further he knowith not.   (signed by mark)

Thomas Bell of Wellington in the parishe of Abbots Rypton in the countie of Huntyngton husbondman of the age of lxii yeres or there abowte, sworen and examyned saithe that Simon Kent before candelmas daye last past had done great waste in felling of woode which grewe in Pottars close and abowte the close but what valor they were of or what number he knowithe nott. And further saythe that he hathe hard his neyghbours saye that Symon Kent hathe fellyd syns candlemas last past wood in the same grownd and caryed yt off of the lords grownd and bestowed yt at his plesure but none upon Oliver Saynt Johns grownd, and also hathe lett fall downe and decayed the lords howsing. And further saythe that William Byrde causid laborers ther in the same towne to fell and cutt downe viii yonge sprynge abowte allhalowtyd last past of the valor wherof he knowith not. Also he saythe that William Stokeley fellyd in a place callyd Bugg grene one okke or twayne syns midsomer last past and the baylyf toke hym fellyng of theym whiche rebukyd hym and he answeryd that he would doo yt and take yt as his owne in the comyn, which this deponent saythe was never usid nor senne in his tyme to be done with owte the lords licence, but he saythe that maple, hasell and thorne they may fell yt as comyn but neyther oke nor ashe. Also further he saythe that he dothe and hathe hard saye that William Baxters grownde ys sore wasted as the woods consumed and howsen fallen downe, which this deponent hathe knowen a plentyfull grownde of woud and the howsing tenants lyke, but what wood he hathe fellyd this deponent knowithe nott, nor further can depose. (signed by mark)

Robert Quene of Wellington aforesayd howsbandman of the age of xlvi yeres sworen and examyned saythe that Symon Kent hathe fellyd syns candlemas day last past xiii trees which were sparr ware, but what they were wourthe this deponent knowithe nott but he saythe they wer ashe and wyche for this deponent dyd se theym and tell theym and more that were fellyd before that tyme of xxti yeres growing or there abowte. And further saythe that William Byrd hathe fellyd syns alhalowtyd dyverse trees wherof this deponent tolde before Christmas last past ix and syns that tyme he hathe fellyd more but the nomber or valor of theym this deponent knowithe not. Also he hathe hard saye by his neighbours that William Stokeley hathe fellyd abowet x^{ne} yong okkes in a platte of grownde callyd Buk grene also he saythe that William Baxter hathe made grete waste in the lords grownde as consumynge of woods and decaying of hys howses, but to what valor this deponent knowithe not nor can depose.[7] (signed by mark)

7 This problem of waste in the tenements and especially on common grounds may properly be seen as part of the same problem from the fourteenth century (see Chapter IX, Section II, above).

BIBLIOGRAPHY

MANUSCRIPT SOURCES

A. Court Rolls

Note : The court rolls are listed under manor and year. 178 or 179 indicates the portfolio heading for the Public Record Office court roll collections under SC 2; the other five digit references are to Additional Rolls in the British Museum. All Ramsey rolls in these collections have been consulted. The following limited list indicates rolls more directly contributing to this volume. When more than one court roll appears for the same year, this usually indicates the survival of the lete as well as the frankpledge roll; occasionally, however, more than one frank-pledge court simply occurred within the limits of the modern year. For account roll bibliography, see *Estates,* pp. 331-2.

ABBOTS RIPTON

1274 - 39586	1339-40 - 179/30	1407 - 179/50
1292 - 34337	Ed. III - 39738	1410 - 179/52
1294 - 39597	Ed. III - 179/28	1411 - 34819
1295 - 179/9	1343 - 179/31	1423-4 - 179/57
1296 - 179/9	1350 - 179/34	1428 - 34370
1299 - 179/10	1356 - 179/36	1430 - 39480
1301 - 179/11	1365 - 39860	1434 - 179/62
1306 - 34895	1369 - 179/38	1440 - 179/63
1306 - 179/12	1370 - 39580	1443 - 179/64
1307 - 179/15	1395 - 179/44	1452-53 - 34827
1308-9 - 39739	1398 - 34817	1455 - 179/67
1313 - 179/17	1300-1400 - 179/45	1462 - 39729
1318 - 179/18	1400 - 179/45	1465 - 179/70
1321 - 179/20	1402 - 179/47	1492 - 178/91
1321 - 179/21	1404 - 179/49	
1332 - 179/26	1405 - 39477	

BARTON

1350 - 179/34	1404 - 179/49	1440 - 179/63
1356 - 179/36	1405 - 179/50	1441 - 179/64
1359? - 179/36	1409 - 179/52	1444 - 179/64
1369 - 39473	1410 - 179/52	1451 - 179/66
1369 - 179/38	1420 - 179/56	1454-55 - 34322
1370 - 179/38	1424? - 179/57	1455 - 179/67
1372 - 179/39	1422 - 179/57	1464 - 179/70
1377 - 179/41	1428 - 179/59	1467 - 179/71
1391 - 174/43	1428 - 34370	1491 - 179/74
1395 - 179/44	1432 - 179/61	1493 - 39731
1400 - 179/45	1433? - 179/61	1518 - 34376

BROUGHTON

1288 - 175/5	1354-6 - 39471	1425 - 34308
1290 - 39754	1359 - 39583	1428 - 34370
1291 - 39849	1360 - 39472	1430 - 39480
1292 - 34335	1365 - 39860	1430? - 179/60
1294 - 34894	136? - 179/37	1434 - 179/62
1294 - 39597	1369 - 39473	1437 - 39481
1297 - 179/9	1369 - 179/38	1446 - 39867
1299 - 179/10	1371 - 39858	1451 - 39482
1301 - 39913	1373 - 179/39	1452 - 179/66
1301 - 34913	1375 - 179/40	1455 - 179/67
1306 - 39459	Ric. II - 39859	1462 - 39584
1306 - 179/12	1378 - 179/41	1464 - 179/70
1306 - 34902	1382 - 34306	1467 - 179/71
1307 - 34916	1384 - 34901	1469 - 34273
1308 - 34304	1386 - 179/42	1473 - 39656
1309 - 34342	1387 - 179/43	1479 - 39483
1311 - 34305	1387-8 - 39474	1483 - 39775
1313 - 34768	1390 - 34815	1488 - 39776
1314 - 39463	1390-1 - 39475	1493 - 39731
1316 - 39464	1391 - 179/43	1495 - 39485
1316 - 39463	1398 - 34817	1496 - 39484
1317 - 34803	1399 - 39476	1503 - 39486
1319 - 34804	1400 - 34920	1504 - 39487
1320 - 39759	1402 - 179/47	1505 - 39488
1321-2 - 179/20	1403 - 39861	1507 - 39489
1322 - 39466	1405 - 39477	1513 - 34310
1322 - 39467	1405 - 179/50	1516 - 39491
1325 - 179/22	1406 - 39478	1524 - 39492
1329 - 39468	1409 - 179/52	1524 - 39493
1331 - 39469	1410 - 179/52	1526 - 39494
1332-3 - 34363	1411 - 34819	1527 - 39495
1333 - 39470	1412 - 39769	1531 - 39496
1334 - 39762	1418 - 179/55	1533 - 39497
1334-5 - 179/28	1420 - 34821	1536 - 39662
1337 - 34899	1421 - 39479	1536 - 39498
1339 - 34808	1423-4 - 179/57	1537 - 39500
1339-40 - 179/30	1424 - 179/57	1586-7 - 34311

BURWELL

1294 - 39597	1326 - 179/22	1411 - 179/52
1299 - 179/10	1347 - 179/33	1419 - 179/56
1301 - 179/11	1350 - 179/34	1438-9 - 179/63
1307 - 179/15	1372 - 179/39	1451 - 179/66
1312 - 179/16	1377 - 179/41	1486 - 179/73
1321 - 179/20	1399 - 179/45	1490 - 179/74
1321 - 179/21	1407 - 179/51	

CHATTERIS

1270 - 179/3
1271 - 179/3
1272 - 179/3
1273 - 179/3

1274 - 179/3
1287 - 179/3
1288 - 179/3
1289 - 179/3

1430 - 39646
1440 - 39772
1452-3 - 34827
1473 - 39656

CRANFIELD

1294 - 39597
1300 - 179/10
1306 - 179/12
1307 - 179/15
1312 - 179/16
1316 - 179/18
1320? - 179/19
1321 - 179/20
1321 - 179/21
1333? - 179/26
1347 - 179/32
1347 - 179/33
1350 - 179/34
1356 - 179/36

1358? - 179/36
1359 - 179/36
1369 - 39765
1372 - 179/39
1377 - 179/41
1391 - 179/43
1395 - 179/44
1399-1400 - 179/45
1404 - 179/49
1405 - 179/50
1410 - 179/52
1420 - 179/56
1422 - 179/57
1429 - 179/59

1430 - 179/60
1432 - 179/61
1433 - 179/61
1434 - 179/62
1443 - 179/64
1454 - 34909
1455 - 179/67
1458 - 179/68
1461 - 179/69
1462 - 39729
1464 - 179/70
1465 - 179/70
1489 - 179/74
1497 - 179/76

ELLINGTON

1278 - 179/4
1290 - 179/7
1292 - 34336
1294 - 39597
1299 - 179/10
1306 - 179/12
1308-9 - 39739
1308 - 179/15
1311 - 179/16
1318 - 179/18
1321? - 179/19
1322 - 179/21
1325 - 179/22
1329 - 39468
1332? - 179/26
1335? - 34320
1340? - 170/30

1350 - 179/34
1356 - 179/36
Ed. III - 34320
Ed. III - 39738
1373 - 179/39
1375 - 179/40
1391 - 179/43
1400? - 179/45
1402 - 179/47
1405 - 179/49
1405 - 179/50
1407 - 179/51
1425? - 179/57
1426 - 179/58
1428 - 179/59
1429 - 179/60
1432 - 179/61

1434? - 179/62
1440 - 179/63
1443 - 34825
1446 - 39867
1447 - 179/65
1450 - 179/66
1452 - 179/66
1453 - 179/66
1454-55 - 34322
1455 - 179/67
1459 - 179/68
1460 - 179/68
1465 - 179/70
1469 - 179/71
1486 - 179/73
1513 - 34310

ELLSWORTH (and Knapwell)

1278 - 179/4
1290 - 179/7
1291 - 179/7
1294 - 179/7
1294 - 39597
1296 - 179/9

1299 - 179/10
1301 - 179/11
1306 - 179/12
1307 - 179/15
1312 - 179/16
1316 - 179/18

1321 - 179/20
1321 - 179/21
  ?   - 179/23
1333 - 179/26
1339 - 179/30
1339-40 - 179/30

1342 - 179/30
1347 - 179/33
1350 - 179/34
1353 - 179/35
1356 - 179/36
1358 - 179/36
1365 - 39860
Ed. II-III - 179/23
1369 - 39765
1365? - 179/37
1369? - 179/37
1373 - 179/39

1375 - 179/40
1399 - 39476
1400? - 179/45
1402 - 179/47
1402? - 179/48
1405 - 179/50
1410 - 179/52
1410 - 179/53
1410 - 179/53
1411 - 179/53
1424 - 179/57
1433 - 179/62

1434 - 179/62
1439-40 - 39771
1448 - 179/65
1452 - 179/66
1456 - 179/67
1457 - 34831
1457 - 179/67
1465 - 179/70
1493 - 179/74
1493 - 179/74

ELTON

1278 - 179/4
1292 - 34338
1299 - 179/10
1301 - 179/11
1306 - 179/12
1307 - 179/15
1312 - 179/16
1313 - 179/17
1316 - 179/18
1318 - 179/18
1320 - 179/19
1321 - 179/21
1325? - 179/22
1331 - 34321
1350 - 179/34
1354 - 179/35
1356 - 179/36
1357 - 179/36

1365 - 39865
1369 - 179/38
1370 - 39580
1370 - 179/38
1375 - 179/40
1386 - 179/42
1387-8 - 39474
1391 - 34816
1402 - 179/41
1405 - 34818
1405 - 179/50
1409 - 179/52
1410 - 179/53
1411 - 34819
1413 - 179/54
1419 - 179/56
1424 - 179/57
1425 - 179/57

1429 - 179/59
1429 - 179/60
1432 - 179/61
1434? - 179/62
1437 - 39481
1440 - 179/63
1443 - 179/64
1446 - 179/65
1447 - 179/65
1451 - 179/66
1452 - 179/66
1453-4 - 179/66
1454 - 34323
1455 - 179/67
1458 - 179/68
1461 - 179/69
1473 - 39656
1547 - 178/86

GIDDING

1290 - 179/7
1294 - 39597
1300 - 179/10
1306 - 179/12
1307 - 179/15
1312 - 179/16
1313? - 179/17
1316-7 - 179/18

1321 - 179/21
1334 - 179/30
1350 - 179/34
1356 - 179/36
1375 - 179/40
1399 - 179/45
1411-12 - 179/53
1413 - 179/54

1419 - 179/56
1441 - 39866
1451 - 179/66
1469 - 179/71
1486 - 179/73
1496 - 179/76
1514 - 179/84
1520 - 179/85

GIRTON

1291 - 179/7
1294 - 39597
1300 - 179/10
1301 - 179/11

1307 - 179/15
1312 - 179/16
1321 - 179/20
1321 - 179/21

1347 - 179/32
1347 - 179/33
1350 - 179/34
1353 - 179/35

1359 - 179/36
1390 - 34814
1391 - 179/43
1407 - 179/51
1412 - 179/53
1419 - 179/56
1424 - 179/57

1426? - 179/58
1430 - 179/60
1441 - 179/64
1446 - 179/65
1452 - 179/66
1490 - 179/75
1491 - 179/75

1492 - 179/75
1493 - 179/75
1494 - 179/75
1495 - 179/75
1496 - 179/75
1497 - 179/75
1498 - 179/75

GRAVELEY

1290 - 179/7
1294 - 39597
1299 - 179/10
1301 - 179/11
1306 - 179/12
1307 - 179/15
1312 - 179/16
1313? - 179/17
1316 - 179/18
1321 - 179/19
1321 - 179/20
1328 - 179/25
1333 - 179/26
1339 - 179/30
1350 - 179/34
1353 - 179/35

1356 - 179/36
1358 - 179/36
1363 - 39857
1369 - 39765
1369 - 179/38
1370 - 179/38
1375 - 179/40
1398 - 34817
1399 - 39476
1400? - 179/45
1402 - 179/47
1402? - 179/48
1405 - 179/50
1410 - 179/53
1410 - 179/53
1411? - 179/53

1424 - 179/57
1433 - 179/62
1434? - 179/62
1439 - 179/63
1446 - 179/65
1448 - 179/65
1453 - 179/66
1455 - 179/67
1457 - 34831
1458 - 179/68
1465 - 179/70
1468 - 179/71
1488? - 179/74
1514 - 34834

HEMMINGFORD ABBOTS

1278 - 179/4
1291 - 179/7
1294 - 39597
1296 - 179/9
1297 - 179/9
1299 - 179/10
1301 - 179/11
1306 - 179/12
1307 - 179/15
1311 - 179/16
1313 - 179/17
1316 - 179/18
1320 - 179/19
1320 - 179/19
1321 - 179/20
1321 - 179/21
1325 - 179/22
1326 - 179/22
1328 - 179/25
1332 - 39582
1332 - 179/26

1339 - 179/30
1347 - 179/32
1347 - 179/33
1350 - 179/34
1356 - 179/36
1359 - 39583
1370 - 179/38
1373 - 179/39
1375 - 179/40
1377 - 179/41
1391 - 179/43
1395? - 179/44
1395 - 179/44
1399-1400 - 179/45
1403? - 179/48
1405 - 179/50
1409 - 179/52
1411 - 179/53
1419 - 179/56
1422? - 179/57
1423 - 179/57

1428 - 179/59
1429 - 179/60
1432 - 179/61
1433 - 179/62
1437 - 179/63
1440 - 179/63
1454 - 34323
1458 - 179/68
1461 - 179/69
1461 - 179/69
1462 - 39584
1465 - 179/70
1469 - 179/71
1483 - 179/72
1490 - 179/74
1514 - 39778
1545 - 178/88
1546 - 178/88
1458 - 178/88

HOLYWELL

1288 - 179/5	1356 - 179/36	1409 - 179/52
1292 - 34337	1359 - 39583	1413 -1 79/54
1294 - 39597	1365 - 39860	1419 - 179/55
1299 - 179/10	1373 - 179/39	1423 - 179/57
1301 - 179/11	1378 - 179/41	1428 - 179/59
1306 - 179/12	1386 - 34778	1430 - 39480
1307 - 179/15	1386 - 179/42	1432 - 179/61
1311 - 179/16	1387 - 179/43	1437 - 179/63
1313 - 179/17	1391 - 179/43	1443 - 179/64
1318 - 179/18	1395 - 179/44	1452 - 179/66
1321 - 179/21	1395 - 179/44	1454-55 - 34322
1326 - 179/22	1398 - 34817	1456 - 179/67
1328 - 179/25	1400? - 179/45	1465 - 179/70
1332? - 179/26	1402 - 179/47	1469? - 179/71
1339-40 - 179/29	1403 - 179/48	1483 - 179/72
1340 - 179/30	1405 - 179/49	1487 - 179/73
1353 - 179/35	1405 - 179/50	1493 - 179/74

HOUGHTON

1274 - 39586	1321 - 179/20	1405 - 179/50
1288 - 179/5	1325 - 34898	1409 - 179/52
1290 - 179/7	1326 - 179/22	1411 - 179/53
1292 - 34338	1328 - 179/25	1419 - 179/56
1294 - 39597	1331 - 39761	1422? - 179/57
1295 - 179/9	1332 - 179/26	1423 - 179/57
1297 - 179/9	1339-40 - 179/30	1424 - 179/57
1299 - 179/10	1347 - 179/32	1428 - 179/59
1301 - 179/11	1347 - 179/33	1429 - 179/60
1306 - 39756	1354 - 179/35	1432 - 179/61
1306 - 179/12	1356 - 179/36	1433 - 179/62
1306 - 179/13	1363 - 39857	1434 - 179/62
1307 - 179/13	1369 - 179/38	1440 - 179/63
1308 - 179/13	1371 - 39858	1453 - 39869
1308 - 179/15	1373 - 179/39	1455 - 179/67
1309 - 179/13	1377 - 179/41	1458 - 179/68
1310 - 179/13	1391 - 179/43	1461 - 179/69
1311 - 179/16	1395 - 179/44	1462 - 39584
1313 - 34324	1400? - 179/45	1464 - 179/70
1316 - 34897	1402 - 179/47	1469 - 179/71
1319-20 - 179/19	1403? - 179/48	1487 - 179/73
1321 - 179/21	1405 - 39477	1543 - 178/89

KING'S RIPTON

1279-80 - 39595	1297 - 179/6	1303 - 179/6
1292 - 34336	1297 - 179/9	1306 - 39459
1294 - 34769	1299 - 179/10	1306 - 179/12
1294 - 39597	1301 - 179/11	1309 - 34770

1309 - 34342
1312 - 34768
1316 - 39464
1322 - 39467
1321-22 - 179/20
1331 - 39469
1332-33 - 34363
1333 - 39470
1347 - 179/32
1350 - 179/34
1357 - 179/36
1360 - 39730
1365 - 179/37

1366? - 179/37
1384 - 34901
1386 - 34771
1390-1 - 39475
1395 - 179/44
1396 - 179/44
1405 - 39477
1409 - 179/52
1411 - 179/53
1412 - 179/53
1419 - 179/55
1419 - 179/56
1421 - 39479

1422? - 179/57
1423-4 - 179/57
1428 - 179/59
1429 - 179/60
1434 - 179/62
1453 - 34828
1455 - 179/67
1479 - 39483
1483 - 39775
1488 - 39776
1493 - 39731

LITTLE STUKELEY

1278 - 179/4
1292 - 34336
1294 - 179/7
1294 - 39597
1296 - 179/9
1299 - 179/10
1301 - 179/11
1303? - 34902
1308 - 179/15
1308-9 - 39739
1313 - 179/17
1318 - 179/18
1321 - 179/20
1322 - 39467

1329 - 39468
1332 - 179/26
1340? - 179/30
Ed. III - 39738
1347 - 179/32
1350 - 179/34
1356 - 179/36
1375 - 179/40
1387 - 179/42
1390-1 - 39475
1395? - 179/44
1405 - 179/50
1407 - 179/51
1424 - 179/57

1426 - 179/58
1429 - 179/59
1432 - 179/61
1434? - 179/62
1437? - 179/63
1440 - 179/63
1453 - 179/66
1454 - 34829
1458 - 179/68
1486 - 179/73
1487 - 179/73
1496 - 179/76
1536 - 39780

OVER

1291? - 179/7
1294 - 39597
1300 - 179/10
1300 - 39600
1301 - 179/11
1305 - 34774
1306 - 179/12
1307 - 179/15

1308 - 179/15
1310? - 179/14
1312 - 179/16
1313? - 179/17
1316 - 179/18
1321 - 179/21
1321 - 39600
1328? - 179/25

1332 - 179/26
1334 - 179/30
1347 - 179/32
1349 - 179/33
1350 - 179/34
1356 - 179/36
1365 - 179/37

SLEPE

1291 - 179/7
1292 - 34339
1294 - 39597
1297 - 179/9
1299 - 179/10
1301 - 179/11
1305 - 34774

1306 - 179/12
1307 - 179/15
1311 - 179/16
1313? - 179/17
1323 - 34777
1325 - 179/22
1328 - 179/25

1332 - 179/26
1322 - 34363
1334 - 179/30
1343 - 179/31
1349 - 179/33
1354 - 179/35
1356 - 179/36

1365 - 179/37	1405-6 - 179/50	1469 - 179/71
1365 - 39860	1420 - 34881	1483 - 179/72
1369 - 179/38	1434 - 39648	1486 - 179/73
1375 - 179/40	1451 - 179/66	1487 - 179/73
1386 - 34778	1455 - 34882	1496 - 179/76
1391 - 179/43	1464 - 179/70	1504 - 179/79
1401 - 179/47	1465 - 179/70	1520 - 179/85
1403 - 34779	1468 - 179/71	1528 - 179/87

SHILLINGTON

1278 - 179/4	1350 - 179/34	1428 - 179/59
1288 - 179/5	1353 - 179/35	1428? - 179/59
1290 - 179/7	1356 - 179/36	1430 - 179/60
1294 - 39597	1358 - 179/36	1432 - 179/61
1300 - 179/10	1369 - 179/38	1433? - 179/61
1306 - 179/12	1370 - 179/38	1451 - 179/66
1307 - 179/15	1372 - 179/39	1452 - 179/66
1313 - 179/17	1377 - 179/41	1455 - 39774
1316 - 179/18	1401? - 179/46	1458 - 179/68
1319 - 179/19	1402 - 179/47	1461 - 179/69
1321 - 179/20	1409 - 179/52	1465 - 179/70
1321 - 179/21	1410 - 179/52	1473 - 39656
1325? - 179/25	1412 - 179/53	1486? - 179/73
1333 - 179/26	1420 - 179/56	1488 - 179/74
1339 - 179/30	1422 - 179/57	
1347 - 179/33	1424? - 179/57	

THERFIELD

1278 - 179/4	1369 - 179/38	1424 - 179/57
1296 - 179/9	1369 - 39473	1428? - 179/59
1306 - 179/12	1370 - 179/38	1439-40 - 39771
1307 - 179/15	1372 - 179/39	1455 - 39774
1312 - 179/16	1377 - 179/41	1457 - 34831
1319 - 179/19	1386 - 34778	1462 - 39584
1321 - 179/21	1390 - 34814	1465 - 179/70
1325 - 179/25	1391 - 179/43	1469 - 179/71
1347 - 179/33	1409 - 179/52	1469? - 179/71
1350 - 179/34	1412 - 179/53	1486 - 179/73
1358 - 179/36	1420 - 179/56	

UPWOOD

1278 - 179/4	1307 - 34799	1322 - 34805
1279 - 34911	1307 - 179/15	1325 - 34806
1294 - 34769	1308 - 34801	1325 - 39851
1295 - 179/9	1311 - 34802	1326 - 34807
1297 - 34798	1313 - 34917	1328-9 - 39852
1299 - 179/10	1318 - 34803	1331 - 34321
1302 - 179/12	1320 - 34804	1332 - 39582

1333 - 34810
1334 - 34809
1339 - 34808
1339-40 - 34811
1344 - 39854
1347 - 34849
1349 - 34850
1350 - 179/34
1353 - 39855
1360? - 179/37
1360 - 34812
1365 - 39860
1365 - 179/37
1369 - 39765
1370 - 179/38
1372 - 39766
1373 - 179/39
1378 - 179/41
1382 - 34306
Ric. II - 39859
1386 - 34813
1387-8 - 39474
1387 - 179/43
1390 - 34814
1391 - 34815
1391 - 24816
1395 - 179/44
14th c. - 34800
1398 - 34817
1402 - 179/47
1403? - 179/48

1405 - 34818
1406 - 39478
1409 - 179/52
1411 - 39863
1411 - 34819
1413 - 34820
1418 - 179/55
1420 - 34821
1421 - 34368
1422 - 34369
1424 - 179/57
1425-6 - 39745
1425 - 39645
1428 - 34370
1428 - 179/59
1429 - 179/59
1430 - 34822
1430 - 39646
1430 - 39480
1435 - 34371
1438 - 34823
1439 - 34824
1441 - 39866
1443 - 34825
1448 - 34826
1450 - 39746
1452-3 - 34827
1453 - 34828
1454 - 34829
1456 - 34830
1457 - 34831

1458 - 179/68
1459 - 34832
1469 - 179/71
1473 - 39656
1483 - 39775
1487 - 39871
1488 - 39776
1496 - 179/76
1497 - 34833
1514 - 34834
1520 - 34835
1533 - 39660
1534 - 39661
1535 - 34377
1536 - 39780
1537 - 34836
1541 - 34837
1543 - 34838
1544 - 34839
1545 - 39876
1554 - 34840
1559-60 - 34841
1568 - 34842
1581 - 34843
1582 - 34844
1584 - 34845
1585 - 34846
1590 - 34847
1591 - 34848

WARBOYS

1290 - 39754
1292 - 34335
1294 - 39755
1294 - 39597
1294 - 34894
1299 - 179/10
1301 - 39850
1301 - 179/11
1305 - 34774
1306 - 34895
1306 - 39756
1309 - 34342
1313 - 34910
1313 - 34324
1316 - 34896
1316 - 34897
1318 - 39757

1320 - 34918
1320 - 39758
1320 - 39759
1322 - 34777
1322 - 179/20
1325 - 34898
1325 - 39851
1326 - 39760
1331 - 39761
1332-3 - 34363
1333 -34919
1333 - 39470
1334 - 39762
1337 - 34899
1339 - 39853
1343 - 179/31
1347 - 39856

1347-8 - 34900
1349 - 39763
1350 - 179/34
1353 - 179/35
1360 - 39764
1363 - 39857
1365 - 39860
1369 - 39473
1369 - 39765
1371 - 39858
1372 - 39766
1373 - 179/39
Ric. II - 39859
1375 - 179/40
1382 - 34306
1384 - 34901
1387-8 - 39474

1387 - 179/43
1390 - 34814
1390 - 34815
1391 - 179/43
1398 - 34817
1400 - 34920
1400 - 179/45
1402 - 179/47
1403? - 179/48
1404 - 179/49
1405 - 39862
1410 - 39768
1411 - 179/53
1412 - 39769

1418 - 179/55
1421 - 39770
1423-4 - 39864
1424 - 39865
1427 - 34370
1428 - 179/59
1430 - 39480
1434 - 179/62
1440 - 39771
1440 - 39772
1448 - 39773
1455 - 39774
1458 - 179/68
1462 - 39729

1469 - 34273
1473 - 39656
1483 - 39775
1487 - 179/73
1488 - 39776
1496 - 179/76
1507 - 39777
1514 - 39778
1516 - 39491
1521 - 39779
1525 - 39872
1533 - 39660
1536 - 39780

WESTON

1290 - 34908
1292 - 34337
1294 - 39597
1300 - 179/10
1302 - 179/11
1306 - 179/12
1307 - 179/15
1308 - 179/15
1312 - 179/16
1318 - 179/18
1320 - 179/19
1321 - 179/21
1325 - 179/22
1350 - 179/34
1354 - 179/35
1356 - 179/36
1358? - 179/36
1360 - 34812

1365 - 39860
1369 - 179/38
1370 - 39580
1370 - 179/38
1372 - 179/39
1375 - 179/40
1386 - 179/42
1387 - 179/42
1391 - 34816
1402 - 179/47
1405 - 179/50
1409 - 179/52
1410 - 179/53
1413 - 179/54
1419 - 179/56
1423-4 - 39864
1424 - 179/57
1425 - 179/57

1429 - 179/59
1429 - 179/60
1432 - 179/61
1434 - 179/62
1440 - 179/63
1450 - 179/66
1451 - 39482
1454 - 34909
1455 - 179/67
1456 - 179/67
1457 - 39870
1460 - 179/68
1462 - 39729
1469? - 179/71
1473 - 39656
1486 - 179/73
1498 - 179/76

WISTOW

1278 - 179/4
1291 - 39849
1292 - 34335
1294 - 39597
1294 - 39755
1297 - 39562
1297 - 34911
1299 - 179/10
1301 - 34913
1301 - 39850
1305? - 34916
1306 - 39755
1307 - 34799

1308 - 34801
1309 - 34342
1313 - 34910
1313 - 34917
1316 - 34896
1316 - 39465
1318 - 39758
1320? - 34915
1320 - 39758
1320 - 34918
1322 - 34805
1325 - 34806
1325 - 39851

1326 - 39760
1328-9 - 39852
1333 - 34919
1333 - 34810
1334 - 34809
Ed. I-II - 34915
1339 - 39853
1344 - 39854
1347 - 39856
1349 - 39763
1350 - 179/34
1353 - 39855
1360 - 39764

1363 - 39857	1406 - 39478	1446 - 39867
1365 - 39860	1408 - 34921	1451 - 39868
1369 - 39473	1410 - 39768	1453 - 39869
1369 - 179/38	1410 - 179/52	1456 - 34830
1370 - 39580	1411 - 34819	1457 - 39870
1371 - 39858	1411 - 39863	1458 - 179/68
1373 - 179/39	1413 - 34820	1461 - 179/69
1375 - 179/40	1418 - 179/55	1465 - 179/70
1378 - 179/41	1420 - 34821	1469 - 34273
Ric. II - 39859	1421 - 39770	1473 - 39656
1384 - 34901	1423-24 - 39864	1483 - 39775
1386 - 34813	1424 - 179/57	1487 - 39871
1387 - 179/42	1424 - 39865	1488 - 39776
1387 - 179/43	1428 - 34370	1516 - 39491
1390 - 34814	1428 - 179/59	1525 - 39872
1391 - 34815	1429 - 179/59	1534 - 39661
1391 - 179/43	1430 - 34822	1536 - 39662
1398 - 34817	1430 - 39480	1537 - 34836
1399-1400 - 179/45	1434 - 179/62	1550 - 39878
1400 - 34920	1436 - 34823	1551 - 39879
1402 - 179/47	1438 - 34823	1585 - 34846
1403 - 39861	1440 - 39771	1591 - 34848
1405 - 39862	1441 - 39866	

B.   *Other Manuscript Sources*

London
>   *British Museum*
>>   Additional Ms 33450
>>   Cottonian Ms Vespas. A XVIII
>>   Cottonian Ms Vespas. E. ii
>>   Eggerton Ms 3663
>>   Harleian Ms 445 (court book)

Norwich
>   *Norwich City Library*
>>   Ramsey Register

PRINTED ORIGINAL SOURCES

A.   *Ramsey Abbey Estates*

Court Rolls of the Abbey of Ramsey and of the Honor of Clare, editor W. O.
    Ault (Yale University Press, 1928).
Cartularium Monasterii de Rameseia, editors W. H. Hart and P. A. Lyons, 3 vols.,
    RS. 79 (1884-93).
Elton Manorial Records (1279-1351), editor S. C. Radcliff, Roxburghe Club
    (Cambridge, 1946).
Select Pleas in Manorial and other Seignorial Courts, I ,Selden Society, II (1889).

B.   Non-Ramsey Materials[1]

Abbreviatio Placitorum, Richard I-Edward II, editors G. Rose and W. Illingworth,
    Record Commission, 5 (1811).
Archaeological Journal, 'Original Documents,' III (1846), 65-6.
Brevia Placitata, editor G. J. Turner, Selden Society, 66 (1951).
Britton, notes and translation by F. M. Nichols (Washington, 1901).
Carte Nativorum, a Peterborough Abbey Cartulary of the Fourteenth Century,
    editors C. N. L. Brooke and M. M. Postan, Northamptonshire Record Society,
    XX (Oxford, 1960).
Casus Placitorum and Reports of Cases in the King's Courts (1272-78), editor
    W. H. Dunham, Selden Society, 69 (1952).
Court Roll of Chalgrave Manor, 1278-1313, edited by Marian K. Dale, Bedfordshire
    Historical Record Society, 28 (1950).
English Historical Documents, editors D. C. Douglas and G. W. Greenaway
    (London, 1953).
Placita Anglo-Normannica, editor M. M. Bigelow (Boston, 1877).
*Royal Writs in England from the Conquest to Glanvill: Studies in the Early
    History of the Common Law,* by R. C. Van Caenegem, Selden Society, 77
    (London, 1959).
Select Cases in the Court of Requests, 1497-1569, editor I. S. Leadam, Selden
    Society, 12 (1898).
Winchester Cathedral Chartulary, editor A. W. Goodman (Winchester, 1927).
Year Books, 13 Richard II, 1389-90, editor T. F. T. Plucknett (The Ames Founda-
    tion, 1929).

SECONDARY WORKS[2]

A.   Monographs

Ault, W. O., *Private Jurisdiction in England* (Yale University Press, 1922).
Benedict, Ruth, *Patterns of Culture* (New York, 1934).
Bennett, H. S., *Life on the English Manor* (Cambridge, 1948).
Beresford, M., *The Lost Villages of England* (London, 1954).
Bloch, Marc, *Feudal Society* (Chicago, 1961).
Cam, H. M., *Liberties and Communities in Medieval England* (Cambridge, 1944).
Darby, H. C., *The Domesday Geography of Eastern England* (Cambridge, 1952).
Davenport, F. J., *The Economic Development of a Norfolk Manor,* 1086-1565
    (Cambridge, 1906).
Dawson, John P., *A History of Lay Judges* (Cambridge, Mass., 1960).
Duby, Georges, *L'économie rurale et la vie des campagnes dans l'occident médiéval:
    France, Angleterre, Empire, IXᵉ-XVᵉ siècles* (Paris, 1962).

---

[1] Only the studies more immediately employed in this volume are listed below. For a
list of edited court rolls, most of which have been consulted for this volume, see E. L. C.
Mullins, *Texts and Calendars; an analytical guide to serial publications* (London, Royal
Historical Society, 1958).
  [2] This selection is largely based upon the works referred to in this volume.

Ekwall, Eilert, *Studies on the Population of Medieval London* (Stockholm, 1956).

Firey, Walter, *Man, Mind and Land* (Glencoe, Illinois, 1960).

Fromm, Erich, *Escape From Freedom* (New York, 1941).

Gray, C. M., *Copyhold, Equity and the Common Law* (Cambridge, Mass., 1963).

Grazia, Sebastian de, *Of Time, Work and Leisure* (New York, 1962).

Hearnshaw, F. J. C., *Leet Jurisdiction in England,* Southampton Record Society, 5 (1908).

Holdsworth, W. S., *A History of English Law,* 12 vols. (London, 1903-38); 7th rev. edition, editors A. L. Goodhart and H. G. Hanbury (London, 1956 ff.).

Homans, George C., *English Villagers of the Thirteenth Century* (Cambridge, Mass., 1942).

Hoskins, W. G., *Essays in Leicestershire History* (Liverpool, 1950).

Hunnisett, R. F., *The Medieval Coroner* (Cambridge, 1961).

Jacob, E. F., *The Fifteenth Century, 1399-1485* (Oxford, 1961).

Keen, Maurice, *The Outlaws of Medieval Legend* (Toronto, 1961).

Levett, A. E., *Studies in Manorial History,* editors H. M. Cam *et al.* (Oxford, 1938).

Levy, Ernst, *West Roman Vulgar Law: The Law of Property* (Philadelphia, 1951).

Lipson, E., *The Economic History of England,* I, 10th edition (London, 1949).

Maitland, F. W., *Domesday Book and Beyond* (Cambridge, 1897).

Martin, G. H., *The Early Court Rolls of the Borough of Ipswich* (Leicester, 1954).

May, Rollo, *The Meaning of Anxiety* (New York, 1950).

Mayhew, Henry, *London Labour and the London Poor,* I (London, 1851).

McKisack, May, *The Fourteenth Century, 1307-1399* (Oxford, 1959).

McLuhan, Marshall, *The Gutenberg Galaxy* (Toronto, 1962).

Mead, Margaret, editor, *Cooperation and Competition among Primitive Peoples* (New York, 1937).

Merton, Robert K., *Social Theory and Social Structure* (Glencoe, Illinois, 1957).

Morris, W. A., *The Frankpledge System* (Cambridge, Mass., 1910).

Orwin, C. S. and C. S., *The Open Fields* (Oxford, 1938).

Plucknett, T. F. T., *A Concise History of the Common Law,* 5th edition (London, 1956).

Pollock, F. and F. W. Maitland, *The History of English Law,* 2nd edition, 2 vols. (Cambridge, 1911).

Powicke, F. M., *Modern Historians and the Study of History* (Odhams, 1955).

Radcliffe-Brown, A. R., *A Natural Science of Society* (Glencoe, Illinois, 1957).

—, *Method in Social Anthropology* (Chicago, 1958).

—, *Structure and Function in Primitive Society* (Glencoe, Illinois, 1952).

Raftis, J. A., *The Estates of Ramsey Abbey,* Studies and Texts, 3 (Toronto, 1957).

Redfield, Robert, *The Little Community* and *Peasant Society and Culture* (Chicago, Phœnix Books, 1960).

Réville, André and Ch. Petit-Dutaillis, *Le soulèvement des travailleurs en 1381* (Paris, 1898).

Russell, J. C., *British Medieval Population* (Albuquerque, University of New Mexico Press, 1948).

Sheehan, M. M., *The Will in Medieval England,* Studies and Texts, 6 (Toronto, 1963).

Tawney, R. H., *The Agrarian Problem in the Sixteenth Century* (London, 1912).

Thirsk, Joan, *English Peasant Farming* (London, 1957).

Thrupp, S. L., *The Merchant Class of Medieval London, 1300-1500* (Chicago, 1948).

Trevelyan, G. M., *Illustrated English Social History,* I (London, 1949).

Vinogradoff, Paul, *The Growth of the Manor,* 3rd edition (London, 1920).
Wagner, A. R., *English Geneology* (Oxford, 1960).
White, Lynn T., *Medieval Technology and Social Change* (Oxford, 1962).

B.   *Articles*

Aston, T. H., "The Origins of the Manor in England," *Transactions of the Royal Historical Society,* 8 (1958), 59-83.
Ault, W. O., "Some Early English By-Laws," *English Historical Review,* 45 (1930), 208-231.
Bosl, Karl, "Uber soziale Mobilitat in der mittelalterliche Gesellschaft," *Viertel-Jahrschrift fur Sozial- und Wirtschaftsgeschichte,* 47 (1960), 306-32.
Cheyney, E. P., "Disappearance of English Serfdom," *English Historical Review,* 15 (1900), 20-37
Colvin, H. M., "Angevin Government," in *History,* 43 (1958), 85-89.
Constant, A., "The Geographical Background of Inter-Village Population Movements in Northamptonshire and Huntingdonshire, 1754-1943," *Geography,* 33 (1948), 78-88.
Fuller, E. A., "Tenures of Land, By the Customary Tenants, in Cirencester," Transactions of the Bristol and Glouc. Arch. Soc., 2 (1877-8), 295-319.
Hallam, H. E., "Some Thirteenth-Century Censuses," *Economic History Review,* Second Series, 10 (1958), 340-361.
Herlihy, D., "The Carolingian Mansus," *Economic History Review,* Second Series, 13 (1960), 79-89.
Hilton, R. H., "Social Structure of Rural Warwickshire in the Middle Ages," *Dugdale Society Occasional Papers,* 9 (1950).
Latham, L. C., "The Manor and the Village," in *Social Life in Early England,* editor G. Barraclough (London, 1960), 29-50.
Latham, R. E., "Minor Enigmas from Medieval Records," *English Historical Review,* 76 (1961), 639-647 (on chevage).
Lennard, Reginald, "The Economic Position of the Domesday *Villani,*" *Economic Journal,* 56 (1946), 244-64.
—, "The Economic Position of the Domesday Sokemen," *Economic Journal,* 57 (1947), 179-95.
—, "The Bordars and Cottars of Domesday Book," *Economic Journal,* 61 (1951), 342-371.
Miller, Edward, "The Estates of the Abbey of St. Albans," *Transactions of the St. Albans and Herts. Arch. Soc.* (1936-8), 285-300.
Packard, Sidney R., review of *Royal Writs in England from the Conquest to Glanvill* by R. C. Van Caenegem, *Speculum,* 36 (1961), 357-9.
Parker, John, "The Manor of Aylesbury," *Archaeologia,* 50 (1887), 81-103.
Peyton, S., "An Elizabethan Inquisition Concerning Bondmen," *Bedford Hist. Soc.,* 9 (1900), 61-74.
Postan, M. M., "The Famulus," *Economic History Review Supplement,* no. 2 (Cambridge, 1954).
Powicke, F. M., "Observations on the English Freeholder in the Thirteenth Century," in *Wirtschaft und Kultur:* Festschrift zum 70. Geburtstag von Alfons Dopsch (Baden bei Wein, 1938), 382-93.
Raftis, J. A., "Rent and Capital at St. Ives," *Mediaeval Studies,* 20 (1958), 79-92.
—, "Marc Bloch's Comparative Method and the Rural History of Mediaeval England," *Mediaeval Studies,* 24 (1962), 349-68.

Russell, J. C., "Mediaeval Midland and Northern Migration to London, 1100-1365,"
    Speculum, 34 (1959), 641-45.
Swynnerton, Charles, "Some Early Court Rolls of the Manors of Stonehouse,
    King's Stanley, Woodchester and Achards," *Transactions of the Bristol and
    Glouc. Arch. Soc.,* 45 (1923), 203-252.
Thrupp, S. L., "Economy and Society in Medieval England," *The Journal of
    British Studies,* 2 (1962-3), 1-13.
Wake, Joan, *"Communitas Villae,"* *English Historical Review,* 37 (1922), 406-13.
Williams, G., "Manumissions of Serfs Extracted from the Records of King's
    College," *Cambridge Antiq. Soc.,* 1 (1959), 359-60.

INDEX

Abbots Ripton, 13, 18, 19, 19 (Distribution of Village Tenements), 22, 24, 25(2), 41, 47, 63, 71, 82, 137(2), 138(4), 144, 148, 164 (table), 170(2), 170n, 171, 173, 174, 178, 181, 182, 182 (table), 185(2), 191, 192, 198, 204, 209, 210; *Texts*, 38, 46, 64-5, 67, 74, 75, 77(2), 81, 85, 88, 107, 113, 115, 119(2), 120(2), 126, 131, 151, 189, 216, 267, 274.

Account rolls, Ch. I, Sect. II, *passim*; 16, 154, 192, 196 (table).

Agreements, involving payments for repairs, fines, etc., 50, 53, 64-5, 66, 71-4, 103; and see *Conventio*.

Alewives, 101n.

Almoner, of Ramsey, 29.

Arlesey, 184 (table).

Ashton, 159(2).

Bailiff, 25(2), 53, 69, 75, 140, 142, 273 (no. 11), App. XXXVI, *passim*.

Barnwell, 181, 184, 184 (table), (3), 185, 267.

Barton, 36, 77, 143, 165 (table), 170(2), 174 (2), 175(2), 179, 180, 180 (table), 184, 184 (table) (3), 185, 186 (table), 192, 193, 197, 199 (table) (5), 199; *Texts*, 37(3), 38, 79, 127, 168n, 202n, 232, 234.

Beadle, 64, 65, 75, 76, 78, 80(2), 85, 86, 87, 140, 274 (no. 12); and see Government by Officials.

Beggar see Vagabondage.

Bentham, Glouc, 177, 180.

Bigging, 25, 171, 173.

Borough English, 55-6.

Brampton, 168, 171, 174(3).

Brewing, 125-7.

Brington, 144, 161, 182 (table), 199 (table); *Texts*, 114, 116, 117, 120; and see Weston.

Broughton, 22, 24, 28, 77, 80n, 89n, 95, 99, 108n, 123, 130, 137(3), 147, 151n, 160 (table), 170(2), 170n, 171, 175, 177, 179, 182, 182 (table), 186 (table), 191(2), 192,

194(2), 195, 198, 199, 199 (table) (3); *Texts*, 37, 75, 103, 108, 112, 117, 118(2), 119, 120, 126, 127(3), 152.

Buckworth, 173.

Burwell, 25, 63, 68, 78, 94, 95, 137, 138, 147, 179, 185, 188, 192, 197, 230; *Texts*, 42, 64, 70, 79, 86, 95.

Bury, 107, 124, 125, 201.

Bury St. Edmunds, 180.

Byelaw, village, see Ordinance.

Bythorn, 88, 143, 161, 182 (table), 185, 199 (table) (4); and see Weston.

Caldecote, 122; and sse Warboys.

Cellarer, 140.

Chamberlain, 38, 81, 85.

Charter, 51, 69, 70(2), 82-8, 95, 200; and see Copyhold.

Chattels, 41 (crop), 46-8, 141; and the tenement, 25; of a house, 45; villein as, 11; withdrawal of by villein, 169; and see Mobility without licence (texts), Crop seized, Agreements.

Chatteris, 24, 40, 49, 52, 77, 149, 163n, 173, 176n, 198, 199 (table) (2), 274; *Texts*, 41, 51, 53, 78, 114, 115.

Chickely, 167, 174.

Colne, 173.

Conventio, 80-1; and see Agreements.

Conveyance, of customary tenements, within family, 63-5, beyond family, 65 ff; and see Tenure.

Copyhold, 199-204.

Cotton, 140.

Court, manorial, 11; rolls, 13-14, and Ch. II-IX, *passim*; ecclesiastical (chapter), 38 (2), 46; autumn, 154; and see Frankpledge, Bailiff, etc.

Cranfield, 43, 52, 59n, 80n, 82(2), 90n, 137(3), 138(3), 140n, 143, 149, 150, 151n, 166 (table), 167, 170(2), 173, 174(2), 176(2), 177(3), 178(3), 180, 180 (table), 185(2), 192,